Denny L. Kimmel
Rte 1, Box 423
Poulsbo, Washington
98370

D1790385

DIRECTORY OF FOOTBALL DEFENSES:

Successful Defenses and How to Attack Them

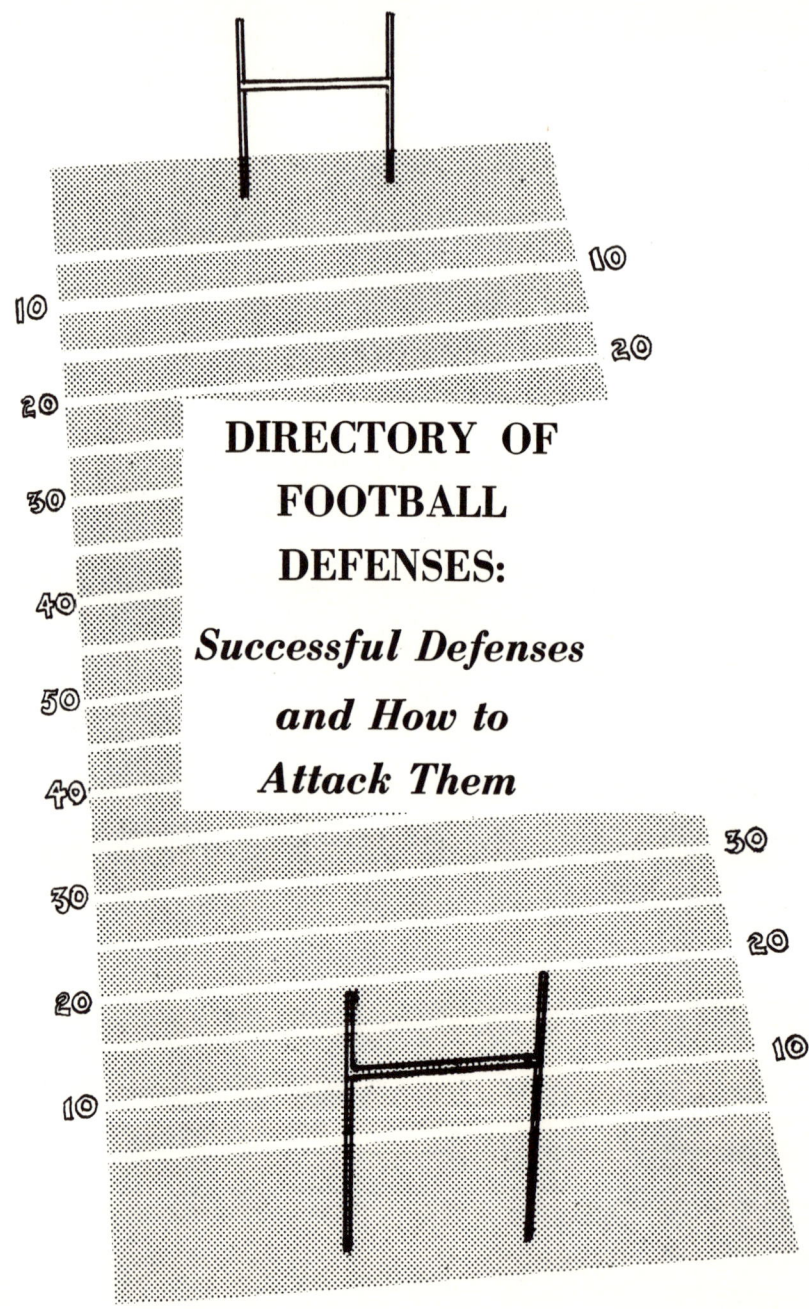

DIRECTORY OF FOOTBALL DEFENSES:

Successful Defenses and How to Attack Them

by

Drew Tallman

Parker Publishing Company, Inc. West Nyack, New York

© 1969 BY
PARKER PUBLISHING COMPANY, INC.

ALL RIGHTS RESERVED. NO PART OF THIS
BOOK MAY BE REPRODUCED IN ANY FORM OR
BY ANY MEANS, WITHOUT PERMISSION IN
WRITING FROM THE PUBLISHER.

Library of Congress
Catalog Card Number: *76–79105*

Third Printing.....February, 1971

PRINTED IN THE UNITED STATES OF AMERICA
BC (13-214841-2)

Dedicated to

MATTY AND ANGIE CERTOSIMO

who have made football an inspiration to so many boys

And to My Family
SUE, JULIE ANN, AND HOLLY SUE

ACKNOWLEDGMENTS

Appreciation is expressed to the many people who assisted and contributed in the preparation of this book. I would like to thank the many author-coaches for permitting the use of quotes from their publications: Jack Curtice, University of California at Santa Barbara; Bobby Dodd, Georgia Tech; Don Fuoss, Middle Tennessee State; Elvan George, East Central State College, Oklahoma; Ray Graves, Florida University; DeWayne King, San Jose State; Noel Reebenacker, Marblehead High School, Massachusetts; and Bud Wilkinson, formerly of Oklahoma University.

Appreciation is due to the many coaches who granted permission for the use of their clinic material and/or sent material for this book: Alex Bell, formerly of Villanova University; Bob Blackman, Dartmouth College; John Bridgers, formerly of Baylor University; Howard Brinker, Cleveland Browns; Bill Crutchfield, Georgia Tech; Glenn Dobbs, formerly of Tulsa University; Bobby Dodd, Georgia Tech; Vince Dooley, University of Georgia; Frank Navarro, Columbia University; Bill Neal, Indiana University of Pennsylvania; Chuck Mather, Chicago Bears; John Pont, Indiana University; Floyd Schwartzwalder, Syracuse University; Leo Strang, formerly of Kent State University; and Bill Tate, formerly of Wake Forest College.

Gratitude is due Mr. John L. Griffith, publisher, *Athletic Journal* and Mr. Herman Masin, editor, *Scholastic Coach* for granting permission to use material from their publications.

I am indebted to Ted Dunn, head football coach of Springfield College who gave me my first opportunity to coach football. Grateful appreciation is due Chuck Klausing, head coach of Indiana University of Pennsylvania and George Paterno, Michigan State University, two of the finest football coaches I have been fortunate to work under who equally gave me the opportunity to coach football and learn much of the game. Many thanks go also to Matty Certosimo, one of the finest coaches in the country who taught me a tremendous amount of football both on and off the field.

A special thanks goes to many people too numerous to mention and yet well deserved who always gave me inspiration. Finally a great deal of appreciation goes to my lovely wife Sue for her unfailing support, faith, and affection.

WHAT THIS BOOK WILL DO FOR YOU

> "It is my feeling that any discussion of offensive football is meaningless unless defensive football in all its basic elements is well understood."*
>
> Bud Wilkinson

The purpose and scope of this book is to give the coach many principles and details of defenses that will enable him to know strategically how and where to attack defenses. Every coach reaches the problem at one time or another of how to attack defenses. Strengths and weaknesses of defenses can change from week to week due to many variables, including such things as different alignments and personnel. Picking a play or blocking scheme out of a hat hoping it will be successful will not work. A coach must understand defenses including the stacks, tandems, angles, stunts, fires, and blitzes if he is going to attack them effectively.

An experienced coach realizes the necessity of correct strategy, and this book gives insight into some strategical ideas. However, this is not the answer to a winning football program. The overall scheme including correct fundamentals and techniques, proper organization, good drills, and psychological aspects must be an integral part of the program if a football team is going to be successful.

This book introduces the *Directory of Football Defenses,* how to make it, the advantages of such a directory, and how it can benefit the coach. A chapter on theories for a proper understanding of all defenses is illustrated. Methods of attacking stunting, angling, and blitzing defenses and how to block tandems and stacks of all defenses are vividly described. The strengths and weaknesses of pass defenses are given and ways of attacking defensive linebackers, ends, and secondaries are explained in detail. Defenses are then discussed with explanations of basic adjustments to offensive formations, defensive maneuvers, and what the defense can jump to easily. The strengths and weaknesses of each defense fol-

---

*Charles (Bud) Wilkinson, *Oklahoma Split-T Football.* (Englewood Cliffs, New Jersey: Prentice-Hall, Inc., 1952), p. 235.

low and how and where to attack the defense up the middle, off-tackle, and outside is illustrated. Blocking combinations and a few plays are shown that can successfully be utilized versus that particular defense.

The information and ideas presented and explained were gathered by the author through readings and research, talks with successful coaches, clinics, and observation of other teams through visits, films, etc. All of the material has been employed at one time or another. What has been successful at one school may not have been successful in other places. However, the information is presented to let the reader realize some of the ideas that *can* be executed.

This book is for the inexperienced as well as the experienced football coach at the junior high, high school, and college level. It is hoped with the information, ideas, principles, suggestions, and methods presented throughout this book a coach will be more capable of understanding, knowing, teaching, and putting these concepts to use. He will not only understand both the principles and details of defenses, but will better be able to plan and organize his strategical attack. Careful study of this book should help the coach become an excellent and intelligent strategist.

DREW TALLMAN

CONTENTS

1. An Introduction to Defenses **1**

    Proper Play Selection   (1)
    Coaches' Directory of Football Defenses   (2)
    Attacking Defenses   (2)
    The Quarterback and Coach   (3)
    Principles of Defense   (4)

        The defensive line • *4*
        The defensive linebackers • *6*
        The containing unit • *7*
        The forcing unit • *8*

    Every Defense Has a Purpose   (8)
    Personnel Makes a Defense Sound   (8)
    The Importance of Successful Teaching   (9)
    Theories of Execution   (9)

        A straight defense • *9*
        A stunting defense • *10*
        A balanced defense (between straight and stunting) • *10*
        An angling defense • *10*
        A balanced angling defense • *11*
        A jumping defense • *11*

Changing Alignments   (11)
Pursuit and Penetrating Defenses   (12)
    The pursuit defense • 12
    The penetrating defense • 13
    Combination of pursuit and penetrating defenses • 13
Attacking Defenses   (16)
    No defense is perfect • 16
    The concept of strengths and weaknesses of defenses • 16
    Attack personnel of the defense • 17
    Improper alignments make a defense weak • 18
    Planning to attack defenses • 18
    Attack one defensive area • 18
    Fifteen ways to take advantage of the defense • 20
    Know the opponent's philosophy of defense • 21

2. Attacking Stacked, Tandem, Stunting, and Angling Defenses ... 22

Importance of Scouting, Films, and Observations in a Game   (22)
The Importance of Drilling   (23)
Attacking Defenses and Their Variations   (23)
The Backfield, Line, and Ballcarrier   (23)
    The offensive line • 24
    The offensive backfield • 24
    The ballcarrier • 24
The Importance of Anticipation   (24)
Seven Variations of the Defense   (25)
    The straight stack • 25
    The straight tandem • 26
    The stunt • 26
    The stunting stack • 27
    The stunting tandem • 27
    The loop or slant • 27
    The fire or blitz • 28
How to Block the Straight Stack   (29)
How to Block the Straight Tandem   (35)
How to Block the Stunt   (38)
How to Block Stunting Stacks   (44)
How to Block Stunting Tandems   (45)
How to Block the Angling Defense (Loop or Slant)   (47)
How to Block the Fire or Blitz   (49)

CONTENTS xi

3. The Pass Offense and Attacking Defensive Linebackers and Ends 51

    The Ingredients of a Good Passing Attack (52)

        The passer • *52*
        The receivers • *53*
        The protection • *54*
        The coverage • *54*

    Importance of Strategy for the Passing Game (54)
    Quarterback Routes and Pass Actions (55)

        The quick drop-back pass • *56*
        The drop-back pass • *56*
        The sprint-out pass • *57*
        The semi-sprint-out pass • *58*
        The roll-out pass • *58*
        The semi-roll-out pass • *59*
        Play-action passes • *59*
        Bootlegs and waggles • *59*
        Delay passes • *59*
        Screen passes • *59*
        Shuffle pass • *60*
        The draw • *60*

    Importance of Films, Scouting, and Observation (60)
    Attacking Personnel (61)
    Attacking Pass Defenses (61)

        The passing tree • *61*

    Attacking All Defensive Secondaries (62)
    Attacking Defensive Linebackers (63)

        The alignment and coverage of linebackers • *63*
        Play-action passes • *65*
        Quick pursuing linebackers • *66*
        Delay passes • *67*
        Check series to ends • *68*
        Check series to backs • *68*
        The check series draw • *70*
        The screen pass • *70*

    Attacking Defensive Ends (72)

        Tight position • *72*
        Walkaway position • *73*
        Double-up position • *75*

4. Attacking Defensive Secondaries 76

Attacking the Deep Secondary   (76)
Disguising Secondaries   (77)
Attacking Zone Defenses   (77)
- The straight zone • 77
  - The two deep zone • 78
  - The three deep zone • 78
  - The four deep zone • 79
- The strength of the zone pass defense • 80
- The weakness of the zone pass defense • 80
- Attacking the straight zone coverage • 80
- The rotation zone • 83
  - The three deep rotation • 83
- Attacking the weaknesses of the rotational three deep • 83
  - The four deep rotation • 85
- Attacking weaknesses of the rotational four deep • 86
- The invert zone • 87
  - The three deep invert • 87
  - The four deep invert • 87
- Attacking the inverts • 88
- The revert zone • 90

Attacking Man-to-Man Secondary Coverage   (90)
- Running plays • 92
- Isolating a receiver • 93
- Extra receivers • 94
- Fake block and release • 95
- Crossing receivers • 95
- Pick passes • 96
- Comeback passes • 96
- Across field routes • 96
- Tackle eligible play • 97
- Quarterback as a receiver • 97
- Delay passes • 97

Attacking the Combination Zone and Man-to-Man • 98

5. The 4–3 Defense 101

The 4–3 Defense   (102)
Adjustments to Formations   (106)

CONTENTS   xiii

    Stunting   (107)
    The 4–3 Tandem   (108)
    Defensive Shifts   (110)
    Attacking the 4–3 Defense   (110)

        The strengths of the 4–3 defense • *110*
        The weaknesses of the 4–3 defense • *111*
        Attacking the areas of the 4–3 defense • *112*

6. The 5–3 In Defense 121

    Playing the 5–3 In Defense   (123)
    Adjustments to Formations   (127)
    Stunting, Blitzing, and Angling   (128)
    Defensive Shifts   (130)
    Attacking the 5–3 In Odd-Diamond Defense   (131)

        The strengths of the 5–3 in defense • *131*
        The weaknesses of the 5–3 in defense • *132*
        Attacking the areas of the 5–3 in defense • *133*

7. The 5–4 Oklahoma Defense 143

    Playing the 5–4 Oklahoma Defense   (145)
    Adjustments to Formations   (147)
    Stunting and Blitzing   (148)
    Defensive Shifts   (150)
    Attacking the 5–4 Odd Box-Corner Defense   (153)

        The strengths of the 5–4 defense • *153*
        The weaknesses of the 5–4 defense • *153*
        Attacking the areas of the 5–4 defense • *154*

8. The Wide-Tackle 6 Defense 165

    Playing the Wide-Tackle 6 Defense   (167)
    Adjustments to Formations   (171)
    Stunts, Blitzes, Fires, and Angles   (172)
    Defensive Shifts   (177)
    Attacking the Wide-Tackle 6 Even-Diamond Defense   (179)

        The strengths of the wide-tackle 6 defense • *179*
        The weaknesses of the wide-tackle 6 defense • *179*
        Attacking the areas of the wide-tackle 6 defense • *180*

9. The Split-6 Defense 193

    The Play of the Split-6 Defense   (195)
    Adjustments to Offensive Formations   (199)
    Stunts, Blitzes, Fires, and Angles   (201)
    Defensive Shifts   (205)
    Attacking the Split-6 Even-Diamond Defense   (207)
        The strengths of the split-6 defense • 207
        The weaknesses of the split-6 defense • 207
        Attacking the areas of the split-6 defense • 208

10. The Gap-8 Goal Line Defense 221

    Playing the Gap-8 Defense   (223)
    Adjustments to Offensive Formations   (226)
    Defensive Maneuvers   (228)
    Defensive Shifts   (230)
    Attacking the Gap-8 Even-Diamond Defense   (230)
        The strengths of the gap-8 defense • 230
        The weaknesses of the gap-8 defense • 231
        Attacking the areas of the gap-8 defense • 231

11. Coaches' Directory of Football Defenses 243

    Advantages of the Defense Directory   (243)
    Why Make a Coaches' Directory of Defenses?   (244)
    How to Make the Coaches' Directory of Defenses   (245)
    Constructing the Directory   (246)
    The Top Card   (247)
    The Bottom Card   (252)

DIRECTORY OF FOOTBALL DEFENSES:

Successful Defenses and How to Attack Them

1

AN INTRODUCTION TO DEFENSES

Football strategy is the science or art of deploying your own attack against an opponent and attempting to outmaneuver him. Knowing the proper methods of how and where to attack a certain defense, against the many variables that can be encountered may denote success or failure during a season. The "Coaches' Directory of Football Defenses" hopes to aid both the high school and college coach in attacking defenses quickly and easily.

PROPER PLAY SELECTION

Bobby Dodd, former head football coach and now athletic director of Georgia Tech, has remarked about the importance of good play selection in his book *Bobby Dodd on Football*: "Football authorities agree that of all factors that produce success in a game, the proper selection of plays is by far the most important. A poor choice of plays will nullify the finest teamwork and will eventually break down the highest morale."[1]

At the American Football Coaches Association meeting, Leo E. Strang, former head coach at Massillon High School and Kent State University, Ohio, began his talk by stating:

> In the past twenty years, or at least since the wide-spread use of movies, football has made great strides in almost every phase. However, I feel one very important phase of football has been neglected. This phase I speak of is organized spotting. By this, I mean taking

---

[1] Robert L. "Bobby" Dodd, *Bobby Dodd on Football* (Englewood Cliffs, N. J.: Prentice-Hall, Inc., 1954), p. 152.

advantage of defense weakness or reactions in an organized manner and not by hit or miss methods. There are probably more games won and lost over these United States by making the right or wrong play-call at the right or wrong times, than by any other single factor.[2]

As can be seen, both Coach Dodd and Coach Strang strongly advocate the importance of this particular phase of the game. Later in his speech Coach Strang mentions, ". . . our teams have lost five out of seventy games played. All five of these were by seven points or less, and all five could have been won by better play calling; on the other hand, I feel at least twenty games have been won because we did a better job of calling plays."[3]

COACHES' DIRECTORY OF FOOTBALL DEFENSES

Since the strategy phase of football is becoming more complex, a device is needed to aid coaches at all levels of the game. Chapter 11 fully describes, explains, and illustrates the makings of the "Coaches' Directory of Football Defenses" which will help the coach in this endeavor. As will be seen, not only is the "Coaches' Directory" used for play selection in games, but also there are several other reasons why it is beneficial to the coach and the entire football program.

ATTACKING DEFENSES

A complete knowledge of all defenses is important for the coach. To attack defenses with the proper play selection he must be able to accomplish the following:

1. Know and recognize defenses.
2. Understand the strengths and weaknesses of the defense and the theories and concepts of it.
3. Attack the weakness areas of the defense with proper play calling.

While recognition of a defense is important, a better understanding comes when the coach knows the individual positions of each defensive player. Bob Blackman, head football coach of Dartmouth College stated before the American Football Coaches Association, "As all of you are well aware, a simple diagram of a defense does not tell too much about it. To really know a defense you must know how each man makes his initial charge, how he reacts from there, how he 'keys', etc."[4] From Coach Blackman's talk, not only is recognition essen-

---

[2]Leo E. Strang, "Defensive Analyzation," *Proceedings of the Thirty-Ninth Annual Meeting, American Football Coaches Association*, Chicago, Illinois, 1962, p. 52.

[3]*Ibid.*, p. 54.

[4]Bob Blackman, "Over-All Team Defense," *Proceedings of the Thirty-Fifth Annual Meeting, American Football Coaches Association*, Philadelphia, Pa., 1958, p. 16.

tial to the defense itself, but the actual responsibilities of each man in the defense are also important.

Floyd B. Schwartzwalder, head coach of Syracuse University, said in a speech to football coaches:

> We have specific game preparation, as everybody does, and we want to study the philosophy of the opponent just as much as we possibly can. We want to get to the point, if we can, where we are thinking just like they are thinking, as nearly as we can, whether they are diamond or box, whether they penetrate or whether they hit and slide. How do they defend on passes; their tendencies; if their deep men really go back quickly; and if the linebackers are crowding or are they loose. Do the linebackers go with the backs, or do they key linemen? Do they synchronize with linemen in groups or do the linebackers function separately?[5]

As can be seen, Coach Schwartzwalder wanted to know the philosophy and tactics of the opponents' defense. Coach Blackman's and Schwartzwalder's speeches, illustrate that there is much more to learn about a defense than just the mere recognition of it. The coach must understand the philosophies, principles, theories, and concepts to grasp fully the idea of a defense. When this has been accomplished, he will develop a better insight into how to attack a defense with better play selection.

THE QUARTERBACK AND COACH

The coach is not the only man who must call plays and understand defenses—the quarterback must also accomplish this. The quarterback must be taught play calling with respect to defenses, field position, down and distance, time of the game, score, wind, weather, and so on, to be able to handle the offense properly. The coach must constantly teach, train, and drill the quarterback on all of these important aspects of the game. To do this coach and quarterback must work together in season and out of season to be fully prepared. The coach should expect the quarterback to think like him about the weaknesses and reactions of the defenses. Don Fuoss, head football coach at Middle Tennessee State University, wrote in the preface of his book *Quarterback Generalship and Strategy:*

> A coach cannot assume his quarterback will call a good game. Although the entire procedure may appear to be relatively clear and simple to the coach, the inexperienced quarterback does not grasp the picture as readily and as clearly. It takes much time and patience to train the quarterbacks, but patience is one of the requirements of a good teacher and a good coach.[6]

---

[5]Floyd B. Schwartzwalder, "Coaching Your Quarterback from Week to Week," *Proceedings of the Thirty-Seventh Annual Meeting, American Football Coaches Association*, New York City, New York, 1960, p. 86.

[6]Don Fuoss, *Quarterback Generalship and Strategy* (Englewood Cliffs, N.J.: Prentice-Hall, Inc., 1958), p. viii.

Following in this chapter are a few principles, philosophies, concepts, and theories of all defenses that will be helpful in recognizing, understanding, and knowing defenses for both the coach and quarterback. While this book will be concerned entirely with assisting the coach on many defenses, their variations, and how to attack each one, it should be stressed that what is learned and understood by the coach can be learned by the quarterback also.

PRINCIPLES OF DEFENSE

A defense will usually be composed of three main units or groups: (a) defensive line, (b) linebackers, and (c) secondary.

    a. The defensive line is primarily concerned with the running plays of the offense and the pass. They rush first and defend against the pass second (Diagram 1–1).
    b. The defensive linebackers are responsible for both the running and passing game (Diagram 1–2).
    c. The defensive secondary have the main responsibility of the pass first and the run second (Diagram 1–3).

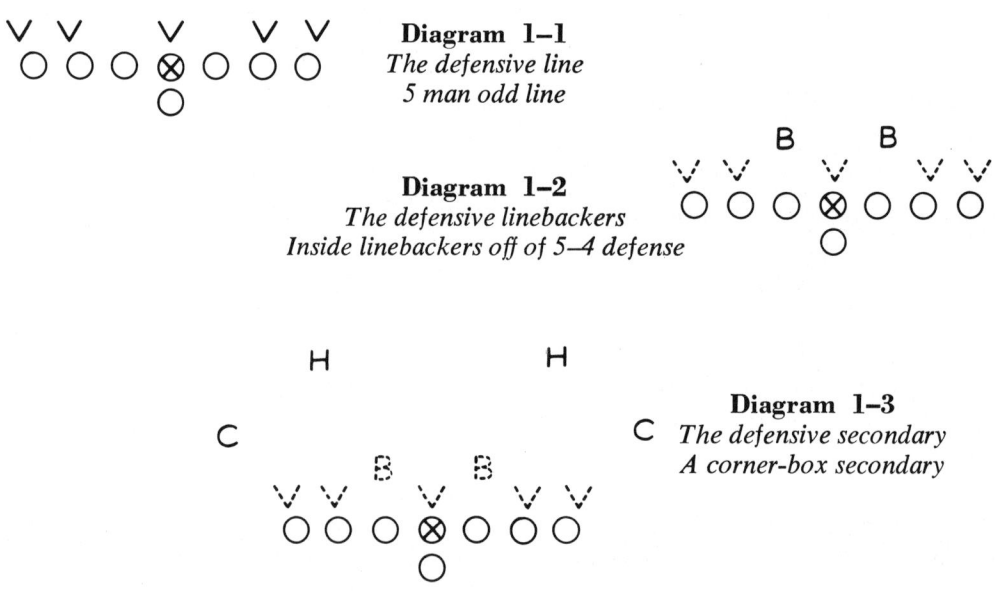

Diagram 1–1
The defensive line
5 man odd line

Diagram 1–2
The defensive linebackers
Inside linebackers off of 5–4 defense

Diagram 1–3
The defensive secondary
A corner-box secondary

THE DEFENSIVE LINE

1. A defensive line will either be an odd defense or an even defense.

Odd
A defense is known as odd when there is a defensive man on the line of

AN INTRODUCTION TO DEFENSES

scrimmage directly over the center or the middle man on the offensive line (Diagrams 1–4 and 1–5).

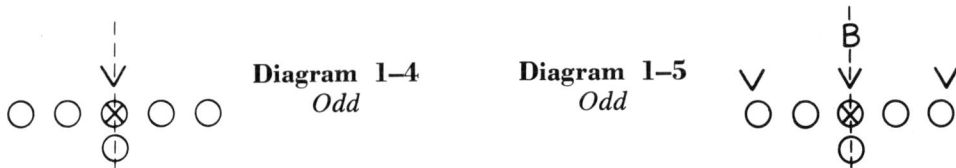

Diagram 1–4
Odd

Diagram 1–5
Odd

Even

A defense is known as even when there is no man on the line of scrimmage directly over the center or the middle man of the offensive line. The defensive linemen will usually be over the offensive guards. A defense can also be termed even if the defensive guards are in the gaps or seams between the offensive center and the offensive guard (Diagrams 1–6 to 1–9).

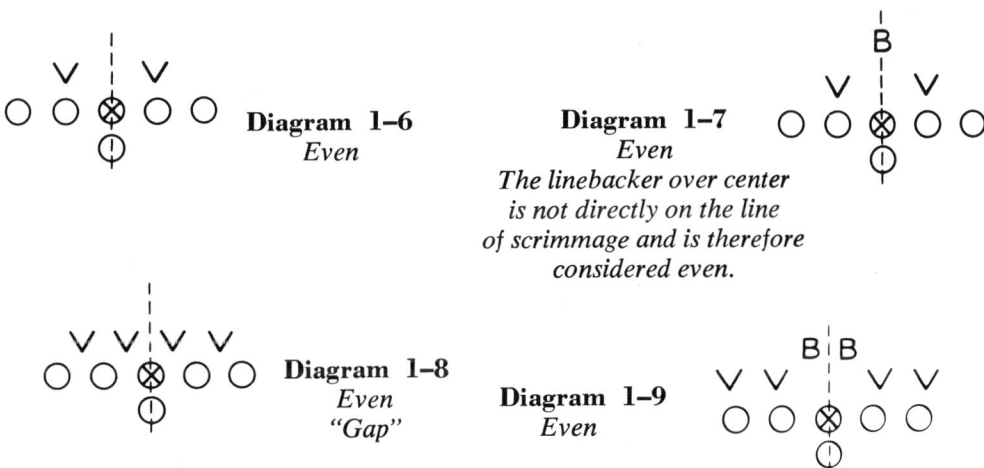

Diagram 1–6
Even

Diagram 1–7
Even
The linebacker over center
is not directly on the line
of scrimmage and is therefore
considered even.

Diagram 1–8
Even
"Gap"

Diagram 1–9
Even

2. A defensive lineman can either be head up, offset either way, or positioned between two offensive linemen (gap).

Head-up position

A defensive lineman is head up when he is directly over the offensive lineman (Diagrams 1–10 and 1–11).

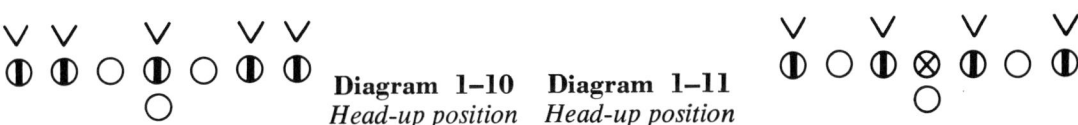

Diagram 1–10
Head-up position

Diagram 1–11
Head-up position

AN INTRODUCTION TO DEFENSES

Offset position

A defensive lineman is offset when he is positioned on an offensive lineman, but not directly over him. He is offset on one side or another (Diagrams 1–12 and 1–13).

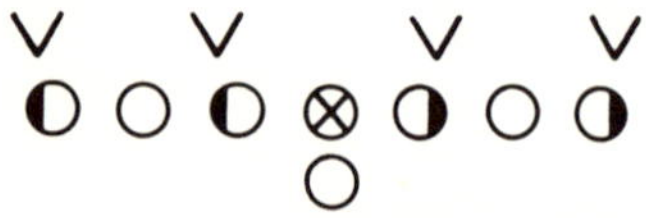

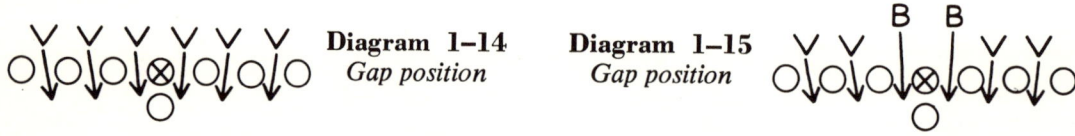

Diagram 1–12
Offset position

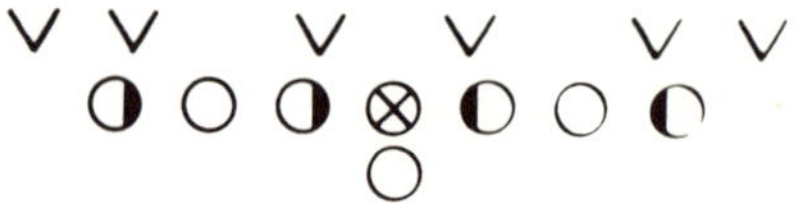

Diagram 1–13
Offset position

Gap position

A gap position occurs when a defensive lineman is positioned between two offensive linemen (Diagrams 1–14 and 1–15).

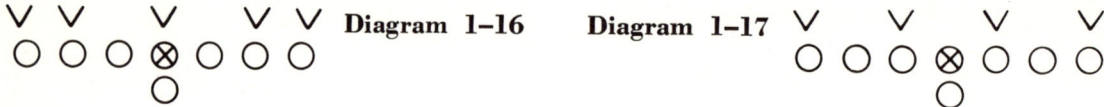

Diagram 1–14
Gap position

Diagram 1–15
Gap position

3. A defensive line will usually have at least one man on every other offensive lineman (Diagrams 1–16 and 1–17).

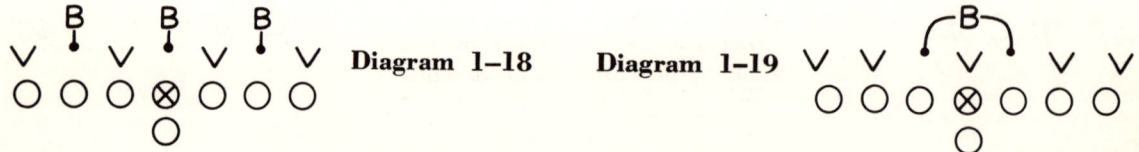

Diagram 1–16

Diagram 1–17

4. A defensive line will usually have at least four men on the line of scrimmage. In some cases, such as a prevent, a three-man line may exist. However, defensive lines usually vary from a four- to a nine-man line.

THE DEFENSIVE LINEBACKERS

1. Linebackers will usually be over offensive linemen that are uncovered, or will be in a position to cover the area or other areas (Diagrams 1–18 to 1–21).

Diagram 1–18

Diagram 1–19

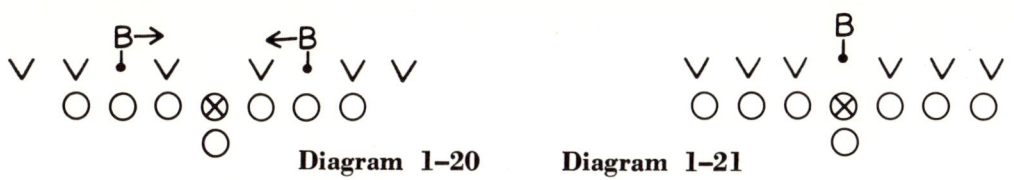

2. When there are an even number of linebackers (2 or 4), each will usually be placed on either side of the middle man of the offensive line. When there are an odd number of linebackers (1, 3, or 5), there will usually be one over the center man (Diagrams 1–22 to 1–25).

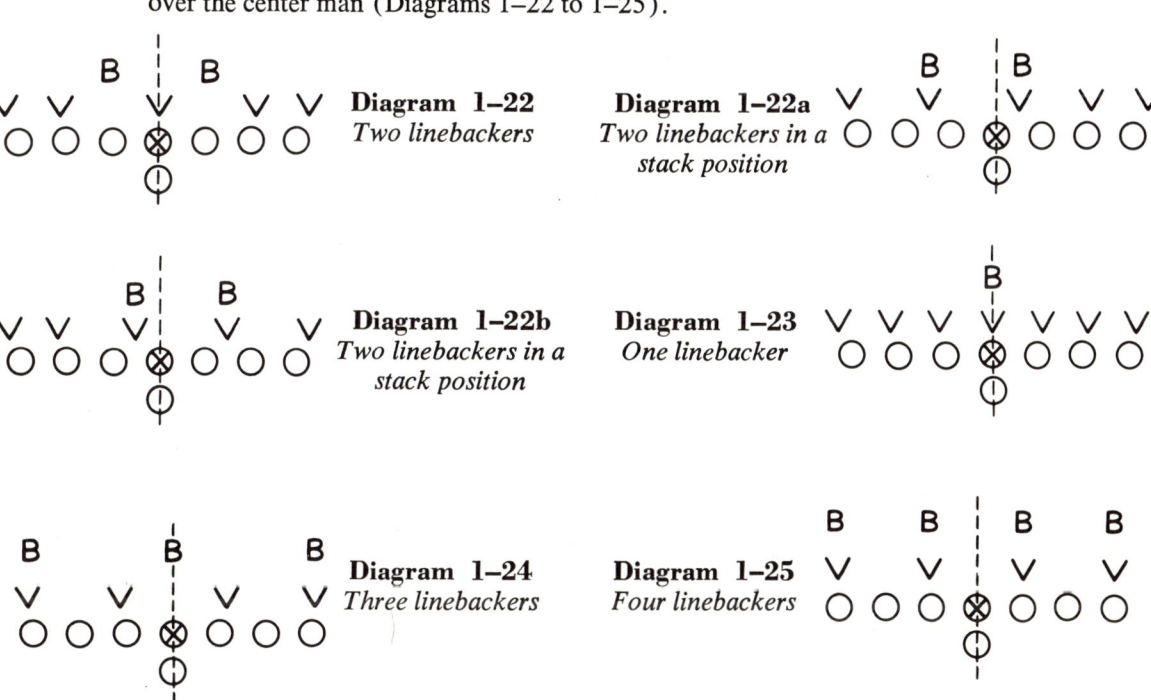

THE CONTAINING UNIT

A defensive secondary will take the form of a two deep box secondary, a three deep diamond secondary, or a four deep umbrella secondary. These secondaries are considered the "containing" portions of the defense (Diagrams 1–26 to 1–28).

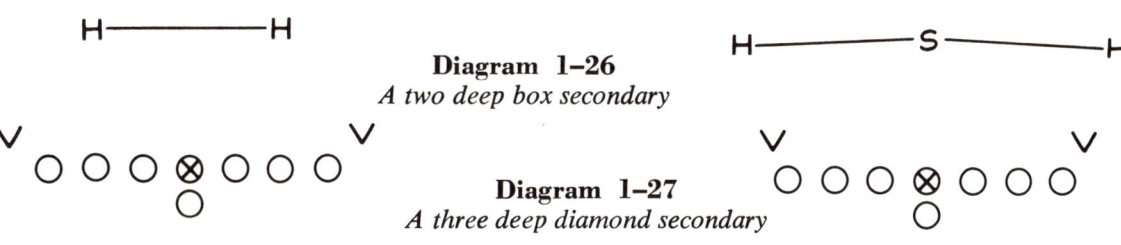

Diagram 1–28
A four deep umbrella secondary

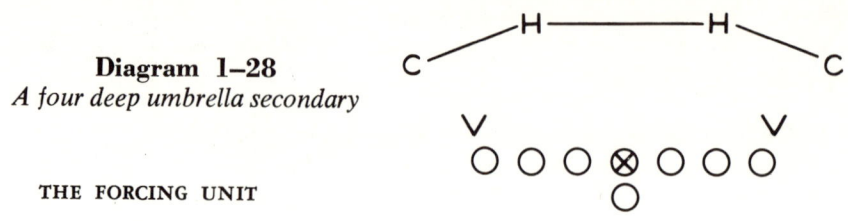

THE FORCING UNIT

A defense will be known as either an eight- or nine-man front. Both are considered to be the "forcing unit" of the defense (Diagrams 1–29 to 1–32).

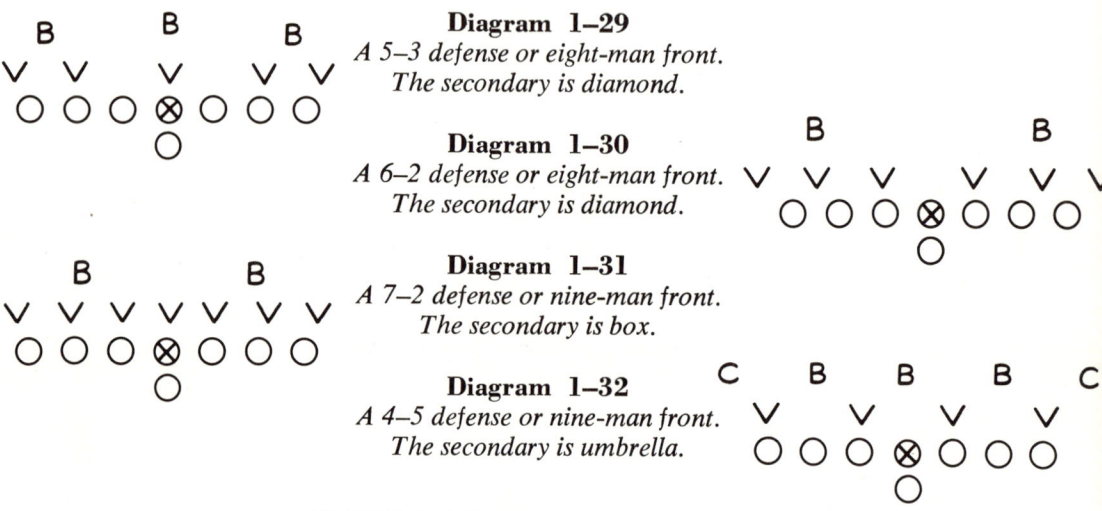

Diagram 1–29
A 5–3 defense or eight-man front. The secondary is diamond.

Diagram 1–30
A 6–2 defense or eight-man front. The secondary is diamond.

Diagram 1–31
A 7–2 defense or nine-man front. The secondary is box.

Diagram 1–32
A 4–5 defense or nine-man front. The secondary is umbrella.

EVERY DEFENSE HAS A PURPOSE

Every defense has a purpose. Defenses and their variations can either penetrate, pursue, penetrate *and* pursue, stunt, angle, veer, loop, slant, fire, etc. However, there should be a sound reason behind utilizing the defense. Is the defense going to stop the running game, passing attack, or both? Does a defense want to stop a team for no gain, throw a team for a loss, or let a team grind out yardage for little gains at a time? Tactical situations will determine greatly when a defense will be employed. Certain defenses can be used on first down, while others may be utilized on second, third, and fourth down situations. The purposes and objectives of defenses should be known and remembered constantly so all can be employed at the proper time.

A team cannot utilize all defenses and their variations because there is only so much that can be taught in a certain amount of time. Basic fundamentals, techniques, alignments, stances, responsibilities, and so forth, must be learned and reviewed constantly if a defense is going to be good. The less he has to learn the better a player will know his assignments and responsibilities.

PERSONNEL MAKES A DEFENSE SOUND

Personnel can make a defense sound or unsound, strong or weak. For example, a team with players who are excellent linebackers would do better to utilize a defense which employs many linebacker positions. However, if a coach decides to use another defense with few linebacker positions, the defense may be unsound due to the type of personnel.

Many teams have tried to copy defenses from bigtime schools and have been unsuccessful. One reason the larger schools enjoy success is that they have the personnel to be successful. With personnel like this, they can just about play any defense and be a winner. Other schools may not have the type of personnel to execute a "successful defense" with the personnel they have available to tap from. A defensive coach should decide what defense will fit his personnel, enabling them to be a winner and experience success. Changing because another team may be successful may sound good in principle, but may not work in reality.

THE IMPORTANCE OF SUCCESSFUL TEACHING

It is what a coach can teach successfully, and get the players to execute successfully, that is important. A coach should not attempt to teach something that has not been successful or has not been tried. It is preferable that the coach go with the "proven" material that he knows best. The better a coach knows and understands his defense and/or offense, the easier he will be able to teach it, and the better his team will execute it.

THEORIES OF EXECUTION

Each defense can be grouped into one of six different theories of execution.

1. A straight defense
2. A stunting defense
3. A balanced defense
4. An angling defense
5. A balanced angling defense
6. A jumping defense

1. A Straight Defense

A straight defense is in operation when the defensive linemen are not angling (slanting or looping) in either direction and the linebackers are not stunting, firing, or blitzing. The philosophy of the defense is to play man against man and challenge the offense to "beat" the defense. The only time the straight defense adjusts is when the offense adjusts. The advantages of the straight defense are: (1) it is very easy to teach and has a great deal of simplicity; (2) it is proclaiming the defensive men are stronger than the offensive men; (3) mistakes are usually held to a minimum; and (4) there is excellent team pursuit in a straight defense. Disadvantages of the straight defense are: (1) a coach cannot rely on the straight defense if he has inferior personnel—sooner or later the defense must stunt, angle, fire, etc. to confuse the opposition; (2) the offense has no trouble in blocking the alignment; (3) the offense is never confused due to defensive maneuvers; (4) the quarterback can easily check-off and automatic when the defense plays straight.

2. A Stunting Defense

A stunting defense is in operation when the defensive linemen and linebackers move from one position to another on the snap of the ball. A defender can move from the nose of the man he is aligned with, to the nose of the next offensive blocker and pursue from there. This is done: (1) to keep offensive linemen from going through on a linebacker or to free a linebacker; (2) to destroy a double-team block; or (3) to help support the defense. (For example, the split-6 linebackers fire the center-guard gaps and the defensive number two men support outside by looping out on to the offensive tackles.)

Also, stunting can be utilized for penetration by shooting the offensive gaps. The advantages of the stunting defense are: (1) it is used as an element of surprise; (2) it confuses the blocking of the offense; (3) it can throw a team for a loss because of its penetration; (4) when penetrating it has great passing rush on the quarterback, if he is setting up in the pocket; (5) it can catch plays from behind; and (6) it is best utilized with the agile football player. The disadvantages are: (1) it is proclaiming to the offense that certain positions on the defense may be weak; (2) a defensive man can stunt himself out of a play; (3) if the stunt is away, pursuit is lost; and (4) if the offensive team has a good cutting ballcarrier, he will be able to cut into many holes that stunting causes.

3. A Balanced Defense (Between Straight and Stunting)

A balanced defense is a combination of the straight defense and the stunting defense. It is a well-balanced attack because it has all the advantages of both defenses. The defense will usually play straight, and when it is necessary to make variations in the defense, it can do so by employing the stunt as a weapon.

4. An Angling Defense

The angling (loop or slant) defense is executed when defensive linemen are in certain defensive positions and, on the snap of the ball, quickly move (loop or slant) toward another position. Each player will square up and either explode into a gap or be ready to hit another offensive lineman. The entire line will either loop or slant right or left. Once the loop or slant has been performed, each lineman will immediately go on pursuit. The advantages of the angling defense are: (1) it can be used as an element of surprise; (2) it will confuse much of the offensive blocking; (3) agile, quick men can be utilized effectively; (4) it can

AN INTRODUCTION TO DEFENSES 11

limit double teaming by the offense; (5) it is excellent for the trap; (6) it can hold up receivers on pass patterns, and so forth. The disadvantages of this defense are: (1) there will not be a good pass rush on the quarterback; (2) it may proclaim that there are inadequacies of personnel on the defense; (3) it can easily loop or slant out of an area where the offense is running; and (4) a good running back will cut and maneuver away from the loop or slant.

5. A Balanced Angling Defense

A balanced angling defense is in operation when the defensive linemen execute a loop or slant and the defensive linebacker performs a stunt or fire in trying to penetrate across the line of scrimmage. This type of defense needs agile linebackers and quick movement of the forcing unit. The balanced angling defense has both the advantages and disadvantages of the angling defense and the stunting defense.

6. A Jumping Defense

A jumping defense is actually a combination of defenses. When the offense lines up for the snap of the ball, the jumping defense will be in one defensive set. On the command by a defensive player, or on the signals of the offensive quarterback, the defensive men will move to another defensive alignment. The defensive linemen can move from a head-up position to an offset, or gap position, and then back to any one of the three, etc. The defense may move as many times as it desires before the snap of the ball. On the snap, the defensive men can play the defense that it landed in, execute an individual or group stunt, or angle in another direction, although this may be hard to accomplish. The advantages of the jumping defense are: (1) it presents an element of surprise; (2) it makes the offensive team go on a quick count; (3) it can confuse the assignments of the offensive linemen; (4) it shows an opening in the defense and is closed by the jump; and (5) it is hard for the offense to automatic a play. The disadvantages of the jumping defense are: (1) a quick count limits the jump; (2) the defense may be caught in the jump on the snap of the ball and may lose some ground; (3) more than one defense is needed; and (4) if defensive linemen and/or linebackers are keying offensive linemen it may be difficult to read quickly.

CHANGING ALIGNMENTS

While changing from one alignment to another may first appear to be simple, it may present teaching problems. This is evident where a defense changes from an eight-man front to a nine-man front or vice versa. For example, a split-6 can adjust to a 5–4 Oklahoma alignment just as any defense can move from one alignment to another. From a split-6 the left defensive end moves to a cornerback position whether on or off the line of scrimmage; the left defensive tackle aligns over the offensive end; the left defensive guard adjusts on the offensive tackle; the left inside linebacker positions over the right offensive guard; the right linebacker aligns over the opposite offensive guard; the right defensive guard adjusts on the center; the right defensive tackle moves on the left offensive tackle, while the right defensive end positions over the left offensive end. The defensive secondary can play in a three deep, with a "monster" corner, or go to a box-corner secondary. As can be seen, a great many alignments, stances, assignments, and responsibilities occur.

However, changing from a 4–3 Box-Corner defense to a 6–1 Box-Corner defense can cause teaching problems also. As an illustration, in a 6–1 defense, usually the defensive guards play on the offensive guards and the defensive tackles position on the offensive tackles. In a 4–3 defense, however, the tackles usually play on the offensive guards. In this case, the defensive tackles must know the keys and reactions of the offensive tackles *and* offensive guards. Also, the guards or ends must now play defensive linebackers. As can be seen, different alignments can adjust easily; however, the responsibilities and assignments will involve different teaching and learning problems for the coach and players.

PURSUIT AND PENETRATING DEFENSES

There are three main areas the defense must control. They are as follows:

(1) Penetration Area
(2) Neutral Zone
(3) Normal Area

There are two defenses that control these three areas. The pursuit defense protects the normal area and the neutral zone, while the penetrating defense controls the penetrating area.

THE PURSUIT DEFENSE

The difference between the normal area pursuit defense and the neutral zone pursuit defense is that the former reads the block of the offensive line and strikes a blow in the normal area. The latter does the same, but first steps into the neutral zone. Both will look for the ballcarrier and go on pursuit. Both are delaying defenses that put great stress on gang tackling. Each allows yardage, but never the long run or long pass. They hope to slow the opponents' attack by forcing them to go the long way for the touchdown. Each defense hopes to punish the offense from down to down and force them into making a mistake, thus stopping their forward progress. Mistakes by the offense that can be made are:

(1) Fumbles   (3) Incomplete passes   (5) Missed assignments
(2) Penalties   (4) Interceptions

AN INTRODUCTION TO DEFENSES 13

THE PENETRATING DEFENSE

The theory of the penetrating defense is to take advantage, attack the offense, and attempt to force the offense into making a mistake. It hopes to throw opponents for a loss and place them in a long yardage situation. The penetrating defense does not wait for the offense to come at them. A penetrating defense will usually be in the gaps between two offensive linemen, ready to explode across the line of scrimmage and get into the offense's backfield. Angling, slanting, or looping into the gaps can be used for penetration also. If the linemen are unsuccessful in penetrating the forward wall, then it is their responsibility, as in the pursuit defense, to go on pursuit as quickly as possible.

The penetrating defense can be employed anywhere on the football field. It can be used as an element of surprise or during passing situations. An excellent time to utilize it is when the opponent is forced, for one reason or another, back to his own goal line. If the defense can force a mistake at this position of the field, it has a good opportunity to score a safety, recover a fumble, or even score a touchdown. The most important time to employ the penetrating defense is when the opponent's offense is on the verge of scoring and possesses the football somewhere short of the goal line. It is imperative to stop the opponent's attack by penetrating the line of scrimmage and halting their backs in their backfield. Diagram 1–33 provides an example of a pursuit defense and Diagram 1–34 illustrates a penetrating defense.

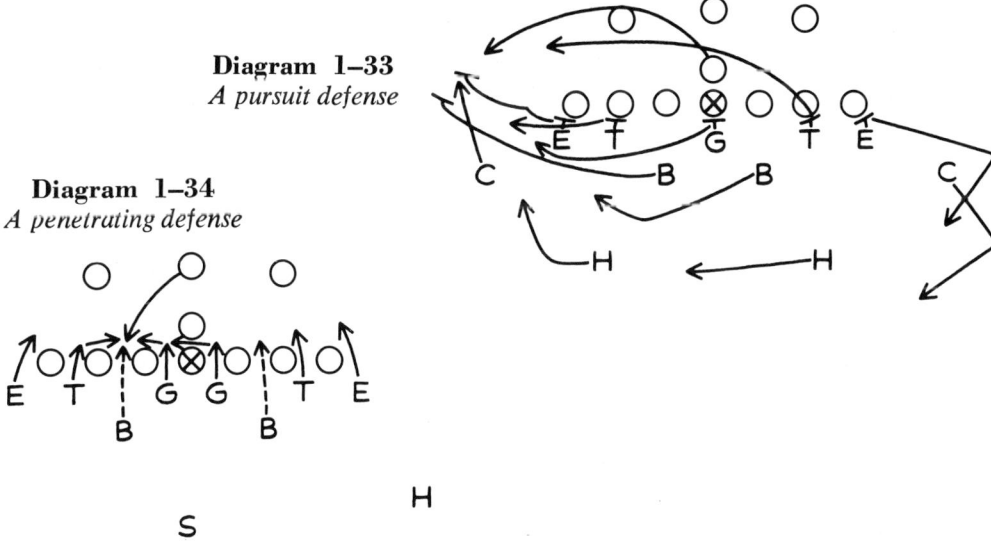

Diagram 1–33
A pursuit defense

Diagram 1–34
A penetrating defense

COMBINATION OF PURSUIT AND PENETRATING DEFENSES

The pursuit and penetrating defenses can be combined. The advantage is that the coach can have both pursuit and penetration as needed. The penetration is usually executed from a pursuit type of defense. The following are examples of pursuit and penetration combinations:

1. A defensive lineman(men) penetrating
2. A defensive linebacker(s) penetrating
3. A defensive safety penetrating
4. A combination of a defensive lineman and linebacker penetrating (blitz or stunt). The blitz is a combination of a firing linebacker and penetrating lineman. (A stunt has already been explained in the stunting defense—both will not be discussed at this point.)

Defensive Lineman Penetrating

When one or more defensive linemen want to penetrate the line of scrimmage, they will usually get into a gap between two offensive linemen and attempt to explode across the line of scrimmage. A boxing or crashing, or angling and looping end is penetration by linemen also. Penetration of defensive linemen from a pursuit defense is illustrated in Diagrams 1–35 and 1–36.

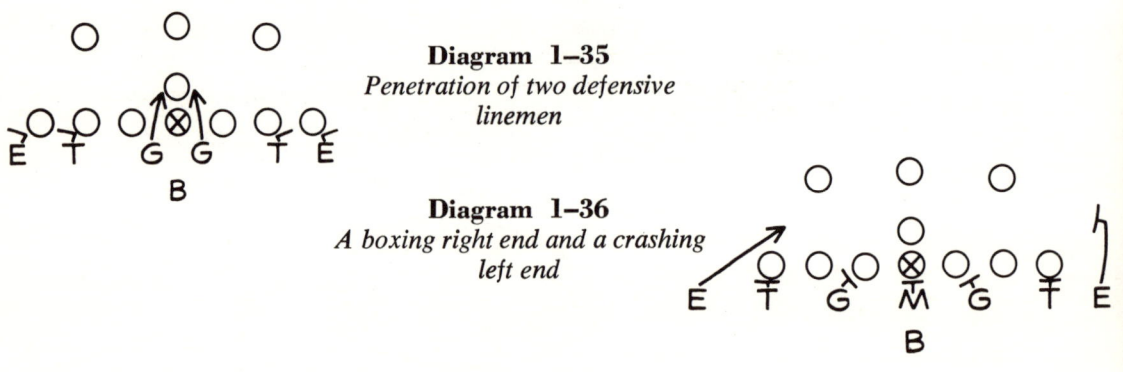

Diagram 1–35
Penetration of two defensive linemen

Diagram 1–36
A boxing right end and a crashing left end

Defensive Linebacker Penetrating

When a defensive linebacker wants to penetrate, it is usually done on a fire or blitz technique. He will move from his position and attempt to get into the backfield to upset the play. He can execute the fire by himself, have defensive linemen open a hole in the offensive line for him, or fire on a reaction of a key (an offensive guard pulling out of the line, when the linebacker's responsibility is to fire over the guard's position on the pull). A firing linebacker is indicated in Diagrams 1–37 and 1–38.

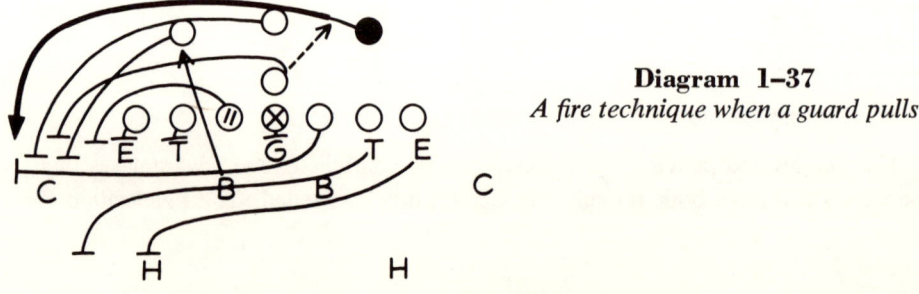

Diagram 1–37
A fire technique when a guard pulls

Diagram 1-38
A fire maneuver with defensive linemen occupying the offensive linemen

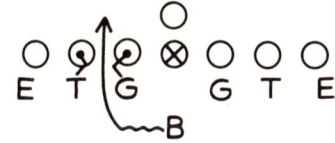

The Scrape-Off Technique

Many linebackers today are involved in a scrape-off maneuver to penetrate and cover an area. They are aligned in one position, but are responsible for another area. The linebackers usually key the ball or someone in the backfield. For example, illustrated in Diagram 1–38a is a 5–4 Oklahoma defense with a fully rotated corner to the right. Since the left side of the defense is considered weak to the outside, the left linebacker's responsibility is to first protect the offensive guard area, and then to scrape-off, penetrate, and force the ballcarrier deep outside. If the play goes in the opposite direction, the left linebacker will go on pursuit. While this is illustrated from a 5–4 defense, the scrape-off technique is employed for off-tackle and middle areas by other defenses also.

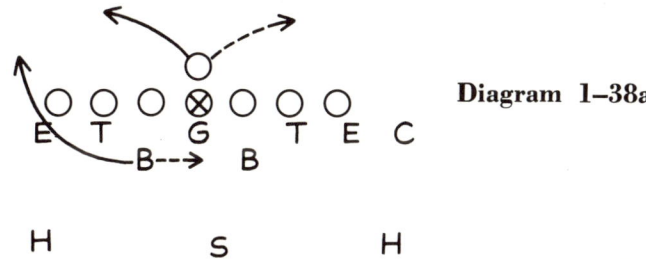

Diagram 1–38a

Defensive Safety Penetrating

A defensive safety penetrating the line of scrimmage is a special maneuver by the defense. It can be executed on any down, but it is best used in a passing situation. The defensive linemen occupy the offensive linemen in the shooting area so the safety will be able to explode free into the backfield. Some part of the pass defense coverage may be weakened, but it is expected that the safety will confuse the offense and stop the play. This is illustrated in Diagram 1–39:

Diagram 1–39
A safety fire

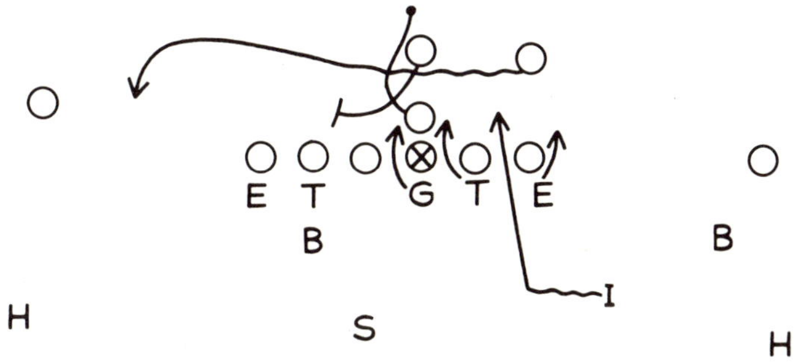

ATTACKING DEFENSES

NO DEFENSE IS PERFECT

It should be realized that no defense is perfect. Coaches throughout the years have thought of and "invented" new defenses and variations to each. However, of all defenses, not one can provide all the answers. A new defense may materialize one year and cause offenses many problems. However, the offenses will eventually "catch up" to the defense with certain blocking combinations, running plays, and passes. The field is simply too large for a defense to be "foolproof." Every defense can be attacked in one way or another and it is up to the coach to find the best method of attacking each one.

THE CONCEPT OF STRENGTHS AND WEAKNESSES OF DEFENSES

Every defense will have certain strengths and weaknesses. A portion of a defense is considered strong when it has all offensive men covered or has more men in the particular area. Diagram 1–40 shows three defensive linemen covering three offensive linemen. This is considered strong.

Diagram 1–40
Three defensive linemen on three offensive linemen

∨ ∨ ∨
O O O

Diagram 1–41 illustrates two defensive linemen and two defensive linebackers against three offensive linemen. Diagram 1–42 indicates another four-on-three ratio, with no men uncovered. Diagram 1–43 shows a three-on-two, which makes these areas of the defense strong in comparison to the offense.

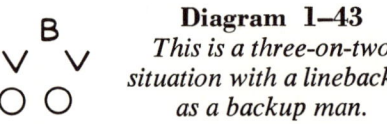

Diagram 1–41
While this area can be attacked, there are four men on three and another man must be brought in for extra blocking assistance.

Diagram 1–42
All three offensive linemen are covered with an extra linebacker. In this situation the offense should run to another area.

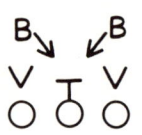

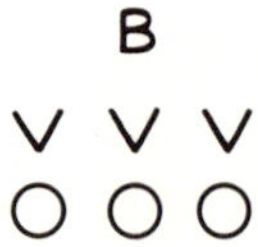

Diagram 1–43
This is a three-on-two situation with a linebacker as a backup man.

One weakness of the defense occurs when there are fewer defensive than offensive linemen in the area, or when a linebacker is off the line of scrimmage. Dia-

AN INTRODUCTION TO DEFENSES

grams 1–44 and 1–45 indicate two-on-three ratios and Diagram 1–46 illustrates a three-on-three with a linebacker.

Diagram 1–44
This is a two-on-three situation. In this case, the middle area is considered weak.

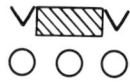

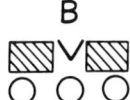

Diagram 1–45
This is a two-on-three situation also. The two side areas are weak.

Diagram 1–46
While this is a three-on-three situation, one is a linebacker off the line of scrimmage and is therefore considered weak.

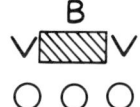

Other areas of a defense are also thought of as weak when a defensive man is in a position that will make it difficult for him to cover another area. An example would be an inside linebacker covering an outside flat. A coach and quarterback should find all of these areas and attempt to attack each one.

Another important factor about all defenses is that each will maneuver and adjust its alignment to meet the adjustments of the offense. If, for example, the offense stations a halfback in a winged position, 1 yard outside the end, the defense can perform a number of movements and shift to meet the offense's strength. An adjustment of a defensive lineman, or linebacker, or a slight rotation with the deep secondary will meet this strength. Other various adjustments to strengths of the offense can be executed by every defense. If the defense does not adjust, then the coach and quarterback must be ready to attack that area. If the defense does, then the offense must be prepared to capitalize on another area of the defense which has been weakened on the adjustment. An offense can do many things to make it difficult for the defense to meet strength with strength. This can be accomplished by shifting the offense before the starting count, split ends, move to slots, put out flankers, put men in motion, go to unbalanced and balanced lines, shift to unusual formations, and so forth.

ATTACK PERSONNEL OF THE DEFENSE

Personnel can be the determining factor in the strength and weakness of a defense. An area which is considered strong, because of the alignment, may actually be inferior in personnel. An area which is thought of as weak may actually be strong. A defense which is also properly taught, trained, and drilled repeatedly will make a defense good, not simply the alignment itself.

It is, therefore, important for the coach and the quarterback to know the personnel of the opponent. This can be secured from scouting reports and observations in a game. Play selection should be aimed at the alignment and its weaknesses first, and when inferior personnel is spotted, the coach and quarterback should attack that area as quickly as possible.

IMPROPER ALIGNMENTS MAKE A DEFENSE WEAK

Improper alignments will make any defense weak. When personnel are aligned in the wrong positions the defense is no longer sound in principle in certain areas. The offense should be aware of any improper alignments that can be quickly seen and should immediately attack them whenever possible. If, for example, a defensive tackle in a 5–4 Oklahoma defense is aligning inside the offensive tackle, the offense should immediately attack outside of him preferably at the off-tackle hole. While the inside may be stronger, the off-tackle hole has definite weaknesses.

PLANNING TO ATTACK DEFENSES

When offensive linemen are blocking defenses, they must fully be prepared to block every conceivable situation that may arise. Blocking rules are usually set up for all defenses in general and then adjustments are made to block particular defenses. Certain blocking patterns, schemes, running plays, and passes must be at a coach's disposal if he is going to take advantage and attack a defense properly and successfully.

To illustrate, against the Notre Dame 6 defense, most rule blocking and offensive plays must be discarded. Once the coach has finished deciphering his material, he has a few blocking combinations and plays that can take care of all the Notre Dame 6 defensive maneuvers. The coach and the entire team now will be able to take advantage of the defense and attack all the defensive movements. This must be done on numerous occasions and the offensive coach should be fully prepared to plan, organize, and teach the team the correct methods of attacking any defense.

ATTACK ONE DEFENSIVE AREA

The offense should direct its attack at the weak areas of a defense. Coach Elvan George, formerly head football coach of Ada High School, and presently athletic director of East Central State College, Ada, Oklahoma, stated in his book *The Split-T in High School Football*:

> Unless the attack is carefully planned, it is unrealistic to assume that the offense is going to move the ball well. Each defense aligns its players so that they have more strength at some points than at others. Should we direct our attack toward the opponent's strong points, we could expect little success unless we were superior in manpower.

AN INTRODUCTION TO DEFENSES

Against strong opposition we must plan carefully to give our players an advantage by directing our attack at the weakness of the defense.[7]

Coach George went on to mention a little later in his book:

The weak point of the defensive formation must be located quickly if it is to be exploited. Most high school coaches have learned long ago that they can't expect the average quarterback to survey the entire playing field and pinpoint the defensive weakness. This is too much for the high school player to accomplish in such a short time. For this reason, I think the best method is to consider only a small area at one time.[8]

This point is important to remember not only for the high school quarterback, but for the college quarterback as well. The quarterback and coach cannot look at an entire defense and attempt to exploit it. One area should be located and attacked. A defense can be divided into four different areas:

1. Middle
2. Off-tackle (right and left of the center)
3. Outside (right and left of the center)
4. Pass defense (right and left of the center)

These areas are illustrated in Diagrams 1–47 to 1–50.

Diagram 1–47
The 4–5 defense

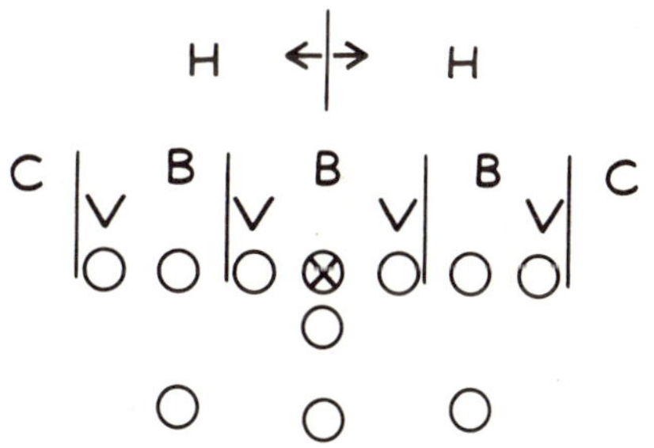

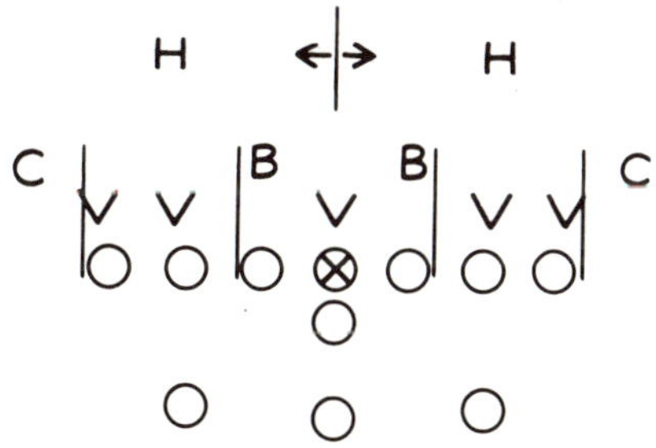

Diagram 1–48
The 5–4 defense

Diagram 1–49
The 6–2 defense

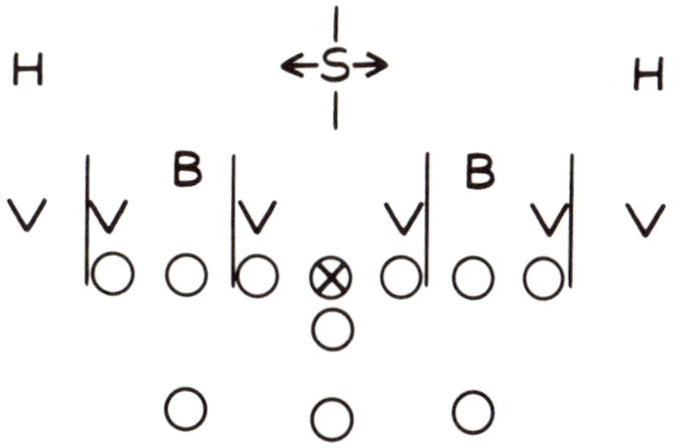

---

[7]Elvan George, *The Split-T in High School Football* (Englewood Cliffs, N.J.: Prentice-Hall, Inc., 1958), p. 148.
[8]*Ibid.*, pp. 155–156.

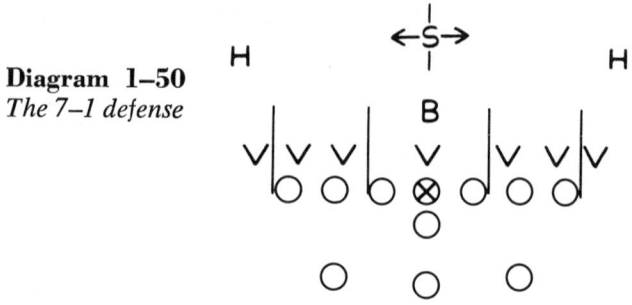

Diagram 1-50
The 7-1 defense

First consider the middle area to see if it can be attacked. The middle area is between the two offensive guards. Next look at the off-tackle hole, and third survey the outside for possible exploitation. Finally search the pass defense on either side of the center to exploit the possible weakness areas.

FIFTEEN WAYS TO TAKE ADVANTAGE OF THE DEFENSE

The following are some general rules for the coach and quarterback to know if they are taking advantage of the different tactics the defense may employ.

1. When the ends are crashing, run pitchouts and sweeps to the outside.
2. When the ends are boxing, run inside of them.
3. When the ends are waiting or floating, run power at them or quickly fake inside and go outside, or fake outside and go inside.
4. When the linemen are penetrating, run traps, draws, screens, or go outside away from the penetration. Run a play-action pass to draw the defensive linemen to the faking ballcarrier.
5. When the defensive men are waiting, run at them with power, wedges, and straight plays.
6. When the defense is tight inside the ends, run outside with runs and passes.
7. When the defense is loose or spread, run inside.
8. When the linebackers are in stack or tandem positions, be ready for stunts or fires.
9. When the defense is stunting, throw quick passes over them. If the offensive linemen cannot block the stunts, run outside, pass, or go inside with wedges.
10. When the defense employs slants and loops, run straight plays at one man and cut off the loop, or run quick counters or reverses. Either pass or run outside.
11. When linebackers are inside the ends, throw in the flat.
12. When linebackers are on the outside of the ends, throw quick hooks between the remaining linebackers.
13. Fully know and recognize rotations, zones, man-to-man, and other combinations to be able to attack them with a good passing game.
14. Split-out ends, flankers, put men in motion, etc., to see how the defense adjusts. Capitalize on the adjustments.
15. Thoroughly know and understand the plays and the series of each in the offense and how each can be employed against every defense.

KNOW THE OPPONENT'S PHILOSOPHY OF DEFENSE

Whether it be in high school, college, or professional football, a coach has his own philosophy of defense. Some coaches believe in using only one defense with absolutely no variations. Others believe in two, three, and four defenses, and some will want to utilize more. While a few strategists stunt and use variations to a limited extent, other coaches try to stunt on every play. Many believe in slanting and looping from a defense and others stunt and fire off the loop or slanting line.

Although every coach does have his own philosophy, he should know the philosophy of his opponent. He should know whether one team utilizes many defenses or only a few. He should understand the stunts and maneuvers that each opponent employs. By knowing this, the coach will be in a better position to meet the many situations which will occur when his team faces the opponent's defense and variations.

2

ATTACKING STACKED, TANDEM, STUNTING, AND ANGLING DEFENSES

Every defense has certain maneuvers that it can utilize in attempting to confuse the offensive blocking. These maneuvers are employed for several purposes: as an element of surprise; as a change of pace; to cover up inadequacies of the defensive personnel; to confuse the offense; and to put a player in a more advantageous position. While all defensive alignments differ and use variations of their own, the maneuvers are basically the same to all defenses and can easily be blocked by the offensive team. Defenses can employ the stack, the tandem, or a stunt from either of these, a fire or blitz, a regular stunt, or an angle (a loop and slanting line). These maneuvers can be utilized anywhere along the offensive line at any time and from all defenses.

The most important point to remember is that every variation can be blocked by the offensive team. It does not matter what the defense employs; if the offense anticipates it, it can be successfully blocked. Some coaches do not mind defensive maneuvers. They feel that if any team does employ any type of angling, looping, slanting, or stunting, the offense will certainly be able to run without any difficulty. It is their contention that the more the defense stunts or angles the better the offensive attack will run.

IMPORTANCE OF SCOUTING, FILMS, AND OBSERVATIONS IN A GAME

If the offensive team is attempting to block the maneuvers of the defense, they must be fully prepared. Scouting reports and the use of films of the opponent are

ATTACKING STACKED, TANDEM, STUNTING, AND ANGLING DEFENSES

very necessary. If possible, the offense must know what the defense utilizes before the game begins. With the employment of scouting and films, coaches know what to expect of the opponent and can teach the offensive blocking patterns they want used for that particular game. If, for example, the defense utilizes the straight stack with no maneuvers from it, then the offense can block it a number of different ways. If the defense stunts from this position though, the offense will have to be prepared to attack the opponent in a different manner. Observation in the game is important also. Once it is learned what the variations and maneuvers of the defense are, the coach will either continue with what the team is doing or make changes because of the different maneuvers and alterations of the defense.

THE IMPORTANCE OF DRILLING

It is of vital importance that the entire team be drilled in blocking the variations the defense employs. The coach cannot go into a game hopefully wishing the team will be able to block the various maneuvers of the defense. The proper time to drill the offense in every situation that may occur in a game is during the first few weeks of preseason. The offense may not encounter any type of stacking or stunting for a number of games, but when the defensive team does employ them, the offense will have been fully prepared. Much drilling and "polishing" of the fundamentals and techniques of the different maneuvers a week before the game is all that will be needed.

ATTACKING DEFENSES AND THEIR VARIATIONS

It must be remembered that offenses have blocking rules against defenses in general, but many of these rules do not hold up against certain variations and maneuvers of defenses. A team may utilize three or four defenses with variations of stacks, tandems, and defensive stunts off each. Therefore, a coach must take from scouting reports and films the alignments and stunts of each defense and the situations when the opponent employs them. He must then make a short list of plays that will successfully be executed against all the defenses and situations that might arise. The offense is then drilled repeatedly during the week, running those plays and blocking the many variations that might arise. In numerous cases, therefore, the coach ends up blocking defenses rather than applying blocking rules, because the rules will not hold up against a few defenses, the many variations to all defenses, and the different defensive maneuvers.

THE BACKFIELD, LINE, AND BALLCARRIER

To attack the various maneuvers the defense employs, the linemen, backfield, and ballcarrier must be entirely ready. The offense must constantly work together to improve the blocking of the play to be run against all defensive maneuvers.

THE OFFENSIVE LINE

Defenses and their variations will probably change from week to week, but the methods of blocking each defensive maneuver will not alter. The linemen must execute the fundamentals and techniques individually and then as groups to coordinate the line in blocking the variations. Examples of group blocking for preparation of the opponent's defense are guards' and centers' blocking stunts and guards and tackles being drilled against stacks, while the tackles and ends execute blocks against the fire and blitz. After individual and group drills, the linemen will come together as an entire unit and continually work every defensive maneuver that was seen in individual and group drills. Every play should be performed against the defensive alignment and its variations to improve the blocking patterns and the plays the offense employs. Blocking rules and line-calls for each should be repeated and improved upon.

THE OFFENSIVE BACKFIELD

Many times, one or more of the players in the backfield must assist the offensive linemen in executing a block on a defensive man. Without a block by the back, the play may not succeed in advancing the ball. As was accomplished by the linemen, the backs must also work individually and in groups. Then the backfield and the line are brought together as a team to execute the play properly.

THE BALLCARRIER

The ballcarrier, although not a blocker, can be the most important individual in making the play and overall team operation perform at its best. Many times when a stunt or another variation is utilized in an area where the play is to be run, a good back who has been drilled on quick cutting and finding an open hole can use this to his team's advantage. In other instances, a stunting linebacker and the linemen may stunt away from the point of attack and again the back can be free. The more drilling of the ballcarrier to run for daylight, the better the play will gain yardage. The ballcarrier, blocking backs, and the offensive line must continually work together against the many situations the defensive team employs. The better trained and drilled the offense is in attacking the various defensive maneuvers, the better the play will be executed, and the more the ball will be advanced.

THE IMPORTANCE OF ANTICIPATION

When blocking the different variations of defenses, the blockers at the point of attack should anticipate what the defense is attempting to do. If the offense

ATTACKING STACKED, TANDEM, STUNTING, AND ANGLING DEFENSES 25

realizes what can occur, especially from scouting reports, films, and observations in the game, it can employ one or more methods to block the maneuver. If, for example, the defense should align in a tandem position and play straight, the blockers can anticipate their move and block it in a number of ways. If the defense tandems and plays straight, but stunts on occasion, the offense must again be anticipating these maneuvers. When such an occasion arises they must block it in a different manner, expecting either one or the other to occur, being able to block each no matter what the defense utilizes.

SEVEN VARIATIONS OF THE DEFENSE

The defense can employ seven different defensive maneuvers against the offense. No matter what the purpose is or what defense is utilized, the offense must think positively and constantly be trained and drilled to block each defender. Once this has been accomplished the offense will have minimal trouble in attacking the maneuvers of the defense. The seven variations of defenses are listed below, with their execution to be discussed:

(1) The straight stack
(2) The straight tandem
(3) The stunt
(4) The stunting stack
(5) The stunting tandem
(6) The angle (loop or slant)
(7) The fire or blitz

(1) The Straight Stack

The straight stack or "stack" is a defensive lineman positioned in a gap between two offensive linemen with a linebacker stationed directly behind him (Diagram 2–1 and Photo 2–1).

Diagram 2–1
A stack

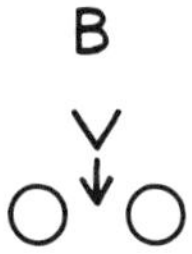

The straight stack is used as a change of pace and a different defensive look. It attempts to get two offensive linemen to block one defensive man. This, therefore, will free a linebacker to move to the point of attack quicker. The lineman in the gap position attempts to penetrate across the line of scrimmage and get into the backfield to upset the play. The straight stack is also used when the linebackers are inexperienced in shedding blockers. The linebacker from this position can cover to the left and right, thereby having two men cover three holes. This is illustrated in Diagram 2–2.

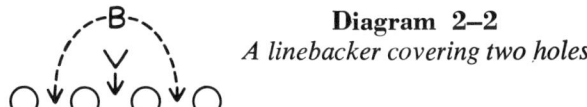

Diagram 2–2
A linebacker covering two holes

(2) The Straight Tandem

The straight tandem or "tandem" is a defensive lineman directly positioned over an offensive lineman with a linebacker stationed behind him Diagram 2–3 and Photo 2–2).

Diagram 2–3
A tandem

```
    B
    V
    O
```

The tandem is found in many defenses and is used as a change of pace for other defenses. At times, it hides a linebacker from being blocked and puts him in a better position to get to the ball. From this position, the linebacker can cover two men instead of one. This is indicated in Diagram 2–4.

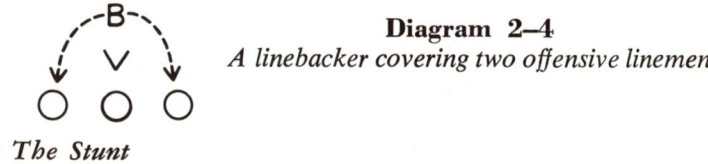

Diagram 2–4
A linebacker covering two offensive linemen

(3) The Stunt

A stunt is usually utilized between a defensive lineman and linebacker. It can be employed by two defensive linemen or two defensive linebackers. Each man is positioned over an offensive lineman and on the snap of the ball changes positions to cover another offensive lineman. A defensive lineman and linebacker stunt is illustrated in Diagrams 2–5 and 2–6.

Photo 2–1

Photo 2–2

ATTACKING STACKED, TANDEM, STUNTING, AND ANGLING DEFENSES 27

Stunts for two defensive linemen and two linebackers are shown respectively in Diagrams 2–7 and 2–8.

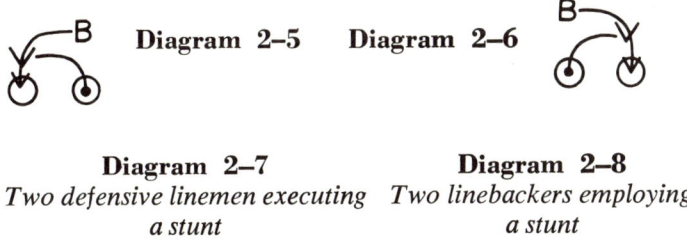

Diagram 2–5   Diagram 2–6

Diagram 2–7
Two defensive linemen executing a stunt

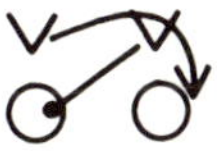

Diagram 2–8
Two linebackers employing a stunt

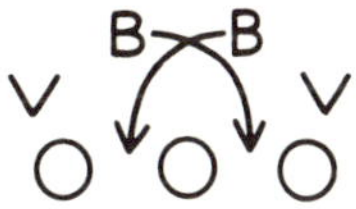

(4) The Stunting Stack

The stunting stack is used when a defensive lineman stationed in the gap will move either right or left to cover one of the offensive linemen on the snap of the ball. The linebacker will quickly move to protect the vacated area. This is indicated in Diagrams 2–9 and 2–10.

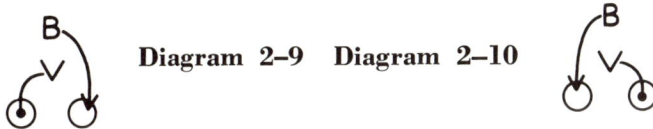

Diagram 2–9   Diagram 2–10

(5) The Stunting Tandem

The stunting tandem is executed when the defensive lineman directly over the offensive lineman moves toward either the uncovered lineman or the man he is covering. The linebacker will shoot opposite the direction the defensive lineman angles. This is illustrated in Diagrams 2–11 and 2–12.

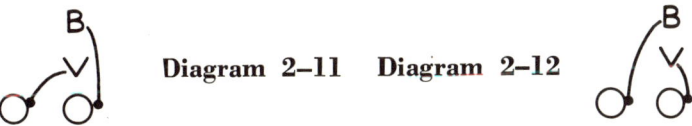

Diagram 2–11   Diagram 2–12

The purposes and advantages of the stunt, stunting stack, and stunting tandem can be referred to in Chapter 1 under the stunting defense.

(6) The Loop or Slant

The angling defense (loop or slant) is usually executed by the entire defensive line, but can be employed by one, two, or three men. On the snap of the ball, the linemen will angle from one position either right or left into a gap or another offensive lineman. The loop is illustrated in Diagram 2–13 and the slant is shown in Diagram 2–14. Refer to Chapter 1 for the advantages and purposes of the angling defense.

Diagram 2–13
A loop to the right

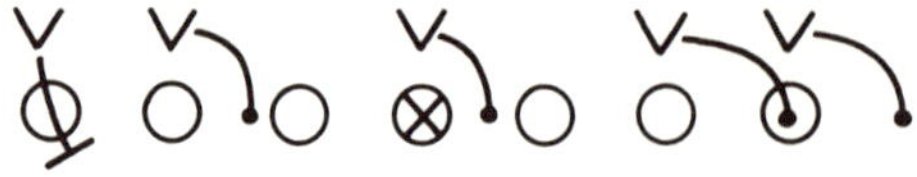

Diagram 2–14
A slant to the left

(7) The Fire or Blitz

The fire or blitz is executed by one or more defensive linemen, linebackers, and halfbacks. On the snap of the ball, one man (fire) or more men (blitz) will move from their positions and explode across the line of scrimmage attempting to upset the play. This can be executed from the tandem and stack defense and from a regular defensive alignment. The fire and blitz is illustrated in Diagrams 2–15 through 2–17.

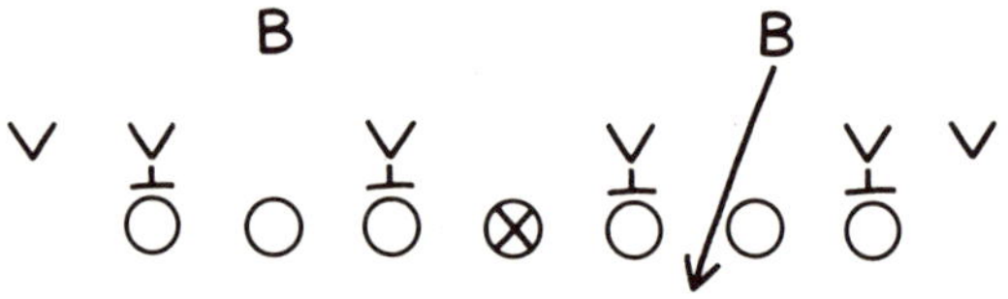

Diagram 2–15
A fire

Diagram 2–16
A blitz

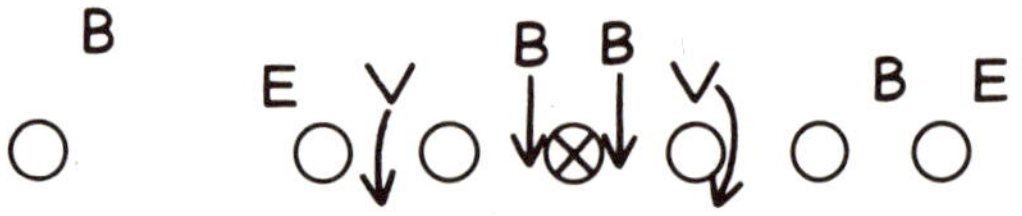

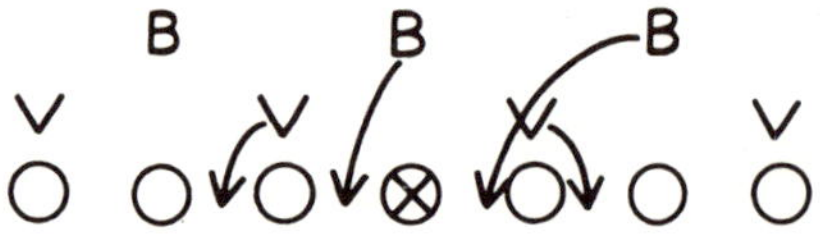

Diagram 2–17
A blitz

The stack, tandem, stunt, blitz, and so forth, were illustrated in the diagrams with two or three men. It must be indicated, however, that each can be executed by more than one or two men and can be used along the entire defensive line. Therefore, it is imperative that every lineman be able to block all variations at any time. The following are a few methods of how to block the defensive maneuvers discussed. No matter what the defense employs, the blocking methods are the same for every defense.

HOW TO BLOCK THE STRAIGHT STACK

The following are four possible ways to block the straight stack:

1. The slide.
2. The swing-around.
3. A backfield man blocking.
4. A lineman blocking.

The Slide

The slide is employed by two offensive linemen. From a good offensive stance the man nearest the point of attack will release from the line of scrimmage, ignoring the man in the gap, and will block the linebacker stationed behind him. He will stay low and under good control, because he will not be hitting a man on the line of scrimmage. The blocker should aim at the linebacker's belt buckle. As he nears the linebacker on the third or fourth step the lineman should remain low, shorten his strides, secure a wide base, keep his head up and shoulders square. Just before the initial blow, the blocker should explode with the legs, back, and arms and make contact in the midsection of the linebacker. The head should be directly in the middle. The feet are foot-firing rapidly, attempting to move the linebacker away from the hole. The head will slide to the side where the ballcarrier is expected to run. If the blocker feels he is sliding to the ground and will lose the block, he should employ the hand nearest the hole to keep himself up and in contact with the linebacker. If he loses the block, he must get up and make contact with the linebacker again. The block should be continued until the whistle has blown.

The lineman farthest from the hole will execute a fill block. On the snap of the ball and from a good offensive stance, he will step toward the hole where the play is being run. He should try to accomplish two things: (1) stop the penetration of the defensive lineman in the gap and (2) attempt to eliminate him from the play. On the first step the lineman should remain low and aim his eyes at the defensive man's near inside hip. If the defensive man explodes across the line of scrimmage, he should position his head in front and as far to the other side as possible, attempting to stop the forward progress of the gap man. The arms will come up to a blocking position. The second step should be taken with the farthest leg. The legs will continually drive to stay in front of the gap man. If possible, the offensive blocker should attempt to position himself on all fours, after stopping the penetration, and execute a scramble block to keep the man from the point of attack.

However, on the first step, if it is noticed that the gap man is not attempting

30   ATTACKING STACKED, TANDEM, STUNTING, AND ANGLING DEFENSES

to penetrate, the blocker must quickly explode across the face of the defensive lineman to execute a crab block on the leg nearest the hole. The offensive blocker should make contact on the second step. He must continually scramble with his hands and dig with his feet to eliminate the gap man from the point of attack. The crabbing will enable him also to stay off the ground.

The slide technique can be employed at the point of attack, but it is best utilized away from where the ball is being run. Diagrams 2–18 and 2–19 illustrate the slide against the stack. The arrow indicates to which side the play is being run (Photos 2–3a, b, and c).

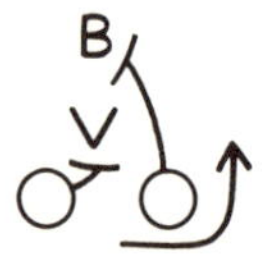

Diagram 2–18 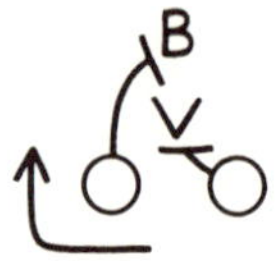   **Diagram 2–19**

Execution of the slide versus the stack. A fill block on the gap man and a straight block on a linebacker is being employed.

The Swing Around

The swing around is used by two offensive linemen against the stacked defensive men. Instead of releasing from the line of scrimmage and blocking the linebacker, the man nearest the hole should execute a down block or a gap block on the man located in the gap. From a good offensive stance, he must step directly toward the gap man. He should remain low, head up, and eyes looking at the near hip. The blocker should be prepared to slide the head either way, depending upon the movement of the gap man. If the gap man attempts to penetrate across the line of scrimmage, the offensive lineman will place his head in front of the penetrator. Then he should explode into the gap man and make contact, with his far shoulder in the opponent's hip. His far arm will come up to form a good blocking base with his head and shoulder. The lineman's other hand

Photo 2–3a

Photo 2–3b

Photo 2–3c

and arm will be used as a stabilizer so he will not go to the ground. His legs should drive hard and rapidly to move the defensive man down the line. If the man in the gap does not penetrate, the blocker's head should slide across the gap man's back and the same blocking movement just described should be executed.

The offensive blocker farthest from the point of attack will execute a quick pull around the block of the man nearest the hole. On the signal by the quarterback, the "puller" will take an open jab step of no more than 6 inches and land on his toes. Simultaneously, his arm is vigorously brought back and kept near the hip, and the opposite foot pivots on the first movement. A short step prevents loss of balance.

On this first movement he remains low to the ground, keeping his head up, and aims in the direction where the play is going. On this step he should be leaning forward, and on the second step a normal stride should be taken. The puller should never break stride after the first step. On the second step his head should be turned inward looking for the linebacker. The toes should be pointed inward and on the third step (which will be the outside foot), he quickly plants, pivots, and turns upfield to execute a block on the linebacker. On the turn upfield he should remain low. The shoulder nearest the line of scrimmage will dip down. A good coaching point is to "grab grass" with the inside hand. This will automatically lower the shoulder making it easier to execute the turn. While facing and aiming downfield, he should look for the linebacker who may or may not have moved from the original position. The pulling lineman must be as quick as possible, but once turned downfield, he must get under control to block the linebacker. To do this he should shorten his stride, remain low to the ground, and have a wide base underneath him. He should make contact with the linebacker and execute the fundamentals explained previously.

The swing around is best employed at the point of attack, but can also be used away from the position where the ball is being run. Diagrams 2–20 and 2–21 illustrate the swing around against a stacking defense (Photos 2–4a, b, and c).

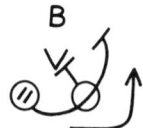

Diagram 2–20   **Diagram 2–21**

Execution of the swing around against the stack with a gap block and a pull maneuver.

A Backfield Man Blocking A Stack

A few plays have been designed for a backfield man to become a blocker on the line of scrimmage. Many times, more than one back will be employed at a stack. The back can either block the gap man or the stacked linebacker. He can be stationed at a wing, slot, halfback, or fullback position. He is utilized either to bring more blockers to the point of attack than what the defense has, or equal the ratio of offensive men to defensive men. An example would be the defense having five men to four of the offense. An extra back will even the ratio, and the play has a better chance of succeeding. Therefore, Diagram 2–22 illustrates five-on-four principles, with a man from a wing position executing a block on a stacked linebacker.

In this case, the end blocks the first man outside of him and the tackle executes a down block on the man in the gap. The guard can do a number of things to

Photo 2-4a

Photo 2-4b

Photo 2-4c

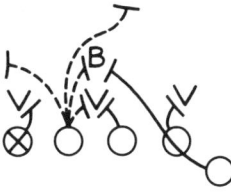

Diagram 2-22

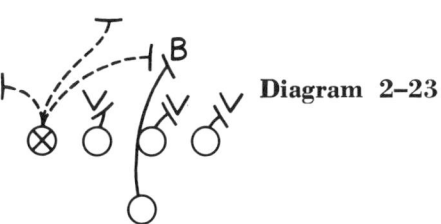

Diagram 2-23

assist the play. If there is a man over him, he must block the defensive players. If there is no man as shown, the guard can assist the double-team on the man in the gap; double-team the linebacker with the wing; release downfield on a defensive halfback coming up for the tackle; or seal to the inside for any pursuit coming to tackle the ballcarrier.

Diagram 2–23 (preceding page) illustrates a stack between the tackle and the end. The end blocks the first man to the outside. The tackle takes the man in the gap, the guard blocks the man over him, and the back who is in a halfback position blocks the linebacker. The center can either seal to the inside, go downfield, or help the back on a double-team.

Diagram 2–24 shows a stack between the guard and center. The left guard takes the man over him, the center blocks the man in the gap, and the fullback executes a block on the linebacker. The right guard can double-team the man in the gap, double-team the linebacker, go downfield, or seal off any defensive men coming to stop the play.

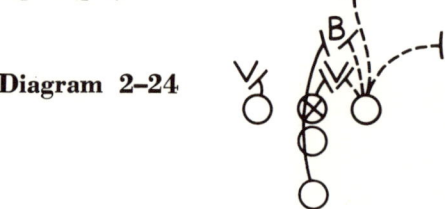

Diagram 2–24

Whether the backs are winged, in a slot, or placed in the backfield, each must execute a hard drive block into the linebacker or lineman. The back must explode from his position and drive hard at the defensive man. When contact is about to be made, the body should be under control, having a wide base and staying low. On contact, the backfield man should drive his feet, keep his head up, and attempt to move the linebacker or lineman away from the hole.

A Lineman Blocking A Stack

The same principle, as with the back employed against a stack, is true for the extra lineman. Diagrams 2–25 and 2–26 illustrate the use of an extra lineman. In this case, the trapping guard can block the man in the gap or the linebacker.

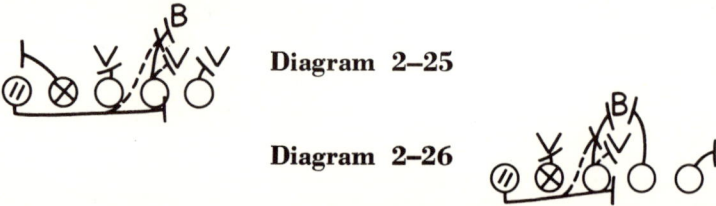

Diagram 2–25

Diagram 2–26

Diagrams 2–27 through 2–29 indicate three plays utilizing the slide, swing around, an extra back, and an extra lineman.

Diagram 2–27

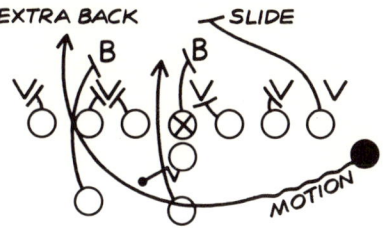

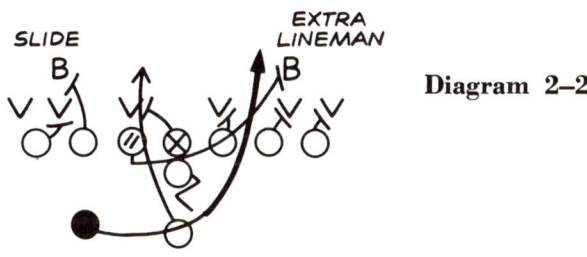

Diagram 2–28

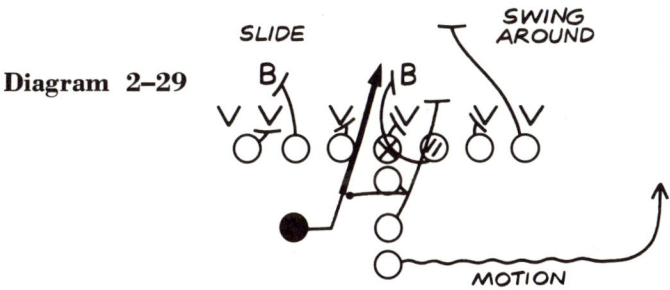

Diagram 2–29

HOW TO BLOCK THE STRAIGHT TANDEM

The straight tandem can be blocked five different ways:

(1) The straight block.
(2) The slide.
(3) The swing around.
(4) A back blocking.
(5) A lineman blocking.

As can be seen, four of the five methods have been employed in blocking the straight stack. These will be discussed along with the straight technique.

The Straight Block

The straight block is a simple drive block by one man on a defensive lineman or a linebacker. It is usually employed at the point of attack and can also be used away from the hole. The straight block is illustrated in Diagrams 2–30 and 2–31.

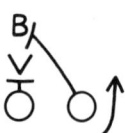 Diagram 2–30   Diagram 2–31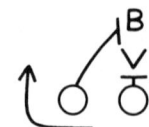

The Slide

The slide is the same in the tandem as it was for the stack, although the fill man must move quickly to cut off any penetration that may occur. If there is a minimum of split by the line, the fill block will become easier. It is seldom used at the hole where the play is being run (Diagrams 2–32 and 2–33).

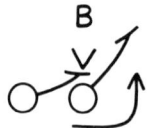 Diagram 2–32   Diagram 2–33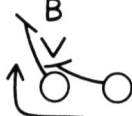

The Swing Around

The swing around is the same as the stack block except that the pulling lineman must go slightly farther to get to the linebacker. This is usually used at the point of attack and away from the hole. The swing around is shown in Diagrams 2–34 and 2–35.

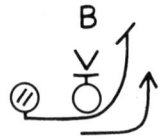 Diagram 2–34   Diagram 2–35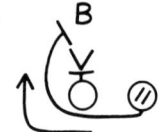

A Backfield Man Blocking a Tandem

Diagrams 2–36 through 2–38 illustrate backfield maneuvers in blocking tandem defenses. The block is employed directly at the point of attack.

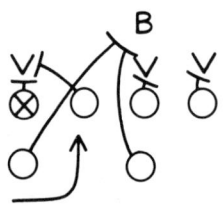   **Diagram 2–36**
Two backfield men on a linebacker

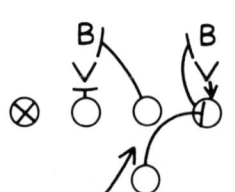   **Diagram 2–37**
A halfback blocking a defensive lineman

Diagram 2–38
With the defense having an advantage (4-on-3) a halfback blocks the linebacker giving the area an even ratio.

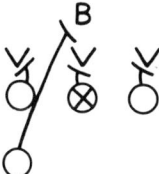

A Lineman Blocking a Tandem

The same can be done with the tandem defense as was accomplished with the stacking defense. Blocking by a lineman is indicated at the point of attack.

Diagram 2–39
A pulling lineman on a linebacker

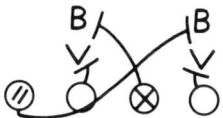

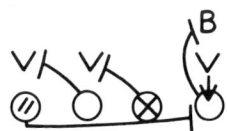

Diagram 2–40
A pulling lineman on a defensive lineman

The five methods for blocking tandem type defenses are illustrated in Diagrams 2–41 to 2–43.

Diagram 2–41

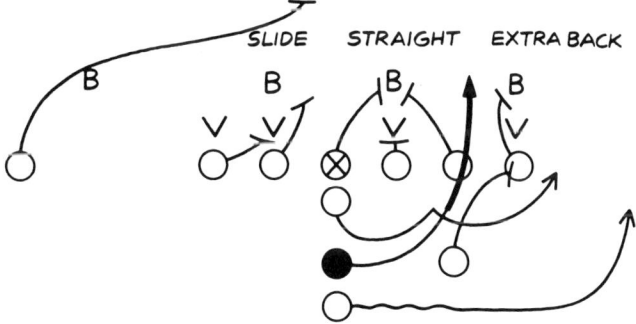

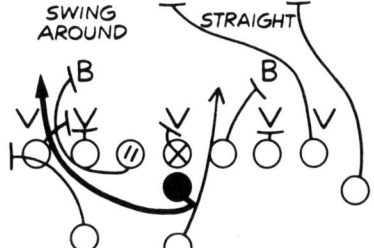

Diagram 2–42

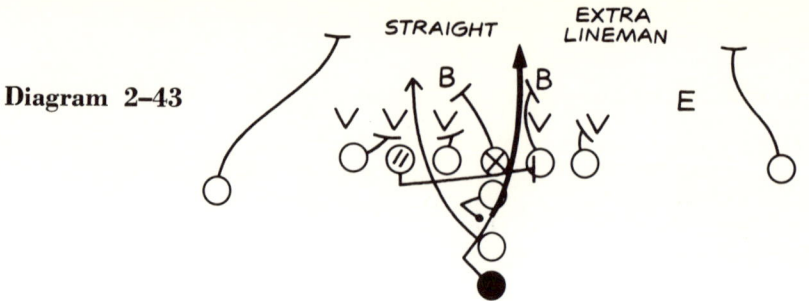

Diagram 2–43

HOW TO BLOCK THE STUNT

When blocking the stunting defense, two things must be accomplished:

1. The block at the point of attack.
2. The block away from the point of attack.

No matter what the defensive alignment is, all stunting can be blocked. As noted, Diagrams 2–5 to 2–8 in the beginning of this chapter illustrated four different defensive alignments and the stunts of two defensive players on two offensive linemen. Blocking the stunt remains the same in all four situations. Anticipation of the stunt is very important, because it puts the linemen in positions to block it. If the offense does not anticipate the stunt, the linemen will not be able to block it and the play will probably not gain yardage.

The Block at the Point of Attack

At the point of attack, each man will step to the inside expecting a stunt. The reason for the step is the tendency of the defensive man stationed over him to angle in that direction or the defensive man down the line, where he is aiming, to angle towards him. If neither occur, the blockers will pivot back for the men positioned over them or other men coming in their direction. If a stunt occurs, each blocker will be in position to pick up the stunt coming into his area. Both men at the point of attack aim their eyes and first steps at the near inside hip of the man down to the inside. This is illustrated in Diagram 2–44. If there is a linebacker stationed over one of the men, the blocker will step down in the same manner as if the linebacker was on the line of scrimmage. If the defense is not

Diagram 2–44

stunting, the blockers will be in excellent positions to pivot on their inside foot and have an inside-out drive block on the defensive player (Diagram 2–45 and Photos 2–5a, b, c, and d).

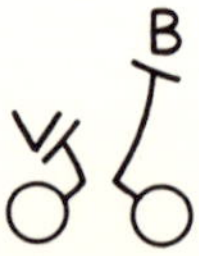

Diagram 2–45

If the defense employs a stunt at the point of attack, offensive linemen will be in excellent positions to block it. Many times, one man will not be blocked but will be picked up by another offensive lineman. The other defensive player will be double-teamed. Diagram 2–46 and Photos 2–6a and 6b (pages 40 and 41) illustrate a stunt and how it is blocked.

Diagram 2–46

Both offensive linemen step to the inside and pick up the stunting defensive lineman. Both will meet the defensive man with a post block and will attempt to drive him away from the hole. The linebacker will be taken by another lineman. If he is not, the linebacker is usually stunting out of the play and will not be able to get to the ballcarrier.

Diagram 2–47 shows the reverse of this, with a double-team on the linebacker. The defensive lineman will be blocked by another lineman. Diagram 2–48 illustrates the same maneuver, and how the blockers separate to pick up each linebacker. This can be accomplished after much work with stunting defenses.

Diagram 2–47   Diagram 2–48

Photo 2–5a

Photo 2–5b

Photo 2-5c

Photo 2-5d

Photo 2-6a

Photo 2-6b

The same aiming points and procedure are accomplished at any hole with all defensive alignments. Diagrams 2-49 and 2-50 illustrate the linebacker and the defensive linemen in a reversed alignment and the blocking by the offensive linemen.

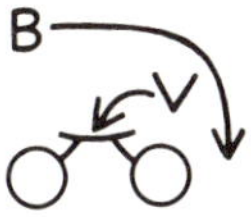

Diagram 2-49   **Diagram 2-50**

The Blocks Away from the Point of Attack

Each offensive lineman aims toward the point of attack when a play is being run down the line from him. Similar to what is done at the running hole, each man steps to the inside anticipating a stunt and aims his eyes and his first step at the inside hip of the next defensive man down the line. This is shown in Diagram 2-51.

Diagram 2-51

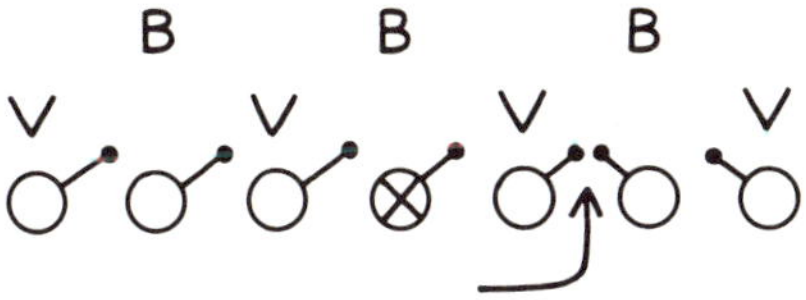

If no stunt occurs, each man will pivot back on the first step he took and block the man positioned over him. The blockers with linebackers positioned over them will continue on and pick up the linebackers' pursuit of the play (Diagram 2-52).

Diagram 2-52

42   ATTACKING STACKED, TANDEM, STUNTING, AND ANGLING DEFENSES

If a stunt occurs away from the point of attack, each offensive lineman will either block the man over him or another defensive player coming at him. Diagram 2–53 illustrates an offensive lineman stepping to the inside toward the hole and picking up the angling defensive lineman and the linebacker being blocked by the offensive lineman stepping back.

Diagram 2–53

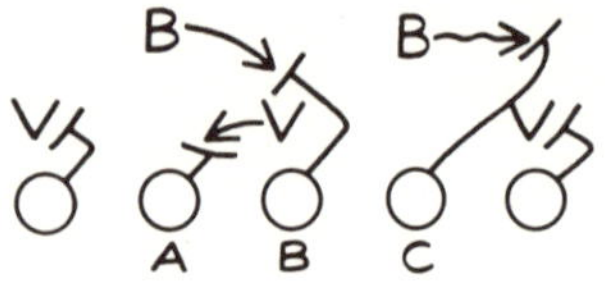

Offensive lineman A will step, anticipating a stunt. When the defensive lineman angles at him, he is in good position to block him. Since his eyes were aimed at the inside hip, the blocker will have a good post block position on the defensive lineman. Offensive lineman B who was anticipating a stunt with the man over him, takes the first step to the inside. When the defensive lineman does not stunt in his direction, he turns to block him. As he realizes the lineman has left, he blocks the linebacker coming into his area (see Photos 2–7a, 7b, and 7c).

Photo 2–7a

Photo 2–7b

Photo 2–7c

If the defensive lineman (Diagram 2–54) stunts in the other direction the offensive blocker B picks up the man over him. He will step to the inside anticipating the stunt and place a post block into the defensive lineman. The blocker

Diagram 2–54

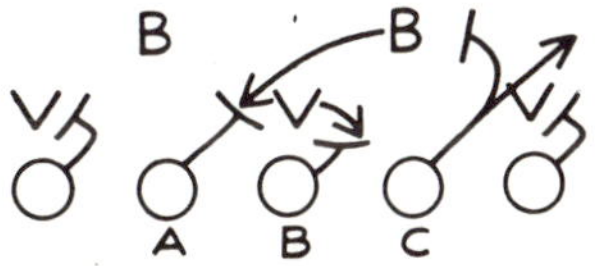

to the left of him, A, will step toward the hole and aim at the inside hip of the man down the line anticipating a stunt from him. Since the defensive man is going in the other direction, offensive lineman A continues on and will either block the stunting linebacker, if the linebacker comes fast, or continue on and block the linebacker who was positioned over him. The offensive lineman, C, will either continue on or turn back and wait for pursuit to come at him, notably the other linebacker.

Diagrams 2–55 through 2–59 are a few illustrations of stunts at the point of attack and away from the hole, and how each can be successfully blocked. As was mentioned in the beginning of this chapter, drilling the fundamentals and techniques is of the utmost importance to block stunting successfully.

Diagram 2–55
4–3 defense
A stunt at the point of attack

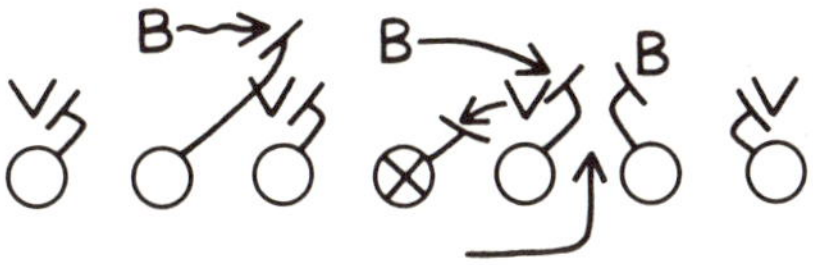

Diagram 2–56
5–2 defense
A stunt at the point of attack

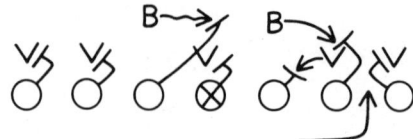

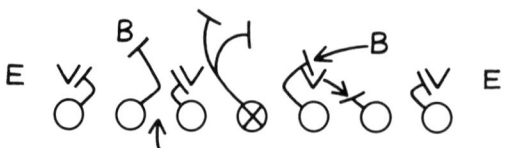

Diagram 2–57
6–2 defense
A stunt away from the point of attack

Diagram 2–58
6–2 defense
A stunt at the point of attack and away from it

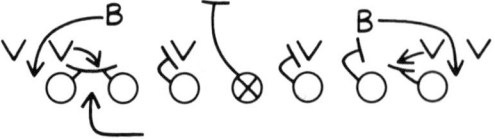

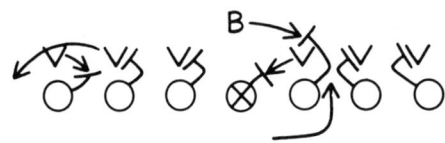

Diagram 2–59
6–1 defense
A stunt at the point of attack and away from it

HOW TO BLOCK STUNTING STACKS

As with stunting, a stunting stack must be anticipated also. The slide or the swing around can be used. Each man must be in such a position that, if the defense stack does not stunt, it can still be blocked. If the play goes to the right of the stack (Diagram 2–60), the man nearest the hole aims his eyes and his first step at the near hip, anticipating that the man in the gap will angle at him. The offensive lineman away from the point of attack aims his eyes and his first step (in this case the right foot) at the inside hip of the defensive man in the gap. Notice the aiming points are the same as in the regular alignment.

Diagram 2–60

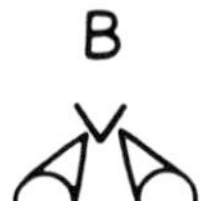

If the gap man attempts to explode across the line of scrimmage, the man farthest from the hole will slip his head in front and stop the penetration. The blocker nearest the hole, seeing no angle coming in his direction, will push off the left foot at the linebacker and place a good drive block on him (Diagram 2–61).

Diagram 2-61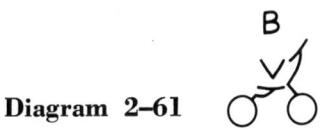

If the man in the gap loops to the left, the man farthest from the hole will be in excellent position for a post block on the defensive lineman. The man nearest the hole will notice the man angle away and should react quickly to the stunt of the linebacker. Each blocker should attempt to move the defensive men from their holes. If the stunt goes in the opposite direction, each blocker picks up the stunt in the same manner. This is illustrated in Diagrams 2-62 and 2-63.

Diagram 2-62
The linebacker stunting to the right and the gap man angling to the left.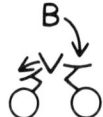

Diagram 2-63
The linebacker stunting to the left and the gap man angling to the right.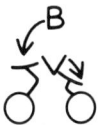

The swing around by a pulling lineman can be employed. The offensive lineman nearest the hole should block down on the man in the gap, whether he angles at him, attempts to penetrate the line of scrimmage, or loops in the opposite direction. The "puller" will block the linebacker if he attempts to stunt in his direction or plays straight. If the linebacker goes in the opposite direction (from where he pulled), the puller should continue downfield for another defensive man. The three situations are shown in Diagrams 2-64 to 2-66.

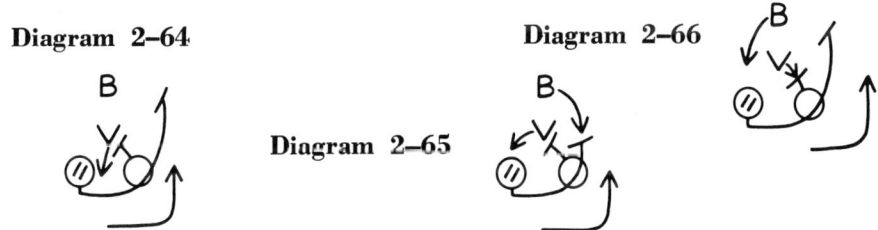

Diagram 2-64

Diagram 2-65

Diagram 2-66

HOW TO BLOCK STUNTING TANDEMS

A stunting tandem can be blocked easily, with the same rules as the regular stunt (Diagram 2-67). The guard and tackle step to the inside where the play is being run. If the tandem is straight, the tackle pivots and blocks the defensive tackle and the guard steps toward the linebacker.

Diagram 2-67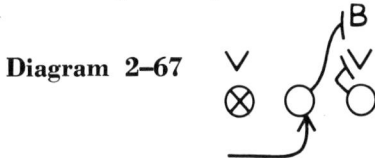

If the defensive tackle angles at the guard, both the tackle and guard will be in position for a double-team on him. If the stunt goes in the opposite direction, the linebacker can either be double-teamed or the offensive tackle can pivot back and place a drive block on the defensive tackle. All three situations are illustrated in Diagrams 2–68 to 2–70.

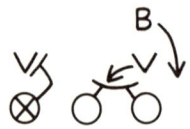

Diagram 2–68
The defensive tackle being double-teamed.

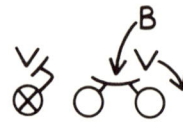

Diagram 2–69
The linebacker being double-teamed.

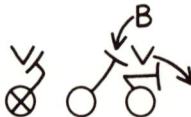

Diagram 2–70
Both the linebacker and the defensive tackle being blocked.

BACKS AND LINEMEN BLOCKING STUNTING STACKS AND TANDEMS

As was explained in the straight stack and straight tandem, the offensive back and trapping lineman can block at the point of attack. If a stunt occurs, each must be prepared to block it. At the running hole, the defense can be blocked in a multitude of ways and the coach must find the best method. The following are a few ways of blocking the stunting stack and stunting tandem with an extra lineman or back being utilized. Each can be blocked by either having a designated man or area (Diagrams 2–71 to 2–75).

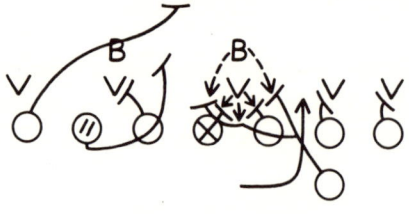

Diagram 2–71
The center and guard double-team the man in the gap, whether he is stunting or not, and the halfback blocks the linebacker wherever he stunts.

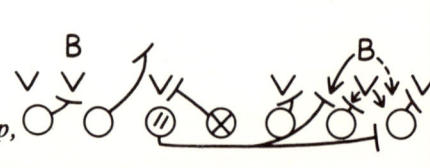

Diagram 2–72
A pulling guard trapping a linebacker. If the linebacker stays in his original position, the puller will turn up the hole for him.

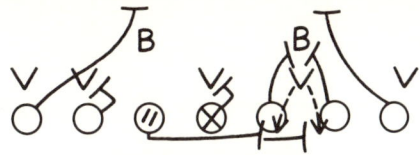

Diagram 2-73
The linebacker is doubled and the guard traps the gap man wherever he goes.

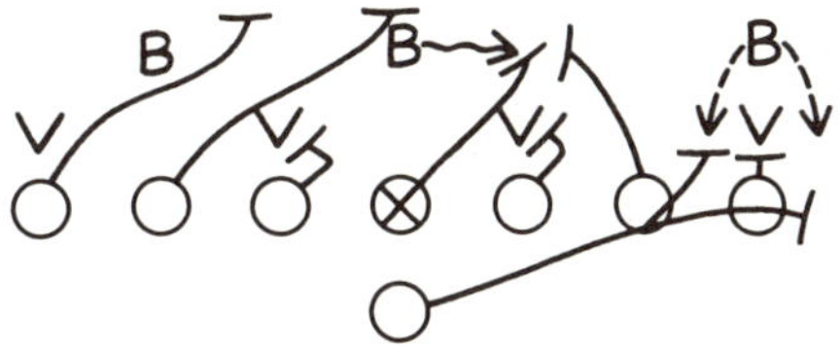

Diagram 2-74
The end takes his man anywhere he angles and the fullback blocks the linebacker wherever he stunts. This can be blocked by area, with the end taking the first man to the inside and the fullback the first man showing to the outside.

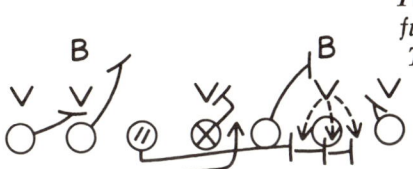

Diagram 2-75
A guard trapping the defensive tackle

HOW TO BLOCK THE ANGLING DEFENSE (LOOP OR SLANT)

The fundamentals and techniques for blocking stunting defenses are applied to the angling defense with simplicity. The first step and the aiming points remain the same. Again, two things must be remembered: (1) the block at the point of attack, and (2) the blocks away from the point of attack. This was explained in the stunting defense. The offensive lineman steps to the inside anticipating the stunt, from either the man down the line angling at him or the man over him, and loops in the direction of the step. His first step and aiming points are at the inside hip of the defensive player down the line toward the point of attack. This is illustrated under stunting defenses in Diagram 2-51.

As shown in Diagram 2-76 the linemen anticipate the angle from an even defense and step toward the point of attack. If the defense does not angle, each blocker is in position to block the defensive players.

Diagram 2-76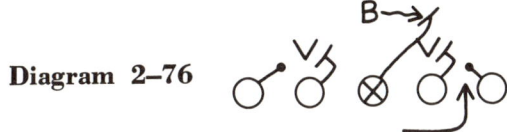

If the angle is toward the hole being run, the linemen will be in good position to block the angle (Diagram 2-77). If the angle goes in the opposite direction,

Diagram 2-77

the left offensive tackle blocks the angle of the defensive guard and the center post blocks the other defensive guard. Because no angle came in his direction, the right offensive guard turns back for the lineman over him. Since he has angled in the other direction, the guard is free to block the linebacker (Diagram 2–78). The left guard is free also and should either turn back on pursuit coming in his direction or go downfield for a block. The same principle in blocking every type of angle applies to all defenses.

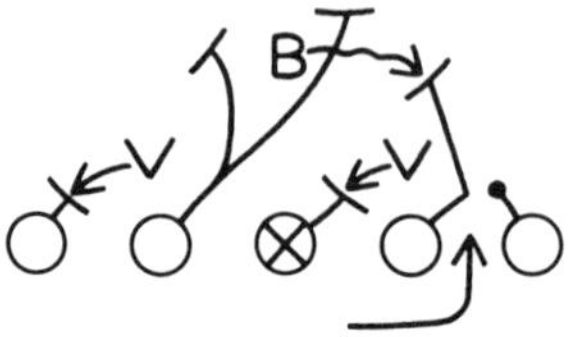

Diagram 2–78

At the point of attack, each man steps to the inside and should apply the same blocking rules used for the stunting defenses. If the loop or slant is in one direction and a linebacker stunts (balanced angling defense), all offensive linemen are in excellent positions to block the defense. Diagrams 2–79 through 2–85 illustrate angling defenses and how each is blocked.

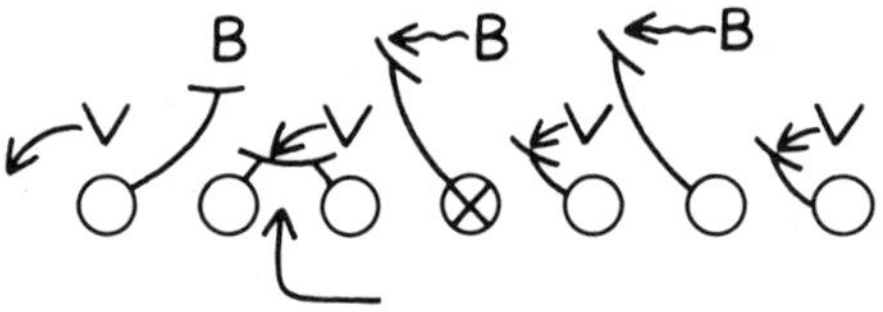

Diagram 2–79
4–3 loop to the left

Diagram 2–80
A 5–2 loop to the right

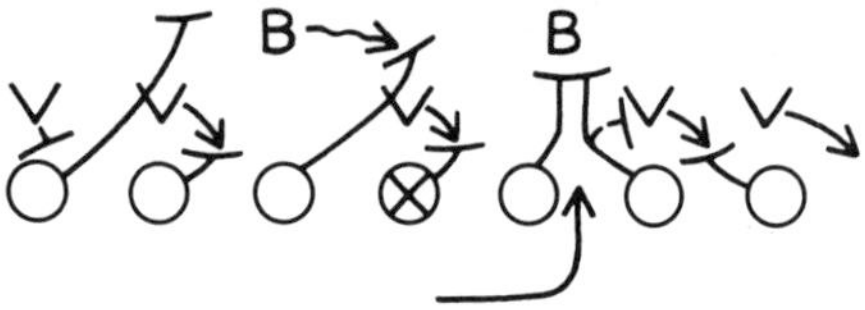

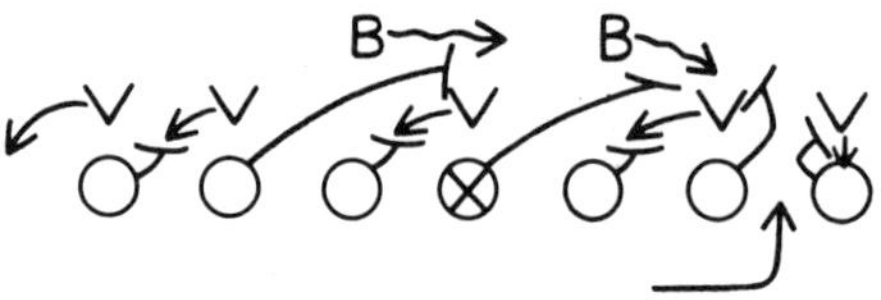

Diagram 2–81
A 5–2 loop to the left

Diagram 2–82
A 5–2 loop to the right

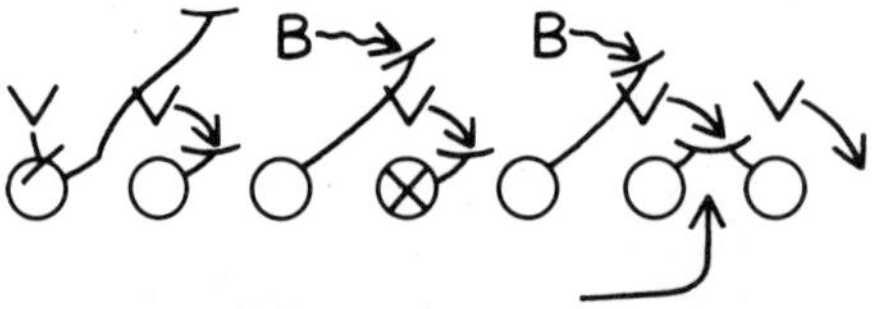

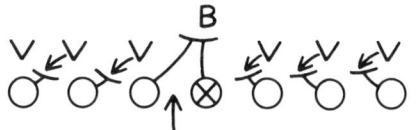

Diagram 2–83
A 6–1 slant to the left

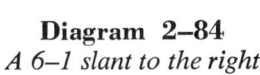

Diagram 2–84
A 6–1 slant to the right

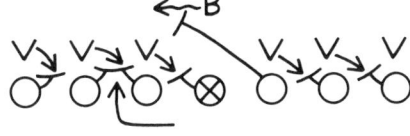

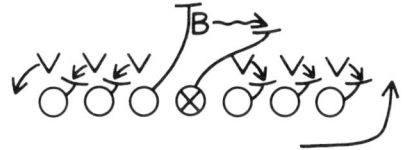

Diagram 2–85
A 6–1 loop to the outside

Another excellent method that can be used is to down block the offensive line away from the point of attack. The offensive linemen block the first men stationed to their inside. If the defense plays straight, each takes his man. If the defense angle toward or away, the line blocks the first man down the line that comes into each of his areas of responsibility. If no man comes they scoot for a linebacker.

HOW TO BLOCK THE FIRE OR BLITZ

The fire or blitz is usually employed against the passing offense or during passing situations. If it is employed during running plays, the offense can block it as if it were an angling defense. However, dropback pass protectors can block fires and blitzes in three other ways:

1. Cup blocking.
2. Man-on-man blocking.
3. Backs on linebackers.

Cup Blocking

Cup blocking requires the five interior linemen to protect the inside (forcing the defense to the outside), regardless of whether the fire or the blitz is being used. The remaining backs block to the outside of the cup, and protect the inside seam also (Diagram 2–86).

Diagram 2–86

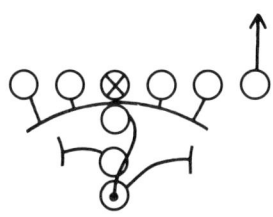

Man-on-Man Blocking

Man-on-man blocking means that each interior lineman blocks the man stationed over him whether he is a defensive lineman or a linebacker, and whether he stunts or not. If the offensive lineman is not covered or if a linebacker does not penetrate, he will assist to his side or in the direction the ball is being thrown.

The remaining backs block the ends on the line of scrimmage (Diagram 2–87).

Diagram 2–87

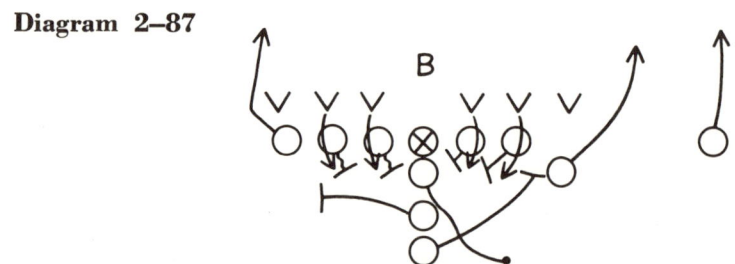

Backs on Linebackers

A good method for protecting the passer is for the remaining backs to step at the linebackers and block them wherever they fire or blitz. However, if the linebackers do not penetrate, the backs will assist the linemen with their blocks. The center takes the man over him if he comes; otherwise, he should help to one side or the other. The guards block the first man down the line. The advantages of this blocking is that the smaller offensive back can usually block the smaller linebacker better than he can block the bigger end. The tackles and guards will now be blocking the bigger defensive linemen (Diagrams 2–88 and 2–89).

Diagram 2–88

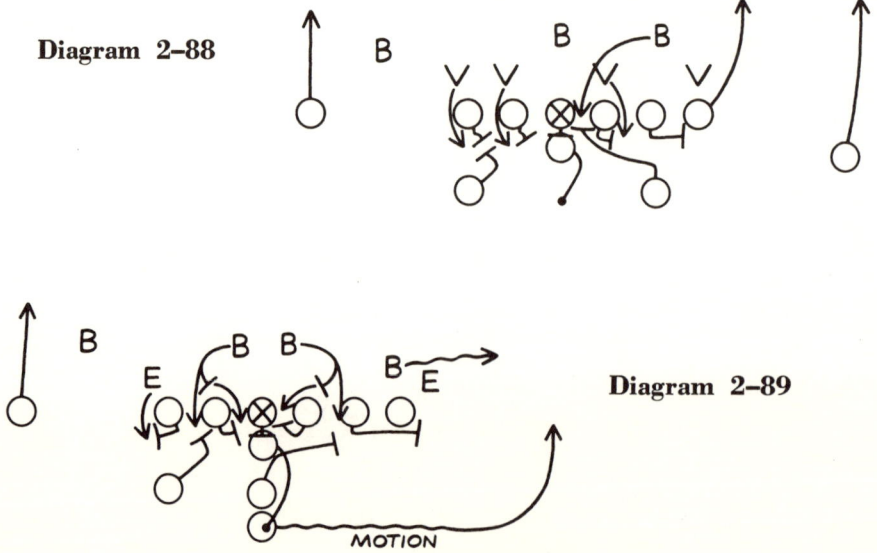

Diagram 2–89

3

THE PASS OFFENSE AND ATTACKING DEFENSIVE LINEBACKERS AND ENDS

There are numerous coaching philosophies on the passing game and the attack of pass defenses. Many coaches use running as a basic attack and the passing game to a limited extent. Some coaches utilize both the running and the passing attacks, while other coaches employ the passing game as their basic offense and use the running as a supplementary attack.

At both the high school and college level, coaches do not advocate the pass as a basic offensive weapon. The positive thought is that only a completed pass is good. Negatively, a pass can either be incomplete with a net gain of no yardage, or it can be intercepted by the opponent. However, the pass has improved the game of football and every team needing yardage at a crucial moment must look to the pass for assistance. But to have a successful passing attack, a running attack is very important. In most offenses the running attack is essential for there can be no passing without it. When a running attack cannot go, the next resort is the passing game. Therefore, when a coach realizes that his team will have a great deal of difficulty in advancing the ball by running, it is wise for him to emphasize that aspect of the game which will bring the greatest returns.

Jack Curtice, head football coach at University of California at Santa Barbara, stated in his book *The Passing Game in Football*, "The idea that passing is always gambling is fallacious. We feel that we can throw all of our short passes with no more danger of an interception than we would of losing a fumble on an off-tackle play."[1] There have been many high school teams that relied on the

---

[1] Jack C. Curtice, *The Passing Game in Football* (New York: The Ronald Press Company, 1961), p. 6.

pass. Coach Noel Reebenacker, whose teams have had much success with passing, mentioned in his book *How to Develop a Successful High School Passing Attack*, "A high school coach should not be afraid to make extensive use of the passing game. . . . High school teams can pass successfully and there are many outstanding teams that rely chiefly on the forward pass."[2]

Coach Glenn Dobbs, former head football coach at Tulsa University, one of the finest passing college teams in the country, remarked at the American Football Coaches Association, "We just didn't worry too much about running first. We were a pass first and will continue to be. Our running attack will go because of our passing. . . . We don't like to try and run over opponents all lined up inside. Let's isolate them, spread them out, throw the football, make them move, and then we will do what we want with the ground attack."[3]

It does not matter what a coach believes in terms of having a running attack, a passing offense, or both. In every offensive attack, some type of passing game is essential. All teams cannot rely on the running aspect of football during the entire season. Therefore, a coach must come forth with a sound passing attack, whether it is used often or to a minimal extent. It is also important that a coach understands and learns the different techniques and styles of his opponents' pass defenses to be able to attack them. Just as there are strengths and weaknesses in every defense, there are strengths and weaknesses in every *pass* defense. To be successful, a passing coach must be able to exploit his offense against all pass defenses; and many times there is just one pass play that can win the game. The pass can win for any team, whether it is employed to come from behind, break open the game, or stay ahead.

THE INGREDIENTS OF A GOOD PASSING ATTACK

Any passing attack, whether it is utilized extensively or to a minimal extent, must function as an entire team process. It is not one or two players that make a team move the ball; it is all 11 men working together to have a successful passing game. There are four important aspects for the pass to be effective:

1. The passer.
2. The receivers.
3. The protection.
4. The coverage.

The Passer

One of the most important parts of any passing attack is the functioning of the quarterback. He must be able to pass the ball to the receivers under any condi-

---

[2] Noel Reebenacker, *How to Develop a Successful High School Passing Attack* (Englewood Cliffs, N.J.: Prentice-Hall, Inc., 1965), p. vi, preface.
[3] Glenn Dobbs, "The Tulsa Passing Game," *Proceedings of the Forty-Second Annual Meeting, American Football Coaches Association*, Chicago, Illinois, 1965, pp. 79–80.

tions. While many coaches believe a quarterback must have the talent to play that position, there have been many passers who do not have the ability to be a great passer, but with proper teaching techniques, practice, drilling, and training have developed into fine quarterbacks.

On any pass, no matter where it is thrown on the field, it must be executed properly. The passer must have a proper stance, receive a good exchange from the center, clear the center quickly, know the proper route where he is to run, get the ball to the "ready" position, and when the moment comes for the pass, be in a good passing position.

The action movement with the arm in throwing the pass is very important. The arm movements can be broken down into five main areas:

The Shoulder. This is used a great deal whenever the ball is thrown hard. If the ball is lofted on a soft pass, the shoulder is not fully utilized.

The Upper Arm. The abductor muscles of the chest act on the shoulder joint to rotate the upper arm toward the midline of the body. The elbow is held above the shoulder in a natural position away from the body. The movement of the upper arm to the midline of the body furnishes the starting force of the pass. The upper arm remains almost parallel to the ground, with the elbow always above, never being lowered or pointed at the ground.

The Forearm. The movement of the forearm from behind and above the ear is initiated at the instant that the elbow is almost, but not pointed toward the receiver. The forearm is snapped out toward the receiver; it is flexed almost fully and extended rapidly with force.

The Wrist. This is a strong factor in the pass. It is cocked in a position so the thumb and the forefinger are toward the radius bone. The wrist becomes involved just before the entire arm is extended. The radius rotates medially and the hand turns outward toward the receiver, with the palm facing him. The action of the forearm flexor muscles snaps the wrist downward.

The Fingers. They coordinate with the wrist and let the ball go with a downward force. The fingers stay parallel to the ground and point toward the receiver. Their downward action on the back end causes the ball to spiral with the nose up. The ball should not be passed nose downward, as it makes for a difficult catch.

All five parts coordinate in a single, continuous, and quick motion. It should never be a jerky or uneven movement. This action of the arm is used for any type of pass thrown from any position on the field.

The Receivers

While many coaches believe the quarterback is the most important person in a successful passing attack, others feel it is the receiver. He must catch the ball to get the necessary yardage. There are many important fundamentals and techniques for the receiver to learn. He must be able to release from the line of scrimmage, run the proper route expected of him, execute good fakes, catch the ball, and run with it. All fundamentals must be continually drilled and practiced if a pass is to be successful.

The Protection

The protection for the passer is of the utmost importance. If the quarterback does not have time to pass the ball, the team will *lose* instead of gain yardage. Therefore, for any pass, whether it is a drop-back pass, quick pass, roll-out or sprint-out pass, the protection for the quarterback is vitally necessary for a successful passing attack. This aspect of the passing game must be constantly drilled with the offensive line. They must realize that if a breakdown occurs, the passing game is stalled. An important aspect of the protection is that the offensive line must know where the quarterback is setting up to pass, know how the defenders rush, and how to cover the pass.

The Coverage

Once the pass is in the air, it is important that everyone sprint to where the ball was thrown. The quarterback should yell "left," "right," or "middle" to indicate to the team, especially to the protection, where the ball is located. The reason for the coverage is twofold. If the ball is caught by the receiver, there will be extra blockers in the area for the receiver to utilize; and if the ball is intercepted, the passing team will be in an excellent position to tackle the interceptor.

These four ingredients of the passing game are vitally necessary in attacking pass defenses. Each aspect must be taught, trained, practiced and drilled every day to make it successful. If one aspect breaks down, the passing game will falter and cause the offense to bog down when needed yardage is essential.

IMPORTANCE OF STRATEGY FOR THE PASSING GAME

While strategy has not been mentioned up to this point, it is probably the most important single aspect of any passing attack. Throwing at the improper time or running poor patterns will nullify all of the work put into the passing game. It is important that the coach put in well-conceived passing patterns to take advantage of the opposition's pass coverage and weaknesses. Certain passing patterns will not be as successful against some coverages. For a good passing game, the quarterback and receivers should be properly drilled as to the type of route and pattern to be run. Also being drilled to read the defensive coverage on the first few steps and then running the proper pattern should be done constantly.

When to pass and when *not* to pass is highly important also. The score, time left in the game, field position, and other tactical and strategical situations have a great deal to do with when to throw and *not* throw the football. For example,

THE PASS OFFENSE AND ATTACKING DEFENSIVE LINEBACKERS AND ENDS   55

in an obvious passing situation with long yardage, the defense is expecting the deep pass. In this case, the defensive secondary has a better opportunity to intercept the football than in any other situation. Passing when the defense is least expecting it, will catch the defense off balance and will gain good yardage for the offense.

Personnel is important also. Since opponents change from week to week, personnel will change. If the personnel in the defensive secondary seem to be excellent defenders, the offense should not think "pass" as long as it can continue to run. However, if the defenders are weak, the offense should exploit that weakness.

QUARTERBACK ROUTES AND PASS ACTIONS

There are a multitude of pass plays to exploit and attack defensive secondaries, whether the pass defense is zone, man-to-man, or a combination. The following are some of the pass actions (including the draw) that can be utilized, and Diagram 3–1 illustrates some of the quarterback routes employed for these passes.

1. Quick drop-back passes
2. Drop-back passes
3. Sprint-out passes
4. Semi-sprint-out passes
5. Roll-out passes
6. Semi-roll-out passes
7. Play-action passes
8. Bootlegs and waggles
9. Delay passes
10. Screen passes
11. Shuffle passes
12. The draw

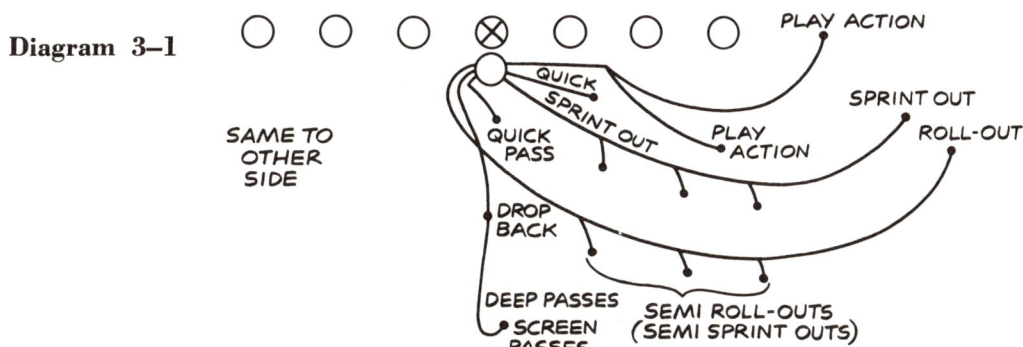

Diagram 3–1

1. The Quick Drop-Back Pass

On the snap of the ball the quarterback will take two steps backward and look for the receiver. The receivers run a quick route, 4 to 5 yards, whether they are tight or split on the offensive line. What pattern is executed is dependent upon the type of secondary, defensive end, and linebacker coverage. The advantage of the quick pass is to hit the receivers before the defense can react.

2. The Drop-Back Pass

The drop-back pass is thrown directly behind the center approximately 4 to 6 yards deep. If the patterns call for the "bomb" or deep pass, the quarterback may have to retreat approximately 7 to 9 yards to have sufficient opportunity to throw the ball. He must get depth as quickly as possible in order to set up and be ready to throw. A quarterback can either employ a crossover step or backpedal technique to get into position.

Backpedal Technique

On the backpedal technique the quarterback should push off with his left (or right) foot. He attempts to get to his required depth as quickly as possible. The ball is taken from the center and brought up to the chest for a good carrying position on the first step. If pushing off with the left foot, the right foot is brought back approximately 1½ to 2 feet. The quarterback should land on his toes so he can push off while the left foot is brought back and behind the right. This is continued until the passer gets to his required depth. The steps are rapid and quick. Since the quarterback is always facing the defense, the ball can be thrown quickly, especially if the quarterback notices any firing linebackers or extra rush. If this is the case, the ball is thrown over the firing linebackers to an end or halfback.

The Crossover Technique

The crossover step technique is also good and is probably employed by more teams than the backpedal method. There are differences of opinion as to the number of steps and the type of technique used. However, the starting technique is similar. On the snap of the ball, the quarterback will push and pivot with his left foot (right) and step back with his right foot. On the first step, the quarterback will turn his shoulders and hips to the sideline, bring the ball up to his chest, and keep his eyes toward the defense by looking over his shoulder. The quarterback can then utilize the five-step method by bringing the left foot in front of the right, stepping with the right foot, crossing over with the left, and then planting with the right foot. Another technique is to utilize the five steps with a hopping motion. In this instance, the passer steps back with the right foot, then utilizes the left, right, left, and then pushes off the left foot and hops on both feet. Another method is to utilize only three steps with a right step back, left, and hop to both feet. It is important, however, that the quarterback get back as quickly as possible so he can set up quickly and have more time to release the football. The receivers usually run an 8- to 15-yard route. The quarterback must hit the receiver when he is about to get open and not when he is already in the clear.

The advantages of the drop-back pass are as follows:

1. A passer who has limited ability as a runner, but is a great passer, can utilize the drop-back pass to an enormous extent.
2. A passer can view the entire field from the drop-back position and can pass to both sides of the formation equally well.
3. The drop-back pass makes great use of the screen, draws, swing passes, and delay passes.
4. If the offense is widened and spread, the receivers can release easier and the widening helps isolate the receivers on the defenders.
5. This widening usually forces a one-on-one situation with the defensive secondary, which makes it easier to complete passes.
6. The deep pass or long ball can be thrown simply from the drop-back pass.
7. The passer can easily read the defense and hit the open receiver with accuracy.
8. The protection knows exactly where the passer sets up to pass the ball and will attempt to force the rushers to the outside.

3. The Sprint-Out Pass

The sprint-out pass is executed with the step-out or face-out open step in the direction where the quarterback is going. If the quarterback is sprinting to the right, he will push off the medial side of the left foot and pivot the right foot in the direction of the route he is to execute. The step is short and "thrown-out." On the first step the eyes focus on the receivers, while on the second, the ball must be in the ready position. The passer sprints to a position approximately 4 to 6 yards deep. The depth is determined by the coach. When the quarterback reaches a position behind the end, he will immediately turn upfield toward the line of scrimmage. If a receiver is open, he will throw the ball quickly. If the passer finds that the receivers are covered, he will run the ball. The advantages of the sprint-out pass are as follows:

1. The sprint-out pass easily ties in with other plays (belly series, counters, bucks, etc.) of the offense.
2. It minimizes the danger of losing yardage. The passer is continually in motion toward the line of scrimmage.
3. All receivers in the pattern are in direct view of the passer.

4. It creates a very simple "read" for the passer. Through constant practice, he can develop proficiency regarding when to pass and when to run.
5. The possibility of a pass on every down causes the secondary men to freeze and hold their positions while deciding whether it is a pass or a run.
6. Persistent pressure is put on the corner man as to whether to defend against the run or pass.
7. Though the defense may apply internal pressure through the employment of shooting and stunting, the quarterback is constantly clearing away from the intended pressure.
8. Since half of the defensive linemen must chase farther for the passer, an extended rush is required, and this may exact a physical toll.
9. The offensive linemen have easier and better blocking assignments, since the defensive linemen have only one way to rush.
10. The defensive secondary must utilize different coverage whenever the ball is in a sprint-out, causing additional problems for them.
11. With a fourth runner in the quarterback, the running attack is greatly expanded.

4. Semi-Sprint-Out Pass

The execution of the semi-sprint-out pass begins like the sprint-out, except that the quarterback will pull up either behind the end, tackle, or guard position. It is meant to look first like a sprint-out, but the quarterback stops and another pattern will be executed by the receivers. It is also utilized to throw back across the field. The advantage of the semi-sprint-out pass is that it can cause much confusion for the defensive secondary, whether to rotate or not and whether it is a sprint-out pass. It causes additional problems for the defensive linemen, who have to chase to different positions instead of one, as with the drop-back pass. The deeper pass can now be employed and the passer has more of a direct view of the entire playing field.

5. The Roll-Out Pass

The roll-out pass is identical to the sprint-out, except that the quarterback, when clearing from the center will execute a roll-out or reverse-pivot technique. If the play is going to the right, the quarterback must spin or pivot on the right foot. The left foot is brought up and around quickly, then planted in the desired direction. The ball is brought to the stomach, with the front of the body temporarily facing the direction opposite that of the intended line of flight. On the second step, the quarterback looks downfield to the receivers. On the third step he has the ball in "ready" position. If the quarterback false steps when clearing the center, the coach must insist he "fall away" from the center at a 45 degree angle in the direction of the roll. The roll-out may put the passer a little deeper into the backfield than the sprint-out. The advantages for the sprint-out pass are the same as for the roll-out.

6. Semi-Roll-Out Pass

The semi-roll-out pass clears the center the same as the roll-out and its purposes and advantages are the same as the semi-sprint-out pass.

7. Play-Action Passes

The play-action pass attempts to fake a running play which will materialize into a passing play. It attempts to freeze the defensive secondary and, at the same time, have the defensive forcing unit go for the faking ballcarrier. The advantages of the play-action pass are that it gives the quarterback a great deal of time to throw the ball, it confuses the secondary as to whether it is a run or pass, and the receivers have a better chance of being open in their route.

8. Bootlegs and Waggles

A bootleg is similar to the play-action pass, except that the passer will fake a play in one direction, and the quarterback will roll back to the other. Some coaches may utilize the term bootleg when the quarterback rolls only to the split end or short side. Another term, "waggle" indicates the quarterback rolling to the side of the tight end, wing, or flanker back position. The advantages of the bootleg and waggle are that it freezes the secondary which must decide whether it is a run or not, and it generally rotates the defensive secondary one way, while the quarterback rolls away from it. Additionally, it gives the quarterback a great deal of time to pass the ball, and the receivers have a better opportunity to get in the clear because of the rotation.

9. Delay Passes

The delay pass is executed by any receiver. All receivers execute one maneuver downfield to minimize the time the secondary has to react to the pattern being run. The delaying receiver will usually block for two or three counts and then will slip into an open area to receive a quick, short pass from the quarterback.

10. Screen Passes

Screen passes are designed to combat a hard-charging defensive line. When the quarterback is having trouble with the protection he is receiving, he will usually call for a screen. The offensive linemen will let the defensive rushers come hard for the quarterback. The quarterback will retreat farther than he normally does to draw the rushing linemen. The offensive linemen will either go to the right, middle, or left on the playing field (according to the screen called). An offensive back or end will delay on the line before getting to his assigned position. As the quarterback retreats, he passes the ball to the receiver at the essential time. Once the receiver catches the ball he will use the blockers to maneuver downfield. The other receivers who ran deep to draw the secondary away from the screen will immediately turn back on the defenders.

11. Shuffle Pass

The shuffle pass is a type of screen pass, yet it develops quicker than a screen. The shuffle pass is usually thrown to a set backfield man who will maneuver up to the line of scrimmage and let the defensive line go by him. The quarterback will quickly shuffle the ball to him.

12. The Draw

The draw can be the most consistent play for a successful passing attack. The draw should be utilized when the defensive linemen are putting a hard charge on the passer. For a more effective passing attack, the draw should be used on every pass play (from the drop-back action), because the defensive linemen usually go to the fake of the draw. This gives the quarterback an extended time to throw the ball. When the fake is no longer drawing the defensive linemen, it should then be employed effectively. The defensive linemen, therefore, will be more aware of the draw and the quarterback will be in a more advantageous position to pass.

IMPORTANCE OF FILMS, SCOUTING, AND OBSERVATION

Although explained in the preceding chapters, it is very necessary that the coach employ scouting to observe how the opponent covers formations with the defensive secondary, linebackers, and ends. The scout should know where the defensive personnel aligns with tight ends, split ends, flankers, slots, wings, and so forth. The scout should know how the opponent covers receivers, whether there is rotation, and if the defense plays man-to-man, zone, or a combination of each. He should observe where the linebackers cover on drop-back, roll-out, and sprint-out passes. How do ends cover against the split end—tight, walkaway, or head-up position? Who covers men in motion to either side of the formation, and is there weakness in the defense for the running game when motion occurs?

To help decide on many of the questions, films are essential. Films of the opponent against other teams are needed. Additionally, the film of the year before may prove valuable.

During the game itself, observation is necessary. The observer should see if the team is covering the offense as expected, or if there are changes in the defense. Other ways of attacking a new secondary should also already be prepared, so the offense will be able to move the team through the air when necessary.

THE PASS OFFENSE AND ATTACKING DEFENSIVE LINEBACKERS AND ENDS 61

ATTACKING PERSONNEL

While personnel has been explained, it must be pointed out again. The coach should attempt to exploit the weakest personnel of the defensive secondary. If a weak pass defender is found, the coach should attempt to strike in his particular area. Flip-flopping of receivers to either side of the formation to attain such a combination is essential. Many times the strongest aspect of the defense can be declared weak because of the personnel in the secondary.

ATTACKING PASS DEFENSES

There are 12 imaginary areas on the field that the passing game can exploit on any defensive secondary. These 12 areas do not have to be attacked, but are mentioned to indicate where a pass offense can release its receivers. The areas are shown in Diagram 3–2. It includes the short middle, the medium middle, and the deep middle. On either side are the short flats, the medium outside, and

Diagram 3–2

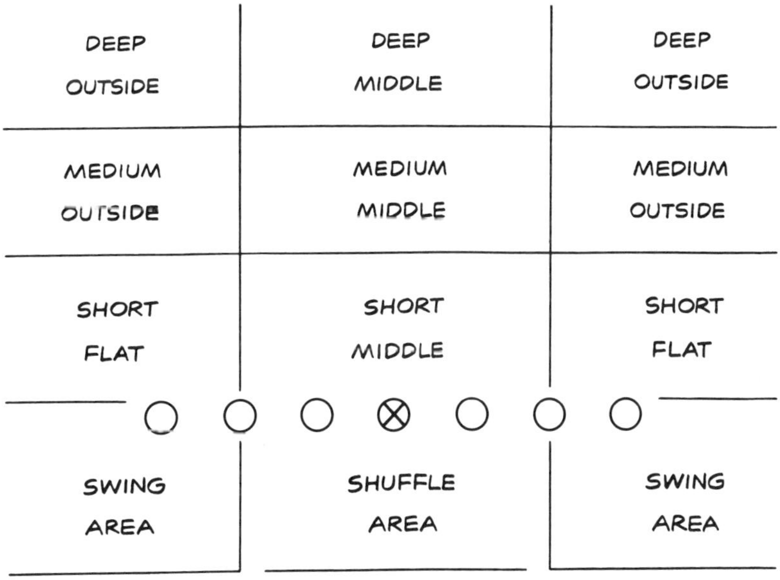

DEEP OUTSIDE	DEEP MIDDLE	DEEP OUTSIDE
MEDIUM OUTSIDE	MEDIUM MIDDLE	MEDIUM OUTSIDE
SHORT FLAT	SHORT MIDDLE	SHORT FLAT
SWING AREA	SHUFFLE AREA	SWING AREA

the deep outside. The other three (swing and shuffle areas) are located on the offense's side of the scrimmage line.

The Passing Tree

The passing tree is illustrated in Diagram 3–3 (next page). It is a combination of different routes which can be executed by the split end, flanker, tight end, and set backs. When utilizing the passing tree the offense should have one set pattern between all receivers. According to the defensive coverage, the offense should capitalize on what the defense is doing and adjust its patterns. For example, if the defensive halfback is aligned with the split end and playing very close or tight on him, the split end can execute the out route once or twice and, when the right moment occurs, employ the out and up pattern attempting to get behind him. Other routes and patterns can be run and altered during the game when the coach and quarterback feel it is essential. It is important that the ends, flankers, and backs run their routes to perfection.

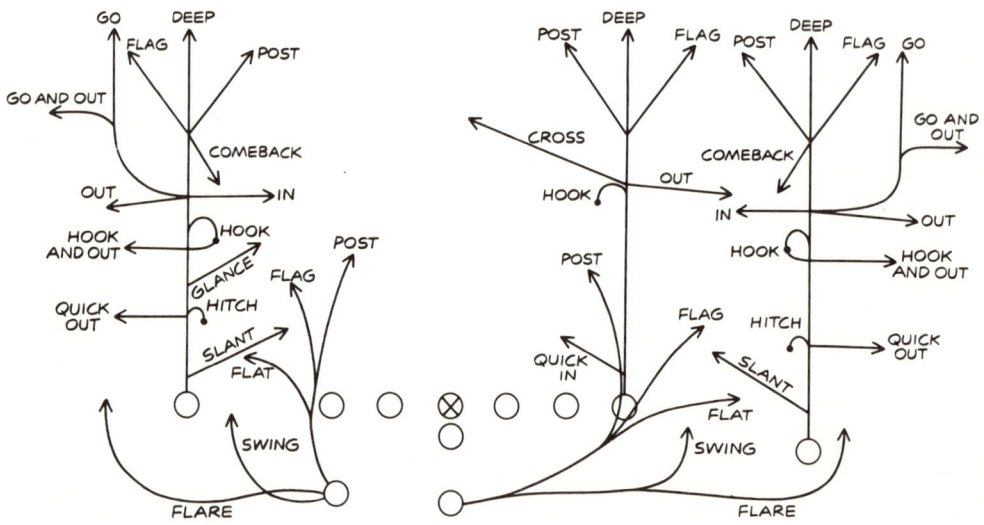

Diagram 3–3
The passing tree

ATTACKING ALL DEFENSIVE SECONDARIES

No matter what pass defense is utilized, there are pass patterns that can be employed against all of them. John Bridgers, former head football coach at Baylor University, has stated: "As far as the secondary coverage is concerned, we throw basically the same patterns against a man-for-man defense as we do a zone. This is perhaps contrary to the thinking of some coaches on the passing game, but we've found our basic cuts have been effective against both coverages."[4]

---

[4] John Bridgers, "Attacking a Zone and Man for Man with the Baylor Passing Game," *Proceedings of the Forty-First Annual Meeting, American Football Coaches Association*, New York, New York, 1964, p. 14.

No defensive secondary wants the long "bomb" completed. Therefore, certain basic and simple individual pass routes can be used. Usually these will be comprised of short pass routes that attempt to force the defensive man in a certain area to retreat deep. The receiver then will execute a quick short pattern. The type of route which can be utilized is the square out, square in, hitch, hook, hook and out, curl, slant, glance, etc. When the defensive pass defender begins to tighten and play closer, the receiver can fake a short route and then run a deep, out and up, hook and go, etc.

ATTACKING DEFENSIVE LINEBACKERS

The defensive linebacker is one of the most important positions of any defense. The linebacker must do a number of jobs well to make a defense good. He must drop back for passes, pursue quickly to the ballcarrier, and fire across the line to rush the passer and break up the running play. In attacking defensive linebackers there are a few ways to exploit these three duties. The following are the methods that will be explained in attacking linebackers:

1. The alignment and the coverage of linebackers.
2. Play-action passes.
3. Quick pursuing linebackers.
4. The delay pass.
5. Check series to ends.
6. Check series to backs.
7. The check series draw.
8. The screen pass.

The coverage of the defensive secondary plays an important role when attacking linebackers also. Usually when there is secondary zone coverage, forcing the coverage deep and throwing around the linebacker can be successful. It must be remembered that if man-to-man defense is being utilized by the secondary, many of the routes and patterns will be covered by defensive backs. However, throwing where the linebackers are *not* covering will help tremendously, even though man-to-man is employed. If linebackers are utilizing man-to-man coverage, a quick back should be able to outmaneuver a linebacker.

1. *The Alignment and the Coverage of Linebackers*

Many passes depend upon the alignments and coverage of the linebackers. No matter where the linebackers align and how each covers on drop-back, roll-out, and sprint-out passes, etc., the pass must be thrown between linebackers or in the vacated areas. Diagram 3–4 (next page) illustrates the gap areas between linebackers on drop-back passes. If the pass is to be a semi-roll-out, semi-sprint-out, or other type of action, the linebackers may be in other positions. A good saying to remember is: "Throw where they're not."

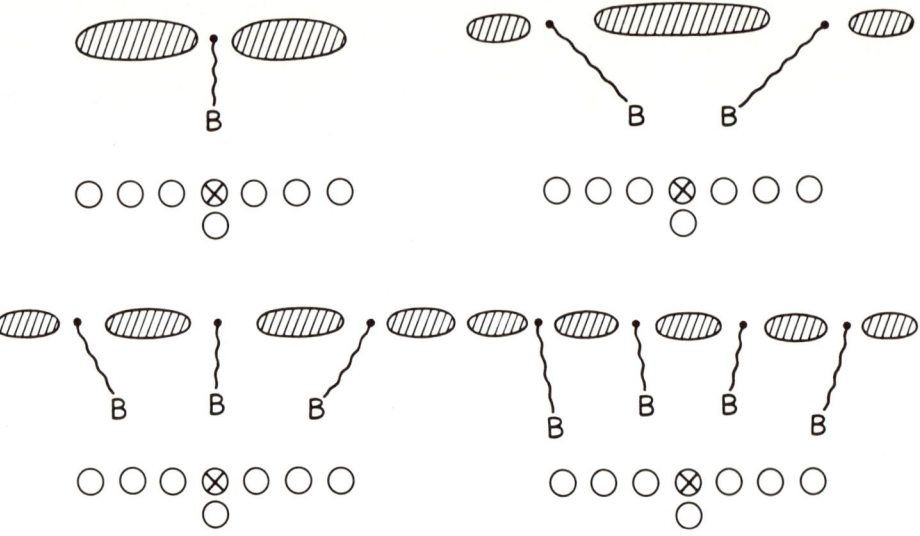

Diagram 3-4

The receivers must run the exact routes required of them. Illustrations 3–5 through 3–8 indicate a few passes that can be utilized against the linebacker, with employment of drop-back, sprint-outs, and semi-sprint-outs. Notice the routes and patterns executed are where the linebackers do *not* cover.

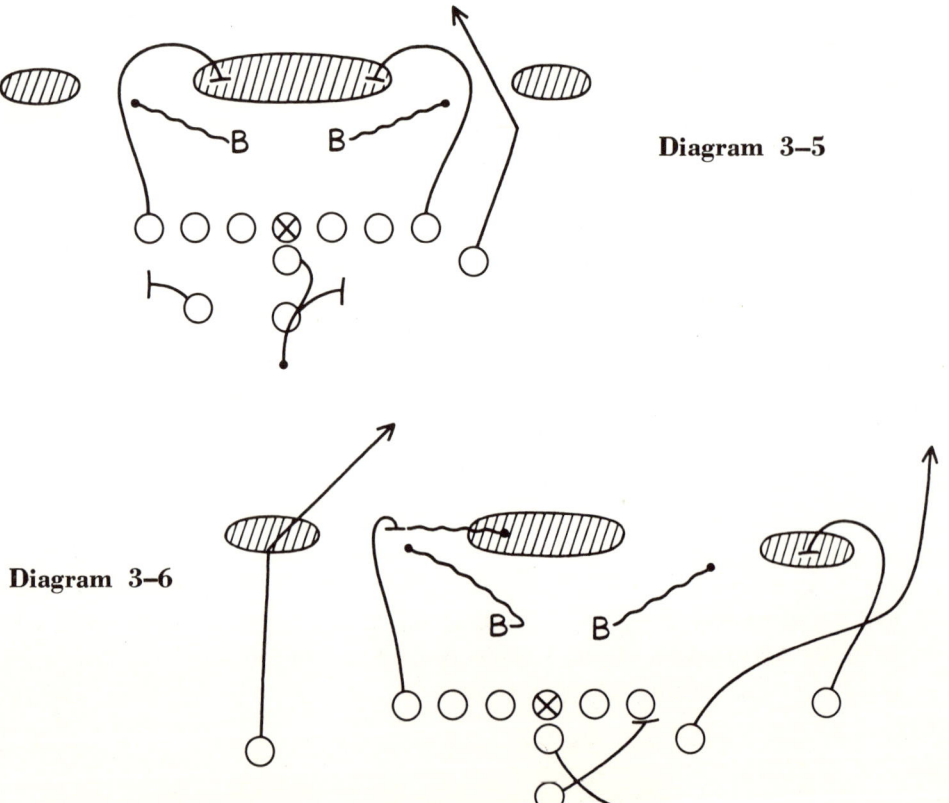

Diagram 3-5

Diagram 3-6

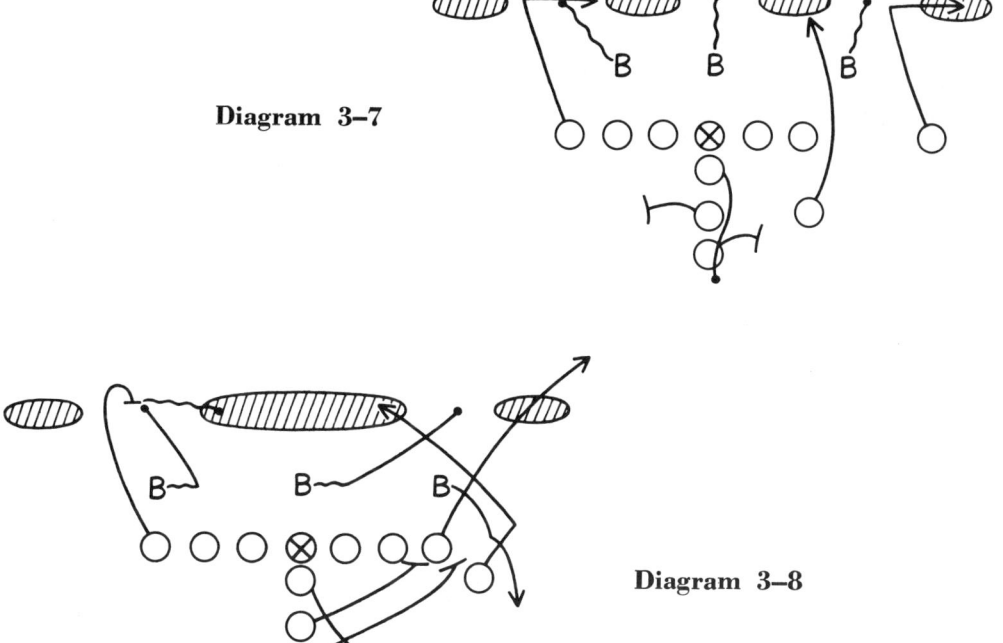

Diagram 3-7

Diagram 3-8

Diagram 3-9 illustrates an unbalanced line to the left. The left defensive linebacker covers the right offensive end and the fullback goes between both linebackers. Notice the right offensive end tries to occupy the left linebacker in this situation.

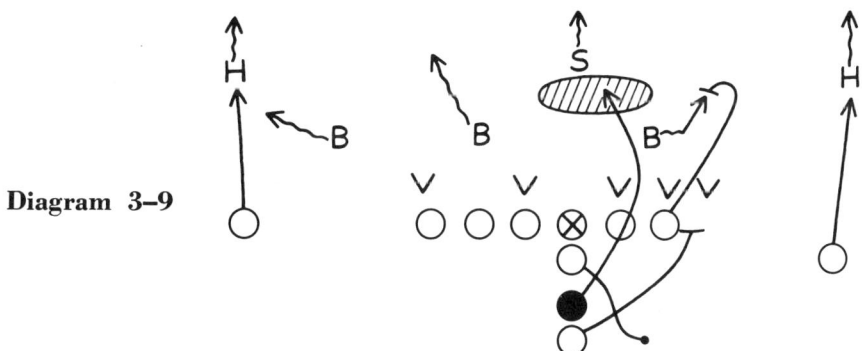

Diagram 3-9

2. Play-Action Passes

Play-action passes are excellent against the linebacker. They tend to draw the linebacker toward the faking ballcarrier. The passer and receivers, therefore, have vacated areas that open wider than usual. A play-action pass is a fake by the quarterback to one of the set backs in the backfield. The passer then sets up and passes the ball to a receiver. Diagrams 3–10 through 3–12 illustrate some play-action passes against the linebacker. While man-to-man secondary coverage may cover the receivers, the passer has a better opportunity to throw over the linebackers in each illustration.

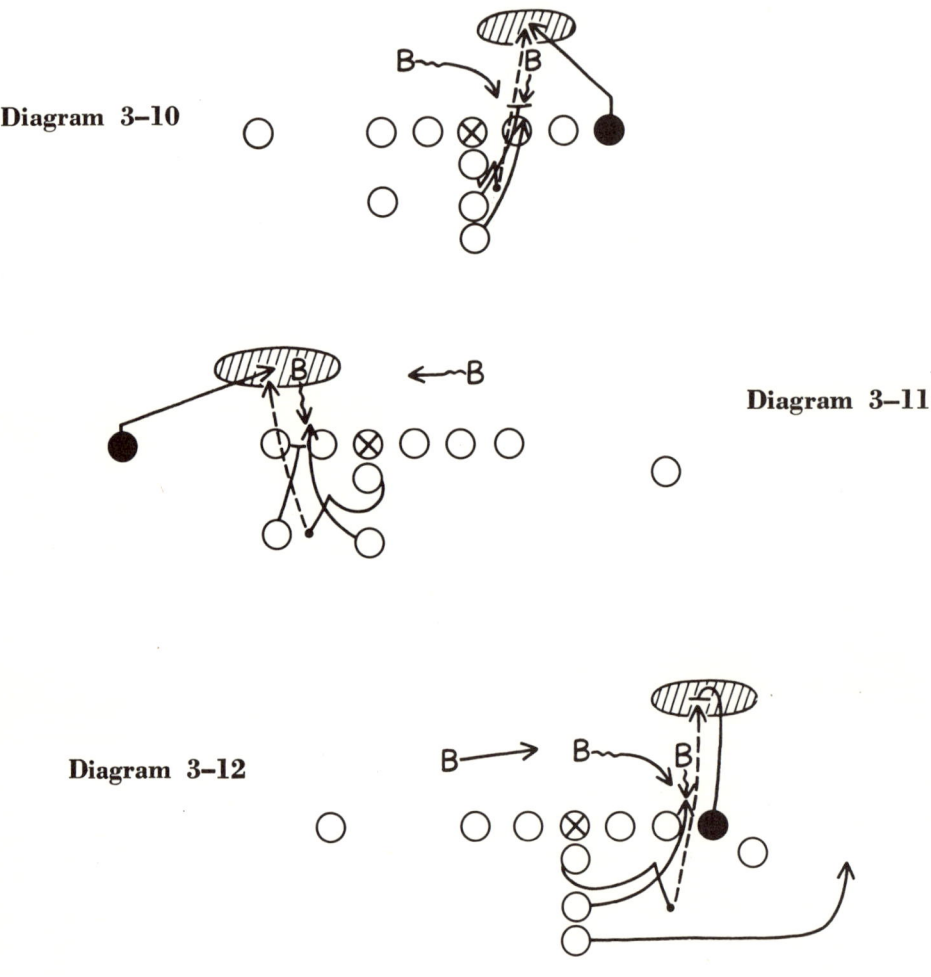

Diagram 3–10

Diagram 3–11

Diagram 3–12

3. Quick Pursuing Linebackers

When defensive linebackers are pursuing fast to the play, the quick throwback pass is excellent. The quarterback will start quickly in one direction, pull up, and hit the receiver. In this case the tight end, away from the intended running direction, receives the ball while the linebacker clears the area. Diagram 3–13 indicates the quick throwback pass.

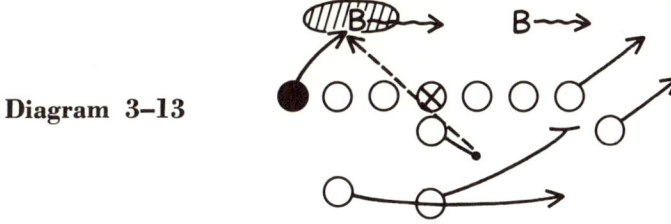

Diagram 3-13

4. The Delay Pass

Another effective method to utilize against the linebacker is the delay pass. Once a pass is shown, the linebackers will immediately retreat to their respective cover areas. This will leave a wide vacated area between the defensive line rushing the passer and the linebackers. The receiver will then run the required delayed route in the vacated area. Diagrams 3-14 and 3-15 illustrate two delaying patterns thrown in front of the linebackers. In Diagram 3-14 the left halfback delays for approximately two counts and slips across the line of scrimmage for

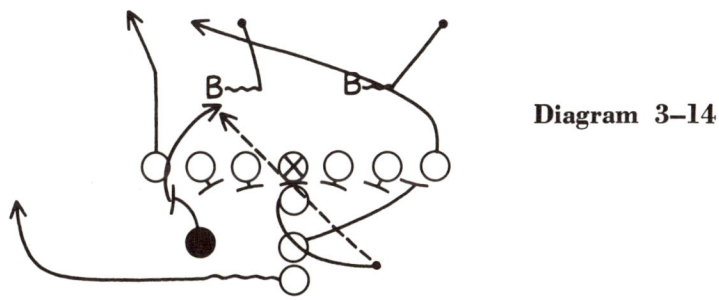

Diagram 3-14

a quick dump pass. Diagram 3-15 indicates a slight roll by the quarterback away from motion. He fakes a throwback and hits a delay pass to the tight end over the middle in front of the linebackers.

Diagram 3-15

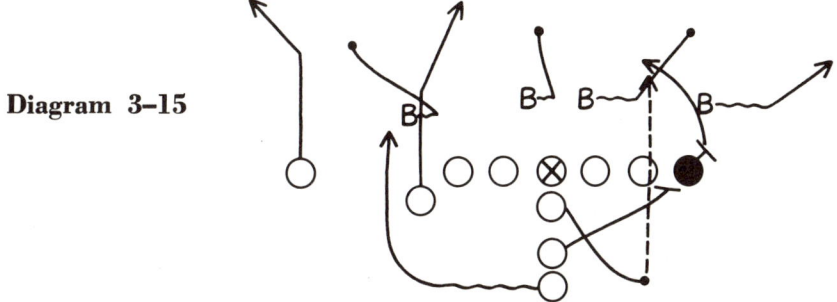

5. Check Series to Ends

The firing linebacker has always been a problem to any passing game. The linebacker has usually put a great deal of pressure upon the passer and many times will be free to tackle him.

One of the finest pass attacks utilized at any time, but excellent against the firing linebacker, is the quick pass. The quick pass is illustrated in Diagram 3–16. The split end and the flanker will run approximately 5-yard quick routes. They will either execute the hitch, out, glance, or slant. The patterns will be dependent on how the defense covers the flanker and split end. The tight end will release from the line and his eyes will be on the nearest linebacker. If the linebacker stunts, the tight end is the safety valve. He will be hit automatically by the quarterback. If the linebacker does not fire, the tight end will continue upfield as illustrated. The protection can be executed in two different ways. The linemen can either fire out and strike the opponent across the line of scrimmage, or the line can quickly set up in a pass protection cup and block the defensive line. The quarterback will take two quick steps backward and key the linebacker. If he should fire, the quarterback will hit the tight end with a pass. Usually the tight end will yell a word such as "Pass-Pass" to alert the quarterback of the firing linebacker. If a linebacker does not fire, the quarterback will pass the ball to either the split end or the flanker, whichever was designated. Another effective method is to have both receivers run the same pattern. When the quarterback steps up to the center, he will look to one side and the other to see if one of the receivers is double-covered. If one is, the quarterback will throw to the other receiver.

6. Check Series to Backs

While the end can be used in the quick pass series, other receivers can also be employed. A halfback who is set in his position can key the linebacker. If the linebacker fires on any type of drop-back pass, he can easily swing out for a pass instead of blocking. In this case the tight end will usually stay in and block. Diagram 3–17 and 3–18 indicate two pass patterns toward the tight and split end with the linebacker firing to stop the play and the halfback swinging out for a pass. Notice in Diagram 3–17 that the fullback can either block or be the third receiver to the split end side. In this situation the other linebacker, who may be covering the tight end and not firing, is away from the play. In Diagram 3–18, the halfback replaces the tight end's assignment for the quick pass, because of the firing linebacker. If a defensive end covers the halfback out of the backfield, swinging another back out can be executed such as is done in Diagram 3–17. A good back should be able to beat a defensive end.

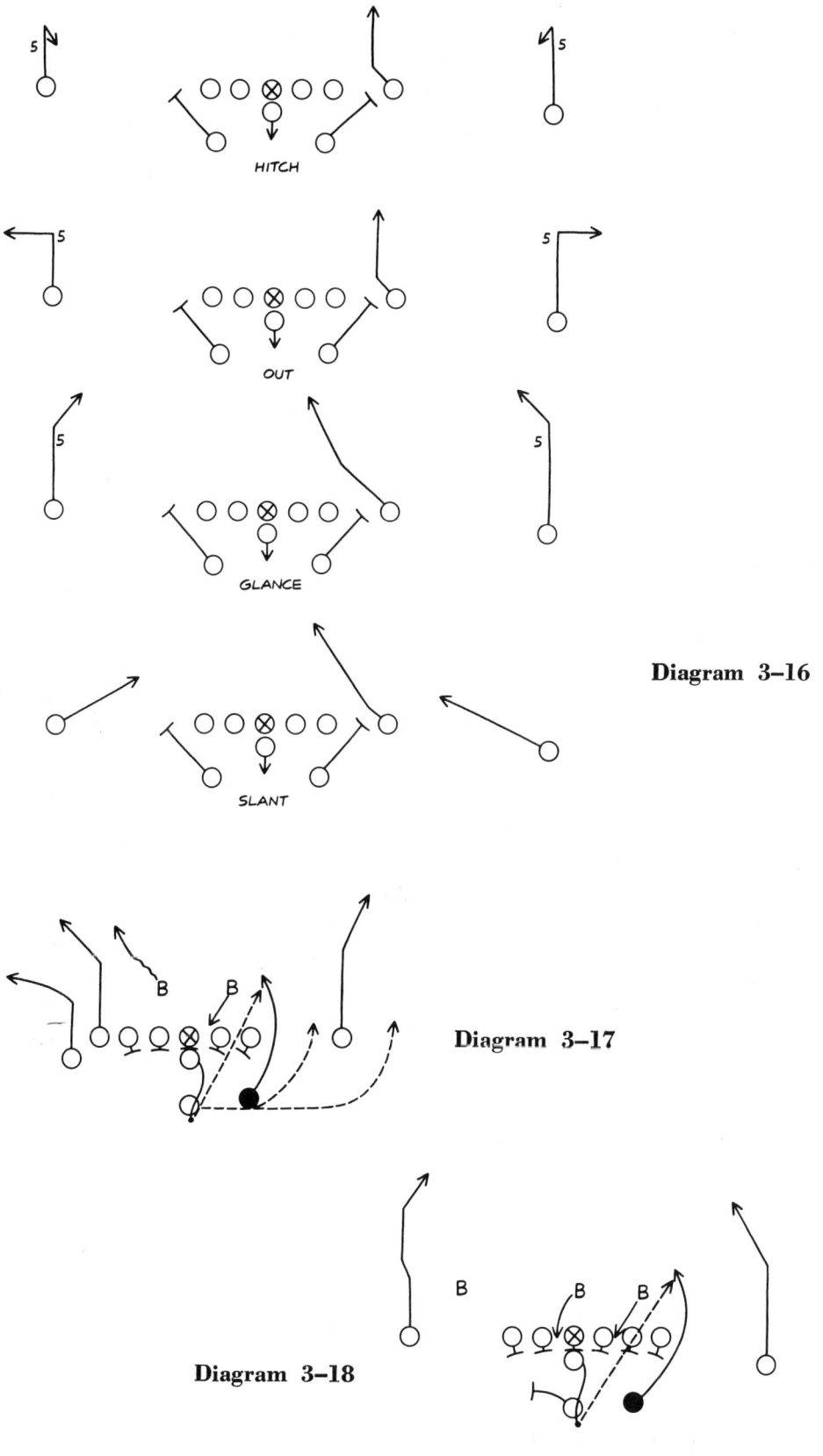

Diagram 3–16

Diagram 3–17

Diagram 3–18

7. The Check Series Draw

Another excellent method when the draw has been called and the linebacker rushes is the check series draw. Bill Crutchfield, football coach at Georgia Tech, mentioned: (Diagram 3–19)

> We use the draw, of course, as everyone else does who uses a passing game to any extent. We feel that we have overcome one of the great problems in running the draw play against a blitzing defense which sometimes makes it a little sticky in there. What we simply have done is incorporated our check series with our draw play. If we have a draw play called, we have the tight end, or the halfback if it is to the weak side, keying the same as he would on any check series play. The instant that we see the linebacker become involved in the pass rush, the quarterback simply pulls up and throws the ball to the check receiver. This is no problem for us since our linemen are using pass protection blocking on our draw and we do not have linemen downfield. The fullback, of course, thinking that he is going to get the ball for the draw, sets for it. But frequently the quarterback, if the blitz is on, will stop short of the handoff point, raise up and throw the ball to one of the check receivers and it will turn into a check series pass rather than the draw.[8]

8. The Screen Pass

The screen is excellent against the defensive linebacker. This is especially evident if the linebackers are executing blitzing and firing. There are many types of screen passes. The coach can employ screen passes to ends or backs and can utilize the screen to the left, middle, or right. A double screen can also be employed. A screen pass to the left is shown in Diagram 3–20. The left tight end will drive the defenders to his side deep. When the screen is thrown, he will turn back and block one of the defenders. The left tackle, left guard, and center will pass-protect for three counts. It is important for these men to strike their opponent two or three times before going to the screen area. The left tackle will sprint out toward the sideline and block anyone coming from the outside. If no man comes, he will turn upfield. The guard will block anyone to the inside. The center will sprint out and turn upfield for any defensive ballplayers. The left halfback will fake a block and release to the screen area to receive the ball. The right guard and tackle will continue to protect the passer's backside. The right end and flanker will release from the line of scrimmage, go across the field, and attempt to get in front of the play. If the screen is to the right, the same techniques are executed (Diagram 3–21).

---

[8]Bill Crutchfield, "Passing Versus the Blitz," *Proceedings of the Forty-Third Meeting, American Football Coaches Association*, Washington, D.C., 1966, p. 96.

Diagram 3-19

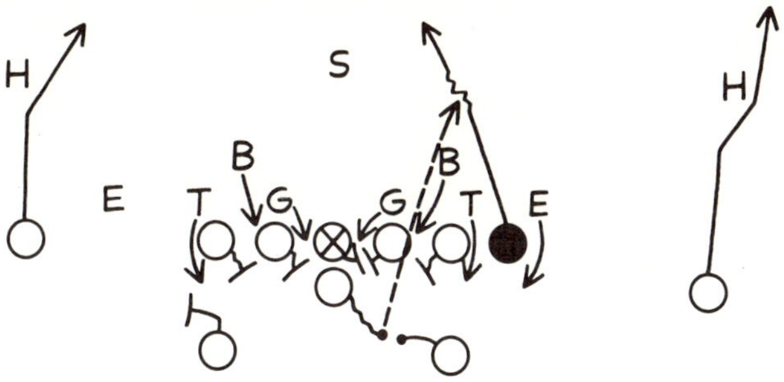

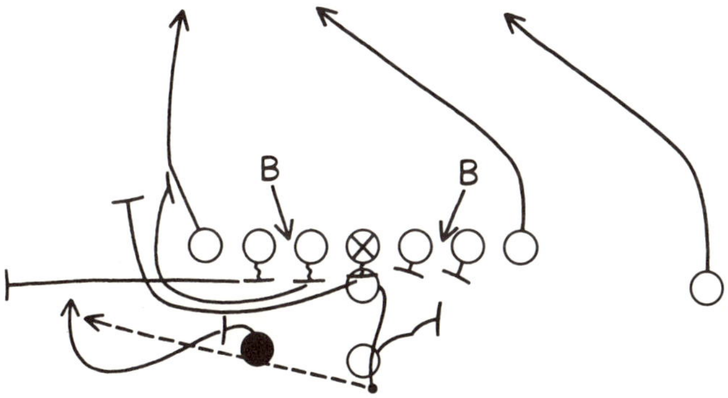

Diagram 3-20

Diagram 3-21

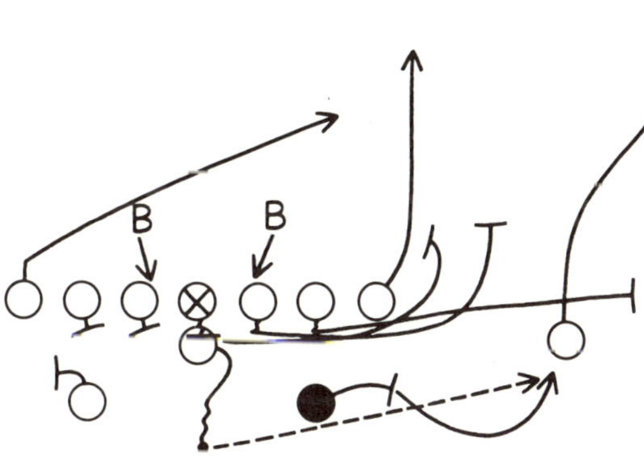

A double screen is shown in Diagram 3-22 against firing linebackers.

Diagram 3-22

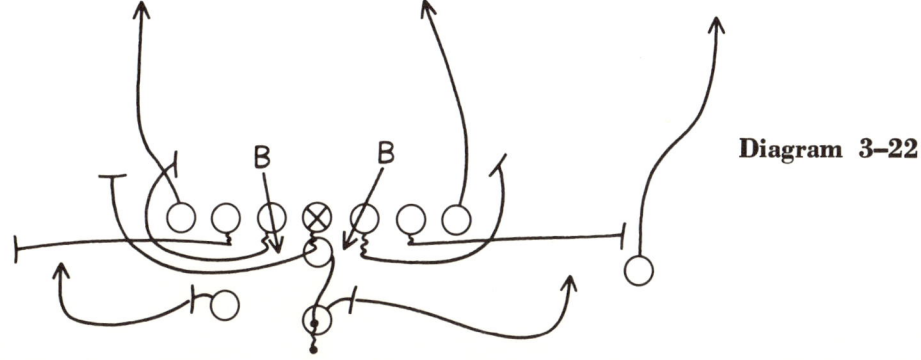

ATTACKING DEFENSIVE ENDS

Defensive ends can play in three different alignments:

1. Tight position.
2. Walkaway position.
3. Double-up position.

Tight Position

A tight position is a defensive end positioned on the line of scrimmage, with an offensive end split-out (Diagram 3–23). This alignment is usually employed when the offense is near to the sideline or the defensive team does not fear the threat of the split end. As can be seen, there is a wide area by the split end for

Diagram 3–23

the maneuver of his routes. As was accomplished with the linebackers, the pass routes should be run where the areas are vacated.

The tight end from this alignment is in a position where he can easily fire across the line of scrimmage on the snap of the ball. But no matter what the play executed, whether it is drop-back, roll-out toward or away from the defensive end, he has the opportunity to sprint to the flat area and cover for passes (Diagram 3–24). The defensive tackle in this case, would be the contain man on any play toward him.

Diagram 3–24

In this situation, one of the best passes is the quick pass to the split end. The split end takes approximately one step across the line, and the quarterback delivers the ball quickly to him (Diagram 3–25).

When the defensive end is in a tight position, the outside patterns (square-out, hook and out, etc.) are excellent passes. If the defensive end is not rushing, but is covering the flat, he will have an exceptionally difficult time covering the

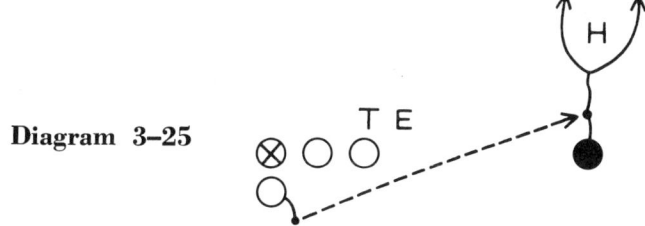

Diagram 3–25

roll-out. The roll-out toward, or the drop-back pass is the best maneuver for the passer with this type of pattern.

Since the end is in tight, he is vulnerable to the play-action pass directed at him. The split end will be able to run any route desired, whether it be inside or outside. If the defensive end commits himself to the faking ballcarrier, the split end can execute hooks, curls, glances, hitches, in routes, out routes, etc. Diagram 3–26 illustrates a play-action pass at the defensive end and the many patterns that can be run.

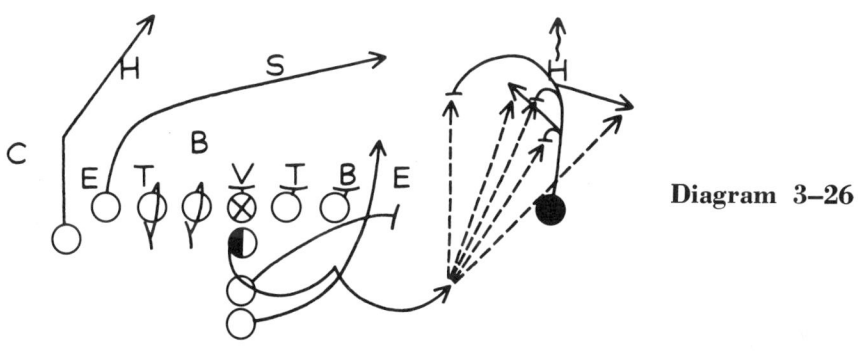

Diagram 3–26

Walkaway Position

The second position is the walkaway position. The defensive end is aligned off the line of scrimmage, approximately 1 yard, and stationed halfway between the split end and the offensive tackle (Diagram 3–27). The best patterns to run when there is a walkaway are out patterns, because the in routes can be easily covered by the defensive end.

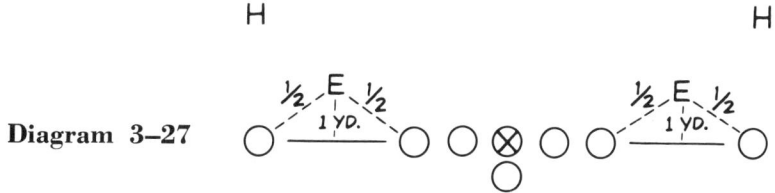

Diagram 3–27

A set back or tailback to the side of the split end can be used very advantageously. If the split end runs his routes to the sideline, the tailback should run inside patterns to keep the walkaway end away from the split end. To throw inside patterns to the split end, (hooks, curls, square-ins) the tailback should

74 THE PASS OFFENSE AND ATTACKING DEFENSIVE LINEBACKERS AND ENDS

run out routes. The tailback can either run flat, flare, or swing patterns to accomplish this (Diagram 3–28 and 3–29).

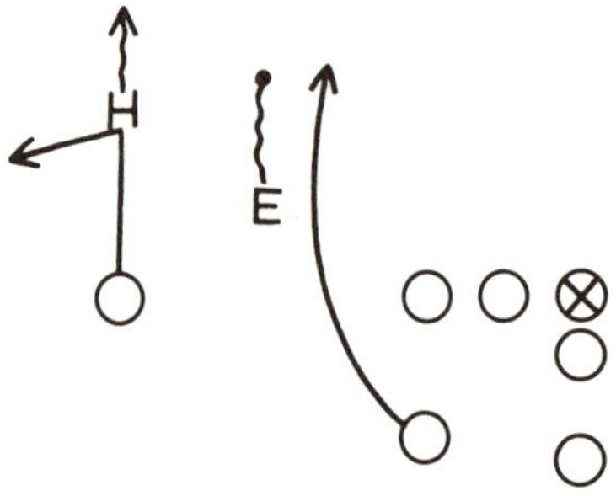

Diagram 3–28

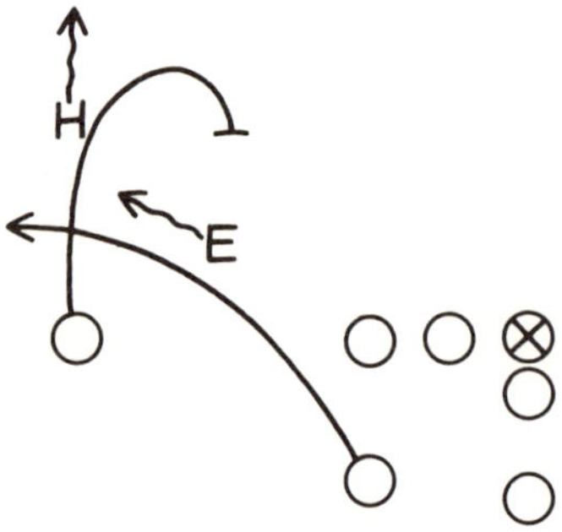

Diagram 3–29

When throwing to the inside, the split end should read the movements of the defensive end and linebackers. What they do will determine where the split end should run his route. Diagrams 3–30 and 3–31 illustrate the walkaway man going to two different positions and the split end varying his route.

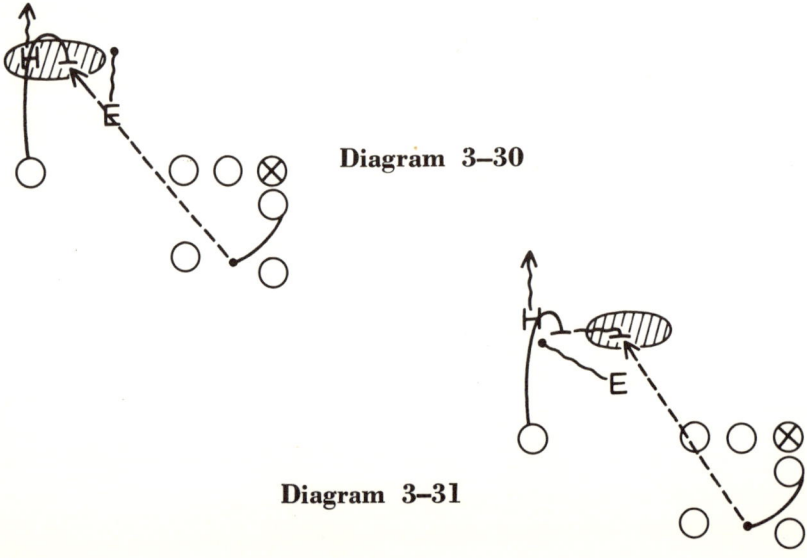

Diagram 3–30

Diagram 3–31

THE PASS OFFENSE AND ATTACKING DEFENSIVE LINEBACKERS AND ENDS

The tailback can accomplish the same if the end covers him close. Diagram 3-32 shows the tailback altering his course to get open.

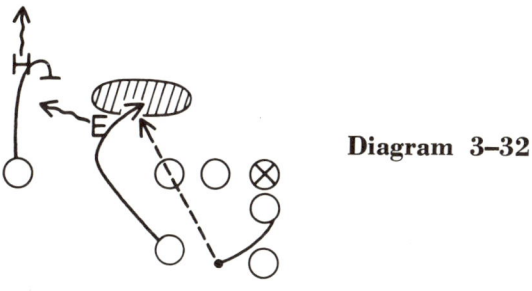

Diagram 3-32

Double-Up Position

The third position a defensive end can play is double up. He can alter his alignment by either being slightly to the inside or outside, according to field position (Diagram 3-33).

Diagram 3-33

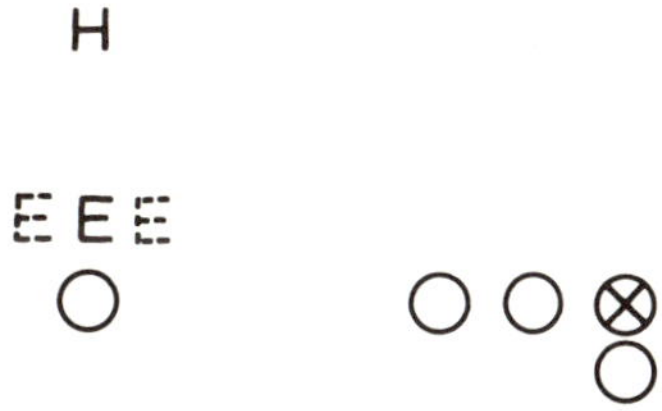

When the split end has a man over him he should run pass routes to the inside (slant, hook, curl, in, etc.). The tailback can run up the seam between the offensive end and tackle if the split end is closely double-covered. The quarterback should then throw to the tailback; the split end can run out patterns. The offense should put men in motion toward the split end to force a one-on-one situation for the split end if possible. If the defensive end does not cover the man in motion, the quarterback can throw to the motion man.

4

ATTACKING DEFENSIVE SECONDARIES

ATTACKING THE DEEP SECONDARY

There are three basic pass defenses; zone, man-to-man, and a combination of each. The coach must be able to attack all three of these defenses. Each defensive secondary has the same basic principles. Their first responsibility is the pass. Each defender must prevent the long pass, the long score, keep completions to a minimum, intercept, and score. All secondary men think "pass" first. Each player should take pride in his job, have enough confidence to get it done, and possess an all-out desire and motivation to play pass defense.

Pass defenses, however, can be played differently and there are many coverages within each secondary. For example, the zone defense employs the two deep zone, three deep zone, four deep zone, rotational zone, invert zone, and the revert zone, with differences in each. The man-to-man utilizes the two deep, three deep, and four deep man-to-man coverage. Some coaches will use man-to-man coverage within the zone, while others will adhere to a strict zone. Other coaches will employ the deep secondary as zone, while the linebackers and defensive ends play man-to-man. This can be altered with the linebackers and defensive ends playing zone and the deep defenders playing man-to-man.

When the coach goes into a game he should know what type of pass defense he will be facing. He should know whether it is a certain type of zone, man-to-man, or a combination of each. Therefore, the coach will be better prepared to attack the weak areas of the defense.

DISGUISING SECONDARIES

There are many defenses that will attempt to disguise their secondary coverage. The reason is, if the offense knows the type of coverage being employed, it will better be able to read and execute the proper routes necessary to beat that particular coverage. For example, if an offense knows the defensive opponent will utilize an invert four deep zone only, then it will better be able to attack the invert. However, if the defense aligns in an invert, but then "reverts" on the snap of the ball, it may confuse both the receivers and quarterback, and the defense in all probability will have the pattern covered.

Therefore, from a defensive standpoint, if an offense has a good passing attack, it should attempt to vary the secondary coverage trying to disguise and confuse the offensive attack. However, the offense should know the secondary coverages the defense employs and practice against *all* the coverages. The receivers then will execute the proper routes and patterns correctly according to what the defense shows.

ATTACKING ZONE DEFENSES

To know and understand zone defenses, it is necessary for the coach to understand some of the basic principles involved. In the zone the deep secondary defenders must stay between the receiver and the goalposts, or play as deep as the deepest receiver. Each must get depth continually, and keep all receivers contained. The defenders should see everything that occurs in front of them. When the ball is in the air, these rules change, and they react directly to the ball. Every defender attempts to play the ball at its highest point and drives through the receiver to play the ball. The zone defenders will either key the ball or a man (receiver). Whatever they were taught as to flow of the ball or maneuvers of the receiver, they will react accordingly.

Numerous coaches teach a strict zone, having the defenders drop straight back into their zones. However, many coaches also teach man-to-man within a zone. Once an offensive receiver enters a zone, the defender picks him up until he leaves the zone area. The defensive back will stay with the receiver all the way through the zone until the ball is thrown.

The zone defense will be separated into four divisions:
1. The straight zone.
2. The rotation zone.
3. The invert zone.
4. The revert zone.

1. The Straight Zone

In the straight zone there are three coverages, basically the same, but requiring a different amount of men. They are the two deep coverage, the three deep coverage, and the four deep coverage.

The Two Deep Zone. The two deep coverage is illustrated in Diagram 4–1. The defensive halfbacks are aligned on the inside shoulder of the offensive end and approximately 7–10 yards in depth. When a pass shows, the two defenders are responsible for the deep pass. Each man will move and be responsible for half of the playing field.

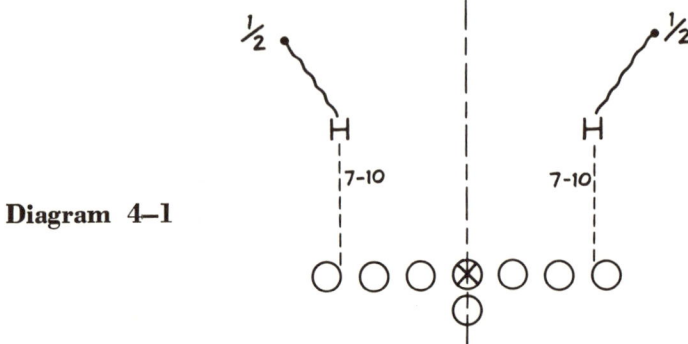

Diagram 4–1

No matter where the ball goes, whether it be left, right, or straight back, the two deep defenders play their zones straight. The two deep zone is not employed widely by many coaches because of the amount of territory each defender must cover on the field. It is basically a special coverage and should never be used if the opposition is expected to pass. A coach may compensate with this type of secondary by running a linebacker down the middle as a safety factor.

The Three Deep Zone. The three deep coverage is shown in Diagram 4–2. The halfbacks align approximately 3–4 yards outside the offensive end with a depth of between 6–9 yards. The halfbacks will usually line up as wide as the widest receiver. Each must be able to cover the widest man on any out pattern. If the receiver is closer than 7–8 yards to the sideline, the halfback will play an inside position on the receiver. No matter where the ball goes, right, left, or drop back, the halfback's responsibility is the 1/3 of the field to his side. The halfback must

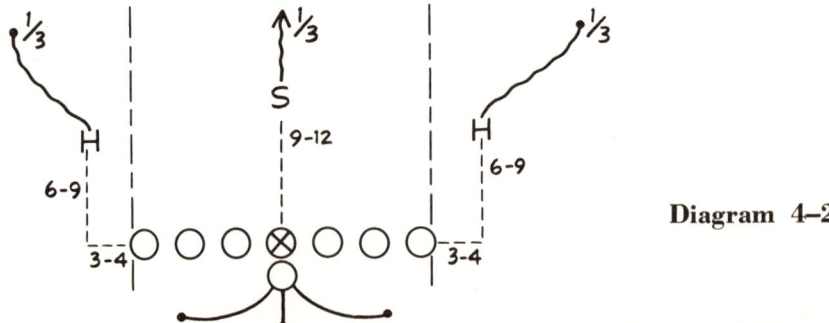

Diagram 4–2

think "pass" first and "run" second. When the halfback is sure it is a run, he must come up and approach the ballcarrier from an outside-in angle. Other coaches may teach an inside-out position depending upon how the defense is executed. If the play goes away from the halfback, he must stay in his zone. After he is definitely sure it is not a pass, he will go across field. The halfback should take a pursuit course that will angle him to intercept the ballcarrier.

The safety man will align directly over the center, approximately 9–12 yards deep. If there is a flanker or a wide side of the field, he should maneuver slightly to that side. The safety's responsibility is the middle 1/3 of the field on any pass and ball flow. If the play is a run, he will be utilized only in a support fashion. The three deep zone is the most widely accepted straight zone coverage and is employed because three men can cover the field fairly well.

The Four Deep Zone. The four deep zone coverage is indicated in Diagram 4–3. There are two corners and two safety men involved. The corner men align approximately 3 yards outside the offensive end and 4 yards deep. The corner men can align deeper with this type of coverage. The safeties align on the inside

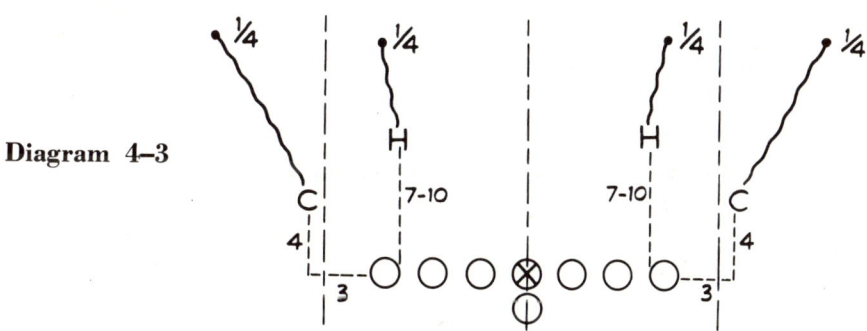

Diagram 4–3

shoulder of the offensive end and about 7–10 yards deep. No matter where the ball flows, the four pass defenders will cover 1/4 of the field. This defensive coverage is not used by many coaches, but it is used by a few teams for simplicity of teaching.

Another reason to use the four deep zone would be for a change-up in defensive coverage. For example, a defensive team may always rotate toward backfield flow. An offense then might fake into the sidelines, causing the defensive secondary to rotate and force one-on-one coverage with a split end, flanker, or wing to the wide or open side of the field. The defense now decides *not* to rotate into the sidelines, but remains in a four deep zone coverage to cover such situations. Still another reason to utilize the four deep zone would be if the offensive opponent continually tries to beat the defenders deep—in which case, the defense remains in a four deep until the offense starts to hurt the defense in the flats. Finally, it can be employed as a prevent coverage when the offense is going to throw the ball deep, definitely trying for the long touchdown pass.

The Strength of the Zone Pass Defense

The strength of the zone coverage is as follows:

1. It can be taught easily, for it is relatively simple for players to learn and understand.
2. It does not need the great athlete at each position.
3. Each defender covers an area and not a man.
4. The players keep their eyes on the ball at all times and react when the ball is in the air.
5. It attempts to get every defender to the ball and punish the receiver.
6. Its main function is to stop the long pass.

The Weakness of the Zone Pass Defense

To attack the zone, it is essential to know and understand the weakness of it. It is essential to remark that one strong aspect of the zone may be weak because of improper coverage of the defenders or of weak personnel. The coach must automatically attack these areas. Other parts of a zone considered weak are as follows:

1. The vacated areas or seams between the defenders. The more defenders, the smaller the seams become.
2. Flooding an area or one section of a zone.
3. All short patterns in front of the defenders (hooks, curls, square-ins, outs, etc.).
4. All flat passes.
5. Diagonal passes across field.
6. The longer the quarterback keeps the ball, the deeper the patterns can get and the defenders must cover more of an area.
7. With linebackers and deep secondary utilizing zone coverage, the more rush desired, the fewer the zones covered.
8. The zone defense is not effective on the goal line when the passes can be quick and the defenders cannot react fast enough.

Attacking the Straight Zone Coverage

The areas to attack a two deep, three deep, and four deep zone pass defense are illustrated in Diagrams 4–4 through 4–6.

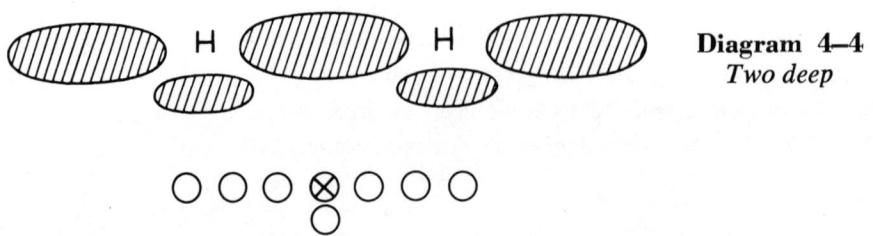

Diagram 4–4
Two deep

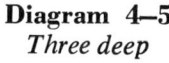

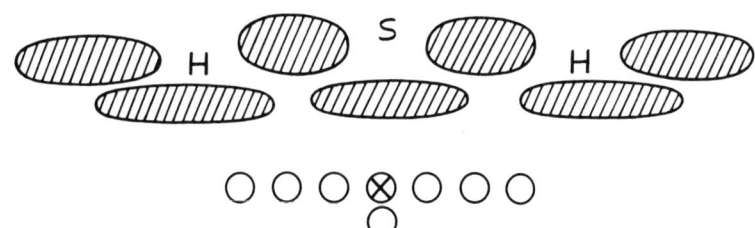

Diagram 4–5
Three deep

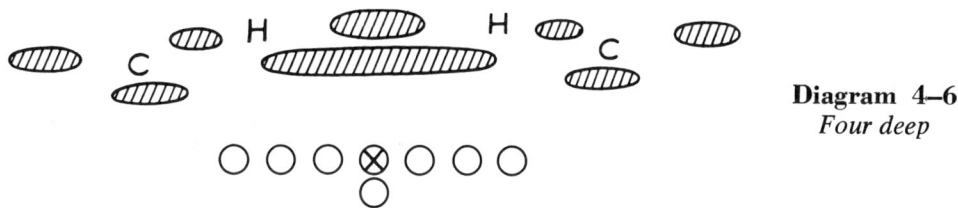

Diagram 4–6
Four deep

The following (Diagrams 4–7 through 4–11) are a few pass patterns that can be employed against the zone pass defense. There are many more patterns that can be utilized and employed. The following are being used for illustrations only.

Splitting the Seams

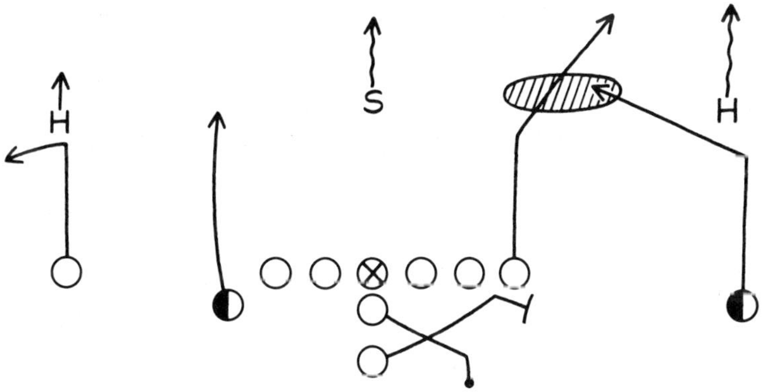

Diagram 4–7
A quick pass in the vacated areas between defenders

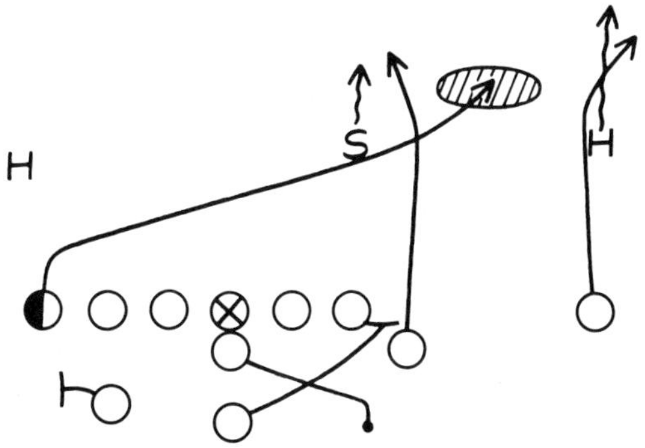

Diagonal Route

Diagram 4–8
Diagonal route cross field

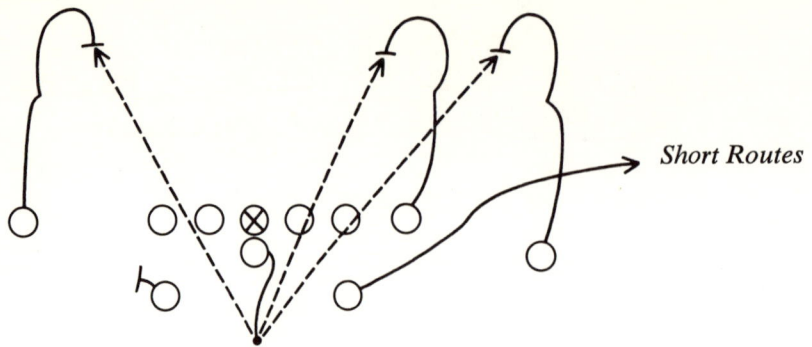

Diagram 4–9
Short routes in front of defenders
On all short patterns the receivers should attempt to drive the defensive halfbacks deep and then execute the required short route.

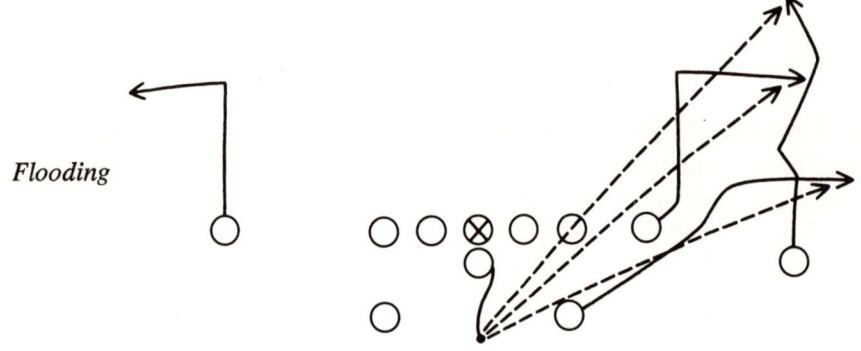

Diagram 4–10
Flooding an area

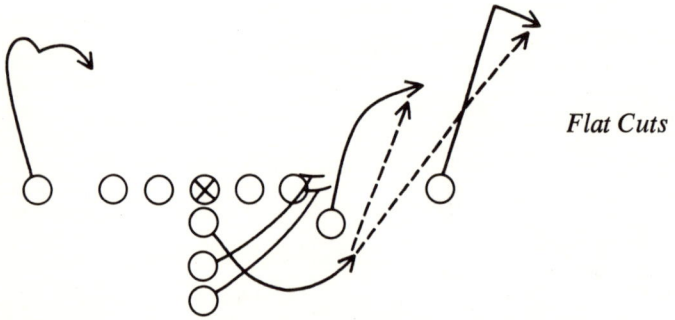

Diagram 4–11
A flat cut
The receiver drives the defender back and then makes a square-out to the sideline.

2. The Rotation Zone
The Three Deep Rotation

A zone that rotates can be accomplished from either a three or four deep secondary. The rotation expects to take advantage of what the offense is doing, especially the roll-out or sprint-out pass. It consists of two or more men leaving an area to cover another section of the field. Rotation by a three deep secondary is shown in Diagram 4–12. The flow of the ball is to the right. The pass defense attempts to flow with it, gaining more strength in that area of the field. The halfback comes up to take the flat and the safety covers the deep outside or the outside 1/3 of the field. In some rotational zones the defensive halfback will not come up until the safety man makes a call to release him. The halfback away from flow will either protect the other 2/3 of the field or will be assisted by another defensive player, i.e., a linebacker. In numerous cases some defenses have their offside linebacker drop back to the middle, or offside 1/3. Another method is for the defensive end to cushion backside or rotate to the deep 1/3 also. If the ball flows in the opposite direction, the rotation of the defensive secondary is the same.

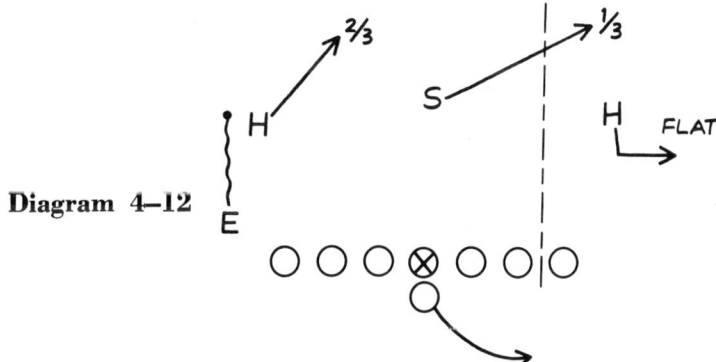

Diagram 4–12

With the rotation, a defensive halfback is now covering the flat area. With this in mind the defense can get a better rush or containment from the outside. For example, if a defensive end, linebacker, or "monster" covers the flat, they can release for containment.

Attacking the Weaknesses of the Rotational Three Deep

The weakness areas of the three deep rotation zones are indicated in Diagram 4–13 (next page). Notice the safety man must travel from his alignment to the deep outside, making a slight weakness in this area. The safety man must take an angle that will be deep, but wide. The defensive halfback covering the flat, leaves an area behind him weak. The away defensive halfback must cover 2/3 of the field, having wide vacated gaps that he must cover. It must be remembered that the weaknesses of the straight zone defense, as were mentioned, relate to every zone defense including the rotation zone and the invert zone, plus the additional weaknesses described.

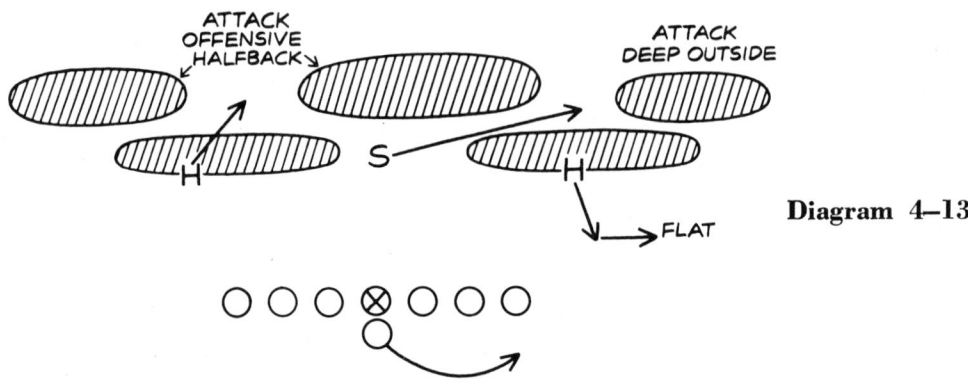

Diagram 4–13

There are a few ways to attack the weakness of the rotation. Diagram 4–14 shows a wingback sprinting to the flat. The tight end reads the move of the defensive halfback. If the halfback should retreat, the offensive end will drive him deep. If the halfback comes up, as in this case, he will cut to the sideline as shown. The safety man has a hard job trying to cover that area. Diagram 4–15 illustrates the offensive end doing the same route, but with the wing starting to the flat and then breaking toward the goalposts.

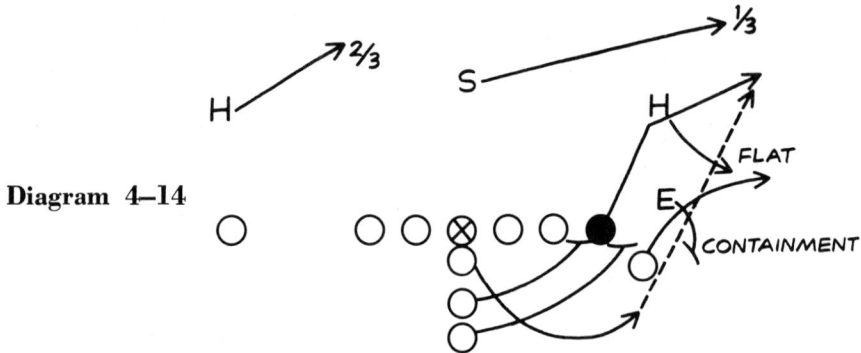

Diagram 4–14

The throwback pass is excellent. The quarterback rolls out, causing the coverage to rotate. The passer will pull up and either hit the end or the tailback releasing to that side (Diagram 4–16). Another effective method is to cause a rotation in one direction and come back the other way (Diagram 4–17). The quarterback sprints out as if he was going to run a sprint-out. He then executes a sharp turn and comes back in the opposite direction. One or two guards can

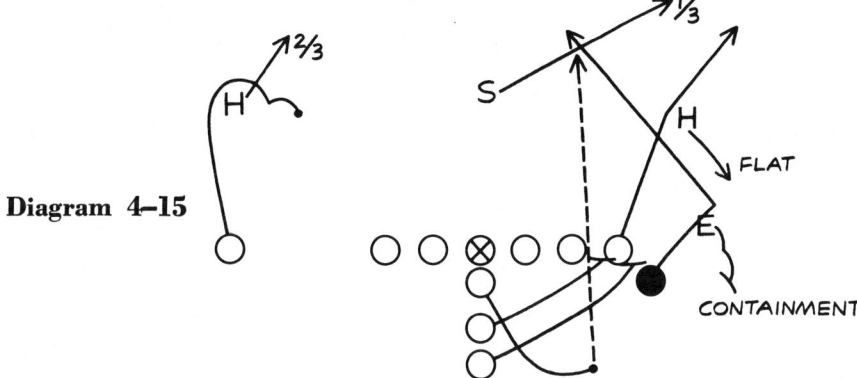

Diagram 4–15

pull for protection. Any pattern can then be run. The safety has already committed to one side and cannot return.

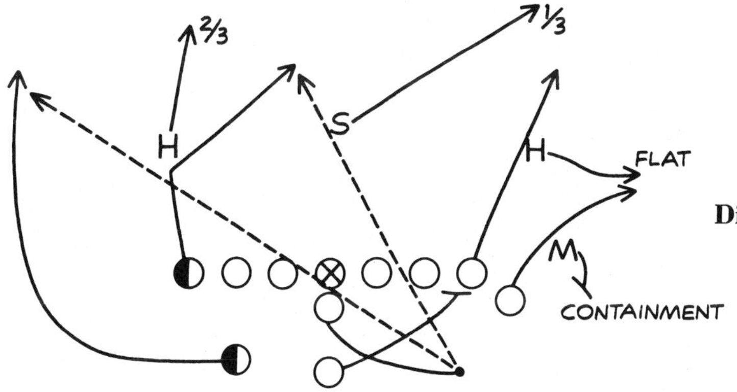

Diagram 4–16

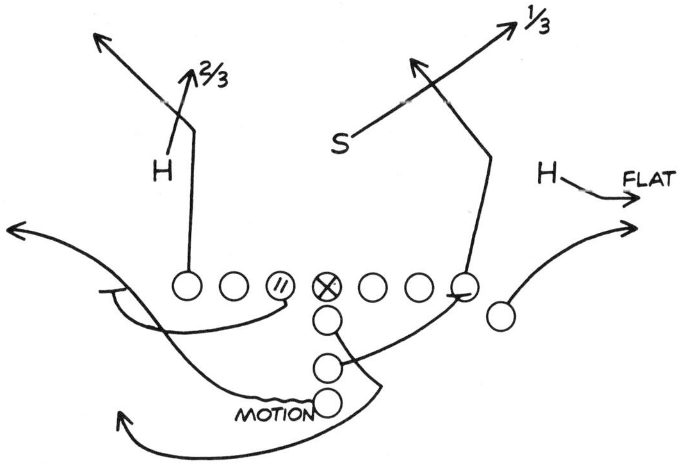

Diagram 4–17

The Four Deep Rotation

The four deep rotation zone is basically the same as the three deep, but it is a better balanced pass defense. Instead of having two men cover the deep passes, it utilizes three men. One man covers the flat while the other three defenders revolve into a three deep zone coverage. Again, the advantage is to try to combine defensive strength with offensive strength. Usually no matter where the ball flows, whether it is right, left, or middle, the four deep rotation will rotate. The defense will make a predetermined call in the huddle, because if a drop-back pass occurs the defenders will know which direction to revolve. Diagram 4–18 illustrates the quarterback flowing to the right and the secondary rotating. The cornerback moves to the flat, the defensive halfback toward flow goes to the deep outside and covers that 1/3 of the field. The away halfback rotates to the deep middle, and the away corner retreats to the deep outside. If the flow were to the left, the secondary would move in the opposite direction.

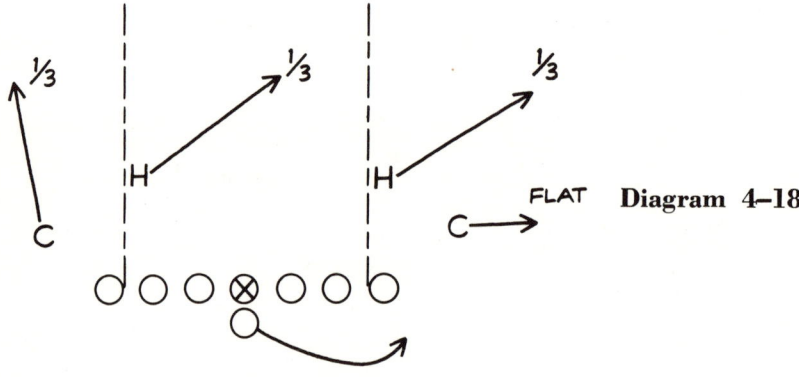

Attacking Weaknesses of the Rotational Four Deep

The weakness areas of the four deep rotation zone are shown in Diagram 4–19. Notice the areas are both in front of the defenders and in the areas vacated between them. There are many pass patterns that can be employed against this

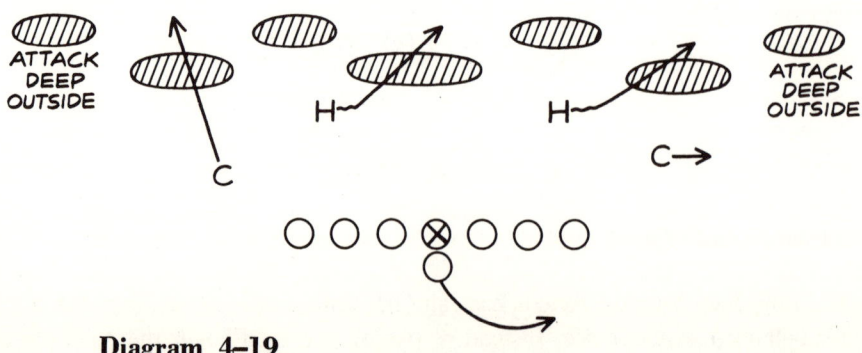

ATTACKING DEFENSIVE SECONDARIES   87

secondary. The coach should find the one or two patterns that can be executed consistently. Patterns should be designed to beat the halfbacks to where they are rotating. The throwback pass is excellent because the corner man has a longer distance to get to the deep outside. A method to make the secondary rotate and then come back in the opposite direction is excellent. The method in attacking the straight zone defense can also be employed.

3. The Invert Zone
The Three Deep Invert

The invert coverage can be accomplished from both the three and four deep coverages. Diagram 4–20 illustrates the three deep pass coverage. The alignment of the three deep is the same as the rotational zone. In this case, the safety and halfback toward the flow of the ball simply change assignments. The defensive halfback's responsibility is the deep outside and the safety moves to the flat. (Again, this is a special coverage for certain situations or teams, etc.) The away defensive halfback's assignment stays the same, the deep 2/3 of the field—unless he is being assisted by another position, such as a linebacker covering down the middle or a defensive end cushioning back for support. The reason for this coverage is that the halfback is in a good position to cover his deep side of the field. The weak area that results from such a coverage is the flat, where the safety must cover. If an offense is finding such a coverage, it should attack the flat area, and use all the methods described in attacking the zone defense and the away side of the flow.

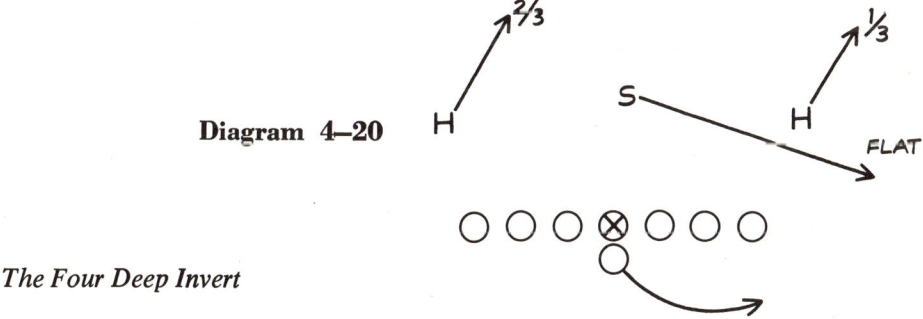

Diagram 4–20

The Four Deep Invert

The four deep invert zone is illustrated in Diagram 4–21 (next page). The invert men are approximately 6 yards deep and directly over the offensive end's position. The deep halfbacks are approximately 8 to 10 yards deep and positioned 3 yards outside the offensive end's position. The invert pass defense was designed for the split end and the wide flanker. The secondary needed a coverage that could align with the wide men with defenders, and yet have a defender that could fill and protect the run. However, the invert coverage can be used against any type of offensive formation. (It must be remembered that an invert coverage is not good against a wingback or tight formation. However, many teams do utilize the invert against such tight offensive formations.) If a strict invert is employed, only two men are used to rotate. The deep halfbacks always cover the deep outside, while the invert men revolve according to the direction of the ball flow. The strength of the defense is that only two men are

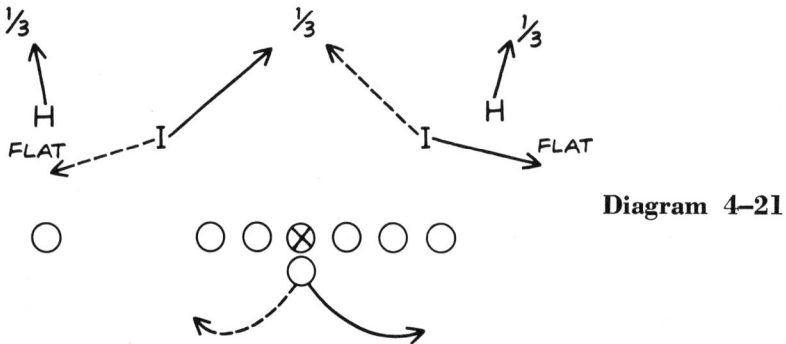

Diagram 4–21

necessary to move and cover all the areas. The weakness of this defensive coverage is that the invert men must be able to cover the flat and still be able to retreat to the deep middle of the field.

Attacking the Inverts

The coach should attempt to attack these two areas of the invert zone coverage: deep middle and flat areas. The weakness areas of the invert zone are indicated in Diagram 4–22.

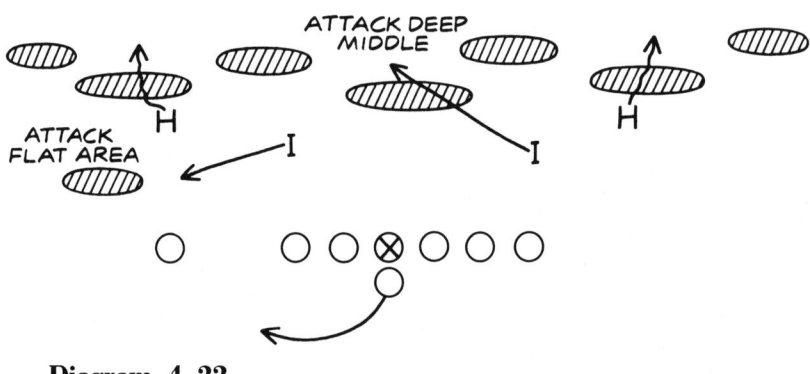

Diagram 4–22

Diagram 4–23 illustrates a deep route for the right slotback. The right split end makes an out route occupying the left defensive halfback, while the slotback sprints directly downfield. Notice that the right defensive invert must travel a long distance to cover this man. If the left defensive halfback covers the slot, the right split end is open for a pass.

Diagram 4–24 shows an invert to the wide slot formation. In this situation, the invert tries to cover the flat. The right split end runs a "curl" route and the slot executes an out-and-up maneuver. If the defensive halfback covers the curl man, the slot will be open and if the defensive halfback plays the slot, the split end is free. The invert tries to cover the slot in the flat which drags him away from the curl position. In many cases, a quick pass to the slot is effective because the invert may not be able to cover him. This is true for the split end also.

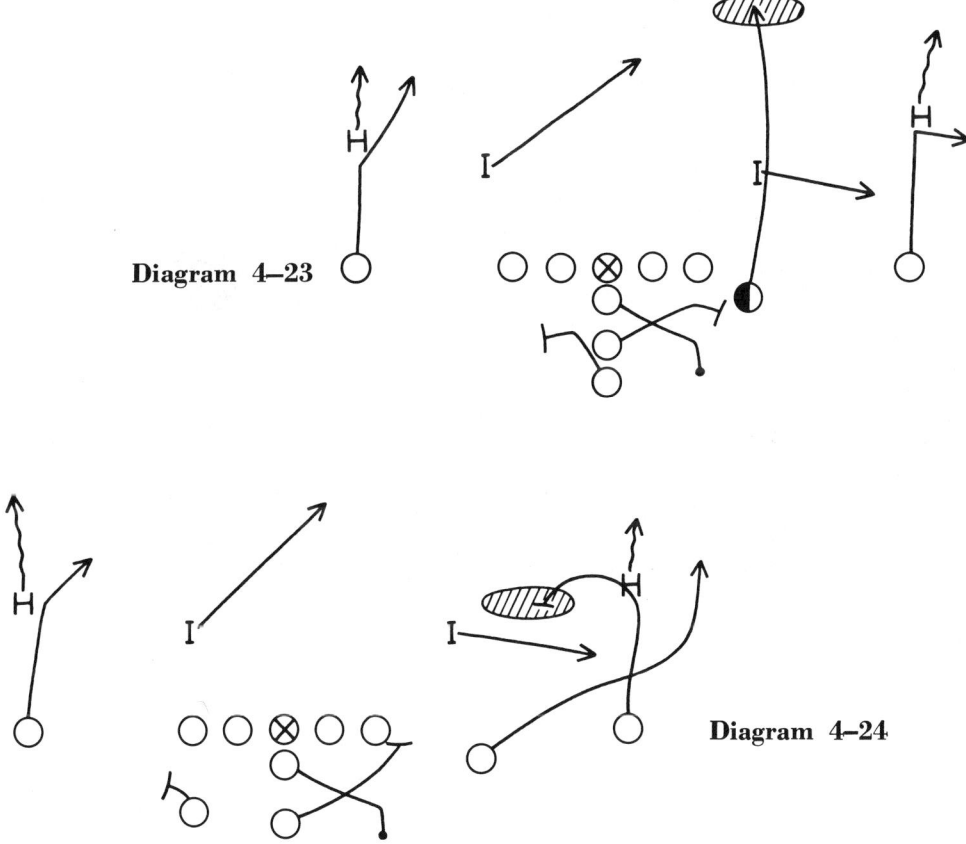

Diagram 4–23

Diagram 4–24

To have the invert men go one way and the play the other is excellent against this coverage. The invert men may key a back on many occasions; if this occurs, Diagram 4–25 (next page) illustrates a way to combat it. A roll-back method as described under the rotation zone is also good. The quarterback fakes to the fullback and comes out sprinting. The invert men are committed to rotate in the other direction and there is only one defensive halfback that can handle three receivers.

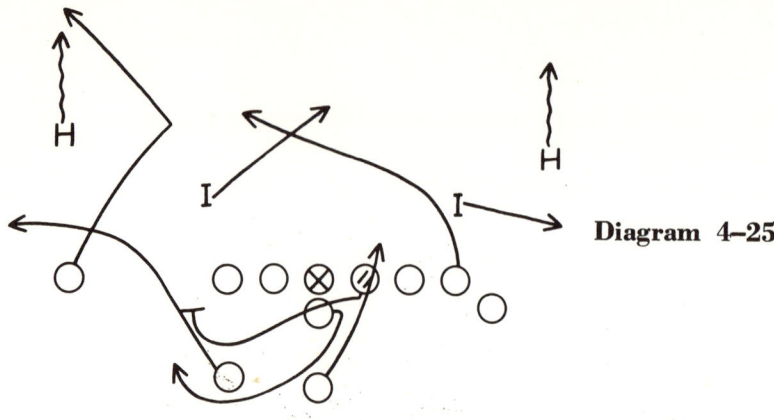

Diagram 4-25

4. *The Revert Zone*

The revert zone will be described briefly. The revert aligns the same as the invert four deep zone coverage, but on the snap of the ball revolves as did the rotation zone (Diagram 4-26).

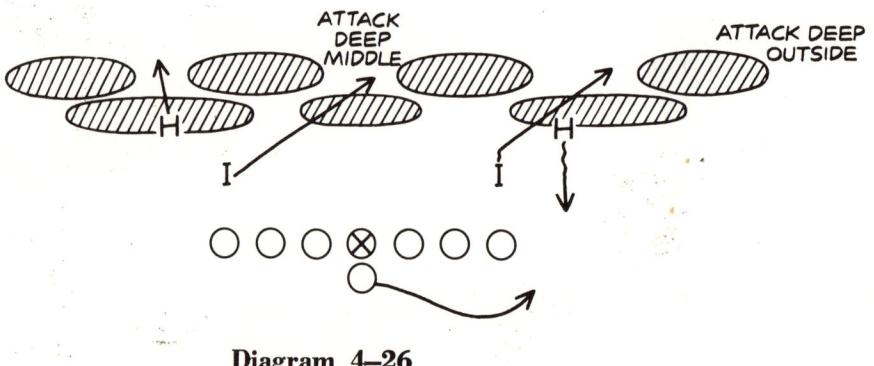

Diagram 4-26

The away invert man and halfback perform the same as the invert coverage. The weakness of this coverage is the same as the rotation zone and the invert zone. The flat is well covered, but the deep outside can be attacked.

ATTACKING MAN-TO-MAN SECONDARY COVERAGE

Man-to-man coverage is a defensive pass defender covering an offensive receiver. The defender will key the eligible receiver. If he blocks on the line of scrimmage, the defender will come up quickly to stop the run. If the receiver releases for a pass, the defensive halfback will take him man-to-man wherever he goes on the field. A man-to-man coverage can be utilized from a two deep, three deep, and four deep secondary. The fewer defenders in the secondary, the more the forcing unit must cover receivers on pass plays. Diagram 4-27 illustrates the three deep coverage and Diagram 4-28 indicates the four deep coverage with their secondary keys.

Diagram 4-27

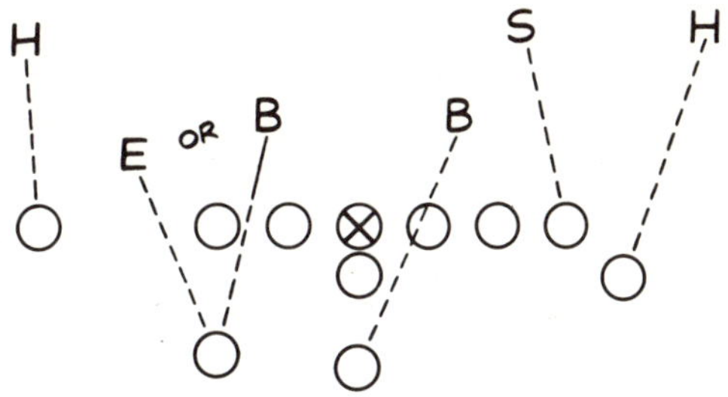

Notice in Diagram 4-27, with the three deep, the defensive linebackers or ends must cover the other eligible receivers. In Diagram 4-28, the defensive right safety keys the tailback. In this situation the safety takes the tailback man-to-man, when he releases for a pass. However, if the left halfback stays in and blocks, the right defensive safety can become a "free safety." He will usually help in the middle or assist in double coverage of another receiver.

A defensive secondary can have a free safety all the time. With this method the right defensive safety, in this case, is always a free safety while a defensive linebacker or end covers the offensive tailback. In one situation a safety is definitely free all the time, while in the other the safety can be free if his man stays in and blocks.

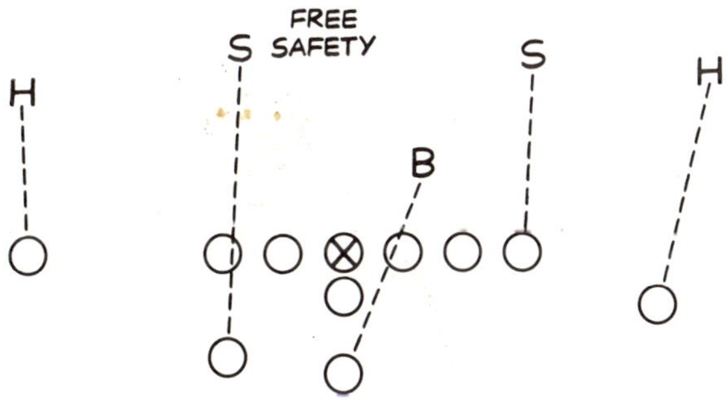

Diagram 4-28

One advantage of the man-to-man defense is that a good defensive halfback can cover a good receiver. An additional advantage is an excellent pass rush can be employed from the forcing unit.

A disadvantage of the man-to-man coverage is that there can be a mismatch of personnel making a weak defender cover a better receiver. Also, with good protection, the quarterback can hold the ball longer and the defenders have difficulty in covering receivers.

There are many things that can be done against the man-to-man. John Bridgers has stated:[1]

---

[1] John Bridgers, "Attacking a Zone and Man for Man with the Baylor Passing Game," *Proceedings of the Forty-First Annual Meeting, American Football Coaches Association*, New York, New York, 1964, p. 14.

We do emphasize several things when facing man-to-man coverage, which are as follows:

1. Receivers will make more use of head and step fakes on their patterns. For example, on a Bend In pattern, our wide receiver might make a jab step to the outside before breaking the pattern to the inside.

2. If our protection is adequate, we will attempt more deep passes. The two deep passes we stress are counters off our basic pattern—the Out and Go, where the receiver will break to the outside from one to three steps, then run a deep pattern staying as close as possible to the sidelines and looking for the ball over the inside shoulder. The other deep pattern we like is Bend In and Corner. The receiver breaks to the inside for three steps and then breaks deep on a corner pattern, looking for the ball over the outside shoulder.

3. Against 4-deep man-to-man coverage, we will stress our patterns to our strong side since our tight end and flanker back will have single coverage. It's to our advantage to keep the ball away from the deep safety.

4. On a 3-deep man-to-man, we will stress throwing to our split end since the safety man who is covering the tight end man-to-man is farther removed from our split end than he is our flanking back.

The following are weaknesses of the man-to-man pass coverage, that can be exploited by the offensive passing game:

1. Running plays with ends releasing (sweeps, etc.).
2. One-on-one situation with defender.
3. Release five receivers against a four deep, or four men against three deep coverage. This will cause a linebacker or defensive end to cover a receiver one-on-one.
4. Play-action passes (fake block and release).
5. Cross patterns between receivers.
6. Pick passes.
7. Comeback passes (comeback routes, curls, hooks, etc.).
8. Across field routes.
9. Tackle-eligible pass.
10. Quarterback as a receiver.
11. Delay passes.

Running Plays

Running plays with the releasing of receivers is excellent against the man-to-man pass coverage. An example would be the "pro sweep." The flankerback releases downfield to drive the defender deep. The tight end blocks the defensive end wherever he goes. The right guard, left guard, and left tackle pull to lead the play (Diagram 4–29).

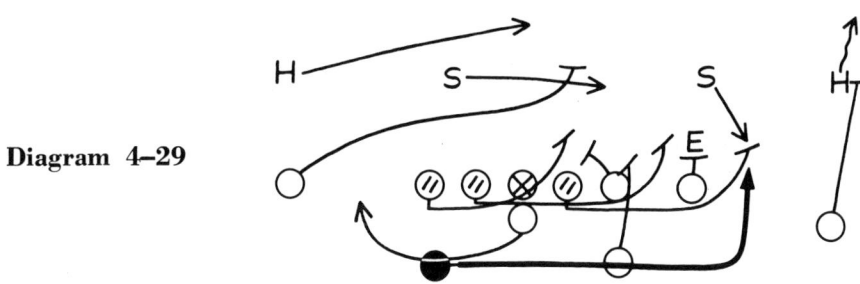

Diagram 4–29

Isolating a Receiver

In attacking man-to-man defenses, it is best to isolate one defender on one receiver. In many instances, a receiver will be covered by two defensive halfbacks. This results from a receiver not releasing for a pass, and a defender (free safety) becoming free to double-cover another receiver. If this should occur, two things can be accomplished to discontinue this: A receiver can release for a pass to force the defender to cover him, or motion by one of the offensive backs can be utilized. This is illustrated in Diagram 4–30. The tailback goes in motion toward the formation. The safety keying the back must continue with him to that side. The left offensive end remains on a one-on-one with the defensive halfback. In this situation, the defensive halfback keying the wingback switches and covers the motion man. The safety keying the offensive tight end switches to take the wingback and the away safety continues across picking up

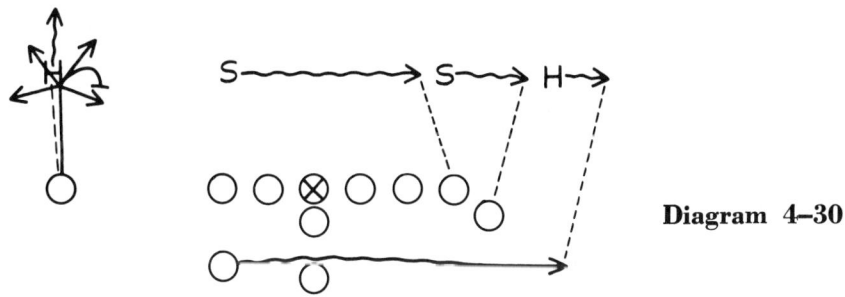

Diagram 4–30

the tight end. The offensive split end can run any pattern desired without being double-covered. The same can be accomplished by flying the wingback and having the tight end remain one-on-one with the defensive halfback. In both cases the motion men can assist in blocking if needed.

While Diagram 4–30 illustrated three men switching on receivers, actually two men could accomplish this. For example, the inside safeties would do the switching. Both halfbacks would remain with their receivers, while the right defensive safety picks up the offensive right tight end and the left safety runs through the defensive halfback's position to cover the motion man. However, in both cases, the motion takes care of the free safety. If the defense utilizes a definite free safety, then a linebacker must cover in the secondary. If this occurs, the offense should attack where the linebackers have vacated or throw to the receiver the linebacker is attempting to cover. Usually linebackers are not as good secondary defenders and a good back or receiver should be able to outmaneuver a linebacker.

Extra Receivers

Releasing an extra receiver, requiring a defensive linebacker to cover him, is an added advantage for the passing attack. An offensive back is usually faster and quicker than the defensive linebacker or end and can get free easier. Diagram 4–31 illustrates a tailback maneuvering deep, on a throwback by the quarterback, against a three deep man-to-man defense.

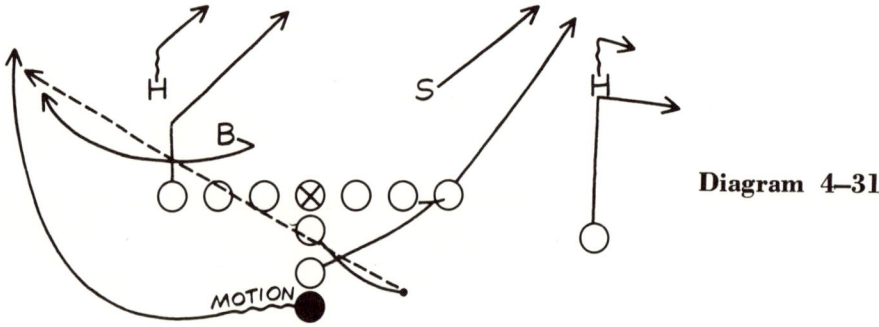

Diagram 4–31

Diagram 4–32 shows the same to a fullback against a four deep secondary. In this situation the left tailback could stay in and block. The free safety would then double-cover one of the deep receivers.

Diagram 4–32

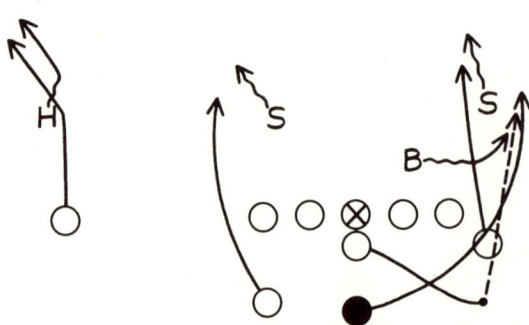

ATTACKING DEFENSIVE SECONDARIES 95

Fake Block and Release

Another effective method against man-to-man coverage is to have a receiver fake a block and force the defender to react to the run. The receiver, however, will release for a pass. Diagram 4–33 indicates an example of a play-action pass, with a fake to the fullback by the quarterback. The tight end blocks down on the defensive tackle for approximately two counts; he then releases, attempting to sprint by the safety man.

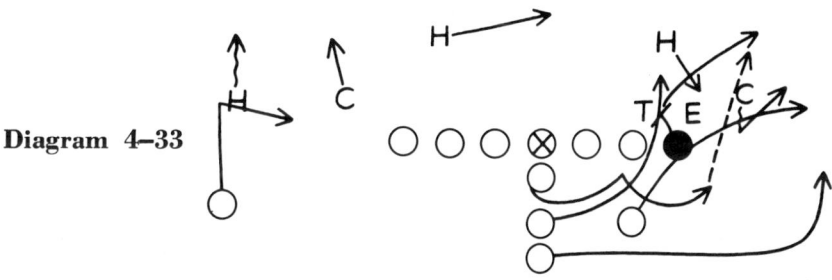

Diagram 4–33

Crossing Receivers

Crossing receivers is an excellent method against the man-to-man. The defensive halfbacks must cross with the receivers, which may cause difficulty. In Diagram 4–34 the tight end and flanker release straight downfield. Approximately 8 to 10 yards deep, they cross, forcing the defenders to cross with them. Diagram 4–35 is another cross pattern against the man-to-man.

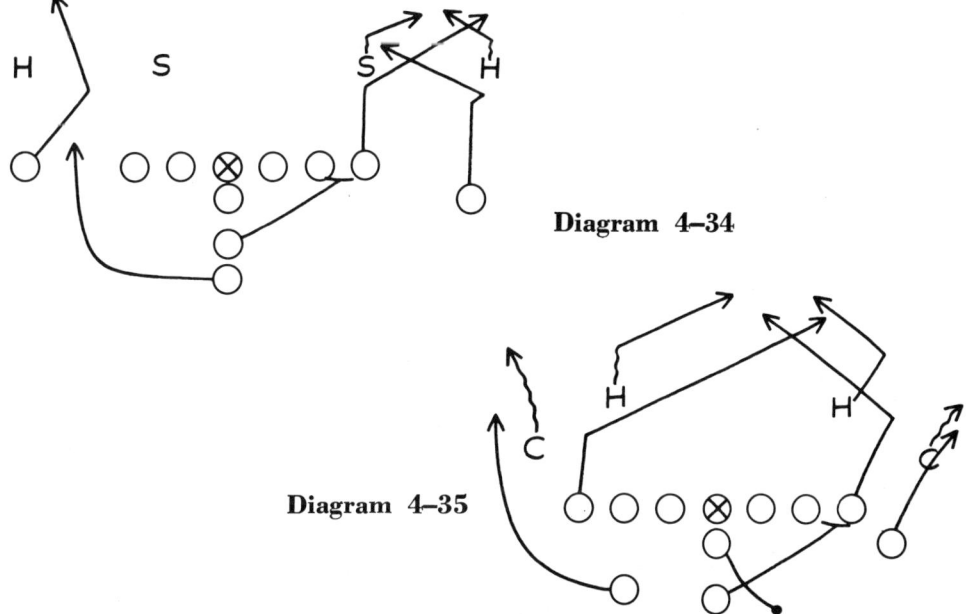

Diagram 4–34

Diagram 4–35

Pick Passes

A pick pass is a receiver releasing from the line and screening off a defensive halfback who must cover another receiver. This is shown in Diagram 4–36. The right end and slotback release downfield. The tight end comes across and screens off the safety man who is attempting to stay with the slotback. The slotback continues toward the sideline for the pass. Other pass patterns with picks can be executed anywhere on the field.

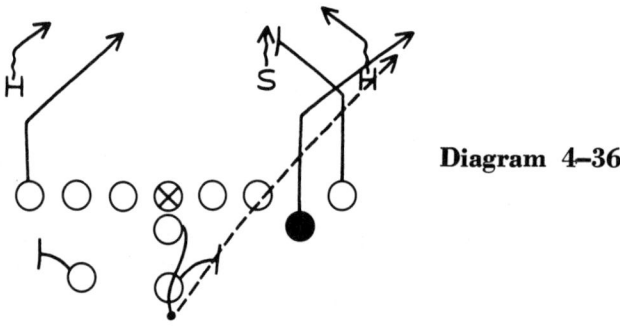

Diagram 4–36

Comeback Passes

Passes which attempt to drive the pass defenders deep and then come back toward the quarterback are excellent routes versus the man-to-man. The receiver releases from the line and sprints to drive the defender deep. When the receiver has the defensive man retreated, he quickly plants and comes back toward the quarterback for the pass. Other excellent routes are hooks and curls back toward the passer.

Across Field Routes

Patterns that begin across field are good. The receiver gains an advantageous position between the defender who has retreated deep and the quarterback. This provides an excellent passing lane between the passer and the receiver. This is illustrated in Diagram 4–37.

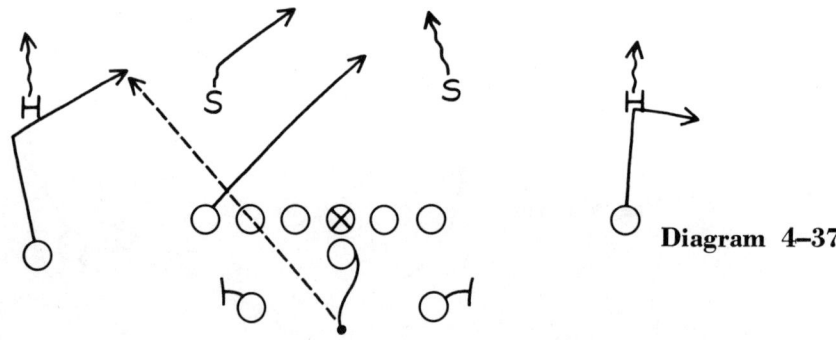

Diagram 4–37

Tackle Eligible Play

The tackle eligible play (outlawed in college) is a surprise element against the man-to-man. It is good when the defense does not recognize it or fails to adjust properly. The split end on the line must step back off the line of scrimmage to make the tackle eligible. The flanker back will then move up into the line. The tight end, therefore, is ineligible to release for a pass. Since there is no defender covering the tackle, he is usually free for the pass. This is illustrated in Diagram 4–38.

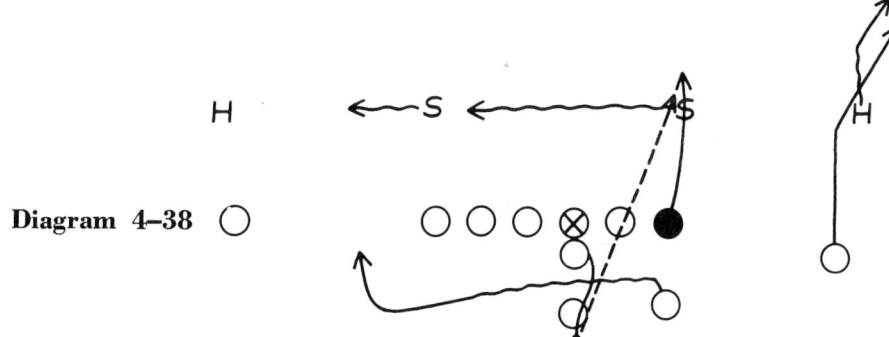

Diagram 4–38

Quarterback as a Receiver

Another unexpected method is the utilization of the quarterback. Usually he is not considered a threat as a receiver, but can be used effectively against the man-to-man. An example of such a pass to the quarterback would be a halfback receiving a pitchout from the quarterback as if he were going to run the ball. The halfback would then pull up and throw back to the quarterback (Diagram 4–39).

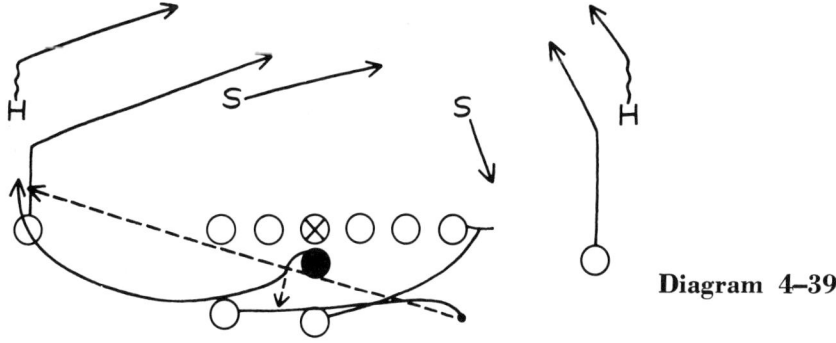

Diagram 4–39

Delay Passes

Another method against the man-to-man is the delay action of a receiver.

When the quarterback shows a pass, the defenders usually drop back to cover the receivers. When the defender sees his key block, he will retreat to assist the other defenders. The delay receiver can release after two or three counts to receive a quick pass from the quarterback (Diagram 4–40).

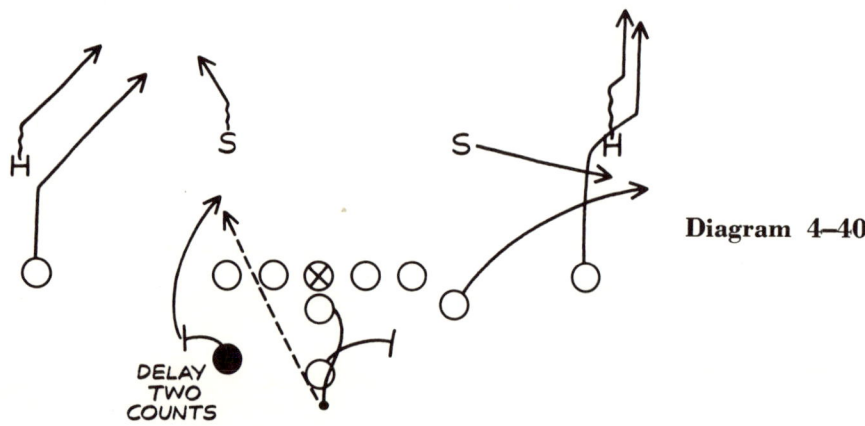

Diagram 4–40

ATTACKING THE COMBINATION ZONE AND MAN-TO-MAN

The combination of the zone and man-to-man is the soundest of all pass defenses. It combines the use of both coverages. There are several different combination man-to-man and zone coverages. DeWayne "Dewey" King, assistant football coach at San Jose State University, stated in his book *Jericho—A Modern System of Pass Defense*, "Certain combination defenses will have specific defenders cover man-for-man while simultaneously the other defensive man will play zone. Another type is to have man-for-man responsibilities within the framework of a zone. Still another combination coverage is to start with a zone and have man-for-man responsibilities within the confines of a zone."[2]

In this case, the combination of zone and man-to-man is a safety and halfback functioning together as a team covering two offensive receivers. This can be applied to both the three and four deep secondaries. In a three deep, the deep safety and a halfback toward the strength of the formation would combine, while in the four deep the safety and halfback to either side would work as a team. In a three deep the halfback not combining with the safety will take the end on his side man-to-man and the linebacker or defensive end will cover the first man out of the backfield.

As the wing and end release from the line, the safety and halfback retreat

---

[2]DeWayne "Dewey" King, *Jericho—A Modern System of Pass Defense* (Englewood Cliffs, N.J., Prentice-Hall Inc., 1963) p. 58.

ATTACKING DEFENSIVE SECONDARIES

keeping peripheral vision on both receivers. The halfback keys the wing while the safety watches the end. At the same time, both are aware of the other receiver. Once the two receivers make their cuts, the reaction must be a quick decision by the two defensive defenders. The receivers can either run "straight" patterns (without crossing), cross, or flood an area to either side. If the patterns are straight with no crossing, the safety and halfback cover the receiver, both keyed man-to-man. If the receivers cross, the defenders will yell "switch" and pick up the crossing receiver. The safety and halfback will then stay with each man.

If the receivers flood to the outside, both defenders will combine to cover it. The halfback should come up to cover the short route, while the safety should take the deep receiver. If the pattern floods to the inside, the safety will cover the short man while the halfback will cover the deep man over the middle. Diagrams 4–41a-f illustrate these coverages.

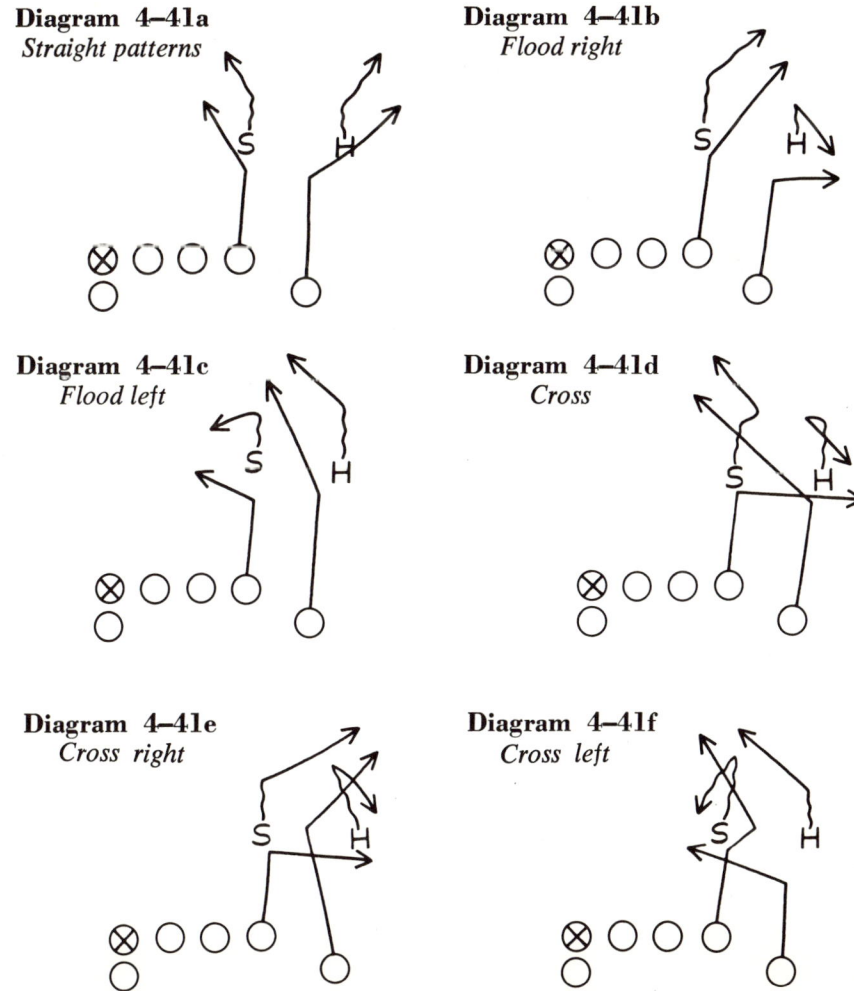

Diagram 4–41a
Straight patterns

Diagram 4–41b
Flood right

Diagram 4–41c
Flood left

Diagram 4–41d
Cross

Diagram 4–41e
Cross right

Diagram 4–41f
Cross left

The advantage of the combination man-to-man and zone is it has the advantages of both the zone and man-to-man coverages. It provides the opportunity for changing responsibility from one receiver to another if necessary. However, it has the disadvantages of both coverages and these should be attacked.

In attacking the combination zone and man-to-man, the basic cuts utilized against all pass defenses can be employed. This would include the square-out, square-in, hook, curl, glance, and so forth.

Another effective method against the combination is forcing the combination to change its coverage by splitting and widening the offensive formation. The pass defense will employ the combination coverage when the receivers are less than 6 yards split from each other. Once the receivers split more than 6 yards the defenders are forced into a man-for-man or other coverage. The coach can then attack the secondary as was mentioned previously, for man-to-man pass defense or other coverages (zones).

5

THE 4-3 DEFENSE

The 4–3 defense is employed by numerous teams throughout the country. It is used by high school and college teams, but is more extensively utilized by the majority of professional football teams. Technically the 4–3 or 4–5 defense is known as the 4–3 Even Box-Corner defense. The defensive tackles (guards) are aligned on the offensive guards; the defensive ends are positioned on the offensive ends; there are *three* linebackers—and thus the name 4–3 defense was assigned to it. The middle linebacker is positioned directly over the offensive center. The outside linebackers (number 2 men) are aligned on the offensive tackles. It is thought of as the 4–5 defense also, because the two corner men are near the line of scrimmage. Diagram 5–1 illustrates the alignment of the entire defense.

It is an even defense without any player aligned directly on the line of scrimmage over the center. It is a containing and pursuing defense. The 4–3 defense is considered a nine-man front with any type of pass coverage employed with the four deep secondary. Since there are four defensive linemen and three defensive linebackers, a multitude of stunting can be utilized by the defense. In many cases, for the defense to be successful, stunting will be necessary.

The defense is usually used by teams that are not fortunate enough to have many strong defensive linemen, but do have quick, versatile linebackers who can pursue the play quickly. The big defensive tackle can be placed over the

Diagram 5–1

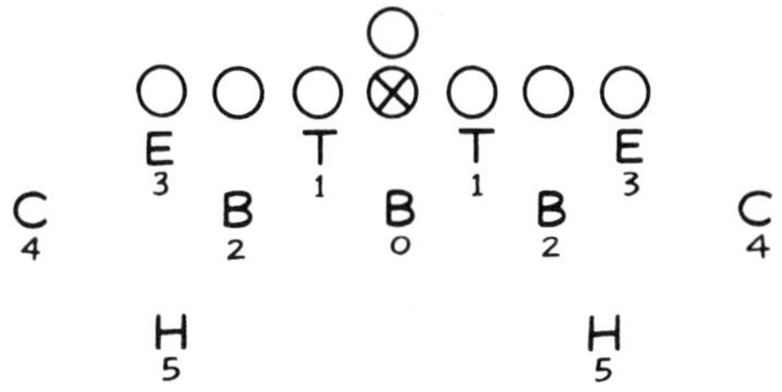

smaller offensive guard to add strength in that area. The outside linebackers can run quickly to the outside from where they are aligned.

The 4–3 is an excellent defense against a passing attack, during passing downs, or at the end of a game when the long pass will be thrown if the offensive team is behind. It can utilize seven men for pass defense (linebackers and secondary) and four men to rush the passer. When more men are essential to rush the passer, a fire or blitz can easily be employed. It is weak against a team that runs consistently if the defense is played straight. This is the result of having only four men positioned on the line of scrimmage. If more men are needed to stop the running game, however, stunting can be utilized. Another important facet is that the defense can easily adjust to the open and spread offensive formations employed today.

THE 4–3 DEFENSE

The following is the straight 4–3 defense used by many coaches throughout the country. Of course there are many alterations and variations within the 4–3 defense that are not mentioned in this chapter. However, this 4–3 is basically the same as other 4–3 defenses.

MIDDLE LINEBACKER (Number 0 Man)

Alignment: Line nose-up position on the offensive center. Toes should be 1 foot deeper than the heels of the defensive tackle.

Stance: Two-point stance with little weight forward.

Execution and Initial Movement: Key the center and read the backfield. Use hands or forearm lift to control center's block. Be in a position to make tackles anywhere along the line of scrimmage.

Responsibility: If center blocks down either way, come up and fill. Watch for isolation and traps. If center fires out, fight pressure and go to ball. Do not let center hook you.

1. Play toward—Make any play straight at you or off-tackle.
2. Play away —Pursue quickly. Take shortest route to ball.
3. Drop Back —Go to required hook areas. Watch for draw and look for screen.

Coaching Points: Play loose so that you can make plays to the off-tackle and outside.

DEFENSIVE TACKLES (Number 1 Men)

Alignment: Line nose-up position, or on the outside eye of offensive guard.

Stance: Four-point stance.

Initial Movement and Execution: Hit blow into offensive guard with forearm shiver. Step up with inside leg and key the guard.

Responsibility: If guard blocks down, shadow him down. Keep him off the middle linebacker. If guard blocks out, fight pressure. If guard tries to hook, get to the outside. If guard pulls, follow him down the line.

1. Play toward —Offensive guard area.
2. Play away —Pursue, do not run around blocker.
3. Drop back —Rush passer from the inside. Watch the draw play.

Coaching Points: Must explode (step with inside foot), immediately bringing outside foot up. Explode upon movement of guard's hand or ball. Watch trap from pulling guard or tackle.

OUTSIDE DEFENSIVE LINEBACKERS (Number 2 Men)

Alignment: Line nose-up position or on the outside eye of the offensive tackle. Toes should be 1 foot deeper than heels of the defensive tackles.

Stance: Two-point stance.

Initial Movement and Execution: Key the offensive tackle and read into backfield (determined by the team and game situation, i.e. keying a halfback or fullback). Strike a blow into tackle with inside forearm. Keep outside leg and arm free.

Responsibility: If tackle blocks down, fill hole and look for isolation from halfback or trap from pulling guard. If tackle blocks out, fight pressure. If tackle tries to hook, go to the outside.

1. Play toward—Offensive tackles position. Must help contain on runs to outside.
2. Play away —Pursue quickly.
3. Drop back —Go to required hook areas.

Coaching Points: Key tackle and read ball flow. Play the run from inside out. Adjust the depth of alignment to down and distance.

DEFENSIVE ENDS (Number 3 Men)

Alignment: Line nose-up position or on the outside eye.

Stance: A low two- or three-point stance.

Initial Movement and Execution: Strike a blow with inside forearm and step with inside leg. Do not let offensive end quick release for pass, or block the linebacker to the inside.

Responsibility: Key the end and read backfield. If end blocks down, shadow him down and look for kick-out by the halfback, pulling guard, or cross block from offensive tackle. If end blocks out, fight pressure. If the end tries to hook, get to the outside.

1. Play toward—Offensive end area, then pursue.
2. Play away —Chase ball, staying as deep as the ball (watch for reverses, etc.).
3. Drop back —Pass shows, rush from outside-in.

Coaching Points: Hit low and keep the outside leg and arm free. Keep the shoulders parallel to the line of scrimmage.

CORNERBACKS (Number 4 Men)

Alignment: Four yards outside of offensive end and 4 yards off line of scrimmage. Make adjustments to perimeter calls.

Stance: Relaxed semi-upright ready position with outside foot back, "toes angling in," weight equally distributed over balls of feet.

Initial Movement and Execution: On the snap of the ball, weight is shifted to outside foot while reading block of near end and back and determining flow of ball. On run play toward, come to the line of scrimmage and meet blocker with inside leg and forearm, shoulders square forcing play wide and deep. Do not open gap between yourself and end. Keep on your feet and skate on outside plays. (Many teams will require corner to force play to the inside.)

Responsibility: 1. Play toward —Outside area on run with "flat" on flow pass.

THE 4-3 DEFENSE

2. Play away —Revolve through deep outside and pursue.
3. Back-up pass—Cover zone designated by perimeter call.

Keys and Coaching Points: Read the block of near end and near back and determine flow of ball.

1. The end and back block and ball flows toward—come up and play run, forcing the play wide and deep.
2. The end and/or back comes downfield without blocking and ball flows toward—drop off and cover flat (¼) zone.
3. The end and/or back comes downfield and ball flows away—sprint back to cover deep outside (⅓) zone.
4. The end and back block and the ball flows away—"shuffle in place" expecting counter or reverse before dropping off and sprinting deep.
5. The end and/or back come downfield and ball flows straight back—move immediately into zone designated by call.

SAFETIES (Number 5 Men)

Alignment: Eight yards deep on outside of end on side of call and over tackle away from call.

Stance: Relaxed semi-upright ready position with outside foot back.

Execution and Initial Movement: On snap of ball shift weight, "shuffle" to outside foot while reading block of near end and back determining flow by ball. Fulfill responsibility of perimeter call.

Responsibility:
1. Play toward —Force all plays from outside-in (inside-out, also). Cover deep outside or deep middle on flow passes.
2. Play away —Revolve and replace on side safety.
3. Back-up pass—Move to your (⅓) zone on first indication.

Coaching Points: Read through near end and back to ball for flow.

1. The end and back block and ball flows toward—come up to outside and play run. Think outside—reach inside.

2. The end and/or back comes downfield and ball flows toward—drop off and out immediately to cover deep (⅓) outside.
3. The end and/or back comes downfield and ball flows away—move to deep (⅓) middle zone.
4. The end and back block and the ball flows away—"shuffle" in place, checking on counter or reverse before moving to middle (⅓) zone.
5. Never let receiver behind you.
6. You must play pass first—run second.

Note—The corner and safety can also employ zone (straight, invert, revert), man-to-man, or a combination if necessary.

ADJUSTMENTS TO FORMATIONS

A defense must adjust its alignment to meet the various formations that are in football today. Adjustments must be made to wings, slots, split ends, flankers, and strong formations. The following are some of the methods used.

If the offense stations a wing, the defensive end aligns, keys, and plays the same. However, he must be conscious of the possible double-team from the end and wing. If this should occur he must fight the pressure to the outside. The four deep secondary will usually rotate slightly toward the wing. The same occurs against the slot, except that the defensive end plays the slot as if he were the end.

There are a number of methods to cover the split end. The defensive tackle remains on the offensive guard, the defensive end positions down over the offensive tackle and keys the tackle as he would the end. The outside linebacker moves out and can either play tandem, tight, walkaway, or double-up position (Diagram 5–2). The tandem position can cause many problems for the offense. The linebacker can align directly behind the defensive end or station 1 yard outside and 1 yard off the line of scrimmage. From this position he can be involved in a stunt inside with the end going outside or vice versa. If the linebacker is directly on the line of scrimmage he can only contain from the outside.

In another example, the linebacker steps up into the line and the defensive end plays the split end in one of the three positions. The defensive secondary must also adjust to cover the split end in the same manner. Diagram 5–3 illustrates two examples of covering the split end with the secondary.

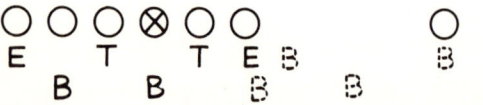

Diagram 5–2

Diagram 5–3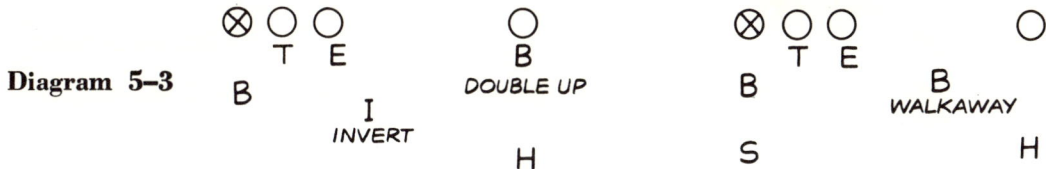

Against the flanker, the defensive end and linebacker align and play the same while the defensive secondary must rotate toward the formation.

If the offense employs a strong formation as indicated in Diagram 5–4, the 4–3 defense can adjust the linebackers to a tandem position against the strength of the backfield.

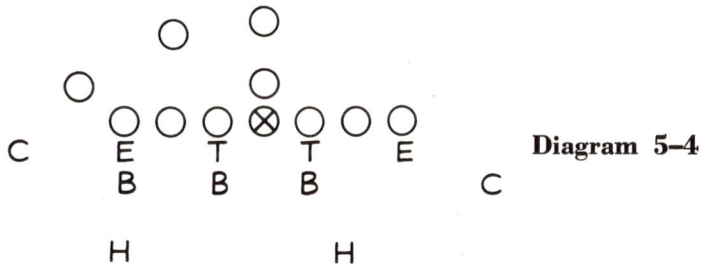

STUNTING

A considerable amount of stunting can be accomplished from the 4–3 defense. Diagrams 5–5 through 5–7 indicate three stunts from the 4–3 defense. Between the two tackles and the middle linebacker, four maneuvers can be employed. A pinch technique is shown in Diagram 5–8. The defensive tackles go through the

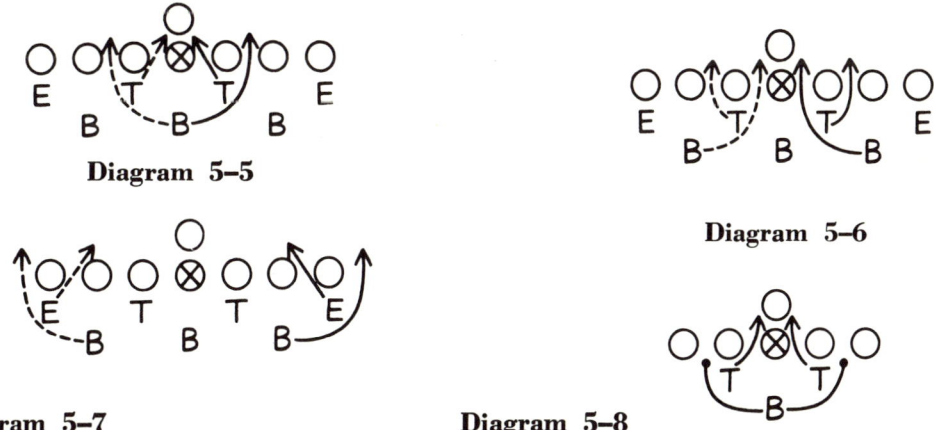

near hip of the center to the quarterback. Both tackles are responsible for the guard-center gap, which they must penetrate and pursue. The middle linebacker

107

keys the fullback, and whichever side the fullback goes, the middle linebacker fills his responsibility as indicated.

Diagram 5–9 illustrates an out maneuver. The tackles explode into the outside gaps and are responsible for the guard-tackle hole. The middle linebacker, on the movement of his key, steps into his hole responsibility.

Diagram 5–9

Diagram 5–10 shows an angling technique by the defensive tackles which can be employed to either side. In this case, the left defensive tackle explodes into the outside gap between the guard and tackle. The right tackle pinches through the near hip of the center to the quarterback. Both tackles will penetrate and then pursue. The middle linebacker will key the fullback and fill in the required direction. Diagram 5–11 indicates the loop to the right.

Diagram 5–10   Diagram 5–11

THE 4–3 TANDEM

Another way the 4–3 defense can adjust its alignment is the employment of the 4–3 tandem defense. This is illustrated in Diagram 5–12.

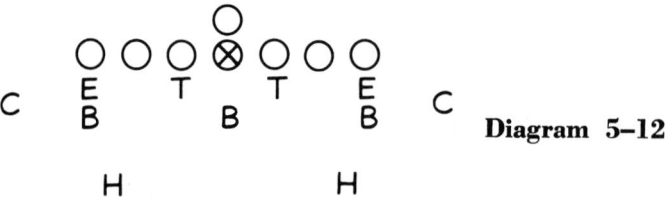

Diagram 5–12

The defensive ends align head up on the offensive ends while the outside linebackers are tandemed directly behind. Stunting from the tandem can then be executed by the linebacker and end. Diagram 5–13 shows the end pinching down through the near hip of the offensive tackle, protecting the offensive tackle area.

THE 4-3 DEFENSE

The linebacker fires to the outside hip of the offensive end and is responsible for the offensive end area. Diagram 5–14 illustrates the opposite movement of the two tandem players. The defensive end plays normally on the offensive end, but the linebacker fires to the outside hip of the offensive tackle. He is, therefore, responsible for the offensive tackle area.

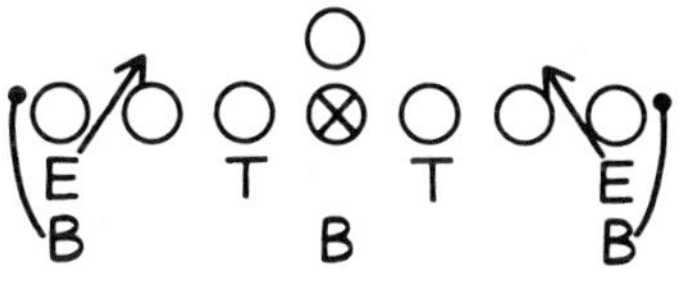

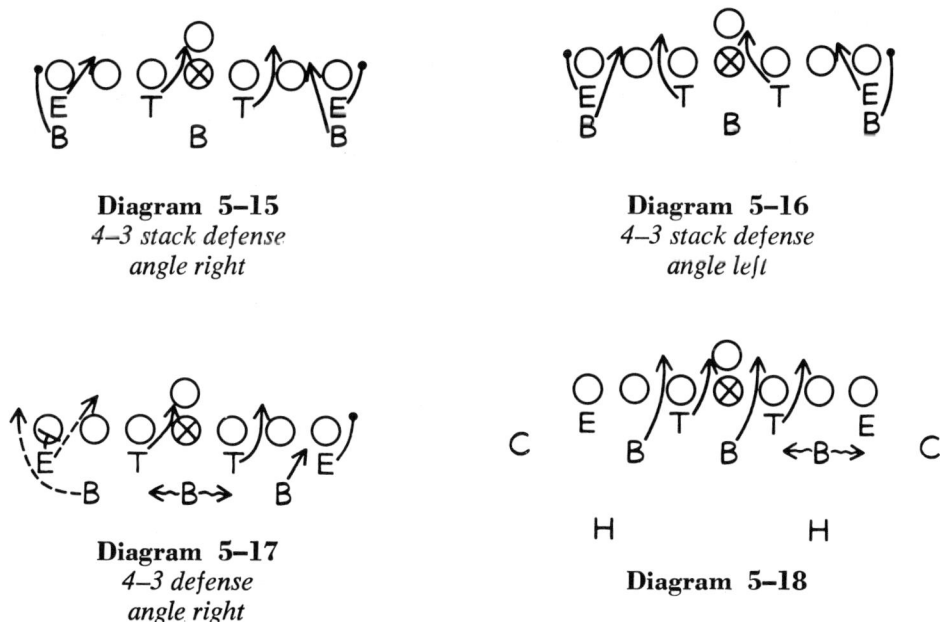

Diagram 5–13

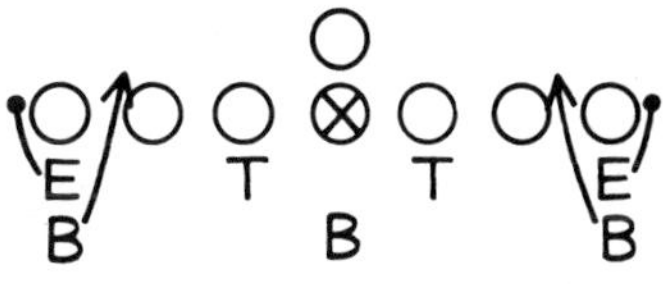

Diagram 5–14

Looping and slanting can easily be accomplished with the 4–3 and the 4–3 stack defense. With the combination of the two defensive tackles, illustrated in Diagrams 5–10 and 5–11, and the stunting of the tandem players just mentioned, an angle can be performed. Diagrams 5–15 through 5–17 illustrate the angling 4–3 defense.

Diagram 5–15
4–3 stack defense
angle right

Diagram 5–16
4–3 stack defense
angle left

Diagram 5–17
4–3 defense
angle right

Diagram 5–18

Blitzing and firing can easily be done with the 4–3 defense to get penetration when necessary and to put a rush on the passer. Diagrams 5–18 and 5–19 illustrate two of many blitzes of the 4–3 defense.

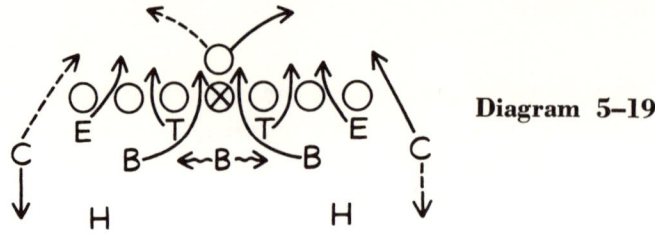

Diagram 5-19

DEFENSIVE SHIFTS

The 4-3 Even-Box defense can easily shift to other alignments before the snap of the ball. The offensive team must be drilled, trained, and prepared for any unexpected change in the defense. The 4-3 can easily shift to the 5-2 Umbrella Odd-Box Corner defense. The middle linebacker steps into the line making a five-man line with two linebackers. Another similar defensive shift is to move both outside linebackers up to the line making a 6-1 Umbrella Even-Box defense. The 6-3 Even Box can be shifted easily. The outside linebackers move into the line, the defensive ends maneuver slightly outward, and the coverbacks align over the ends in linebacker positions.

The 4-3 can easily shift to the 5-4 Oklahoma defense. The middle linebacker steps into the line, the defensive tackles move onto the offensive tackles, and the outside linebackers align on the offensive guards. Other defenses the 4-3 can shift to are the 5 Eagle Odd-Box Corner, the Snake-Eye 5, the 5-4 Inside, the 7 Box Odd-Box, the 7-2 Odd-Box, and so forth. It must be remembered that almost any defense can be adjusted with simple, elementary changes. Also, these defenses are quite similar in keys, responsibilities, and can be shifted quickly with little maneuvering.

ATTACKING THE 4-3 DEFENSE

THE STRENGTHS OF THE 4-3 DEFENSE

It is necessary to understand the strengths of a defense if an offense hopes to attack it. The strongpoints of a defense can then be avoided in order to concentrate on its weaker aspects. Howard Brinker, defensive coach of the Cleveland Browns, listed a few ideas, from a defensive viewpoint, about the strengths of the 4-3 defense:

1. The positions of the linemen and the linebackers in the 4-3 defense permit line charge variation.
2. A charge to the strong side can be used to meet offensive strength to that side.
3. A charge to the weak side is utilized to meet the strengths of the weak side.
4. An inside charge meets the strength to the inside. This is true for the outside charge also.

THE 4-3 DEFENSE

5. The 4-3 defense allows for many pass coverage variations—zone, single, double, and combination.
6. It provides an opportunity to rotate the deep backs to meet the offense's passing strength.

Other strengths of the defense include:

1. A nine-man front is employed.
2. The guard area where the bigger defensive tackle is aligned on the smaller offensive guards.
3. The end area—where the defensive end can hold up the receiver.
4. The double-team is eliminated off-tackle for the offensive tackle and end.
5. The 4-3 defense is generally stronger outside than inside.
6. The 4-3 is stronger against a passing team, especially the short passing game.
7. The defense is strong in the flat areas.
8. The defense is strong in the hook areas (smaller vacated gaps).
9. The linebackers can flow and pursue the ball quickly.
10. A multitude of stunting and blitzing can be employed.
11. Linebackers can flow and cover the stunts of other players.
12. It is strong against the delayed play.
13. It can jump to other defenses quickly and easily.

THE WEAKNESSES OF THE 4-3 DEFENSE

Coach Brinker stated some of the weaknesses of the various charges that were executed:

1. There are weaknesses created by the various line charges.
2. A charge to the strong side creates a running weakness to the weak side.
3. This is true, also, with a charge to the weak side creating a running weakness to the strong side.
4. An inside charge causes weakness to the outside, with a weakness in the pass rush.
5. In order to fill the running charge, the coverage of the defensive secondary is limited.

The weaknesses of the 4-3 defense also include the following with the weak areas illustrated in Diagram 5-20.

1. The middle or center area can be attacked.
2. The off-tackle area—the bigger offensive tackle on the smaller linebacker.
3. The outside area at the corner.
4. Generally weaker inside than outside.
5. There are many players off the line of scrimmage (soft men or linebackers).

6. The 4–3 is weak against a running team, especially to the inside.
7. It is weak against a quick-hitting team.
8. The defense must rotate the secondary.
9. Stunting can cause weaknesses.

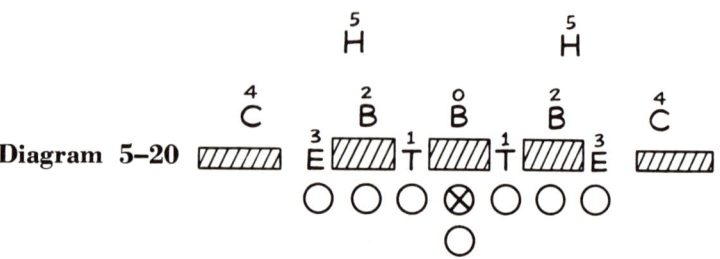

Diagram 5–20

ATTACKING THE AREAS OF THE 4–3 DEFENSE

As can be seen from Diagram 5–20, the middle area should be attacked. The sneak and wedge plays are excellent. A quick-hitting trap on the defensive tackle, with the fullback carrying the ball, is also effective. The fullback trap is shown in Diagram 5–21. Notice the move of the right guard to the outside, with the right tackle coming across on the middle linebacker. The center has an angle block down, and the guard pulls to trap the defensive tackle. If the right offensive tackle is having difficulty in blocking the middle linebacker (i.e. linebacker stepping up into hole) then the right offensive guard, instead of moving out, should come inside and block the linebacker (Diagram 5–21a). Trapping with the offensive tackles and utilizing counters and inside reverses can be executed also. The draw, screen, and shuffle pass in the middle should be employed when the quarterback is being rushed hard.

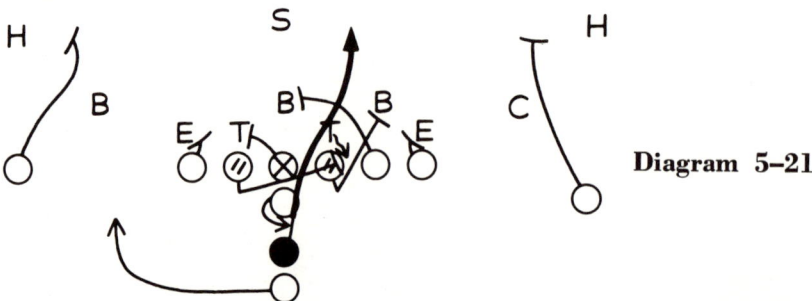

Diagram 5–21

Straight ahead blocking is essential along the entire offensive line, since the linebackers are already off the line of scrimmage. Quick dive plays with the

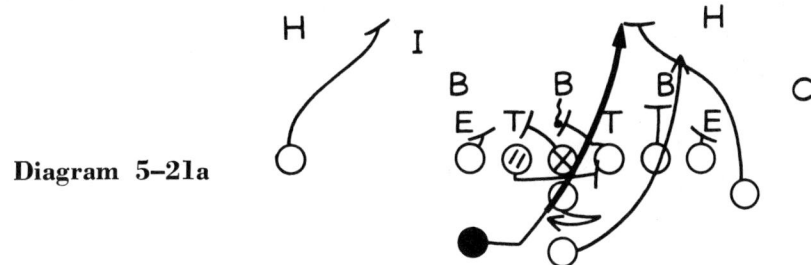

Diagram 5-21a

fullback and halfback can be employed effectively. Diagram 5–22 illustrates the offensive guard taking the tackle anywhere he goes (a scramble block is good, especially against the bigger defensive tackle), and the fullback cutting either way off the block. The halfback dive, over the offensive tackle at the linebacker, should be utilized. This is especially true with the bigger tackle on the smaller linebacker.

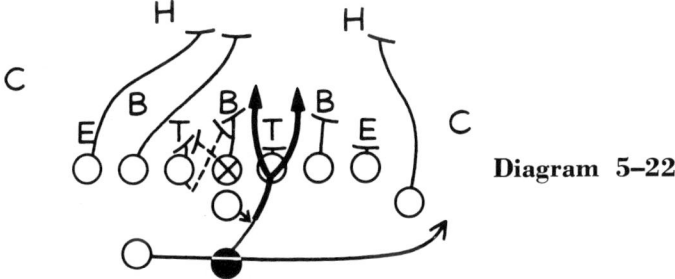

Diagram 5–22

Angle and cross blocking should be used, especially between the center, guard, and tackle. There are excellent angle blocks for the tackle and center on the defensive tackles, with the guards pulling on the linebackers. Fold blocking, which can be employed too, is a type of cross block used in keeping defensive linemen away from the hole being run. It is used when the ballcarrier cannot find a hole and cuts back for daylight. This block may create a bigger hole for the cutting ballcarrier. Diagram 5–23 illustrates this maneuver. The fullback cannot find an opening and breaks back over the center. If the middle linebacker steps up into the hole, then the fullback should continue his regular course looking for daylight.

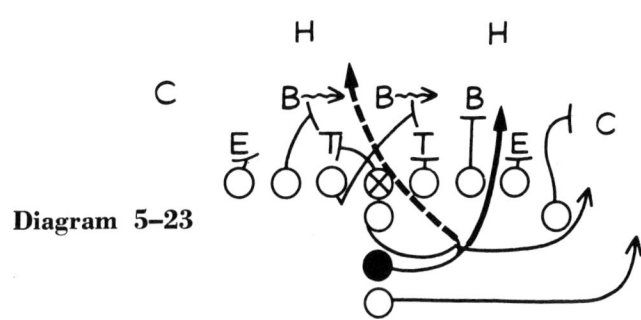

Diagram 5–23

Since there are only four men on the line of scrimmage and three linebackers, many isolation and power plays should be utilized against the linebackers. This would include double-teaming on the defensive linemen. For example, a power play executed at a defensive outside linebacker is shown in Diagram 5–24. The right guard and right tackle double-team the defensive tackle. The right end blocks the defensive end (the key block), and the wing, with the assistance of the fullback, isolates and double-teams the outside linebacker.

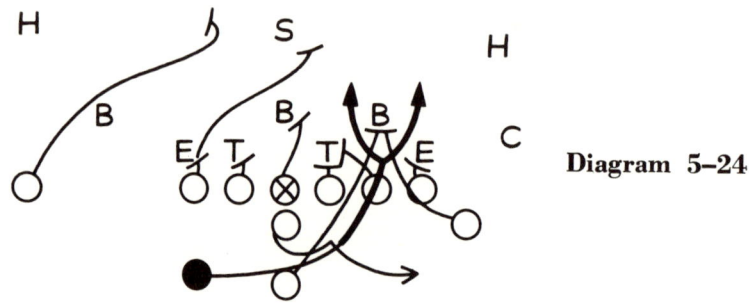

Diagram 5–24

Bill Neal, coach at Indiana University of Pennsylvania, submits two isolation plays which give him "headaches" against the stacked 4–3. However, both can be run at the straight 4–3 defense. Diagrams 5–25 and 5–26 illustrate both plays. The rules are as follows:

End: Blocks out on defensive end. If defensive end pinches, end will post and tackle will drive block.
Tackle: Block out. If end pinches, double-team with end. If linebacker comes in, block him.
Halfback: From set or wing position. Lead block at hole. Block first man that shows.

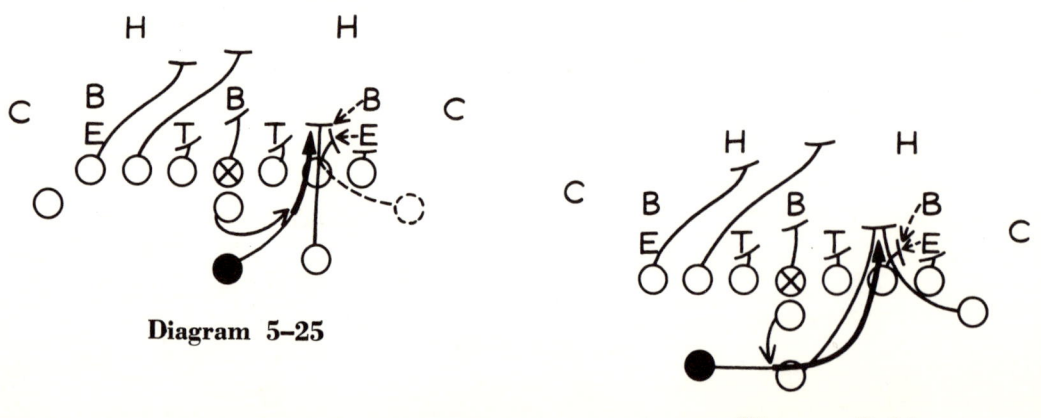

Diagram 5–25

Diagram 5–26

THE 4-3 DEFENSE

Trapping the end off-tackle is effective. The tackle has a good angle block on the defensive tackle, the end blocks down on the linebacker, and the guard pulls to trap the defensive end.

To attack the corner, sweep plays with pulling can be employed. The end and wing should double-team the defensive end. It must be remembered that if the defensive end plays more outside, the offense should attack inside off-tackle. When the defensive end starts aligning nose-up to the inside, the offense should attack outside. With less men off the line of scrimmage, more pulling can be utilized. Another method to attack the corner area is with the option run-pass (sprint-out, roll-out, etc.). Attacking the corner with a faking ballcarrier (fullback belly fake) and the quarterback rolling out with a trail man is excellent. If the corner attacks the quarterback, the quarterback will pitch to the trail man. If the corner goes to the trail man, the quarterback will keep the ball.

The offense should split its ends against the 4-3 defense. If the defensive end aligns to the inside (tight or walkaway positions), the offense should go outside. The split end has a good angle on the defensive end. Diagram 5-27 illustrates a power sweep toward the split end side. The split end blocks to the inside on the walkaway man.

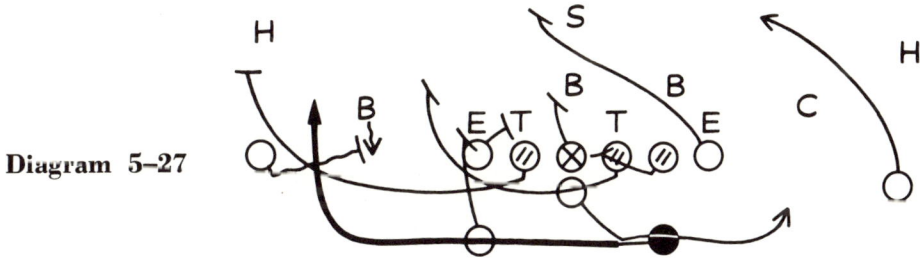

Diagram 5-27

The left tackle blocks down and the left guard pulls on the defensive halfback. The left halfback blocks the number 2 man. The quick pitch is an excellent play to this side also.

The offense can option (Diagram 5-28) the walkaway or tight end. The split end angles down as if to block the defensive end, but then runs past him. The split end seals to the inside picking up anyone; i.e., linebacker, safety fill, etc. The left halfback goes for the outside contain man. In this case, it is the defensive halfback.

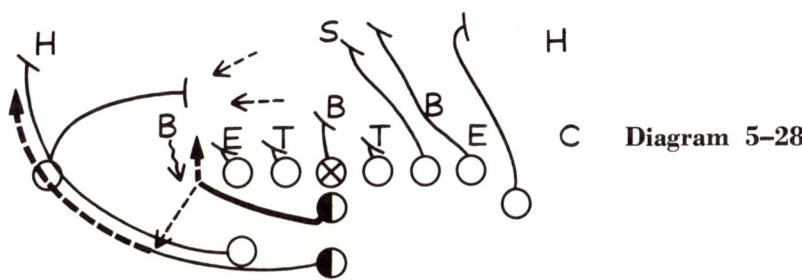

Diagram 5-28

The quarterback sprints down the line at the number 3 man and options off him. If the defensive end attacks the quarterback, the quarterback pitches to the fullback. If the defensive end goes for the fullback, the quarterback keeps and runs the ball. The key block with this play is the offensive left tackle. His first responsibility is not to give any penetration and then, if possible, to turn the man to the inside.

Other option plays can easily be employed. A fullback fake up the middle to either side of the center, with a wingback coming back in motion as the option man, is excellent. In Diagram 5–29 the fullback fakes to the right. This tends to hold and freeze the linebackers.

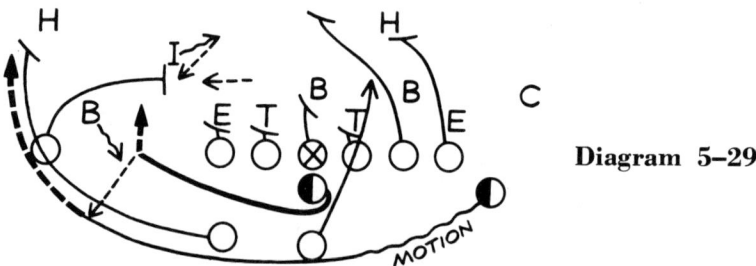

Diagram 5–29

Also, if there is an invert man, the fake may tend to drive him toward the deep middle of the field. The blocking, as mentioned previously, remains the same.

If the defensive end plays in a double-up position, the offense should run inside of him. Diagram 5–30 illustrates the same power sweep shown in Diagram 5–27, except that the defensive end, or number 3 man, is in a double-up position.

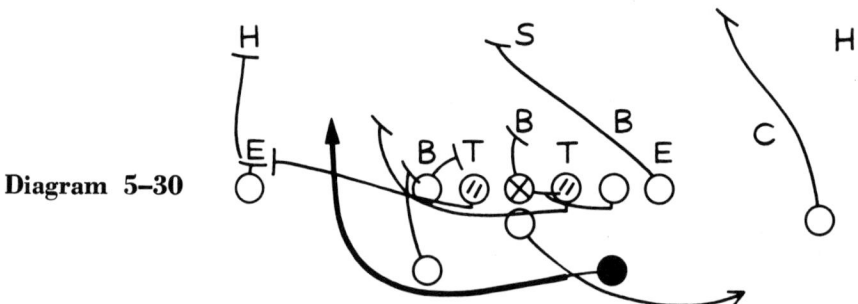

Diagram 5–30

In this case, the split end should block the number 3 man, then release on the defensive halfback. The left guard now pulls and "traps" the double-up man. As can be seen, both men exchange assignments. Everyone else remains the same. The right tailback, however, should look more to the inside for his cut, than outside. Many other plays can be run toward the split end, and the plays mentioned are used as examples only.

The offense should attack the split end with the passing game. The routes of

THE 4-3 DEFENSE

the split end should be run according to where the number 3 man aligns; i.e. tight, walkaway, or double-up position. Look to Chapter 3 for a more detailed account in attacking the defensive end.

Since there are a number of linebackers in the 4–3 defense, frequent faking to one ballcarrier and giving to another tends to freeze the linebackers to the faking ballcarrier. The fake drive series to the fullback over the guard and, then the handoff to a halfback is an example. Quick counters up the middle and scissors off-tackle are essential in attempting to get the linebackers to start one way while the ballcarrier goes in the opposite direction. If the linebackers are reacting quickly to the ball, inside and outside reverses can be used effectively. If the linebackers are pursuing quickly to the outside on a sweep play, the ball can be handed back to a wingback coming in the opposite direction. The offensive linemen can then execute peel blocking back on the linebackers and the defensive linemen.

The play-action pass is effective to get the linebackers to the faking ballcarrier. The quarterback can then set up and throw to a receiver.

Since there are a number of linebackers, a great deal of stunting can be performed. The offensive linemen should be ready to area block, if this occurs. Going on the quick count is effective also. The quick pass or check pass over the stunting linebackers is excellent. If the offense is having difficulty handling the stunts, wedge blocking is good. Running and passing outside can be employed against internal stunting. The splitting of ends and flankers will minimize stunting to some extent.

Diagram 5–31 illustrates a brief outline of the strengths, weaknesses, plays, and comments on the 4–3 Even Box-Corner defense. Diagram 5–32 (page 120) illustrates the "card" for the Coaches' Directory of Football Defenses with the stunts, defensive shifts, strengths, weaknesses, and best blocking against this 4–3 defense.

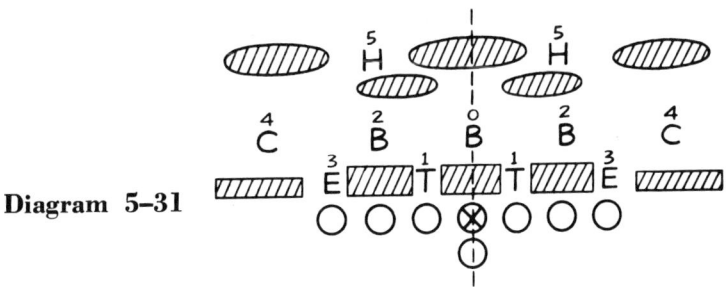

Diagram 5-31

Strength: This defense is stronger outside than inside. It is a nine-man front. It is stronger against the passing game than the running game. Linebackers give freedom to pursue quickly. A great deal of stunting and blitzing can be employed.

Weakness: Certain personnel and improper alignment can make it weak (number 1 or 3 man aligned inside). Generally weaker inside than outside. It is weak against the running team or a quick-hitting team. The offense should attack the middle square and off-tackle square.

Best Plays Against This Defense:

1. Attack the middle square with sneaks, traps, wedges, counters, and straight drive plays.
2. Execute the straight block along the offensive line with quick dives by the fullback and halfbacks.
3. Employ cross blocks at linemen and linebackers (can easily fold block).
4. Run isolation at the linebackers (number 3 men) with power.
5. Double-team the defensive linemen (center and guard, guard and tackle, tackle and end) and execute isolation and traps.
6. Trap the defensive tackles and ends (angle block down).
7. Execute faking plays to freeze the linebackers.
8. Run quick counters up middle and off-tackle.
9. Run outside and inside reverses against quick-flowing linebackers.
10. Pull offensive linemen to go outside and turn up through holes.
11. Option run-pass the corner.
12. Fake to fullback and go outside with option to trail man.
13. Put out flankers, wings, and split ends and go outside. Utilize double-team with wing and end. Angle down with split end and flanker.
14. Utilize play action passes against the linebackers and secondary.
15. Employ the quick pass against the stunt (check pass).
16. Area and wedge block against the stunt. Go outside against internal stunting.
17. Split ends and flankers to minimize the stunting game.

Comments: For this defense to be strong, the defensive tackles and ends must be good. The linebackers must be able to fill on running plays. Attack the defensive secondary according to the coverage being employed.

SUCCESSFUL RUNNING PLAYS

TO THE LEFT	TO THE RIGHT

SUCCESSFUL PASSING PLAYS

SUCCESSFUL ACTION PLAY PASSES

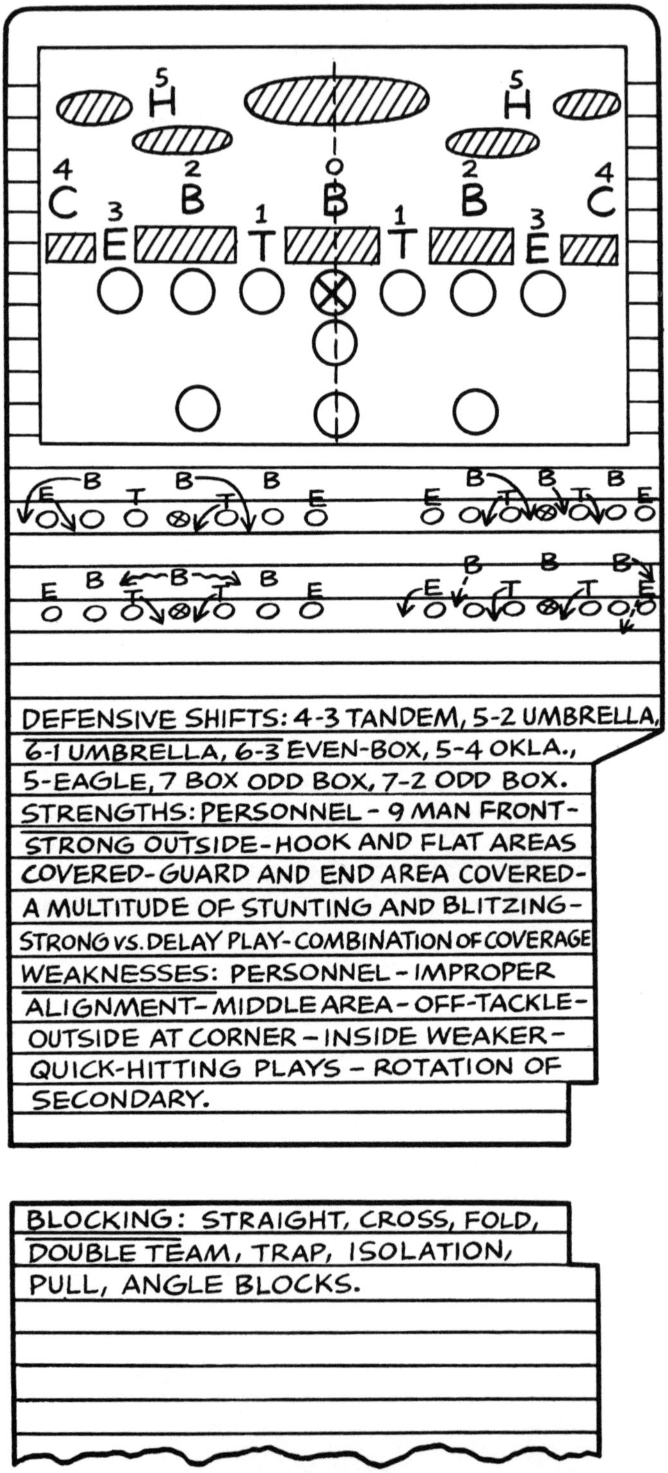

DEFENSIVE SHIFTS: 4-3 TANDEM, 5-2 UMBRELLA, 6-1 UMBRELLA, 6-3 EVEN-BOX, 5-4 OKLA., 5-EAGLE, 7 BOX ODD BOX, 7-2 ODD BOX.
STRENGTHS: PERSONNEL – 9 MAN FRONT– STRONG OUTSIDE–HOOK AND FLAT AREAS COVERED–GUARD AND END AREA COVERED– A MULTITUDE OF STUNTING AND BLITZING– STRONG VS. DELAY PLAY–COMBINATION OF COVERAGE
WEAKNESSES: PERSONNEL – IMPROPER ALIGNMENT– MIDDLE AREA – OFF-TACKLE – OUTSIDE AT CORNER – INSIDE WEAKER – QUICK-HITTING PLAYS – ROTATION OF SECONDARY.

BLOCKING: STRAIGHT, CROSS, FOLD, DOUBLE TEAM, TRAP, ISOLATION, PULL, ANGLE BLOCKS.

Diagram 5–32
The 4–3 even box-corner

6

THE 5-3 IN DEFENSE

The 5–3 In defense utilizes a five-man line with three linebackers. The outside linebackers are positioned inside the defensive ends; therefore, the defense is known as the 5–3 "In." It is an eight-man front with a three deep diamond secondary, in which a middle guard is positioned over the offensive center, and a middle linebacker is stationed directly behind the middle guard. The defensive tackle can align in one of three positions according to what the coach wants accomplished by the defense. The tackle can align on the inside shoulder of the defensive tackle, head up, or on the outside eye of the offensive tackle. An outside linebacker is positioned over the defensive end, approximately 1 yard off the line of scrimmage, and he can align either on the inside shoulder, head up, or outside eye of the offensive end. The defensive end aligns according to the positions of the defensive tackle and the outside linebacker. If the linebacker and defensive tackle are positioned more to the inside, the defensive end will move closer to the offensive end. If the defensive tackle and outside linebacker align more to the outside, the defensive end will position wider, approximately 2 yards. Diagram 6–1 (next page) illustrates the three different alignments of the 5–3 In defense.

The 5–3 In defense is mainly a pursuing and containing defense from which stunting can easily be accomplished. The middle guard and the middle linebacker can "deal" one way or the other, and this gives penetration up the middle and attempts to cause confusion with the offensive line. Stunting can also be employed between the defensive tackle, outside linebacker, and defensive end. The defense usually uses stunting against any offensive attack, especially with the tandemed players.

If the 5–3 In defense is to be strong, the middle linebacker must be good. He should be quick and fast and able to react to either side of the center when the play develops. If a play is not executed up the middle, the middle linebacker should be able to scoot off-tackle and outside for support on containment. Another responsibility of the middle linebacker is pass defense, where he must drop back to the middle hook zone area on drop-back passes and onside hook areas with roll or sprint-out passes. If a stunt is executed between the middle guard and the middle linebacker, the linebacker has no pass responsibilities except for rushing the passer, but at this time he must be alert for the draw and middle screen.

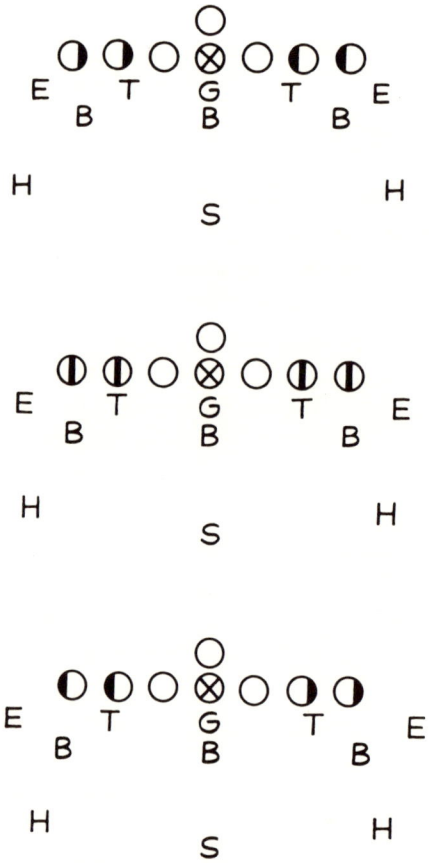

Diagram 6–1

THE 5-3 IN DEFENSE

The defensive tackles should be strong, since there is no man over the offensive guard and only a middle linebacker to assist in that area; they must help to the inside when possible. Yet the defensive tackle should be able to assist outside for support off-tackle and around end. Also the 5–3 employs a three deep secondary. The three deep can use rotation but usually will not because of the alignment and responsibility of the three linebackers who can cover the flats and hook areas adequately.

PLAYING THE 5–3 IN DEFENSE

The following defense is the head-up alignment of the 5–3 In Odd-Diamond defense with descriptions of the inside and outside alignments of the defensive tackle, linebacker, and defensive end.

MIDDLE GUARD (Number 0 Man)

Alignment: Line nose-up position on the offensive center, tight on the ball.

Stance: Four-point stance.

Initial Movement and Execution: Must be able to hit center with either forearm. Step into center and deliver a forearm blow. Look for the ball.

Responsibility: Play center's head and go to the ball. If double-teamed by the guard and center, fight through the pressure.

    1. Play toward—The center area. Be able to assist over the guards.
    2. Play away —Pursue. Play the ball on the option.
    3. Drop back —Rush the passer hard from in front. Look for the draw play and middle screen.

Coaching Points: Do not be blocked by the center. Hit and react quickly to the ball.

MIDDLE LINEBACKER (Number 1 Man)

Alignment: Line up approximately 3 to 4 feet directly behind the middle guard.

Stance: Two-point stance.

Initial Movement and Execution: The middle linebacker keys the center, quarterback, and fullback. He must be alert for a double-team on the middle guard and he should react to the movement of the two offensive guards.

Responsibility: If a double-team develops on the middle guard, the middle linebacker must fill in the hole, plus be alert to a trap by another lineman. If a guard blocks out on one of the defensive tackles, the linebacker must fill in the hole. If guard blocks at him, he must fight the pressure. If both guards pull, he should pursue to the off-tackle hole.

1. Play toward—Center guard area.
2. Play away —Pursue. Go to the off-tackle hole, then outside.
3. Drop back —Drop back 8 yards to the middle hook area. If the play is an action pass, go to the hook area on that side.

Coaching Points: The middle linebacker must be one of the best ballplayers on the defense. He must be able to react quickly to the play and remain low when filling the holes in order to tackle the ballcarrier.

DEFENSIVE TACKLE (Number 2 Men)

Alignment: Line nose up with the offensive tackle.

Stance: Four-point stance.

Initial Movement and Execution: Step and strike a blow into the offensive tackle. Key his movements. Play his head. If the offensive tackle goes down, move down. If he tries to hook, go outside. If he blocks out, fight pressure. (If aligned to the inside, step into the offensive tackle with the outside shoulder, keeping shoulders square to the line. Key remains the same.) If the offensive tackle blocks in on the defensive tackle, the defensive tackle must fight pressure to the outside, but should never run around the offensive tackle.

Responsibility:
1. Play toward—Tackle area. Play the fullback on the option.
2. Play away —Pursue to the ball.
3. Drop back —Rush passer on a 45 degree angle.

Coaching Points: He should never be blocked by the offensive tackle. Hit, key, and react.

OUTSIDE LINEBACKER (Number 3 Men)

Alignment: Head up on the offensive end approximately 1 yard off the line of scrimmage (this will vary).

THE 5-3 IN DEFENSE

Stance: Square two-point stance. Keep the body square to the line and stay low to the ground. Good football position.

Initial Movement and Execution: Read and key the head of the offensive end. If end blocks out, strike a blow with the inside forearm keeping the outside leg and arm free.

Responsibility: Read and react to the head of the offensive end. If end blocks down on the tackle, step up and meet the play and be aware of the trap. If end blocks out, fight pressure and meet him aggressively. If end releases downfield, hit him hard attempting to slow him up. Do not let end get a clear shot at the middle linebacker. If aligned inside, step up into end with outside shoulder keeping square to line and be responsible for the off-tackle area.

1. Play toward—The off-tackle area.
2. Play away —Pursue. Keep end off defensive halfbacks.
3. Drop back —Go to respective hook areas.

Coaching Points: Must be able to support to the outside on sweeps and quick pitchout plays.

DEFENSIVE ENDS (Number 4 Men)

Alignment: Line up approximately 1 to 2 yards outside of the offensive end. (This will be determined by the alignment of the outside linebackers on the offensive end.) The farther inside the linebacker positions, the closer the defensive end must align.

Stance: Two-point stance with outside leg back.

Initial Movement and Execution: The end can either play a crashing or boxing type of end play. If crashing, the end comes across hard, shutting off the off-tackle area, but he must contain the play coming in his direction. When the end is crashing hard, the outside linebacker can support more to the outside to assist the end. If boxing, the end takes two steps across the line of scrimmage forcing all plays to the inside. The outside linebacker in this case will definitely be responsible for the off-tackle area.

Responsibility: If the end crashes, he must come across hard, tough, and contain all plays his way.

1. Play toward—Contain and protect off-tackle area.
2. Play away —Chase play looking for the counters, reverses, bootlegs, etc.
3. Drop back —Rush the passer. There is no pass defense responsibilities.

If boxing:
1. Play toward—Force all plays to the inside. Take the quarterback on the option.
2. Play away —Rotate back and around. Look for the bootleg and throw-back pass.
3. Drop back —Rush and contain the quarterback.

Coaching Points: The 5–3 In usually employs a crashing charge by the defensive end. If crashing, the end should not delay. The charge is made immediately. He should not run around blockers.

DEFENSIVE HALFBACKS (Number 5 Men)

Alignment: Line up 3–4 yards outside offensive end and 7–10 yards deep. Line up as wide as the widest receiver.

Stance: Two-point stance with outside leg back.

Initial Movement and Execution: Watch your required key (end?). On snap of ball, weight should be shifted back to outside foot on reading the key.

Responsibility: React to run, if end blocks. Approach the ballcarrier from an outside-in position. On plays away, look for pass and then pursue. Must watch for the fake block. If offensive end pass protects or releases downfield, play pass first, then react to the run.

1. Play toward—Deep outside one-third unless indicated otherwise.
2. Play away —Deep outside one-third unless indicated otherwise.
3. Drop back —Deep outside one-third unless indicated otherwise.

Coaching Points: Play the man when he is in the zone. Be as deep as the deepest receiver. When the ball is thrown, go quickly and play the ball at its highest point.

SAFETY MAN

Alignment: Directly over the center, 9–12 yards in depth.

Stance: Two-point stance.

THE 5-3 IN DEFENSE   127

    Initial Movement
    and Execution: Watch your required key. On snap of the ball, the first step should be back.

    Responsibility: On any play the safety must think "pass" first and "run" second. The safety only assists on runs when it is definitely a run and not a pass.

        1. Play toward—Deep middle one-third of field unless indicated otherwise.
        2. Play away —Deep middle one-third of field unless indicated otherwise.
        3. Drop back —Deep middle one-third of field unless indicated otherwise.

    Coaching Points: Must think "pass" first and "run" second. Play as deep as deepest receiver. Sprint to the ball and go through the receiver to the ball.

As can be seen, the 5–3 In defense can align, play, and execute in different ways. With the 5–3 In defense, a crashing end is usually employed. However, there are many exceptions and variations to the type of defensive line play and the offensive coach should know exactly how the defense is being executed if he is going to attack it properly.

ADJUSTMENTS TO FORMATIONS

When offensive line splits become wider, the defense must adjust into the gaps. The defensive tackle should align in the guard-tackle gap, the outside linebacker should station in the tackle-end hole, and the defensive end should be on the outside shoulder of the offensive end.

If the offense splits an end, the 5–3 In can adjust in many ways. The defensive tackle could align on the offensive guard and the defensive end positions on the offensive tackle. The outside linebacker would play either tight, walk-away, or double-up position on the split end. The middle linebacker can stay in the same alignment or he can position over the uncovered offensive guard. Another method in adjusting to a split end is to have the defensive tackle remain the same, the defensive end align outside of the defensive tackle, and the outside linebacker position on the split end. The middle linebacker, in this case, would remain in his similar alignment behind the middle guard to protect both center-guard areas.

If a wingback is stationed outside the offensive end, the defense can adjust in one or two ways. The outside linebacker can adjust on the outside eye of the offensive end and the defensive end can position on the outside shoulder of the wingback. The defensive tackle could slightly adjust and align on the outside eye of the offensive tackle. Another method is the defensive end positioning on the offensive end and the outside linebacker aligning over the wingback. The defensive secondary adjusts accordingly. The same method can be applied to a flanker back. The outside linebacker can either play a tight, walkaway, or double-up position according to what the situation warrants.

Another method in adjusting to a flanker is the middle linebacker aligning outside of the offensive end. In this situation, the defensive tackle would align in the guard-tackle gap, the linebacker positions in the tackle-end hole, and the end stations outside of the offensive end. This is illustrated in Diagram 6–2. The three deep must adjust to the flanker. If a slot occurs, the same method of

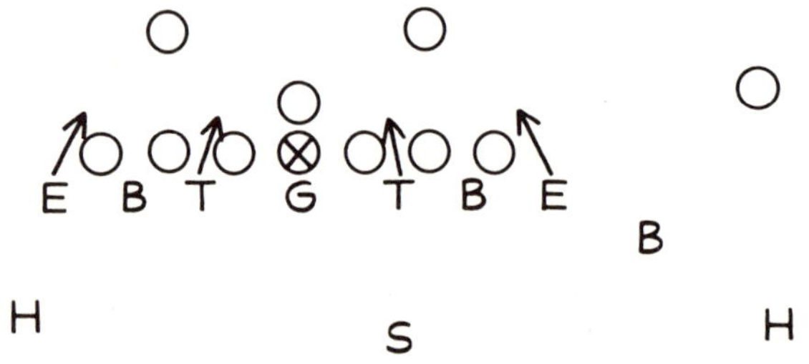

Diagram 6–2

adjusting can be done as if the offensive end were a wingback. However, the middle linebacker can adjust as was accomplished against a flanker back. Diagram 6–3 indicates the middle linebacker over the slotback.

Diagram 6–3

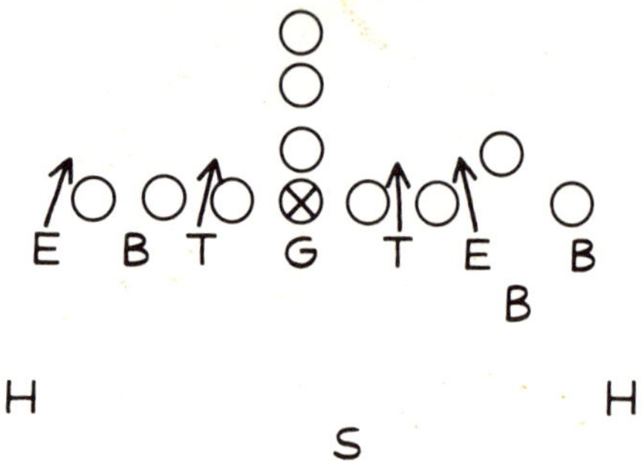

STUNTING, BLITZING, AND ANGLING

Because of the alignment of the middle tandem, a great amount of stunting should be executed between the middle guard and the middle linebacker. The middle guard could fire to the right in the center-guard gap while the middle linebacker stunts to the left. The same stunt can be reversed, with the middle guard charging to the left and the linebacker stunting to the right. The defensive tackle, outside linebacker, and end can coordinate in executing different stunts in their respective areas. The defensive tackle could charge from an alignment

THE 5-3 IN DEFENSE

over the tackle through the guard-tackle gap with the linebacker covering the tackle-end gap.

Another excellent stunt can be executed between the outside linebacker and the defensive end. Diagram 6–4 illustrates the end crashing to the inside hard while the linebacker loops outside on an "X" charge.

Blitzing into a Gap 8 is shown in Diagram 6–5, one example of the many combinations of blitzes and stunts which can be accomplished from the 5–3 In defense. The middle guard and linebacker fire the guard-center gaps, the tackles

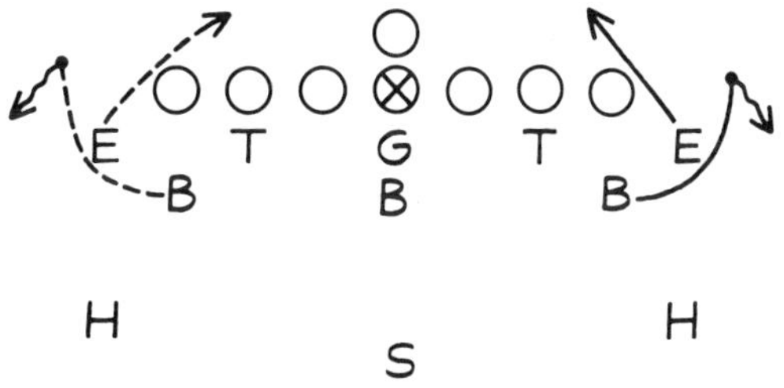

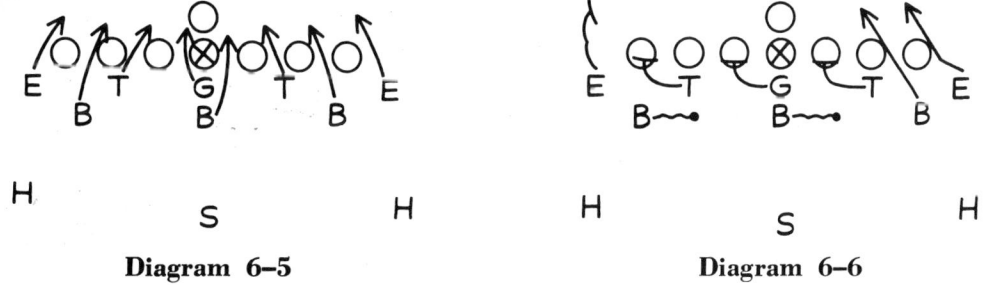

Diagram 6–4

explode through the guard-tackle hole, the linebackers shoot the tackle-end area, and the defensive end crashes the line of scrimmage.

Angling and looping from the 5–3 In defense can easily be employed. The angling line to the left is illustrated in Diagram 6–6 with brief explanations as to the forcing unit assignments. Angling right is shown in Diagram 6–7 (next page).

Diagram 6–5 **Diagram 6–6**

Left End—Set two steps upfield and turn everything in. Play away, rotate back and around.

Left Tackle—Angle over end stopping his release on the outside linebacker.

Middle Guard—Angle left over guard stopping his release on the middle linebacker.

Right Tackle—Angle left over guard stopping his release on middle linebacker. Play away, chase.

Right End—Play regular crashing end.

130   THE 5-3 IN DEFENSE

Right Outside Linebacker—Fire the tackle-end gap. If you cannot "bust," take the regular angle of pursuit.
Middle Linebacker—Take one step to the right. Protect over the middle, then off-tackle and end run to the right.
Left Outside Linebacker—Drop back and step to the inside. Play wide-tackle-six linebacker.
Halfbacks and Safety—Play regular secondary assignments.

DEFENSIVE SHIFTS

Diagram 6–8 illustrates a Gap 5–3 In defense. The ends align in a three-point stance and charge through the outside shoulder of the offensive end to close off the off-tackle hole. The defensive tackles position on the inside shoulder of the offensive tackles and charge through the outside shoulder of the offensive guards, staying low and aiming for the hips of the quarterback. The middle guard loosens slightly, but plays the same 5–3 In defensive responsibilities. The outside linebackers align on the inside shoulder of the offensive ends. The outside line-

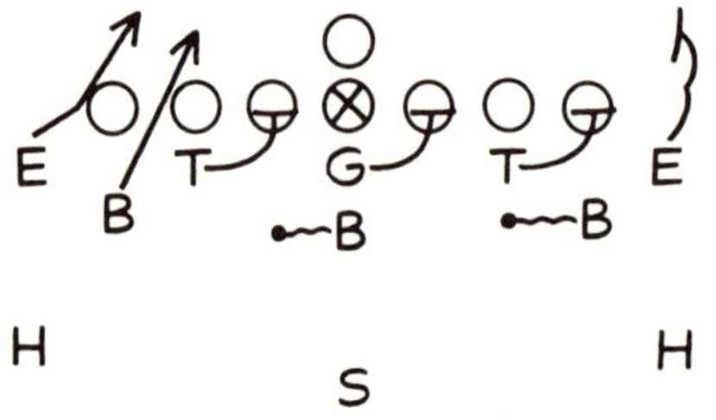

Diagram 6-7 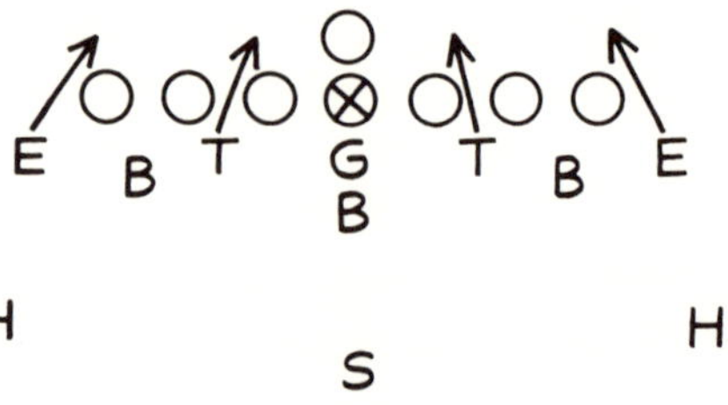   **Diagram 6-8**

backer should not be blocked in and should continually make it tough for the receiver to release from the line of scrimmage. The middle linebacker can remain in his similar position, but can adjust to wings, flankers, and slots, as was illustrated in Diagrams 6–2 and 6–3.

Tandeming the linebackers behind the defensive tackles can be accomplished and this is shown in Diagram 6–9. Also, stunting off the tandem can easily be done. The defensive tackles can charge either left or right, with the outside linebackers dealing in the opposite direction of the tackle's charge.

Another excellent defensive shift was sent by Charles Mather, assistant football coach of the Chicago Bears. Coach Mather employed this variation of the 5–3 In defense while he coached high school football in Ohio. The defensive ends align nose up on the offensive ends and the outside linebackers position directly behind the ends. This is shown in Diagram 6–10. Coach Mather also illustrated stunts and charges from this alignment. The defensive ends can charge

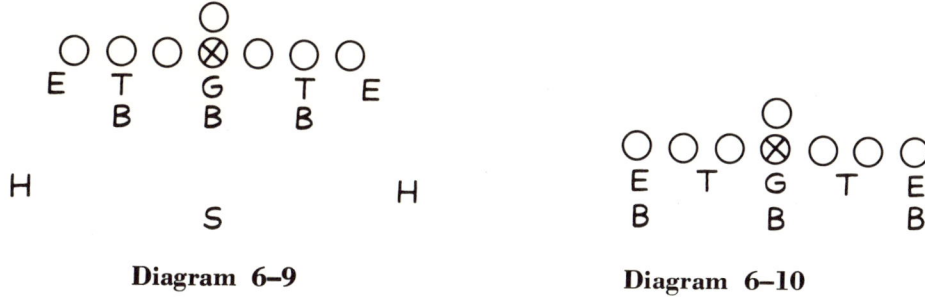

Diagram 6-9 **Diagram 6-10**

to the inside and the linebackers can fire to the outside. This stunt can be executed opposite with the defensive end going to the outside and the linebacker charging to the inside. The defensive tackles can either play straight and pursue or can shoot the guard-tackle hole. The middle guard aligns off the line slightly and plays the movements of the quarterback. Diagram 6-11 (next page) indicates a few maneuvers from the Tandem 5-3 In defense.

The 5-3 In Odd-Diamond defense can easily shift to other defenses. Since it is an eight-man front, it can shift and jump to other eight-man fronts. The 5-3 Out Odd-Diamond defense is one such defense. The defensive ends align over the offensive ends and the linebackers position outside the offensive ends. The 7-1 Odd-Diamond defense is another quick shift. From the 5-3 In defense the linebacker can move directly over the offensive ends in a three- or four-point stance making a seven-man line. Other various 7-1 alignments and variations can also be jumped to quickly.

The Gap-8 Even-Diamond defense can be shifted with the middle guard aligning in one center-guard gap and the middle linebacker positioning in the other. Other defenses can be shifted and jumped to with little maneuvering. Such defenses include Loose or Wide Tackle Six Even-Diamond, the Tight Six Even-Diamond, the Tandem 6 Even-Diamond, the Notre Dame 6, and others.

ATTACKING THE 5-3 IN ODD-DIAMOND DEFENSE

THE STRENGTHS OF THE 5-3 IN DEFENSE

The strengths of the 5-3 In defense are as follows:
1. The off-tackle area is basically strong, considering there are three defensive men to two for the offense.
2. The defense is strong around end if the defensive end is boxing and forcing everything to the inside.
3. The 5-3 In defense is strong off-tackle if the defensive ends are crashing.
4. The 5-3 In defense employs a three deep pass coverage.
5. The offensive ends can be held up from releasing the line of scrimmage.
6. The hook areas of the pass defense are well covered by the three linebackers.
7. A considerable amount of stunting and blitzing can be done with the linemen and linebackers.

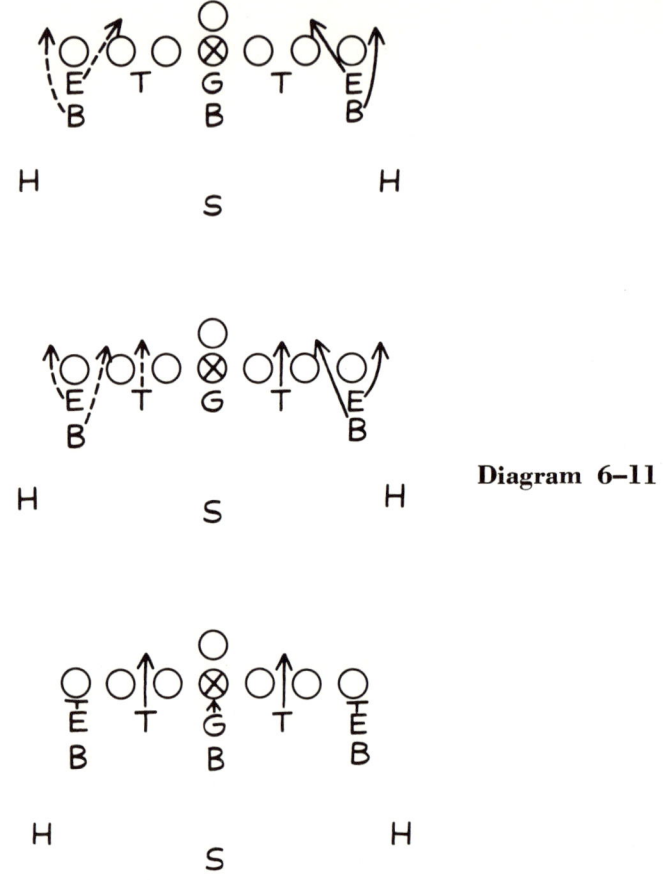

Diagram 6-11

8. Stunting can cause confusion for the offensive blocking in the middle area. This may reduce pulling by the guards.
9. The 5–3 In defense can adjust to other defenses easily.

THE WEAKNESSES OF THE 5–3 IN DEFENSE

The weakness areas of the 5–3 In defense are illustrated in Diagram 6–12, with the weaknesses of the defense listed as follows:

1. Defense is weak if offense takes wide offensive splits.
2. The middle area is weak with three offensive linemen on two defensive players.
3. The outside linebacker aligned off the end is weak against the running game.
4. Is the offensive end bigger and stronger than the outside linebacker? End may have a good angle block on the outside linebacker.
5. If the defensive end is boxing, the inside running game is effective.
6. If the defensive end is crashing, the outside is weak.

THE 5-3 IN DEFENSE

7. The flat areas for the passing game can be attacked.
8. Stunting by the middle defensive players limits pursuit to the outside.
9. Stunting causes weaknesses in the middle hook areas.
10. Attack the weak area of the three deep pass coverage.

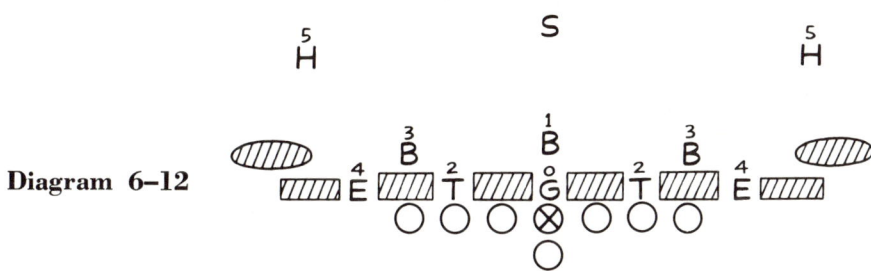

Diagram 6–12

ATTACKING THE AREAS OF THE 5–3 IN DEFENSE

The middle area of the 5–3 In defense should be attacked. The center and two offensive guards can easily occupy the middle guard and linebacker. Straight blocking can be used in this area with the center blocking the middle guard one-on-one and the two guards double-teaming the middle linebacker. However, this will be dependent on the alignment of the defensive tackle. If the defensive tackle is aligned nose up on the offensive tackle, the defensive tackle can easily be blocked. If the defensive tackle is positioned inside, then one of the offensive guards will be needed to block him.

If straight blocking cannot be used, cross blocking can definitely be employed. This would be done between the guard and tackle. No matter where the defensive tackle is aligned, the offensive guard can block out on him. The offensive tackle will then step behind and block the middle linebacker. Cross blocking by both guards and tackles is illustrated in Diagram 6–13 with a halfback counter. If the play is going in the opposite direction, fold blocking can be utilized also. The guard and tackle execute the same technique as described with the cross block. If the ballcarrier cuts back, a wider hole may be there for him.

A pull-around technique can be employed by one of the guards and this is illustrated in Diagram 6–14 (next page). The center blocks the middle guard. The right guard can either block out on the defensive tackle, if the offensive

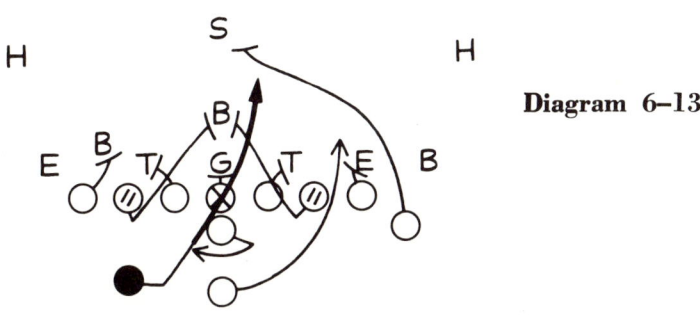

Diagram 6–13

tackle cannot block him alone, or the right guard can assist the center with a double-team block. The left guard pulls out of the line and turns up off the right guard's block for the middle linebacker.

With the blocking that has been described, different and various plays can be used. The quick dive play over the guard, with the fullback and halfbacks, should be employed. Any quick opener in this area is effective.

One of the best methods to attack the middle area is with counters, scissors, and cross-bucks of some type. A counterplay, to make the middle linebacker start in one direction away from where the ball is actually going, is excellent. The simple counter from the two back "I" formation is shown in Diagram 6–15. The fullback fakes a handoff over the left guard and the quarterback hands back to the deep tailback. It is hoped that the fake will hold the middle linebacker so he cannot react and fill the hole easily.

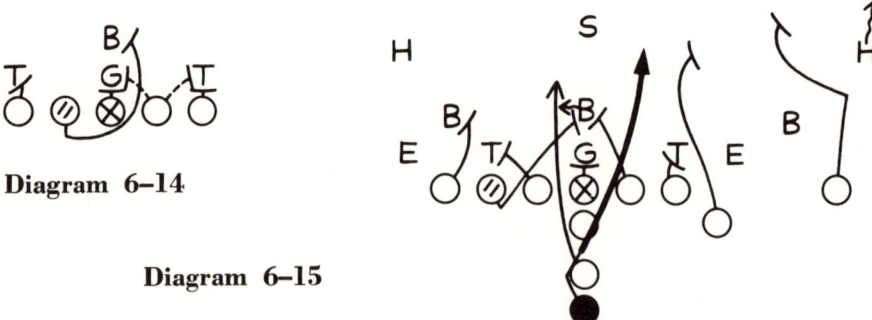

Diagram 6–14

Diagram 6–15

Isolation and power blocking up the middle at the linebacker should be employed. Double-teaming the middle guard with a center and guard is effective with a back or slotback driving to the inside and blocking the middle linebacker. Another method is to double-team the defensive tackle with the guard and offensive tackle and employ a back on the linebacker. In this situation the center would block the middle guard alone. Another method is to block out, with the guard on the defensive tackle, the offensive tackle on the outside linebacker, the center on the middle guard, and a back to isolate and power on the middle linebacker. Counters with isolation can be used also. This is shown in Diagram 6–16, with blocking out by the offensive linemen.

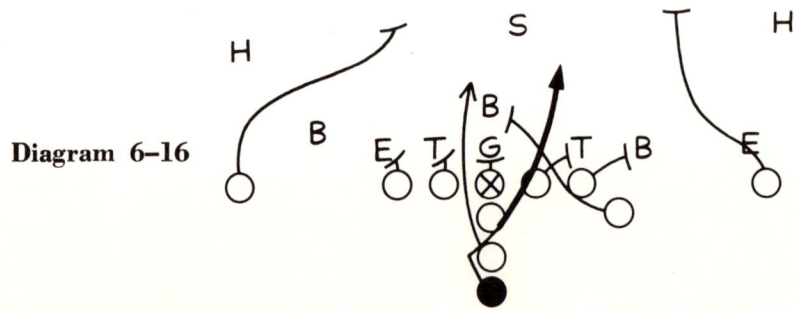

Diagram 6–16

Faking plays are important, especially against the middle guard and middle linebacker. Faking a fullback drive series up the middle and handing off to another back is effective. It tends to slow the pursuit of the middle guard and linebacker to the off-tackle hole and outside.

Play-action passes are effective against the middle linebacker. A quick pass over the middle area, with the middle linebacker going to the faking ballcarrier, should be employed.

Stunting is utilized a great deal, especially with the two middle tandem defensive players. When the linebacker and middle guard stunt, it results in both center-guard gaps needing to be filled. The offensive linemen must block this stunting with area blocking. Wedge blocking is good also. This can be executed with both the sneak and fullback wedge play. Utilizing the draw and the middle screen in this area is effective. Trapping can be employed against stunting. If the stunting continues up the middle, the offense can run more outside, away from the internal harassment. Another excellent method is to put out flankers and detach ends to see if the defense adjusts—this may minimize stunting.

Trapping the defensive tackle is effective, especially when the tackle is pinching or coming across the line hard. Trapping with the off-side guard or tackle can be utilized. An inside reverse, with a trap by the off-side guard or tackle can be used. An inside reverse, with a trap by the off-side tackle, is illustrated in Diagram 6–17. The left end blocks out and goes for the near-side halfback. The left tackle moves out and blocks the outside linebacker. The left guard blocks the middle linebacker and the center takes the middle guard one-on-one. The fullback fakes over the guard, hoping to draw both the middle guard and linebacker to the fake of the fullback, and attempts to make the block on these men easier. The right guard blocks out on the linebacker and the right tackle pulls and traps the defensive tackle. The right end goes for the safety man. The wingback comes directly for an inside handoff and cuts off the tackle's block. The quarterback reverse pivots and hands back to the wingback.

The offense should attack the alignment and movement of the defensive tackle. If the defensive tackle aligns and plays to the inside, the attack should go outside of him. If the defensive tackle plays more to the outside, the offense should go inside. Plays that fake inside of the tackle to draw the defensive tackle to the

Diagram 6–17

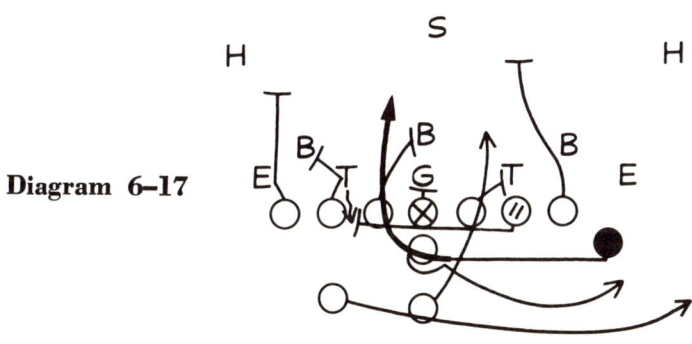

fake are excellent. The quarterback can then hand off outside or keep and go outside of the defensive tackle. The inside belly series is an example.

The off-tackle area is considered strong. There is a defensive tackle, outside linebacker, and defensive end positioned on the offensive tackle and end. This gives a three-on-two situation for the defense. In order to attack the off-tackle area, the offense must include an extra back or lineman to give a three-on-three ratio of offensive men to defensive players. In many instances, a double-team will be needed in the area, and a fourth offensive player will be necessary.

Straight blocking can be utilized. The offensive tackle blocks the defensive tackle and the offensive end takes the outside linebacker. A halfback or fullback is employed to kick out on the defensive end. Another method is for the offensive end to block down on the defensive tackle and the offensive tackle to step behind on the outside linebacker. This is shown in Diagram 6–18. A halfback or fullback again kicks out on the defensive end.

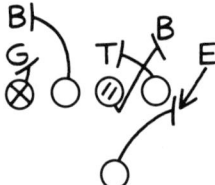

Diagram 6–18

A wingback can angle block down on the outside linebacker while the offensive tackle blocks the defensive tackle and the offensive end takes the defensive end. This is illustrated in Diagram 6–19.

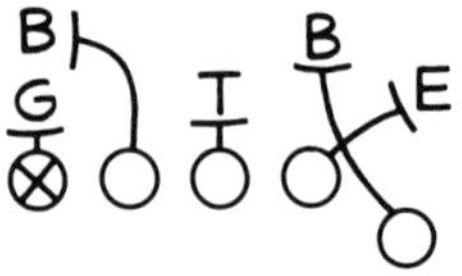

Diagram 6–19

Another method to attack the off-tackle hole is to add a fourth blocker in the area and put a double-team on the defensive tackle. This is indicated in Diagram 6–20. The offensive end and tackle double on the defensive tackle, the halfback kicks out on the defensive end, and the fullback blocks the linebacker.

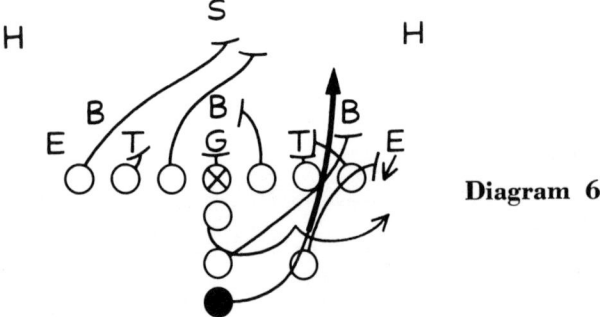

Diagram 6–20

Diagram 6–21

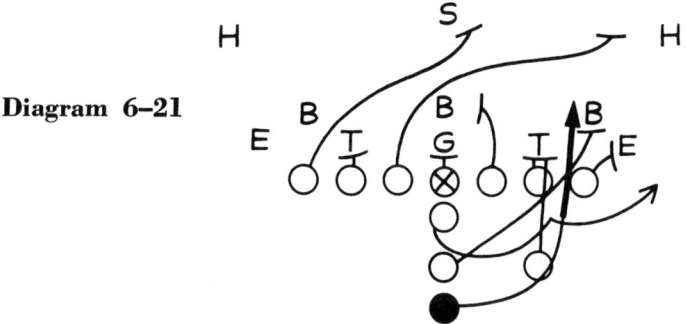

Another method is for the end to switch assignments (Diagram 6–21). The halfback assists on the defensive tackle while the end blocks out on the defensive end.

A double-team can be executed on the outside linebacker. The tackle blocks the defensive tackle, and the end takes the defensive end. The offensive guard pulls on the linebacker and the wing doubles with the guard. Diagram 6–22 illustrates this, with the fullback filling up the middle where the right guard is pulling. With this maneuver the fullback could pick up any middle stunting or slanting by the middle guard. This would hold the defensive middle linebacker and tackle inside also, and the fullback could assist with the offensive tackle on the defensive tackle.

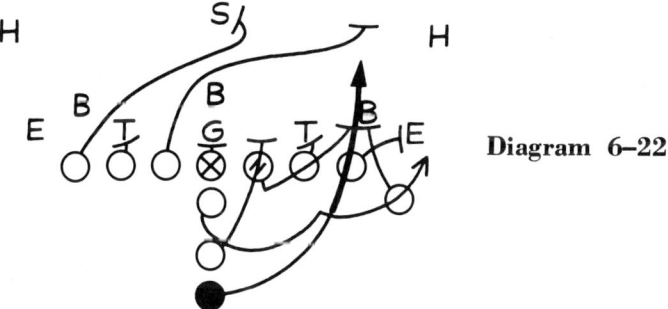

Diagram 6–22

Trapping the end can be done with either the onside or offside guard. If the onside guard is employed, the tackle blocks the defensive tackle, and the end takes the outside linebacker. The onside guard pulls and traps the defensive end. Another back penetrating on the middle linebacker or the offside guard pulling on him can be utilized (Diagram 6–23). A cross-buck, to hold the middle linebacker, could be employed with the type of blocking just mentioned being utilized.

Diagram 6–23

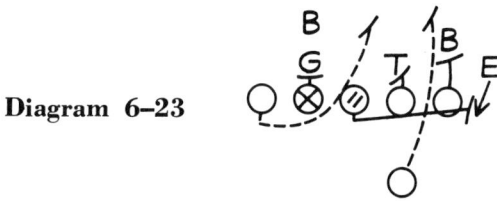

If the defensive tackle, outside linebacker, and defensive end position in a gap alignment, the offensive linemen should angle block down and kick out the defensive end with a halfback or fullback. If the defensive alignment positions to the inside, the offense should attack the outside and if the defense aligns outside, the offense should attack the inside.

When attacking the end area, the offense should know the type of defensive end play employed. Most consistently with the 5–3 In defense, the defensive end will be crashing down the line. The linebacker can then assist to the outside. If this is the case, the offense should go outside with sweeps and quick pitches. The alignment of a wingback gives an added advantage to the outside because the defense must adjust to the strength of the wingback. Doubling down on the number 3 man is effective. The offense should utilize the outside belly series. Faking to the fullback and keeping, is effective if the defensive end starts committing to the fullback. Optioning to the next widest man, in this case the halfback, off the outside belly series can be accomplished once the defensive end commits. Optioning the crashing defensive end and pitching to the trailing halfback is good. The split "T" running attack should do well against this defense.

The option run-pass is effective against the defensive halfback. Throwing in the flat areas is important. The linebackers have a difficult job in covering the flat well. Swing, flare, and quick flat routes are excellent in this area. A screen to the outside can be employed, especially with the crashing defensive end.

If the defensive end is boxing, floating, and forcing everything to the inside, the offense must run inside. The defensive end usually boxes when the linebacker plays closer to the line of scrimmage on the offensive end. It would be difficult for the linebacker to get outside from this alignment; therefore the end boxes. Plays that look as if they are going wide, but end up inside, are good. The outside belly and optioning the boxing end can be employed. If the end goes for the halfback, the quarterback keeps the ball. If the defensive end commits to the quarterback, he pitches the ball to the trailing halfback. Trapping the end can be utilized also. This can be executed with inside reverses. Reverses are good for getting the middle linebacker flowing in one direction and then having the ballcarrier go in another.

The offense should put out flankers, detach ends, and run and pass accordingly. If the defense positions inside the wide receiver, the offense should angle block down and go outside with power sweeps, pitchouts, reverses, and option plays. If the wide men are doubled up, the offense should go inside with a back or lineman kicking out on the wide defensive player. The offense should attack the three deep secondary and linebackers according to the coverage (Chapters 3 and 4).

Diagram 6–24 illustrates the weakness areas of the 5–3 In defense, with the strengths, weaknesses, best plays against this defense, and comments listed after it. Diagram 6–25 (page 141) indicates the 5–3 In defensive card that should be installed within the "Coaches' Directory of Football Defenses."

Diagram 6–24

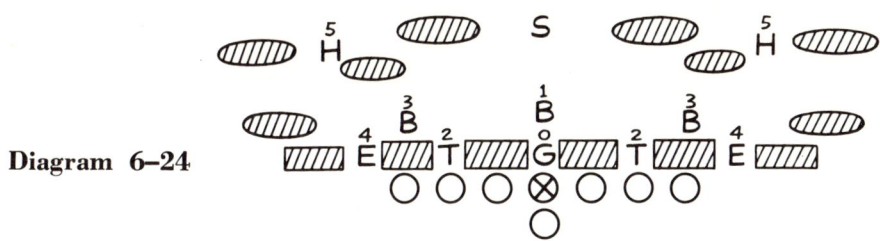

Strengths: The off-tackle area is strong. The offensive ends can be held up on the line from releasing for passes. The three linebackers cover the hook areas adequately. The 5–3 In defense employs a three deep pass coverage. Stunting can be employed with the middle guard and linebacker to get penetration up the middle.

Weaknesses: The middle area is considered weak with three offensive linemen to two defensively. The outside linebackers can be attacked. The flat area is a weakness. Around end is weak if the defensive end crashes. Attack inside if the ends are boxing.

Best Plays Against the 5–3 In Defense:

1. Attack the middle area. Employ straight, cross, and fold blocking.
2. Utilize quick-hitting plays over the guard area.
3. Employ all types of counters, scissors, and cross-bucks at the middle area.
4. Isolation and power blocking at the middle linebacker are effective. Use double-teams and out blocking.
5. Faking plays over the middle to hold the middle linebacker should be used.
6. The inside drive series is excellent against the defensive tackle.
7. Attack the defensive tackle's alignment. Go outside if the tackle moves inside and go inside if the tackle plays outside.
8. Attack the off-tackle area with extra backs and linemen.
9. Straight and cross blocks, with the offensive end and tackle on the defensive tackle and outside linebacker, are effective.
10. Isolate and power block the outside linebacker. Double-team the defensive tackle.
11. If the defensive end crashes, go outside with sweeps, quick pitch-outs, and options.
12. If the defensive end boxes, go inside with kick-outs, traps, reverses, counters, etc.
13. Employ both the outside belly option keep-pitch and the split "T" option play on the number 4 man.
14. Release the offensive tight end to the outside and employ the option run-pass against the defensive halfback.
15. Attack the flat areas with swing, flare, and quick flat routes.
16. Screen to the outside.
17. Utilize play-action passes against all linebackers.

SUCCESSFUL RUNNING PLAYS

TO THE LEFT	TO THE RIGHT

SUCCESSFUL PASSING PLAYS

SUCCESSFUL ACTION PLAY PASSES

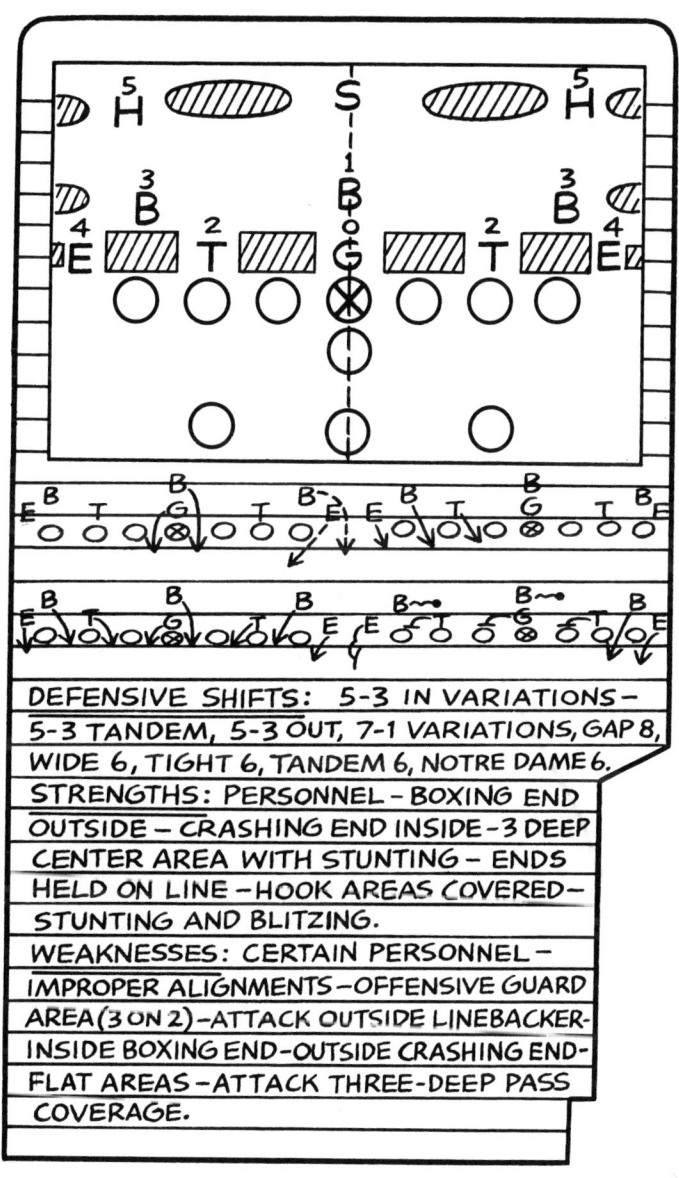

DEFENSIVE SHIFTS: 5-3 IN VARIATIONS – 5-3 TANDEM, 5-3 OUT, 7-1 VARIATIONS, GAP 8, WIDE 6, TIGHT 6, TANDEM 6, NOTRE DAME 6.

STRENGTHS: PERSONNEL – BOXING END OUTSIDE – CRASHING END INSIDE – 3 DEEP CENTER AREA WITH STUNTING – ENDS HELD ON LINE – HOOK AREAS COVERED – STUNTING AND BLITZING.

WEAKNESSES: CERTAIN PERSONNEL – IMPROPER ALIGNMENTS – OFFENSIVE GUARD AREA (3 ON 2) – ATTACK OUTSIDE LINEBACKER – INSIDE BOXING END – OUTSIDE CRASHING END – FLAT AREAS – ATTACK THREE-DEEP PASS COVERAGE.

BLOCKING: AREA (STUNTING) – STRAIGHT CROSS (FOLD) DOUBLE TEAMS – ISOLATION – POWER – OUT BLOCKING, TRAPS, ANGLE BLOCKING.

Diagram 6–25
The 5–3 In odd-diamond defense

18. If the defense stunts up the middle, use the draw and middle screen. Must be able to area block for the running and passing game.
19. Use the sneak wedge and the fullback wedge play up the middle if stunting.
20. Put out flankers and split ends to minimize the stunting game. Go outside against internal stunting; go on the quick count, etc.

Comments: The 5–3 In defense should not be able to stop the split "T" running attack, unless the defensive personnel is superior. Check the alignments of all defensive men for possible exploitation against improper alignments. Attack weak personnel.

7

THE 5-4 OKLAHOMA DEFENSE

The 5-4 Odd Box-Corner defense, known nationally as the 5-4 Oklahoma defense, has been one of the most prominent defenses used in the last few years. One reason the 5-4-2 is employed is because of the widely known and successful split "T" offensive attack. While the split "T" was enjoying great success, a need arose for a defense to combat it and the 5-4 was such a defense. Coach Ray Graves, head football coach of Florida University, stated in his book *Ray Graves' Guide to Modern Football Defense*, "In 1950 at Georgia Tech we were having our troubles stopping the split 'T' offense. Coach Bobby Dodd called Coach Bud Wilkinson and asked him how you stopped this monster he and Don Faurot had created. After several phone calls Coach Wilkinson tried to give us the Oklahoma 5-4-2 defense...."[1]

Since that time, the split "T" offense has not been used as extensively as others, and offenses with other variations have now become more successful. However, the 5-4 has remained because adjustments from it can be made to combat such changes as open formations, isolations, power plays, trapping, cross blocking, and so forth. A multitude of high schools and colleges are now using the 5-4 throughout the country. The professional football teams, however, have not seemed to stress its use.

The 5-4 Odd Box-Corner utilizes a four deep secondary coverage. The zone, man-to-man, free safety, and combinations can easily be installed. While it has only five men on the line, the two linebackers represent a seven-on-seven rela-

---

[1] Ray Graves, *Ray Graves' Guide to Modern Football Defense*. (West Nyack, New York: Parker Publishing Company, Inc. 1966), p. 27.

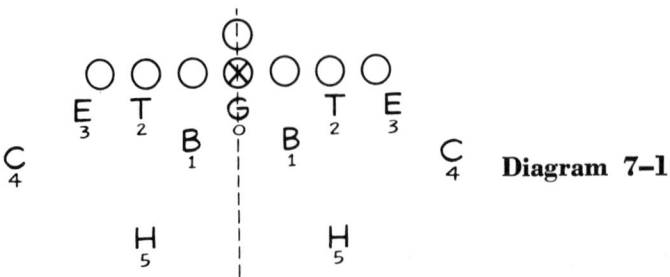

Diagram 7-1

tionship with the offensive line. The cornerbacks give it a nine-man front. It is a pursuing and containing defense. Diagram 7-1 illustrates the alignment of the 5-4-2 Oklahoma defense.

There are many theories as to the execution, movements, and responsibilities of the Oklahoma 5-4-2 defense. Some coaches look for a quick middle guard, who can cover an area between the two offensive guards, but can be quick and fast to pursue outside and make the tackle. Other coaches will utilize the big, strong, but slow middle guard whose responsibility is to cover the middle area only.

Most coaches desire the two linebackers (number 1 men) to protect the areas over the offensive guards. However, the linebackers must make tackles off-tackle and be secondary contain men when the play moves to the outside. Some coaches have the linebackers key and react to the guards' movements, while others key into the backfield and disregard the offensive guards. Other coaches have the linebackers read through the guards into the backfield. The keys and responsibilities of the linebackers will be determined by what the defensive coach wants and how the defense is executed. Most linebackers should be strong enough to stop plays up the middle, be quick and fast to assist outside, and be able to get back to their respective hook areas.

The defensive tackles usually key the offensive tackles and pursue the ballcarrier. The tackles must continually be aware of the offense's trapping game. The tackles should be strong enough to protect against the running game off-tackle, must be responsible for the dive play, and must fight the double-team from the offensive tackle and end. With a drop-back pass, the defensive tackle should be strong and quick enough to attack the passer either inside or outside, according to the calls and responsibilities.

Many coaches have the defensive ends align and play the offensive end areas in different manners. The end can key the offensive end, read the backfield's movements, and carry out his responsibilities. Other coaches have the end wait on the line of scrimmage and key the backfield only, while other coaches desire that the defensive end step across the line a yard and execute a box maneuver. In many instances, coaches have the defensive end crash down at the near halfback attempting to disrupt the play and throw the offense for a loss. The defensive end must be strong, quick, able to assist off-tackle, get outside and contain, hold up receivers, rush on passes, chase, and cover passes in the flat areas.

As can be seen there are many ways to play the 5-4 Oklahoma defense, and the material that follows describes these methods.

PLAYING THE 5–4 OKLAHOMA DEFENSE

MIDDLE GUARD (Number 0 Man)

Alignment: Head on center, 6 to 18 inches off the ball.

Stance: Four-point stance, feet parallel.

Initial Movement and Execution: Destroy center's block with forearm or hand shiver, and locate ball. Read center's head and follow flow of ball.

Responsibility:
1. Play toward—Offensive center area.
2. Play away—Pursue; do not run around.
3. Drop back—Play draw and delay rush.

Coaching Points: Learn to play with either forearm. Keep arm free to side of remaining back.

LINEBACKERS (Number 1 Men)

Alignment: Outside shoulder of offensive guards with feet approximately 2 yards *off the ball*. If middle guard moves to gap your side to take away split, "stack" while linebacker away moves up to line of scrimmage.

Stance: Balanced "ready" position with feet even or inside foot forward, no more than "toe-heel relationship."

Initial Movement and Execution: Short jab step with inside foot while striking blow with "hand-shiver" or "forearm lift" to destroy block.

Responsibility:
(1) *Play toward*—Offensive guard area, then pursue—you become second-contain when ball gets outside of contain man. Use inside-out approach in pursuit.
(2) *Play away*—Check counter and pursue—do not overrun. Get some depth in your pursuit.
(3) *Back-up Pass*—Flyback to hook. Check late flat. You have secondary responsibility for screen and draw (all passes are back up until the passer is outside the offensive tackles). Set up 8 to 10 yards deep in offensive end's running lane.

Coaching Points: Read the block of the guard and key the ball flow:
1. Never be hooked by guard.
2. Keep outside arm free.
3. Always play run from inside out. Do not overrun.
4. Be a leader on defense.

5. Be aggressive at all times.
6. You are *responsible* for correct alignment of linemen your side.
7. Adjust depth to down and distance.
8. Play quarterback's eyes.
9. Anticipate pass.
10. Make use of peripheral vision.
11. Be ready when quarterback is ready to throw.
12. React to throw.
13. Play blocker's head.

DEFENSIVE TACKLES (Number 2 Men)

Alignment: Outside shoulder of offensive tackle 10 inches off ball. Vs. abnormal guard-tackle split—Tackle will move into gap.

Stance: Four-point with feet slightly wider than hands. Inside foot in normal or slight stagger.

Initial Movement and Execution: Explode into tackle with inside forearm, keeping him off your linebackers. Key tackle's block and read ball.

Responsibility: Tackle goes down—you go down—keep tackle off linebacker. Watch for trap and isolation blocking. If tackle blocks out, fight pressure. If he tries to hook, get outside.

(1) *Play toward*—Play tackle area and locate ball. Ball moves to outside, pursue from inside out.
(2) *Play away*—Pursue. Do not run around blocker.
(3) *Drop back*—Rush passer best way possible.

Coaching Points: Must explode (step with inside foot) immediately, bring up outside foot while keeping outside arm free. Keep shoulders parallel. Explode upon movement of tackle's hand or the ball.

DEFENSIVE ENDS (Number 3 Men)

Alignment: Outside shoulder of offensive end about 18 inches off the ball.

Stance: Two-point upright with inside foot forward.

Initial Movement and Execution: Jab step with near foot into man. Hand or forearm shiver the end, keeping him off your defensive tackle. Do not let the end hook you or release to the outside. Read his block and key the ball.

THE 5-4 OKLAHOMA DEFENSE

Responsibility: (1) *Play toward*—Play end area.
                             (2) *Play away*—Go to flat.
                             (3) *Back-up Pass*—Outside rush. Responsible for screen.

Coaching Points: Meet flow with inside foot up the field and with outside arm free. Keep shoulders parallel to line of scrimmage and turn tail slightly inside. Keep leverage on the ball.

DEFENSIVE CORNER BACKS (Number 4 Men) Same as 4–3 defense (Chapter 5)

DEFENSIVE HALFBACKS (Number 5 Men) Same as 4–3 defense (Chapter 5)

The 5–4 defense can play more of a "reaction" and "keying" defense also. In this type of play the forward front wall does not strike a blow, but keys, reads, and reacts to the movement of the offensive linemen. A forearm blow is not struck unless the offensive linemen drive straight out at the defensive linemen.

ADJUSTMENTS TO FORMATIONS

Against a wing alignment the defensive end should widen slightly. However, the defensive end should still key the offensive end and react according to the assignment and responsibilities given. The defensive end must be aware of the double-team between the wingback and the offensive end. Once pressure is felt, the defensive end should fight to get outside. The defensive secondary should adjust according to the coverage being employed. Against the slot formation, the end plays the slotback as if he were an end. Against a split end, the defensive end will play head up from 2 to 4 yards, and on the inside shoulder from 4 to 6 yards. Beyond the point of 6 yards, he can either play a tight, walkaway, or double-up position. Another method to play the split end is to have the defensive tackle move down onto the offensive guard, the defensive end align on the offensive tackle, and the number 1 man (linebacker) move outside and play the defensive end's assignment, i.e. tight, walkaway, or double-up position. Again, the defensive secondary must adjust to the split end. Against a flanker, the forcing unit remains the same and the defensive secondary will adjust.

If a strong formation presents itself, usually the defensive secondary will adjust by rotating the entire defensive backfield into a three deep and having the cornerback step up and be directly on the line of scrimmage. This would be known as a "monster" or "rover" player. (The monster man can and usually will play this way at times against any formation and be used according to defensive philosophy.) The linebackers could adjust as illustrated in Diagram 7–2 (next page). In this case, the right linebacker aligns over the middle guard and the left linebacker positions directly behind the left defensive tackle.

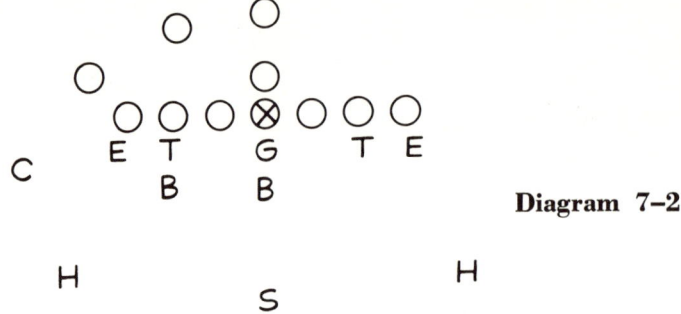

Diagram 7-2

STUNTING AND BLITZING

There are many stunts that can be executed from the 5-4 Oklahoma defense. While the 5-4 is not a total stunting defense, it is widely used as an element of surprise. It is mainly utilized when the basic defense is not stopping the offensive attack and something (stunting) is needed. One of the basic items of the 5-4 defense is the stunt with the middle guard and one of the linebackers. Diagram 7-3 illustrates the middle guard shooting the center-guard gap and the left linebacker firing across the center into the opposite hole. In this case, the right linebacker adjusts over the middle and goes in either direction determined by the flow of the ball. The same stunt by the right linebacker is shown in Diagram 7-4.

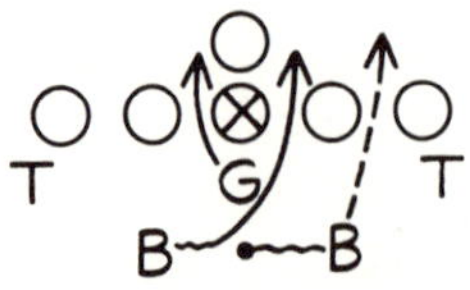

Diagram 7-3

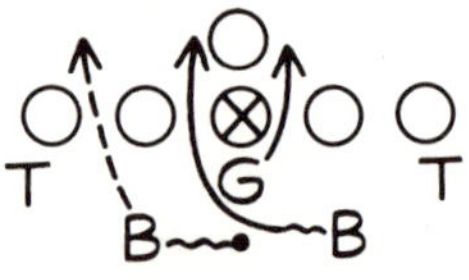

Diagram 7-4

Another charge can be executed between the linebacker and the defensive tackle. The defensive tackle slants down into the outside shoulder of the offensive guard and the linebacker stunts over the offensive tackle. Both stunters should look for the ball and pursue (Diagram 7-5).

A stunt between the linebacker, tackle, and end can be performed. The tackle charges down over the guard, the defensive end fires at the outside shoulder of the offensive tackle, and the linebacker stunts outside, over the end (Diagram 7-6). This is especially good when the defense expects a tough running play inside.

Another stunt can be performed by the defensive tackle and defensive end. The defensive end slants down into the offensive tackle while the defensive tackle steps out and around, into the offensive end (Diagram 7-7).

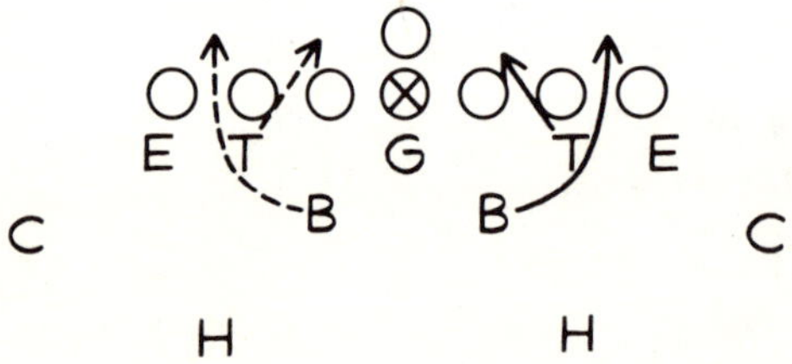

Diagram 7-5

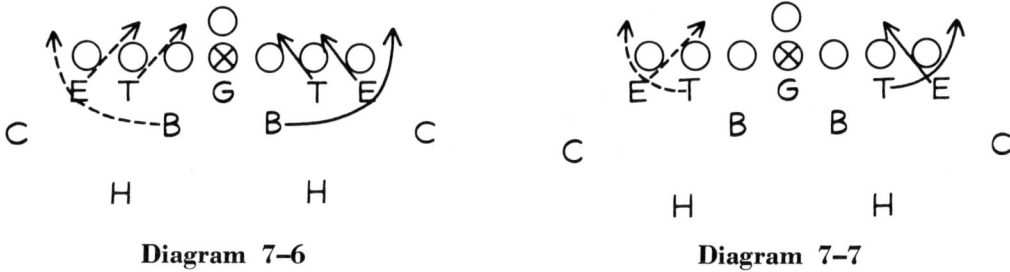

Diagram 7-6   **Diagram 7-7**

Many coaches desire the linebackers to go all out on their charge maneuver whatever the direction of the ball. However, a few coaches have the linebackers key a backfield man, i.e. quarterback. As illustrated in Diagram 7-8, if the quarterback should flow to the right, the linebacker would continue to the right. If the flow of the ball goes in the opposite direction, the linebacker would read his key and go on pursuit. In this case, the defensive right end should use an anchor technique to keep the offensive left end off the stunting linebacker.

Diagram 7-8

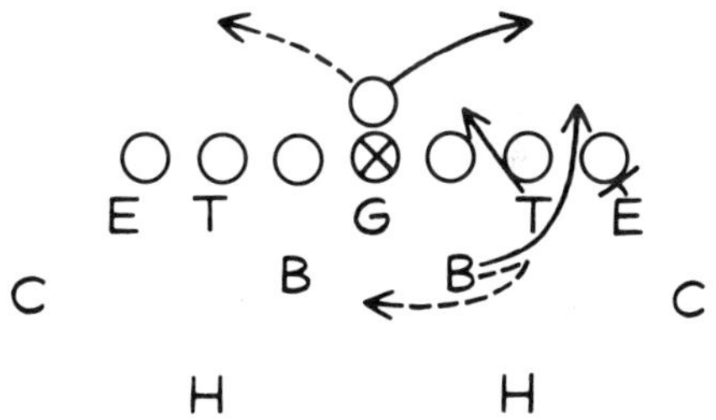

A combination of stunts can be employed between the two linebackers and the five defensive linemen. Diagram 7-9 illustrates this. The middle guard loops on to the offensive right guard (can penetrate gap if rush is needed) and the linebacker stunts in the opposite direction. Together with this stunt, the right linebacker loops outside while the defensive tackle and end slant to the inside.

Diagram 7-9

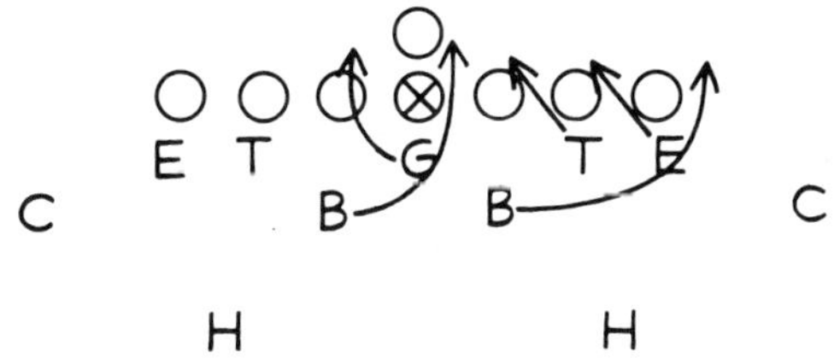

The following safety blitz is an excellent element of surprise against the passer. Diagram 7-10 (next page) illustrates the middle guard looping to the left and the linebacker firing the center-guard area. The defense reverts to three deep while the rover man shoots the guard-tackle hole to create extra pressure on the passer. The left linebacker adjusts over the middle and the defensive ends charge from the outside in.

Many other combinations of stunts can be employed according to what the defensive coach desires. The offensive coach should know the correct stunts and blitzes of his opponent so he will have his team drilled and prepared to meet the various situations (stunts and blitzes) that will occur in the game.

DEFENSIVE SHIFTS

The 5–4 Oklahoma defense can easily shift to other alignments, especially alternations from the basic defense. One of the most famous is the "monster" defense. A cornerback, designated the monster, steps directly on the line of scrimmage, making a six-man line. The defensive secondary rotates into a three deep. This is illustrated in Diagram 7–11. Usually the end to the side of the monster can play either inside shoulder (step into the end), head up, or outside shoulder (fire through outside hip). His assignment is to never be blocked in, delay the receiver, and keep the end off the linebacker. The defensive end away from the monster plays head up to outside shoulder and should move out to protect the short side. Another method is to have the middle guard, tackle, and end away from the monster angle outside.

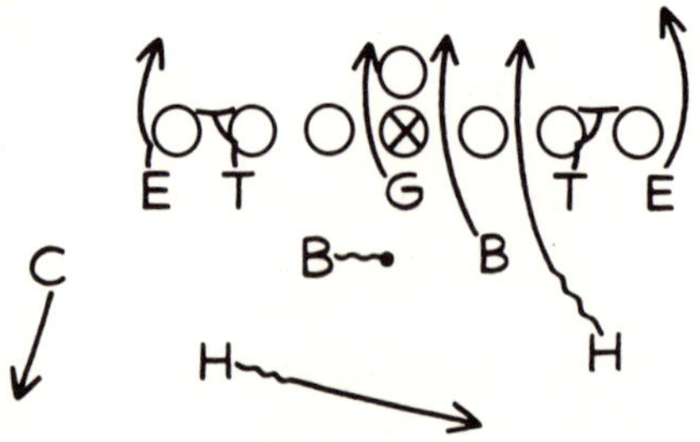

Diagram 7–10 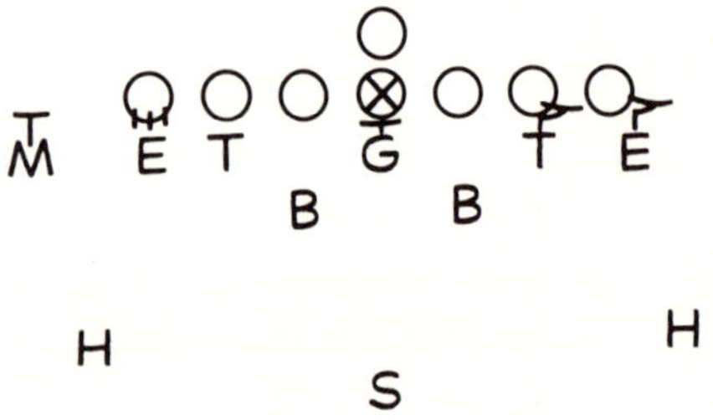   **Diagram 7–11**

When a short yardage situation occurs, the 5–4 "tough" can be employed. The two linebackers step up into the line in either a low two-point stance or four-point stance. The pursuit outside, however, is not as sufficient. The linebackers play the guards, strike a blow and protect their area before going on pursuit. Diagram 7–12 illustrates the 5–4 "tough" defense.

Another method in executing the 5–4 defense is to align the linebackers into a tandem position directly behind the defensive tackles (Diagram 7–13). The defensive ends line up directly on the offensive ends. Their responsibility is the same as the regular defense. If the play goes to the outside, the defensive ends

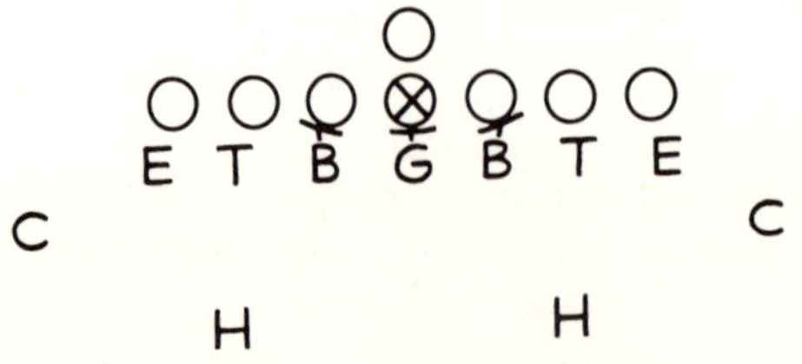

Diagram 7–12

THE 5-4 OKLAHOMA DEFENSE

must fight in that direction. The defensive tackles should charge into the offensive tackles to defeat their block. The middle guard plays the same as in the 5-4 defense. The linebackers look through the guard to the center and quarterback. If the offensive play drives up the middle, the linebacker must fill. However, he is in good position to pursue quickly outside from where he is aligned.

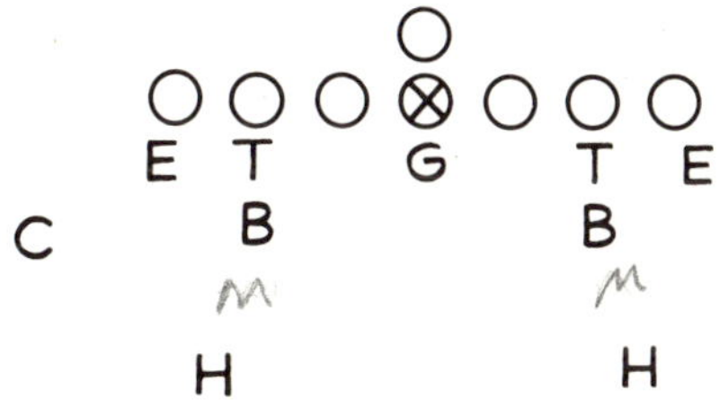

Diagram 7-13

Stunting can be used from the 5-4 Tandem defense. As shown in Diagram 7-14 the tackle slants down into the near shoulder of the guard closing off the inside. The linebacker is responsible for the off-tackle hole. In Diagram 7-15 the tackle pinches down on the guard, the defensive end pinches into the near hip of the offensive tackle closing off the inside, and the linebacker loops out to protect the end area. The middle guard in both situations plays the same as in the basic 5-4 Oklahoma defense.

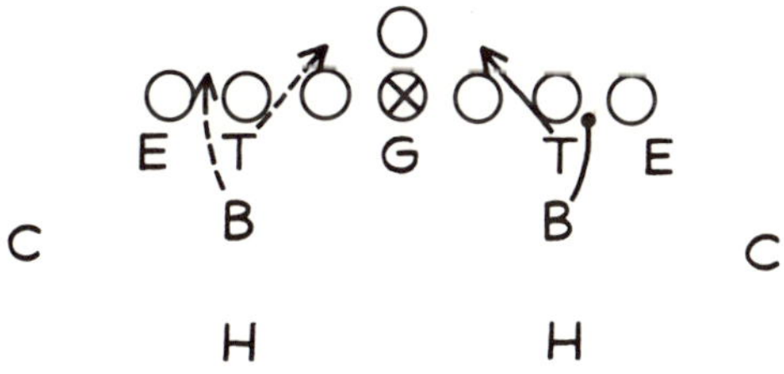

Diagram 7-14 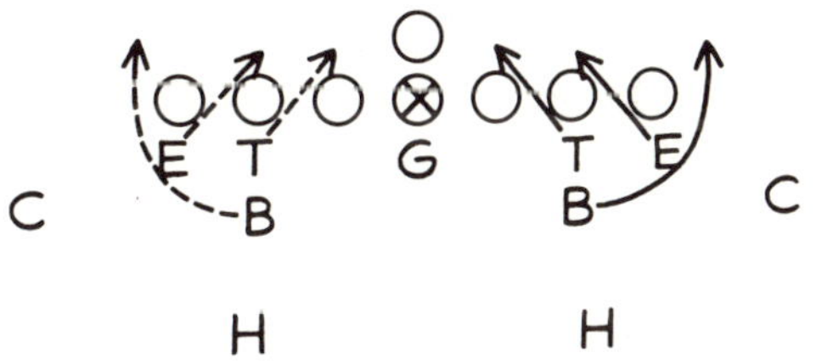   **Diagram 7-15**

Diagram 7-16 indicates another movement from the 5-4 Tandem defense. In this situation, the ends and tackles step to the outside and recover to the inside. The ends play the halfbacks coming in their direction. Both will rush the passer if a pass develops. The linebackers step to the inside and look for the dive, isolation, or trap plays. They should read through the guards to the center and quarterback.

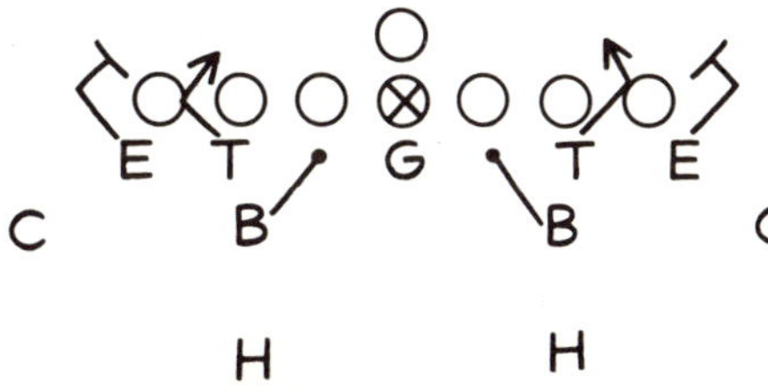

Diagram 7-16

The front five linemen can easily go into the gaps at times to create different defensive looks. Diagram 7–17 shows a stack right, with the middle guard and right linebacker. All other players have the same assignments and responsibilities. Diagram 7–18 indicates a stack left, with the middle guard and left linebacker. The middle guard, in both situations, aligns into the center-guard gap. He will explode across the line trying to go for the quarterback and get penetration. The linebacker reads the blocks of the two adjacent blockers. If the center blocks the middle guard, the linebacker will be ready to fill toward the center area. If the offensive guard blocks down on the middle guard, the linebacker will be ready to fill in that area also. At all times he will be prepared to pursue the ballcarrier.

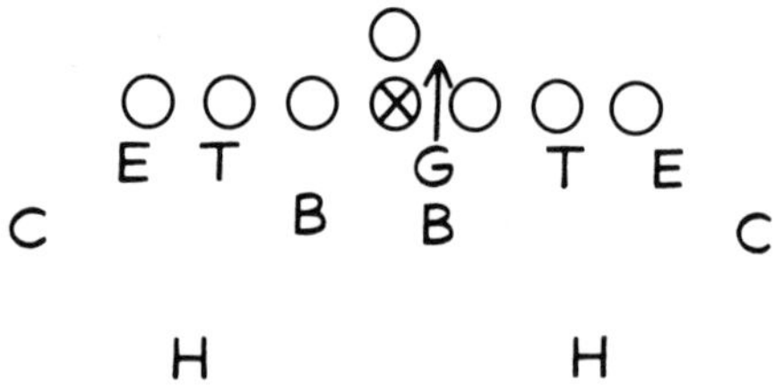

Diagram 7–17

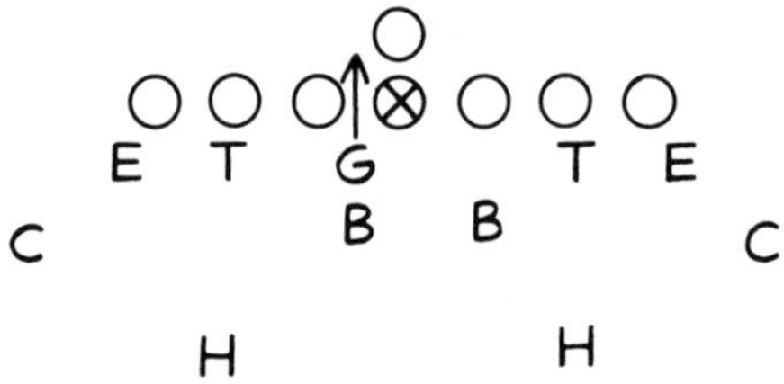

Diagram 7–18

Diagram 7–19 is an example of the tackle and linebacker stacking to the left, and Diagram 7–20 illustrates both tackles and linebackers stacking. Diagram 7–21 shows the middle guard and tackle in the gaps, with the linebackers stacked behind each one.

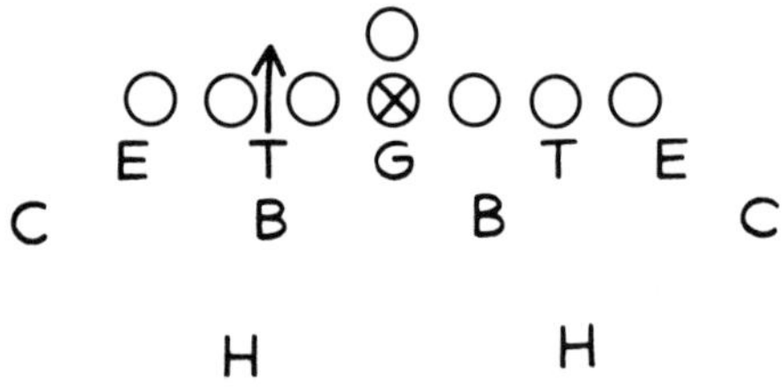

Diagram 7–19

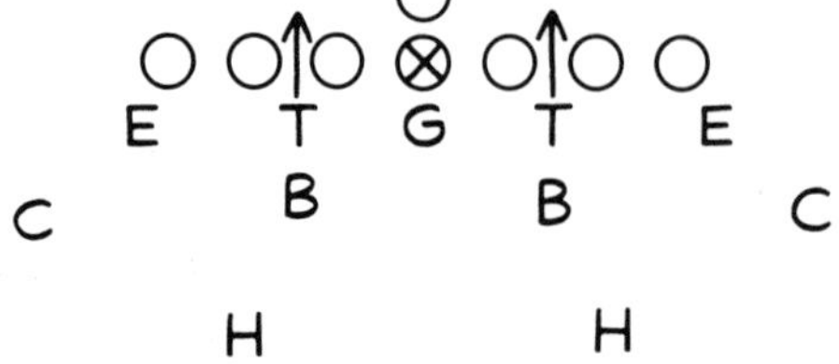

Diagram 7–20

Diagram 7–21

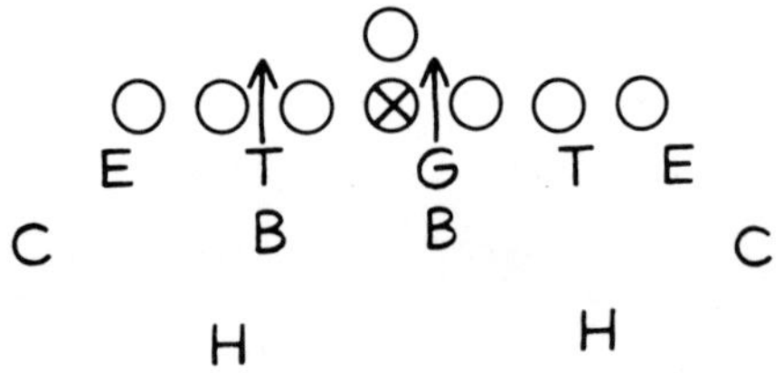

THE 5-4 OKLAHOMA DEFENSE

The 5–4 Oklahoma defense can shift to other defenses quickly and easily. The linebackers can stack behind each other, over the middle guard, creating the Snake-Eye 5 defense. From the 5–4 defense, the defensive tackles can move down over the guards, or inside shoulder of the tackles, making the 5–2 Umbrella Odd-Box Corner defense. From this position the linebackers can align on the inside shoulders of the ends, creating the Eagle-5 Odd Box-Corner. The 6–1 Umbrella Even Box-Corner, 4–3 Even Box, 7–2 Odd-Box, and the 7 Box-Odd-Box can be easily adjusted and shifted from the 5–4–2 Oklahoma defense.

ATTACKING THE 5–4 ODD BOX-CORNER DEFENSE

THE STRENGTHS OF THE 5–4 DEFENSE

The strengths of the 5–4 defense are listed as follows:

1. Over the tackle area.
2. Over the end area.
3. The defense can use a variety of secondary coverages: zone, (invert, rotation, straight), man-to-man, combination, etc.
4. It is a nine-man front with every offensive man covered.
5. It is a good containing defense.
6. It is an excellent running and pursuing defense.
7. The flat and hook areas are well covered for the short passing game.
8. If the linebackers are good, the defense is strong.
9. The defense is strong against straight blocks and the split "T" offense.
10. The defense can stunt easily against the running and passing game.
11. The 5–4 can shift and jump to other defenses easily.

THE WEAKNESSES OF THE 5–4 DEFENSE

The 5–4 defense can easily be attacked with many different blocking variations. The weak areas to attack the defense are illustrated in Diagram 7–22 (next page) and the weaknesses are listed as follows:

1. Attack over the guard areas.
2. Attack the off-tackle hole with blocking combinations.
3. Attack the outside area at the corner men with the running game.
4. Good angle blocking can be accomplished with the guards, tackles, and ends against the 5–4 defense.
5. Splitting the line widens the running areas up the middle.
6. The defensive secondary must rotate with the flow of the offense. If it does not the deep middle is weak with no safety covering the middle area.
7. Stunting may cause weaknesses in the defense.

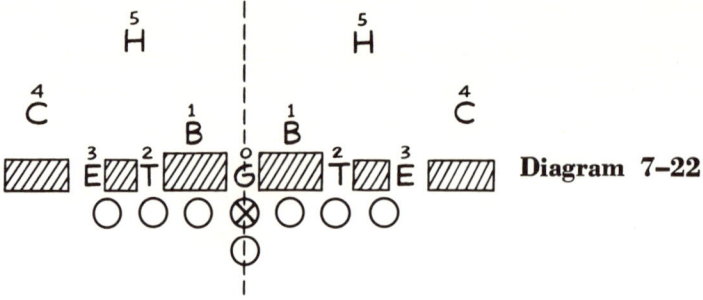

Diagram 7-22

ATTACKING THE AREAS OF THE 5-4 DEFENSE

One of the vulnerable areas in attacking the 5-4 defense is the middle area, from offensive guard to guard. While there is a three-on-three situation, there are two linebackers positioned off the line of scrimmage, creating a definite weakness in this area. Straight blocking can be used especially if the offensive linemen are bigger and stronger. Are the offensive guards stronger than the linebackers? Angle and power blocking are excellent in this area also.

The fullback quick dive and the halfback hand-off over the offensive guard area can be employed. The tackle blocks out on the defensive tackle, the guard fires into the linebacker, and the center can scramble block on the middle guard.

Cross blocking between the center and guard on the middle guard and linebacker can be used. This is excellent because of the angle blocks utilized. The offensive guard angle blocks down on the middle guard and the center steps behind the guard to block out on the linebacker. The halfback and fullback quick-dive play with cross-angle blocking can be used. Cross blocking between the guard and tackle can be employed also. Either offensive blocker could go first, which would be determined by the offensive coach and the type of play being executed. While cross blocking can be easily used, the fold block is effective also. This is utilized when the play starts in one direction and the ballcarrier, finding the hole is plugged, cuts back inside where the fold block was employed. For a more detailed account of the fold block, see Chapter 5 (the 4-3 defense).

Coach Bill Tate, former head football coach at Wake Forest College, sent this excellent play (Diagram 7-23) which has been very successful. It is a fold or cross block between the tackle and guard. In this situation, the guard blocks out on the defensive tackle and the offensive tackle steps behind and fires on the linebacker. The play is actually a predetermined cutback by the fullback. The quarterback reverse pivots as if to ride the fullback to the right, and the fullback cuts back quickly over the left guard. It is hoped from the first movements of the quarterback and fullback that the linebacker and middle guard will flow with the fullback creating a wider hole in the opposite direction. The left guard has a good angle on the defensive tackle and the offensive left tackle blocks the linebacker flowing away from the play.

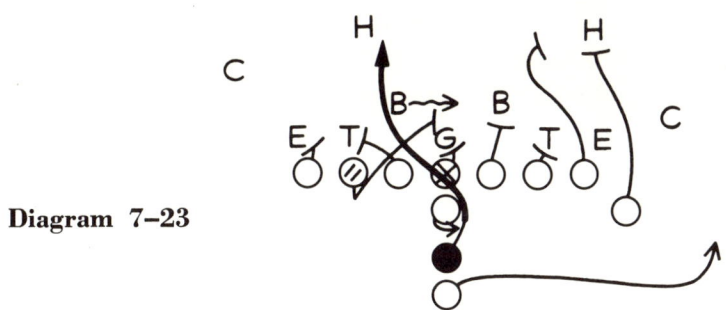

Diagram 7-23

Another excellent play with the same type of blocking is a quick fake to the fullback. The quarterback keeps the ball and counters through the guard and tackle fold block. This is illustrated in Diagram 7-24.

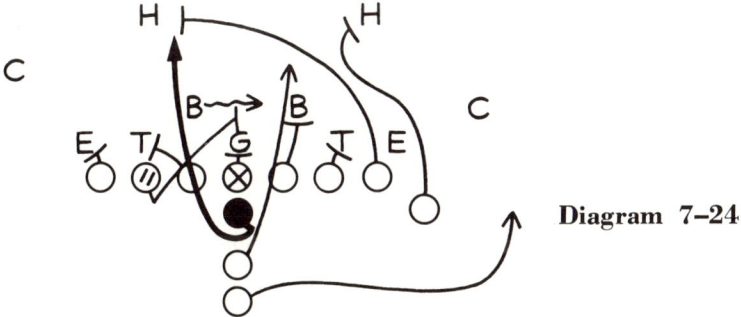

Diagram 7-24

A double-cross between both guards and tackles can be used. This is illustrated in Diagram 7-25 where the quarterback fakes a pitch to the right halfback and hands back to the tailback. The tailback looks for daylight.

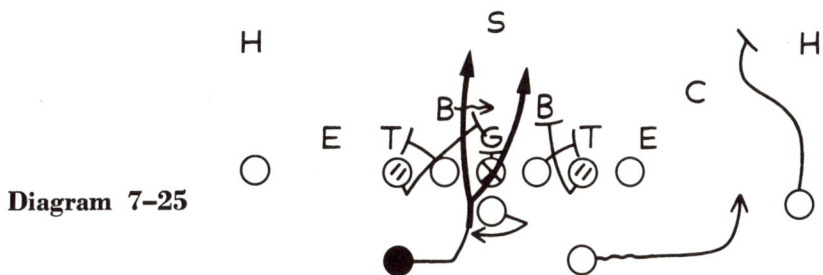

Diagram 7-25

Other excellent blocking variations up the middle are double-teaming, power, and isolation blocking. An excellent method is to double-team down on the middle guard with the center and offensive guard. Either one or two backs can isolate and power on the linebacker. Diagram 7-26 illustrates a play with two backs blocking. The linebacker is doubled by the halfback and fullback and the deep "I" back-runs over guard to find daylight. One man is shown isolating a linebacker from a slot formation in Diagram 7–27.

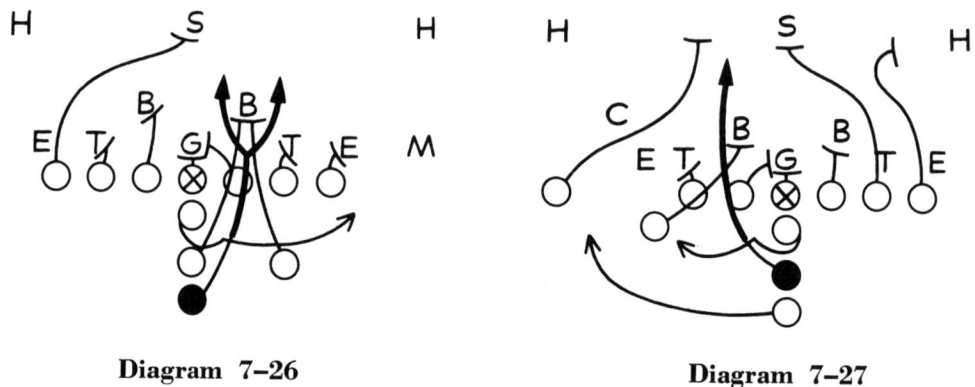

Diagram 7–26   Diagram 7–27

In this area of the defense, counters, scissors, and cross-buck plays are excellent. All methods and variations of blocks can be employed with the counters; i.e., power, isolation, angle blocking, straight, etc. Any plays that cause the linebackers and middle guard to start in one direction while the play goes opposite are excellent—blocking becomes easier for the blocker and the holes widen and enlarge for the ballcarrier.

Another method of double-teaming up the middle is for the guard to block out on the defensive tackle with the offensive tackle, and a back would then isolate the linebacker. While this can be run with a straight handoff, Diagram 7–28 illustrates it with a counter. The quarterback steps out to fake the fullback. The deep "I" back initiates one step to the left, then cuts back for the ball over the right guard. The right halfback blocks the linebacker.

Another method in blocking the middle area is out blocking with the offensive guard on the defensive tackle, the tackle on the defensive end, and the end block on the corner man. A back will then isolate the linebacker. Again this play is excellent as a counter and scissor type of play (Diagram 7–29).

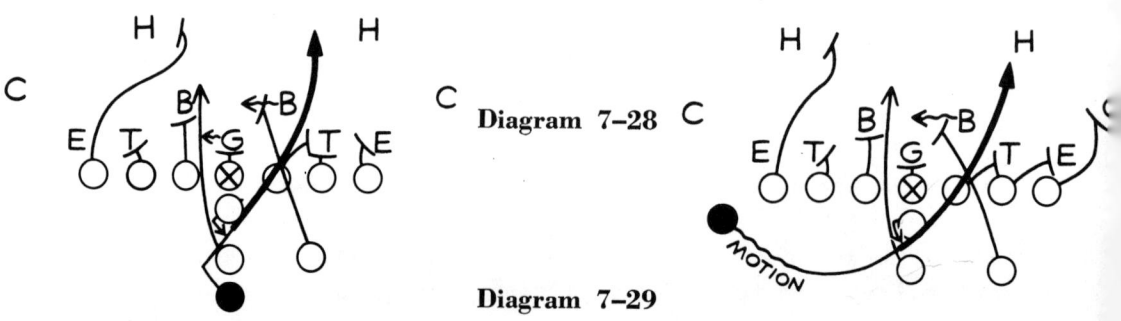

Diagram 7–28

Diagram 7–29

If the offensive coach finds the linebackers keying the offensive guards, such a play as the following may be effective: Diagram 7–30 illustrates a pull maneuver by the offensive guard to draw the linebacker in one direction. The wingback then executes a block on the linebacker and the center blocks the middle guard one-on-one. The quarterback fakes a pitch to the halfback and then steps back to hand off to the fullback.

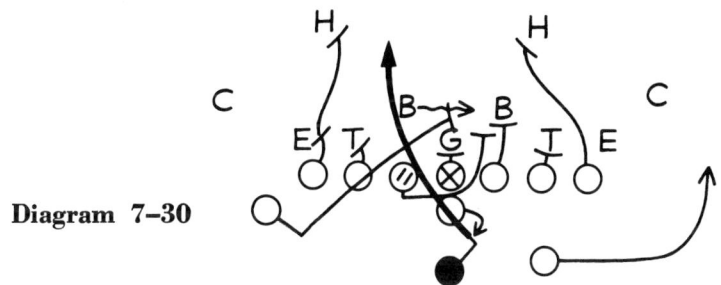

Diagram 7–30

The wedge play with the halfback or fullback carrying the ball over the guard area can be employed. Trapping the tackle with down blocking is excellent. The offensive tackle blocks down on the linebacker, the offensive guard blocks on the center, and the center angles on the linebacker. The far guard pulls and traps the defensive tackle. This can be used with straight plays, cross-bucks, and counterplays.

Bobby Dodd, former head coach of Georgia Tech University, sent this excellent countertrap (Diagram 7–31) for the 5–4 defense, that is used successfully from the Georgia Tech slot formation. The center blocks the middle guard, and the right guard and end double-team the linebacker. The right tackle moves out and blocks the defensive end, while the slotback fires out for the corner man. The left guard pulls from the line and traps the tackle. The fullback fakes over the pulling guard, and plugs the hole while the quarterback reverse-pivots and gives an inside handoff to the tailback.

Other plays can be executed up the middle area. The draw play is illustrated in Diagram 7–32 (next page) with a cross block between the right guard and center. Both ends and the flanker release downfield to drive the pass defenders

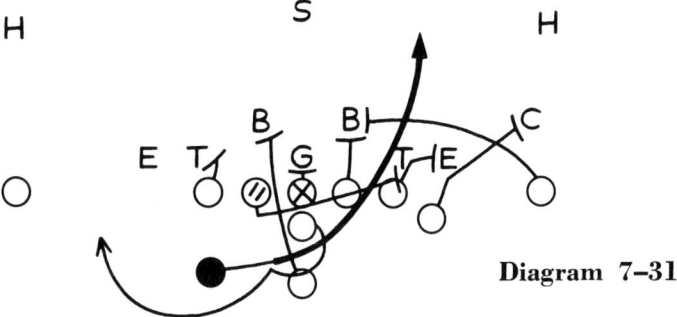

Diagram 7–31

deep. The left tackle, left guard, and right tackle drop back as if to pass protect, but after a quick count, fire out on their respective defensive men. The right guard drives down on the middle guard with a good angle block and the center steps around and fires for the linebacker. The fullback receives the ball and runs for daylight looking for the guard-center hole.

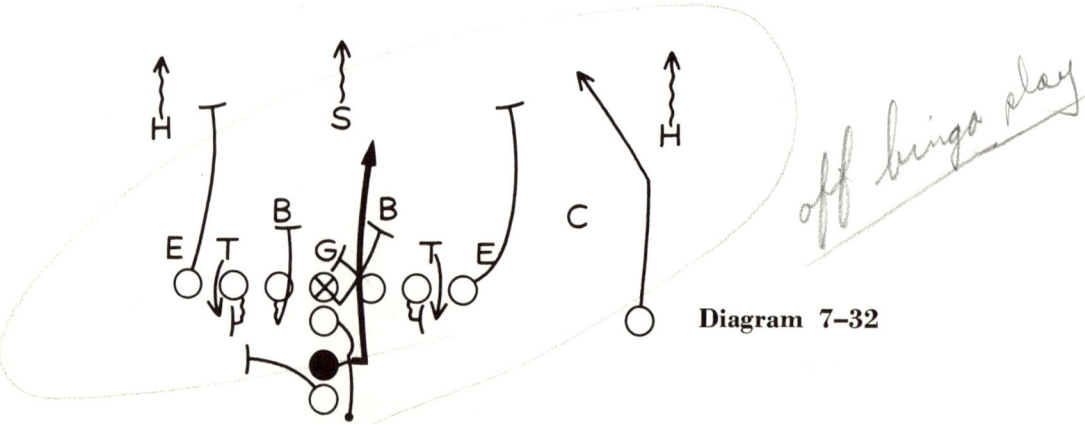

Diagram 7–32

Improper alignments must be attacked by the coach and quarterback. The quarterback should be continually aware if such errors exist. If the number 1 man (linebacker) is aligned on the inside shoulder of the guard, the play should run outside of him. If the linebacker is positioned far to the outside, the quarterback should run plays to the inside.

One of the best methods of attacking the off-tackle hole against the 5–4 defense is the double-team block by the end and tackle on the defensive tackle. One back, two backs, onside guard, or offside guard can easily block the defensive end out. Diagram 7–33 illustrates the offensive tackle and end executing a two-on-one block with the two "I" backs power blocking the defensive end. The offside guard pulls through the hole to become an extra blocker.

Another power play is illustrated in Diagram 7–34. The slotback receives the pitch and will run for daylight wherever the hole opens, either off-tackle or outside. This is an excellent play, especially with the rotation of the backfield toward the formation.

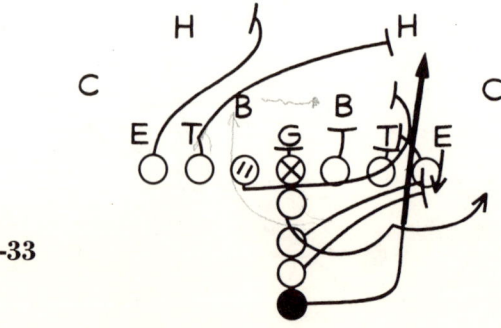

Diagram 7–33

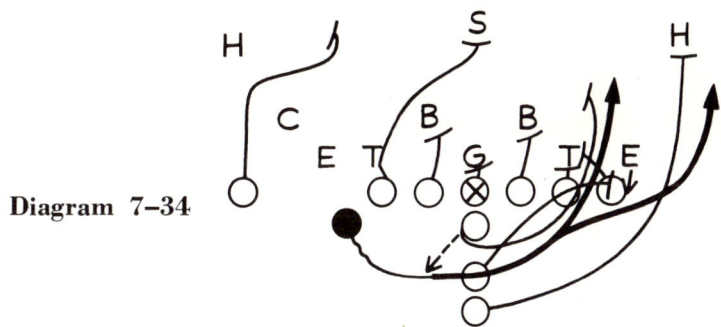

Diagram 7-34

Another excellent double-team can be executed by the offensive tackle and wingback. The end blocks the defensive end and any play (drive series, counters) off-tackle can be executed. An example would be the fullback belly off-tackle play with the quarterback faking the pitch to the trailing tailback. A fullback fake over the guard and a give to the halfback off-tackle, with the same blocking combination, is effective. In many instances the double-team is very successful because the defensive tackle commits to the faking fullback inside.

Angle blocking down with the offensive end and tackle on the defensive tackle and linebacker respectively, with the guard pulling on the defensive end, can be employed. Any backfield maneuver can be executed, including counter and scissor actions.

A combination of double-teaming and trapping can be used. Diagram 7-35 illustrates an inside reverse with a double-team block on the defensive tackle and a trap block by the offside guard on the defensive end. The right tight end opens up and gets approximately 2 yards in depth to turn through the hole. He looks for any linebacker or cornerback coming to the ballcarrier.

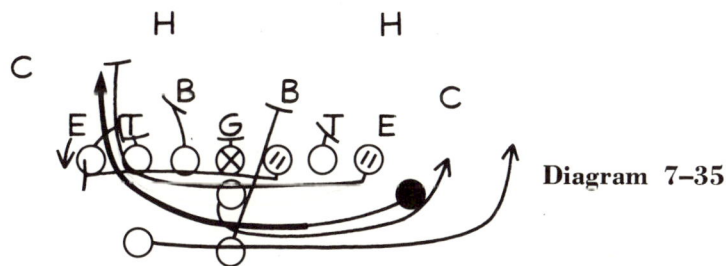

Diagram 7-35

Another excellent trap play with a slot formation is illustrated in Diagram 7-36. The slotback runs to the flat, attempting to draw the defensive end out, while the inside guard pulls out and traps him. The fullback leads through the hole for the linebacker.

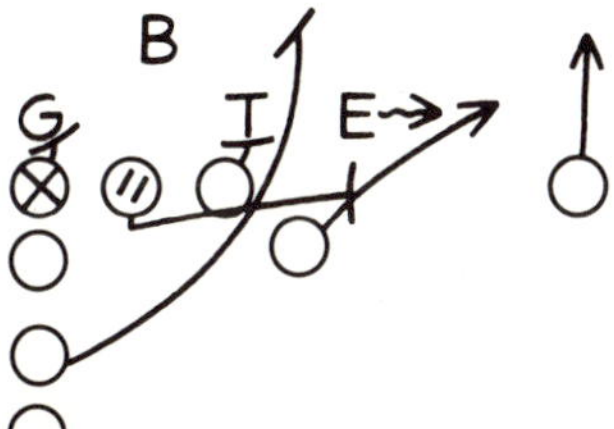

Diagram 7-36

Cross blocking can be used effectively between the end and tackle at times. If the defensive end utilizes a boxing technique, a cross block is good. If the defensive end moves down well to the inside, the cross block is not as effective. However, a good method to go outside is for the end to block down and, while the defensive end moves down to protect the inside, the tackle pulls out and hooks the defensive end. Again, the coach and quarterback must attack the alignment of the defensive tackle. If he aligns to the inside, the running attack should go outside. If the tackle is committing outside, the offense should go inside.

There are many methods in attacking the outside. Bobby Dodd of Georgia Tech University sent his power sweep (Diagram 7–37) from a slot formation. The end and slotback double-team on the defensive end, the right tackle, right guard, and center scramble block, and the left guard pulls and leads upfield. The quarterback reverse pivots and flips the ball to the tailback. The fullback blocks out on the number 4 man or cornerback.

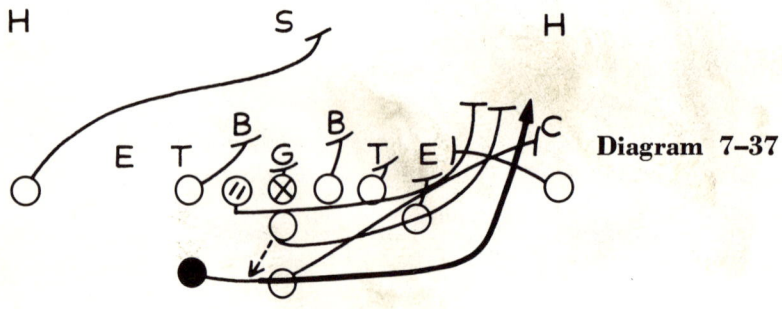

Diagram 7-37

The same power sweep can be executed with a wingback and tight end. Other blocking patterns and variations can be employed. Angle blocking down can be used. The wingback blocks the defensive end, the end blocks the defensive tackle, and the center scrambles the middle guard. One or both guards can pull. Any action in the backfield can be executed.

The fake off-tackle, with the fullback ride series and optioning on the corner man, is excellent. The option run-pass against the corner man can be utilized, also. Putting out flankers and spreading the offense to see how the defensive backfield adjusts should be done. The offense should attack the weaknesses of the coverages as described in Chapter 4. If the defense rotates fully, the defense can attack away from the flanker back.

With the split ends and flankers, the offense should run and pass accordingly. If the defense covers inside, the offense should utilize out patterns with the

THE 5-4 OKLAHOMA DEFENSE

passing attack. Going outside with the running, utilizing power, option, quick pitches, and reverses are excellent. However, if the coverage is outside, the passing patterns and running game should be geared inside of the wide defensive men.

If stunting is being employed by the 5–4 defense, all the methods to attack the stunts and blitzes should be used. Area blocking must be used with the offensive linemen. Check passes, quick passes, and jump passes against firing linebackers are essential. Wedge blocking, going outside away from internal stunting, spreading flankers, and splitting ends to minimize the stunting game can all be employed.

Diagram 7–38 illustrates the weaknesses of the 5–4–2 Oklahoma defense, with the strengths, weaknesses, best plays, and comments listed after it. Diagram 7–39 (page 163) indicates the coaches' defensive card that can be installed in the "Coaches' Directory of Football Defenses."

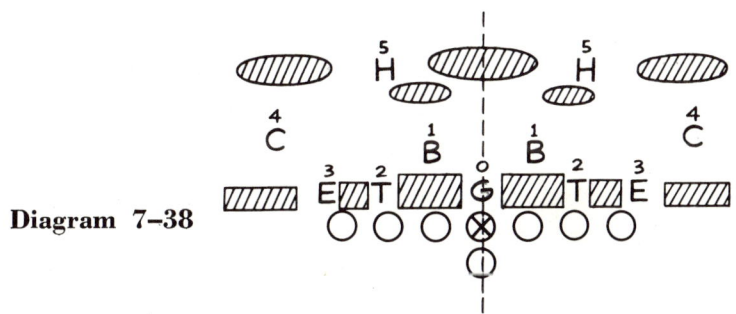

Diagram 7–38

Strengths: The 5–4 is an excellent running, pursuing, and containing defense. It is a nine-man front. The hook and flat areas are well covered. The defense is excellent against the split "T" offense. If the linebackers are strong, the defense is good.

Weaknesses: Over the middle and guard area. Attack off-tackle and corner men with the running game. Angle blocking and double-teams are good. Attack inferior personnel and improper alignments.

Best Plays Against the 5–4 Defense:

1. Attack the middle area with straight and cross blocking.
2. Double the middle guard and power the linebacker.
3. Double the defensive tackle and power, or isolate the linebacker.

SUCCESSFUL RUNNING PLAYS

TO THE LEFT	TO THE RIGHT

SUCCESSFUL PASSING PLAYS

SUCCESSFUL ACTION PLAY PASSES

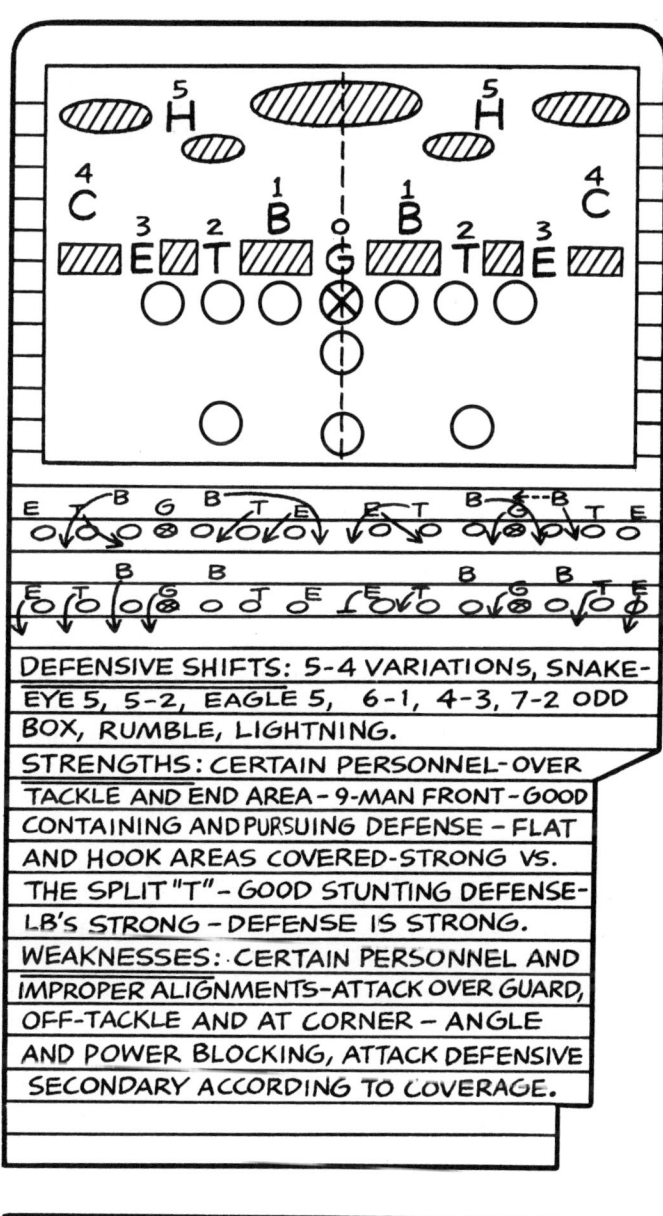

DEFENSIVE SHIFTS: 5-4 VARIATIONS, SNAKE-EYE 5, 5-2, EAGLE 5, 6-1, 4-3, 7-2 ODD BOX, RUMBLE, LIGHTNING.

STRENGTHS: CERTAIN PERSONNEL-OVER TACKLE AND END AREA - 9-MAN FRONT - GOOD CONTAINING AND PURSUING DEFENSE - FLAT AND HOOK AREAS COVERED - STRONG VS. THE SPLIT "T" - GOOD STUNTING DEFENSE - LB'S STRONG - DEFENSE IS STRONG.

WEAKNESSES: CERTAIN PERSONNEL AND IMPROPER ALIGNMENTS - ATTACK OVER GUARD, OFF-TACKLE AND AT CORNER - ANGLE AND POWER BLOCKING, ATTACK DEFENSIVE SECONDARY ACCORDING TO COVERAGE.

BLOCKING: STRAIGHT, CROSS, DOUBLE, ISOLATION, POWER, OUT BLOCKING, TRAPS, ANGLE BLOCKING - PULL LINEMEN - AREA BLOCK IF STUNTING.

Diagram 7-39
The 5-4 Oklahoma odd-box-corner defense

4. Utilize out blocks on the defensive alignment and isolate the linebacker with the wingback.
5. Employ all counters, scissors, and cross-bucks with any blocking patterns to freeze and hold the middle guard and linebackers.
6. Use faking plays to hold the linebackers.
7. Utilize the false key against the linebacker.
8. Attack improper alignments of the linebackers.
9. Trap the defensive tackle with straight, quick-hitting, and counterplays.
10. Utilize straight and cross blocking with the guard and tackle.
11. Double-team the defensive tackle with the tackle and end, and kick out with the halfback, fullback, or trapping lineman.
12. Double down with the wing or halfback and tackle on the defensive tackle and block out with the end on the defensive end.
13. Angle down with the end and tackle and trap out with the pulling guard.
14. Block straight, pull the onside guard, and trap the defensive end while an end or slotback influences the defensive end out.
15. Utilize options against the number 3 men or defensive ends.
16. Go outside with double-teaming on the defensive end.
17. Angle down and pull the offensive guards to go outside.
18. Employ the option run-pitch to the trailing halfback on the corner man. Attack the corner with the option run-pass also.
19. Utilize all counters, inside reverses, and reverses to hold and freeze the linebackers.
20. Utilize the play-action pass against the linebackers and the defensive secondary.
21. Split the offensive line to widen the defense if possible.
22. Split ends and put out flankers, and pass and run according to the coverage of the defense.
23. If the defense stunts, area block, go outside, wedge block inside, use check quick passes, split ends, and put out flankers.

Comments: Attack the 5–4 defense with angle, double-team, and power blocking. Straight blocking can be used especially when the defensive personnel are superior. Find the pass coverage of the secondary (invert, fully rotated, man-to-man, free safety, etc.) and attack accordingly.

8

THE WIDE-TACKLE 6 DEFENSE

The Wide-Tackle (Loose) 6 defense is an even six-man line with two linebackers stationed off the line of scrimmage (an eight-man front) and a three deep diamond secondary. Defensive linemen are aligned over the offensive guards and ends. The defensive guards are positioned over the offensive guards either in an inside, head up, or outside offset alignment. The defensive guards should keep a constant distance from each other whether the offensive line splits wide or not. The defensive tackles are aligned over the offensive ends and are either in an inside shoulder, head up, or outside shoulder position. The alignment of the defensive guards and tackles will be determined by the execution of the defense, the splits of the offensive line, the type of offense that is run at the defense, etc. The defensive ends are positioned on the line of scrimmage outside the offensive ends approximately 1 to 2 yards. This will depend on the alignment of the defensive tackle, the way the defense is executed, etc. The defensive linebackers are stationed over the offensive tackles approximately 1 to 3 yards off the ball according to the down and distance, and the other variances of the game already mentioned.

The Wide-Tackle 6 is a containing and pursuing defense. The defensive ends are in excellent position to contain the roll-out pass and run easily. The Wide-6 is an excellent stunting defense also. Another advantage of the defense is it can adjust to different offensive formations with minimum defensive movements. The defense can (although not mandatory) remain in a three deep secondary and does not have to rotate. The Wide-6 creates a good four-man rush on passing plays, with the three deep and four short zones adequately covered. Diagrams

8–1 and 8–2 illustrate the Wide-Tackle 6 in an inside shoulder and head-up alignment. The defensive personnel can align on the outside shoulder of their offensive counterparts if the offensive linemen's splits are closed down tight.

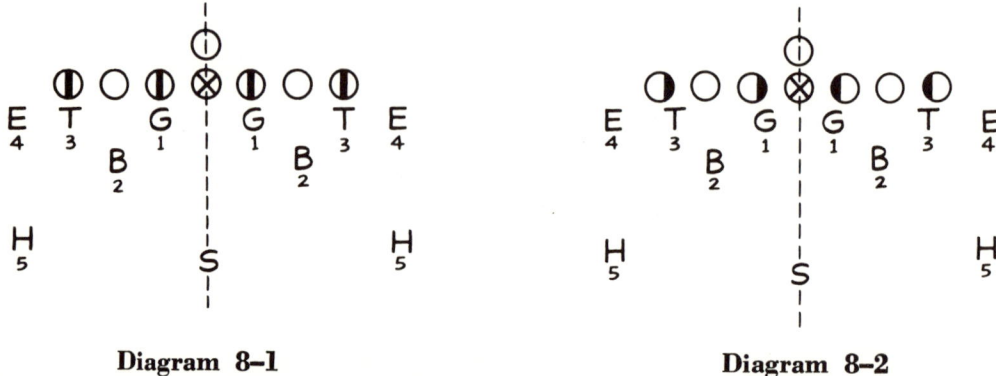

Diagram 8–1 **Diagram 8–2**

The type of personnel essential for the Wide-Tackle 6 defense will vary. Many coaches desire the defensive guards to be big and strong and to shut off the inside running attack of the offense. These men should particularly be aware of the middle trapping game. The defensive tackles positioned over the offensive ends should have adequate speed, react both inside and outside, rush the passer hard, and be able to chase the ballcarrier from behind. The defensive ends must be strong and fast to protect and contain the outside running attack of the offense and assist quickly on the passing game also. The defensive linebackers should be quick and fast for both the running and passing game, but strong to meet the offensive tackle when the play comes toward them. Diagram 8–3 illustrates the pursuing angles and responsibilities when the flow of the ball goes to the left; if the flow of the ball is to the right, the opposite would occur.

In Diagram 8–3 the defensive left end, tackle, linebacker, and guard attack the play directly, as quickly as possible. The defensive right guard and end takes proper pursuit angles to the ballcarrier. The defensive right tackle chases the play behind the line of scrimmage looking for the reverse, bootleg, cutback, etc.

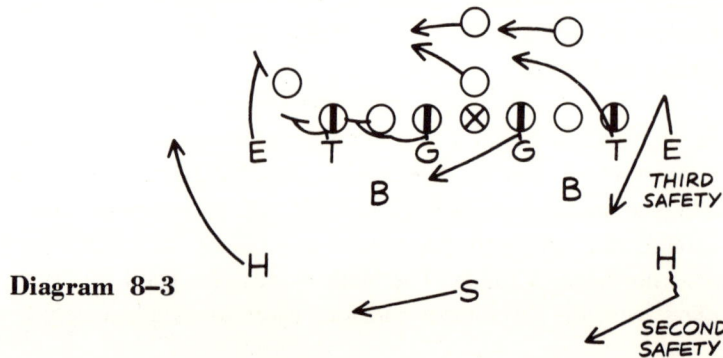

Diagram 8–3

THE WIDE TACKLE-6 DEFENSE

The left halfback attacks the play directly, while the safety and right defensive halfback are the first and second safety men respectively.

PLAYING THE WIDE-TACKLE 6 DEFENSE

The following is the alignment, stance, initial movement and execution, responsibilities, and coaching points of each position in the Wide-Tackle 6 defense:

DEFENSIVE GUARDS (Number 1 Men)

Alignment: Line nose up, inside shoulder, or outside shoulder of the offensive guard. Can automatically line up in either of the three positions even if splits are normal. Align 1 to 4 feet off the guard according to defensive play.

Stance: A low three- or four-point stance, with feet parallel or in a toe-instep relationship.

Initial Movement and Execution: Step with the outside foot, and forearm shiver with the outside shoulder and arm. Some coaches teach stepping with the inside foot first and hitting with the outside shoulder. Stay low and read and react to the movements of the offensive guard and center.

Responsibility: Responsible for the inside, sneak, quick trap, wedge, and draw plays. Should not be taken by a fake in backfield.

1. Play Toward—(1) Stop trap first—Offensive guard pulls past center step laterally to the nose of the center, fight block and play trap.

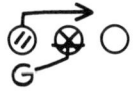

If guard pulls toward end, step in the direction of the pull. If no pressure, step to inside and play trap.

If pressure from outside (offensive tackle), read backfield action and fight outside pressure.

(2) Defeat the single block of the offensive guard. Fight double-team pressure from both offensive center and guard, or tackle and guard.

2. Play Away—Play offensive guard area, then pursue. If sprint-out is away, look for the draw.
3. Drop Back—Rush the passer. One or both guards can be conscious of the draw. If one guard has the draw the other rushes the passer hard.

Coaching Points: Strike a hard blow into the offensive guard. Do not run around the block. First responsibility is the inside, then go outside.

DEFENSIVE LINEBACKERS (Number 2 Men)

Alignment: Align head up with the offensive tackle approximately 2½ to 3 yards off the ball. This will depend on the tactical situation and strategical planning.

Stance: A low two-point stance, with either the feet parallel or in a toe-instep relationship.

Initial Movement and Execution: Read and key the movement of the offensive tackle, then react to the play.

Responsibility:
1. Play Toward—Step up and meet the offensive tackle with a low forearm shiver. If the offensive tackle blocks out or in, step up, stay low, and be prepared for isolation, power, and trap plays.
2. Play Outside—Protect area, then pursue. If sprint-out or roll-out pass, can either sprint to the flat and cover that area or slide down the line, pick up the offensive end, and stay with him to the hook area (slightly wider than the drop-back pass). Secondary containment of the quarterback if end or tackle loses containment.
3. Play Away—Check for the counter, then pursue to the ball. Stay at your position if the backfield divides, then pursue. If sprint-out or roll-out away, check for the draw and drive back picking up crossing receivers (or to hook zone).

THE WIDE TACKLE-6 DEFENSE

    4. Drop Back—Sprint to the hook area approximately 10 to 15 yards in depth. Play any receiver in your area. Stay alert for screens, draws, etc.

Coaching Points: Stay low and meet offensive tackle low, hold ground. Second, contain man on running plays to the outside. Be quick and fast on pursuit.

DEFENSIVE TACKLES (Number 3 Men)

Alignment: Line nose up to inside or outside shoulder of the offensive end approximately 12 to 18 inches off the ball.

Stance: A three- or four-point stance.

Initial Movement and Execution: Step with the outside foot and deliver a blow with the outside shoulder and forearm. (May step with inside leg first and on the second step strike a blow with the outside shoulder and forearm.) Read and react to the offensive end and tackle movements.

Responsibility: Responsible for off-tackle area and inside.
    1. Play Toward—Play territory and protect against the straight dive. If outside, fight through the end's block and attempt to force the pitch on the option play.
    2. Play Away—Read the offensive end. Be alert for the trap, then chase looking for the reverse, bootleg, etc.
    3. Drop Back—Hit end and never let him release to the inside. Be contain man and rush from outside-in.

Coaching Points: Strike a hard blow into the offensive end and stay square to the line of scrimmage. Do not penetrate when there is no pressure; be aware of the trap. When hitting end, do not overextend in executing the charge.

DEFENSIVE ENDS (Number 4 Men)

Alignment: Line up approximately 1 to 2 yards from the defensive tackle. This will depend on the alignment of the defensive tackle, down and distance, sideline, etc.

Stance: A low two-point stance with the outside leg back.

Initial Movement and Execution: On the snap of the ball, jab step with the inside foot and react to the play.

Responsibility:
1. Play Toward—Contain on all wide plays. Drive across line. Force everything to the inside. Do not give ground. "Ball comes, I come."
2. Play Away—Drop back to the flat area and look for the reverse, throwback pass, bootleg, cutback, etc., then pursue to the ballcarrier. "Ball go, I go."
3. Drop Back—Go immediately to the flat zone and turn to the outside. Cover area and sprint to ball.

Coaching Points: Push everything to the inside when the play comes toward. Be tough and hold ground. Meet play with inside shoulder and leg, keeping the outside leg and arm free. Keep shoulders parallel to the line of scrimmage.

(under the 5–3 In Odd-Diamond defense) for a detailed account of the defensive halfbacks.

DEFENSIVE SAFETY Look to Chapter 6 (under the 5–3 In Odd-Diamond defense) for a detailed account of the defensive safety.

Diagram 8–4 illustrates the defensive coverage for the passing game when the quarterback rolls to the defense's left. The opposite or mirror would be true if the quarterback rolled in the other direction. The diagram indicates that the defensive backs are in a drop-back zone. However, the defensive secondary can utilize other coverages, such as rotational, man-to-man, etc. If rotation or man-to-man occurs, both the defensive end and linebacker can put pressure on the contain man, while the defensive halfbacks and safety cover their respective assignments.

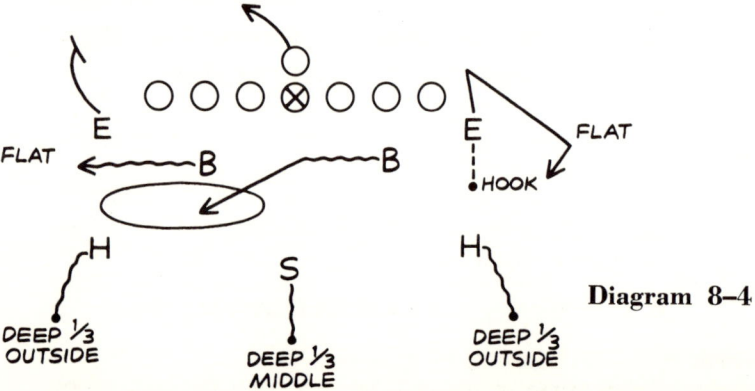

Diagram 8-4

ADJUSTMENTS TO FORMATIONS

If the offense splits an end, there can be numerous adjustments made by the Wide-Tackle 6 defense. The defensive guards will maintain the same position on the offensive guards. When the offensive end splits, the defensive end will cover him. The defensive end will play on the outside shoulder of the offensive end up to a point of 4 yards. Beyond this position the defensive end will play in a double-up, walkaway, or tight alignment. The defensive tackle can maintain the same relative position as if the offensive end were tight and should not be hooked by the offensive tackle from this position. From this alignment, the defensive tackle can be the contain man on all roll-out and/or sprint-out passes while the defensive end can cover in the flat zone. The defensive linebacker will play in his normal position. If a roll-out is to the linebacker's side, he does not have to cover the flat, because the defensive end has taken that responsibility. The defensive linebacker, therefore, can cover on passes in the flat or hook areas, or can be a contain man with the defensive tackle on outside plays. The three deep secondary must maintain defensive position on the split end.

Another split end coverage occurs when the defensive tackle aligns on the offensive tackle, while the defensive linebacker can either align between the defensive guard and tackle or stack behind one of these defensive men. The defensive end can play double-up, walkaway, or tight position. The linebacker, however, can play the walkaway position while the defensive end positions double-up with the split end. Still another method is for the defensive end to play one of the three positions on the split end while the defensive linebacker aligns over the offensive center and becomes a middle linebacker.

If a slot formation occurs, the defensive guards will align in the same relative position. The defensive ends will play the widest man in the slot formation up to 5 yards and will maintain the same responsibilities. If the widest man (split end) is spread more than 5 yards, the defensive end will split the difference between the split end and the slotback. If the slotback is more than 2 yards split from the offensive tackle, the defensive end will align on the outside shoulder of the slot man. In this situation, the defensive end will cover the flat on roll-outs toward him. The defensive tackle will align head up to the slot man if he is 2 yards or less from the offensive tackle. If the slotback is more than 2 yards split from the offensive tackle, the defensive tackle can either align head up to the inside shoulder of the slotback or can position on the offensive tackle. Again the defensive linebacker will play in his normal position or will stack behind the defensive guard or tackle, maneuver to the outside for a certain defensive alignment, or will station over the offensive center, as previously stated.

If a wingback is positioned outside the offensive end, the defensive end can position on the outside shoulder of the wingback. The defensive tackle will align more in a head-up position on the offensive end. The defensive tackle will read the wingback, offensive end, and tackle. The wing and tackle read will depend upon the offensive team and the type of plays run in that area.

If the offensive team stations a flanker, the defensive end will play outside the flanker, up to a point of 4 or 5 yards. If wider than this point, the defensive end will come back to his normal alignment and execute his responsibilities. It must be remembered, in the above situations, that the defensive secondary must adjust to all of the wide and diversified formations.

If the offensive line begins to split and attempts to spread the defense, the defensive line and linebackers must adjust accordingly. The defensive guards can position in the center-guard gaps, the linebackers will station in the guard-tackle seams, and the defensive tackles will align in the tackle-end gaps. The defensive ends will adjust down to the outside shoulder of the offensive ends.

If long motion is executed by the offense, the defense can disregard it, unless the offense continually hurts the defense with it. If this is the case, the defense may have to adjust with the defensive end or linebacker to the side of the motion. Numerous methods can be used, and the offense should find the defensive adjustments, and attack the weaknesses created by the motion man from there.

STUNTS, BLITZES, FIRES, AND ANGLES

The Wide-Tackle 6 defense is an excellent stunting and blitzing defense. Many defensive maneuvers can be executed with the six-man line and the two linebackers. Diagram 8-5 illustrates a fire charge by the defensive linebackers. On the snap of the ball, the linebackers will drive hard over the offensive tackles, but keep the same keys. If the flow of the ball is toward him, the linebacker must not go to either side of the offensive tackle, but should play tough and stop the dive man. If the ballcarrier should go wider, the firing linebacker must hit the offensive tackle and slide outside with the play. If the flow of the ball is away, the linebacker must strike a blow and pursue quickly to the ballcarrier. If the offensive tackle pulls, the linebacker should be free and should sprint in the direction of the ball. The interior guards, with the firing technique, should be extra careful and conscious of the trap. The defensive tackles can align slightly wider and hold up the offensive ends. The linebacker must rush the passer hard, because he has given up the hook zone.

A stunt can be executed between the defensive guards and linebackers. Diagram 8-6 illustrates the defensive guards driving through the guard-tackle gaps

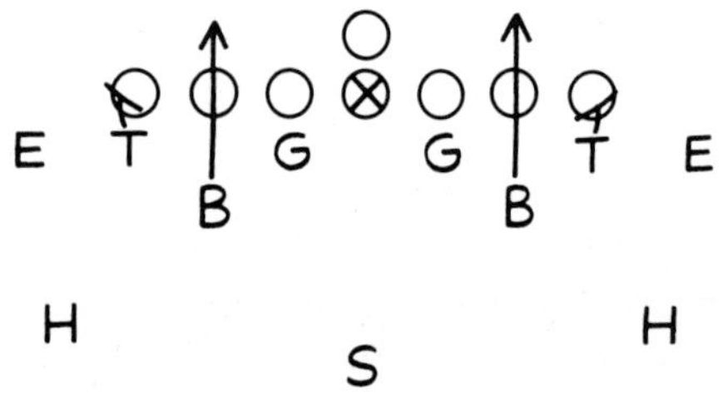

Diagram 8–5

THE WIDE TACKLE-6 DEFENSE

while the linebackers fire the center-guard seams. Diagram 8–7 indicates a safer stunt with the linebackers charging in the same manner, but the defensive guards angling out on the offensive tackles. The defensive guard, in this situation, should strike a blow with the inside shoulder using a forearm lift. On contact, the defensive guard should square up to the line of scrimmage, stay low, and be in a position to move quickly. The defensive tackles will strike a blow with the outside shoulder and will not allow the offensive end to block them in. The defensive tackles should stay square to the line of scrimmage and fight to the outside.

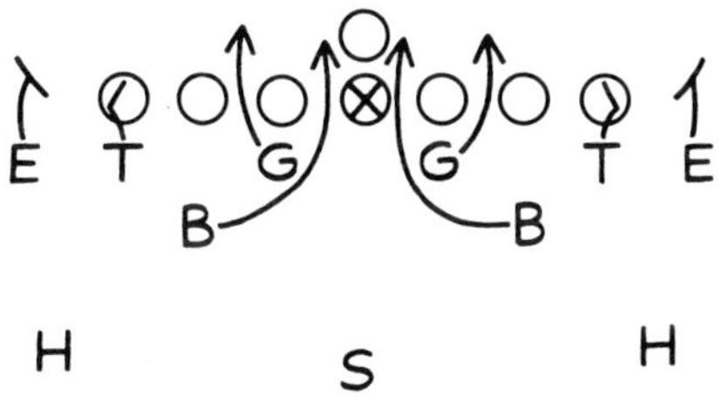

Diagram 8–6 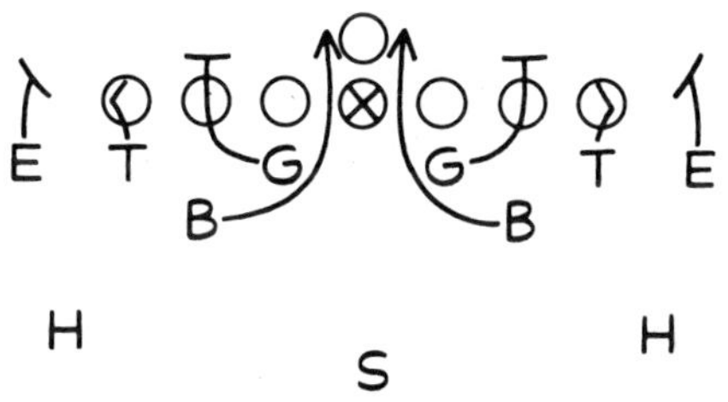   **Diagram 8–7**

A blitz is shown in Diagram 8–8. One side of the line, or both sides of the line, can execute the blitz. The defensive guard and linebacker can fire, or one entire side can blitz. Any desirable amount of players can be employed for the defensive charge.

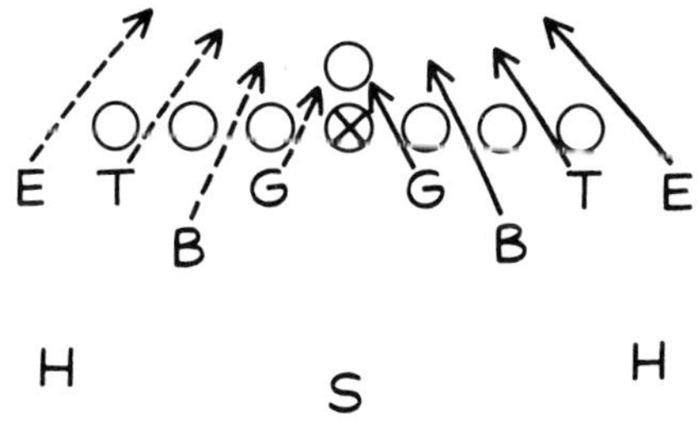

Diagram 8–8

A stunt executed by the defensive tackle and linebacker is illustrated in Diagram 8–9 (next page). The defensive tackles initiate a slant charge through the neck of the offensive tackle protecting over the offensive tackle area. The defensive tackle's responsibility is not to be blocked out by the offensive tackle, not to be cut off by the end, to fight for containment, rush on drop-back pass, and chase on flow away. The defensive linebacker's responsibility is to maintain the same key in the backfield, be prepared to meet the offensive end if the offensive backs come in that direction, drive over the end when flow comes toward, and pursue to the ball. The defensive guards will utilize an inside charge into the offensive

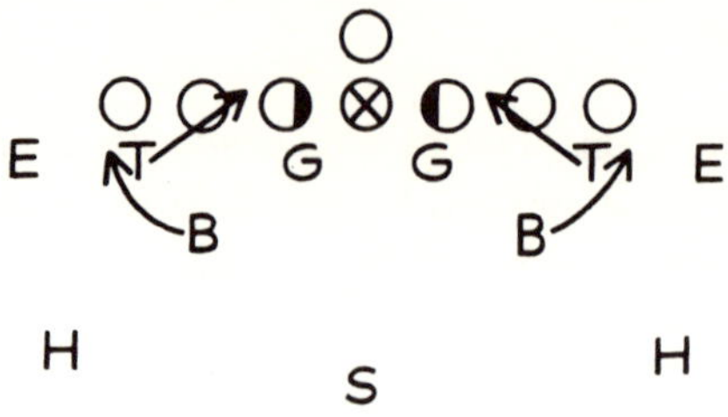

Diagram 8–9

guards and will be extra careful of the trap play. The defensive ends play a normal Wide-6 end. The same type of charge, but with a different aiming point can be executed with the defensive tackle. Instead of aiming at the neck of the offensive tackle, the defensive tackle should make an aggressive charge at the outside hip of the offensive tackle and play that position as previously mentioned. The disadvantages of this stunt are the turn-out block by the offensive tackle, the containment on drop-back passes, weakness in the end area, and the defensive linebacker cannot assist on trap plays up the middle area. The advantages of such a charge are that it protects well over the offensive tackle area and is a change of pace maneuver.

Another stunt can be executed by the defensive tackle, end, and linebacker. As illustrated in Diagram 8–10 the defensive tackle slants down through the neck of the offensive tackle as previously mentioned. The defensive end will drive hard through the outside hip of the offensive end, aiming for a point in front of the offensive fullback. The defensive end is responsible for the off-tackle area and any cut maneuver by an offensive back outside. The defensive end will contain on a drop-back pass, force everything toward him deep if the tackle cannot be made, and chase if the flow of the ball is away. The defensive linebacker keys the triangle of the halfback, fullback, and quarterback and moves outside for containment if flow comes toward him. If flow goes away, the linebacker checks for a counter, bootleg or reverse and then pursues the ballcarrier. On a drop-back pass the linebacker covers the outside hook zone, and on a roll-out toward him, he covers the hook if the defensive end contains. The linebacker plays normal if the roll of the backfield is away, but plays the halfback if the backfield splits. The disadvantages of this stunt are the trap play and the poor coverage in the flat area. However, it creates a good outside rush and is good against the off-tackle power and belly play.

A stunt between the tackle and end is illustrated in Diagram 8–11. The defensive end has the same technique and responsibilities as indicated in Diagram 8–10. The defensive tackle, however, steps around the driving end and comes to a point approximately 1 yard deep in the backfield and outside the original

Diagram 8–10

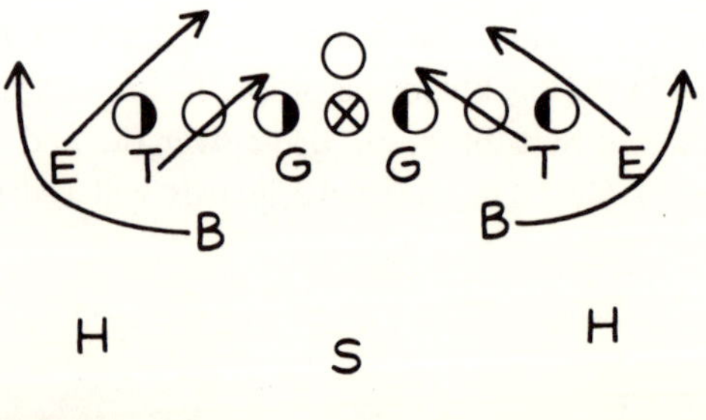

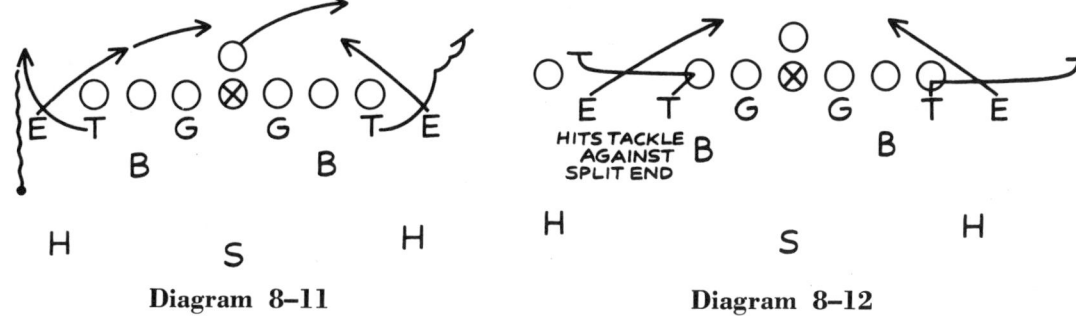

Diagram 8–11   Diagram 8–12

alignment of the defensive end. The defensive tackle will contain on flow toward, cushion if flow is away, and cushion about 15 yards deep on the drop-back pass. If a bootleg occurs, the tackle will cushion first and contain second, if the ballcarrier gets around the defensive end. The disadvantages of this stunt are the flat area on drop-back passes and poor containment on a bootleg pass. However, it creates a good rush for the bootleg, a good outside rush on a pass play, and forces the play quick on both the option and power sweep.

Another type of "X" charge is illustrated in Diagram 8–12. The defensive end crashes hard and fast into the backfield for the fullback. If a wing is positioned outside the offensive tight end, the defensive end will crash over the wing's outside hip. The defensive tackle will deliver a blow into the offensive end and attempt to hold the end up. The defensive tackle will maintain outside leverage on the offensive end and immediately release to the outside to cover against the screen pass. The defensive tackle is the secondary contain man if the ballcarrier gets outside the defensive end.

Angling from the Wide-Tackle 6 can easily be accomplished. Diagram 8–13 illustrates an angle to the right (Wide-6 "rumble") with the explanations as to each position's assignments and responsibilities. The opposite or mirror would be the same for each position to the left (Wide-6 "lightning").

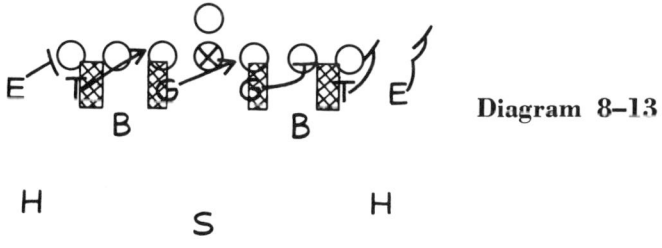

Diagram 8–13

LE: On the snap of the ball, slide to the inside and tighten up on the offensive end. Deliver a hard blow into the offensive end and do not let him release on the linebacker. Execute a 5–4–2 defensive end play.

LT: Slant charge through the offensive tackle protecting over the tackle area. Chase play when flow of ball is away.

LG: Slant charge through the offensive center and drive through him hard if he attempts to turn out.

RG: Line up slightly deeper off the ball and execute a loop charge to a head-up position on the offensive tackle. Key the offensive guard's block and do not be hooked by the guard's gap charge if there is a big split between the offensive guard and tackle.

RT: Execute a loop charge to the outside shoulder of the offensive end and force flow toward. Contain the sprint-out and bootleg pass, chase on flow away and do not be cut off.

RE: Secondary contain man when the offensive tackle and/or guard loses it. Cover the flat on the sprint-out, drop-back, and bootleg pass. Cushion on flow away.

Linebackers: Key the backfield triangle and cover the squared areas. Read the flow and go to your responsibility. However, be aware of the cut outside by the offensive back, sneak, or fullback slant over the offensive guard, and the trap play. The pass coverage on the Wide-6 "rumble" is the same as the regular Wide-6 defense.

The greatest danger of the angling line is the flow away from the angle; however, the advantages are the motion coverage and the defensive end coverage in the flat area.

Diagram 8–14 illustrates another angling maneuver from the Wide-Tackle 6 defense. In this situation, however, not all the defensive linemen will angle.

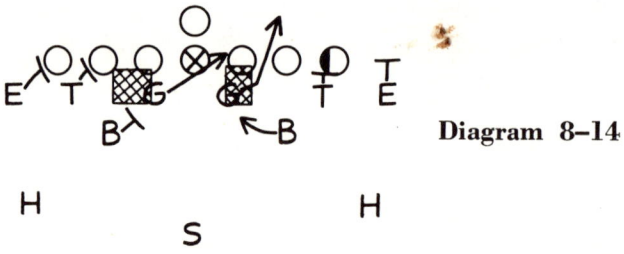

Diagram 8–14

LE: The defensive end plays the same as the Wide-6 "rumble," but does not get as tight to the offensive end.

LT: The left tackle plays the same Wide-6 tackle, but steps into the offensive tackle instead of the end. He will key both blockers as before, but will be careful of the trap play.

LG: Same execution of the Wide-6 "rumble" defense.

RG: Gap charge between the guard and tackle. Do not be cut off by the guard when 1 yard depth is reached.

RT: Execute normal Wide-6 tackle play.

RE: Execute normal Wide-6 end play.

THE WIDE TACKLE-6 DEFENSE

LLB: Key the triangle and be responsible for the squared area. Key flow for dive, sneak, and trap toward. Execute the same pass coverage as the Wide-6 defense.

RLB: Key the triangle and be responsible for the squared area. Key flow for the fullback slant and trap toward. Same pass coverage responsibilities.

The weakness of this angling charge is the flow away from the slant and the quick handoff play. Advantages to this defense are that it stops the trap in the middle area and can be used toward the field without showing overshift by the defense.

DEFENSIVE SHIFTS

The defensive linebackers can easily shift behind the defensive guards, as illustrated in Diagram 8–15. The tandemed defensive players can easily stunt and angle as was illustrated previously. Diagram 8–16 shows the linebackers in a tandemed position firing the center-guard gaps. The defensive guards shoot the guard-tackle holes (or can loop out on the offensive tackles) while the defensive tackles and ends can execute an "X" maneuver. If the defensive ends and tackles cross, they must protect the off-tackle area, because the linebackers are going hard to the inside.

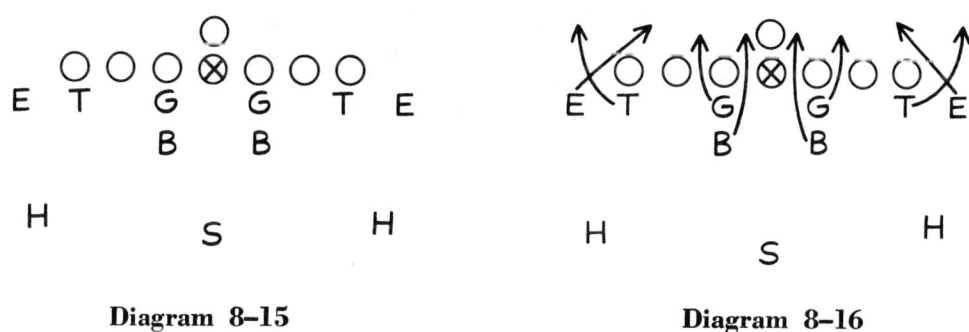

Diagram 8–15   Diagram 8–16

Diagram 8–17 indicates the defensive guards in the gaps and the linebackers stacked directly behind. Angling and stunts can still be accomplished.

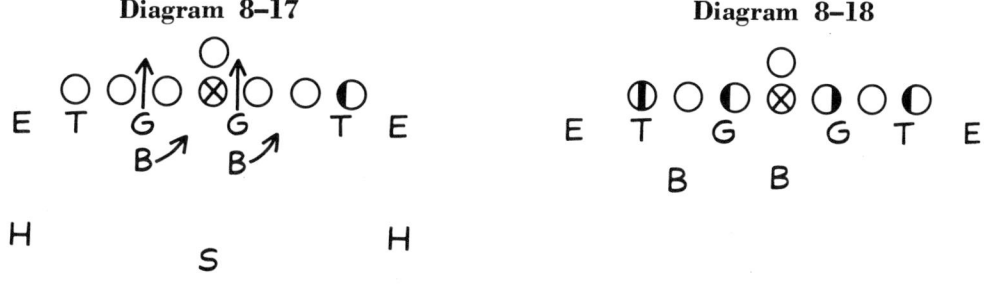

Diagram 8–17   Diagram 8–18

The defensive linebackers can overshift to one side of the defensive line especially against a strong formation as illustrated in Diagram 8–18. In this situation the left linebacker has remained the same, but the right linebacker has adjusted over the offensive center. The left end plays normal and the left defensive tackle aligns in a head-up position. The left and right defensive guards play on the outside shoulder of the offensive guards and the right defensive tackle aligns on the inside shoulder of the defensive end. From this alignment the right defensive tackle can adjust on the offensive tackle and the defensive end can align on the offensive tight end. Another defensive shift is the right defensive tackle position head up to the offensive tight end and the defensive end "stack" behind him. The defensive end in this situation will key the triangle and if the flow is toward will support to the outside. On the option, the tackle should take the quarterback, while the end takes the pitch man. If the offense sprints out, the defensive end is the second contain man while the tackle is the first. The linebackers can adjust to the right (opposite that of Diagram 8–18) and the same adjustments can be made to the left with the left end tandeming behind the tackle. When the linebacker overshifts, the disadvantage is toward the weak side.

Stunts can easily be done with the overshift and new stunts can be executed with the middle three; i.e., defensive guards and middle linebacker. The defensive guards can execute a gap charge through the center-guard gaps while the middle linebacker can support to either guard-tackle hole. Angling away from the overshift by the two interior defensive guards can easily be accomplished also.

A regular 6-2-3 defense can be shifted to from the Wide-6 defense. The defensive tackles align on the offensive tackles and the defensive ends adjust over the offensive ends. The two linebackers maneuver anywhere along the line of scrimmage (Diagram 8–19).

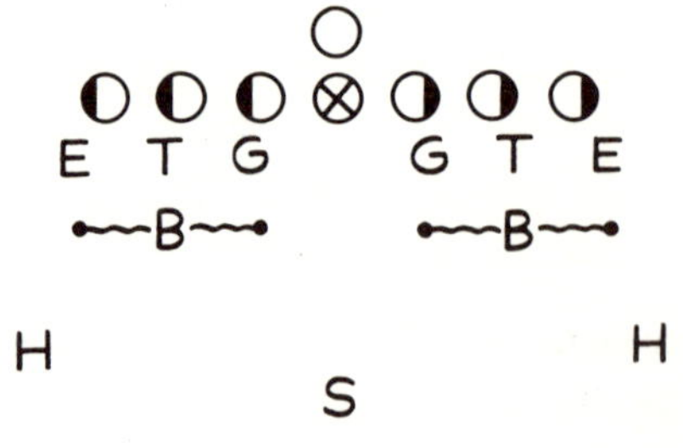

Diagram 8–19

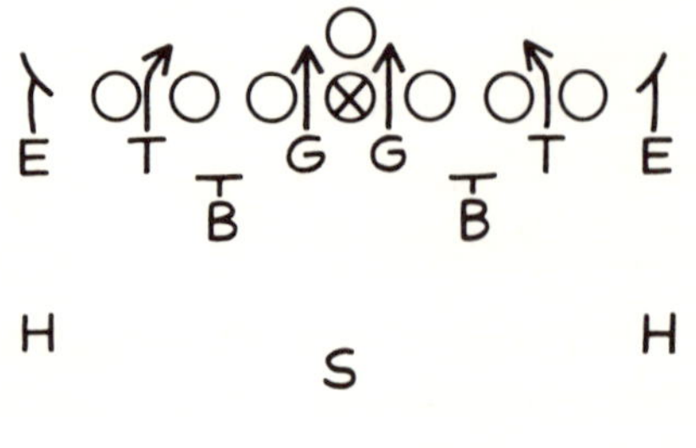

Diagram 8–20

As mentioned previously, the Wide-6 can easily adjust into the gaps and this is illustrated in Diagram 8–20. It gives the defense more strength inside and reduces the splits of the offensive line. Other defenses to which the Wide-Tackle

THE WIDE TACKLE-6 DEFENSE

(Loose) 6 Even-Diamond defense can shift easily are the 4–4 Even-Diamond defense with its many variations, the 4–4 Tandem Even-Diamond defense, the Tight-6 Even-Diamond, the Split-6 Even-Diamond, the Gap-8 Even-Diamond, the Stack or Tandem-6 Even-Diamond, the 5–3 In (Out) Even-Diamond, the 7–1 and its variations, etc.

ATTACKING THE WIDE-TACKLE 6 EVEN-DIAMOND DEFENSE

THE STRENGTHS OF THE WIDE-TACKLE 6 DEFENSE

The strengths of the Wide-Tackle 6 defense are as follows:

1. The defensive guard area is strong.
2. The end area: Is there a bigger defensive tackle on the offensive end? The defensive tackle can hold up the offensive end from releasing the line for a pass.
3. The Wide-Tackle 6 defense is relatively stronger outside than inside.
4. The defense eliminates the double-team power block over the off-tackle area.
5. The defensive ends are in good position for containment on the running and passing plays outside and off-tackle.
6. The Wide-Tackle 6 employs a three deep secondary.
7. The hook areas and the long passing game are adequately covered.
8. The defense is effective against a delaying offense.
9. The linebackers are in a position to pursue quickly and easily.
10. The Wide-Tackle 6 is a good stunting defense.
11. The Wide-Tackle 6 can make overall adjustments to offensive formations easily.
12. The defense can jump to other defenses quickly and easily.

THE WEAKNESSES OF THE WIDE-TACKLE 6 DEFENSE

The weaknesses of the Wide-Tackle 6 defense include the following, and the weakness areas are illustrated in Diagram 8–21 (next page).

1. Wide offensive splits can hurt the defense.
2. The middle area or over the offensive center: There is a three-on-two relationship wtih the center and two offensive guards against the two defensive guards.
3. Over the offensive tackle: Is the offensive tackle bigger and stronger than the linebacker? Linebacker must stop the dive play.
4. The flat areas for the passing game are relatively uncovered by the position of the defensive ends and linebackers.

5. The inside is relatively weaker than the outside for the running game.
6. The defense is vulnerable to traps if played straight.
7. There is a seven-on-six relationship for the offense from end to end.
8. Power and isolation at the linebackers.
9. Quick-hitting plays are effective against the Wide-Tackle 6 defense.
10. The split "T" running attack is effective.
11. Stunting may cause certain weaknesses.
12. The short middle zone between the linebackers for the passing game.
13. Attack the three deep pass defense secondary according to its coverage.

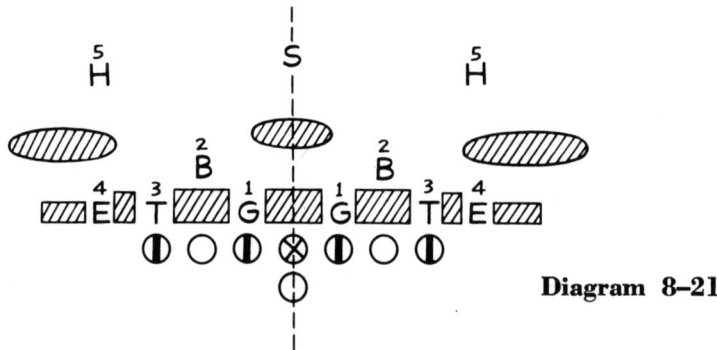

Diagram 8–21

ATTACKING THE AREAS OF THE WIDE-TACKLE 6 DEFENSE

The offense should attempt to spread the defense wider. This is apparent in the middle area of the defense. The offensive guards should take a wider split than usual to force the defensive guards out, creating a wider hole. The defensive guards will either align in a head-up, outside, or inside position on the offensive guard. This will probably be determined by the split of the offensive line. The offensive guards should make a study of their opponent to see how the defensive guards align in certain situations. If the defense is slanting and looping, the offensive guards should attempt to locate a tip-off or cue giving the defense away.

In the middle area of the Wide-Tackle 6 defense, over the offensive center and guards, there is a three-on-two situation in favor of the offense. If the defensive guards are in a head-up alignment, straight blocking can be used. The offensive guards block the defensive guards and the offensive center goes downfield or picks up an offside linebacker.

Double-team blocking can be utilized with the center and guard blocking on one of the defensive guards and the opposite guard taking the other defensive guard. Diagram 8–22 illustrates the double-team block, with a counter-action in the backfield.

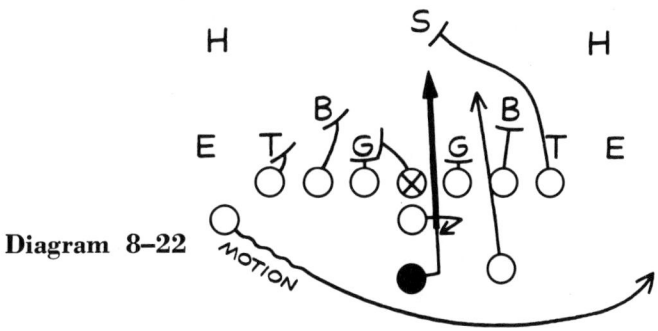

Diagram 8–22

The right tailback fakes a dive play over the offensive tackle hoping to hold or freeze the left defensive guard. This creates an easier block for the right offensive guard. The offensive center and left guard double on the right defensive guard. The same type of play can be employed, but with a slightly different blocking adjustment: Instead of doubling on the number 1 man, as illustrated in Diagram 8–22, the left offensive guard can pull to the left and block the defensive number 2 man or linebacker. In this case, the left offensive tackle can block out on the defensive tackle and the left end can release for a downfield block. The offensive center blocks the defensive guard one-on-one. The same procedure can be executed, but the left offensive guard can assist in a double-team block on the linebacker with the left tackle. It must be remembered, however, that some type of fake is essential on the other side of the line to hold or "freeze" the defensive left guard and linebacker.

The type of play to be utilized in the middle area, with straight and double-team blocking, can be quick-hitting fullback and halfback plays with a quick handoff by the quarterback. The quarterback sneak is effective also. Any type of counter-action in the backfield to freeze the defensive linemen and linebackers should be employed.

Another excellent method in attacking the middle area is the employment of the pull-around technique. Coach Bill Tate, formerly of Wake Forest College, Winston-Salem, North Carolina, sent the following play (Diagram 8–23) with the pull-around maneuver. The right offensive guard blocks the number 1 man, the center angles down on the right defensive guard, and the left offensive guard pulls around and blocks on the linebacker. In this situation, the fullback steps toward the guard-tackle gap and the quarterback reverse pivots as if to ride the fullback wide. This tends to hold, again, the left defensive guard and linebacker for a slight instant. The fullback then cuts back over the middle area. The left tackle can either block the linebacker or block out on the defensive tackle.

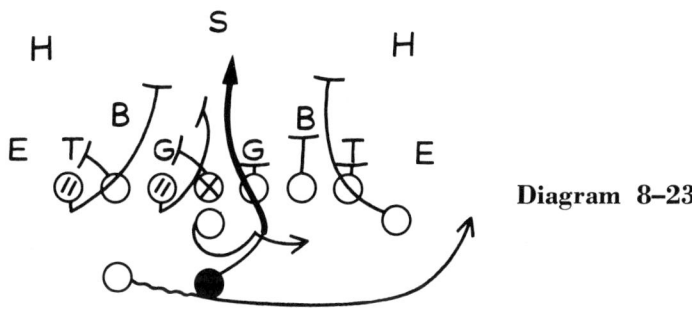

Diagram 8–23

Another method in blocking up the middle area is to angle block down, with the center on the number 1 man. The offensive guard, for whom the center is blocking, will pull out and block the opposite defensive guard. This type of block would be a double-team, because the other defensive guard would stay in and block. This type of blocking action is good whether the defensive guards are in a head-up, inside, or outside shoulder alignment. Any action in the backfield can be employed.

One of the most effective blocks up the middle area is the short trap executed by one of the offensive guards. This type of block can be employed whether the defensive guards are aligning head up on the inside or outside shoulder. Any type of backfield action can be utilized with the blocking up front. As illustrated in Diagram 8–24, the center angles down on the number 1 man and the left offensive guard pulls and traps the left defensive guard. The right offensive guard pulls and blocks the linebacker, and the right offensive tackle comes across the center and blocks the far linebacker with the left offensive tackle. In this situation, the quarterback reverse pivots and hands quickly to the fullback. Any other backfield action can be utilized, especially with some counter-action to hold the defensive line and linebackers.

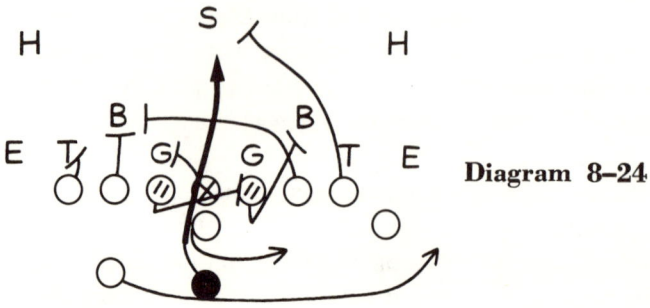

Diagram 8–24

The right guard who pulls to the right can block out on the defensive tackle also, and the right offensive tackle, instead of going for the far linebacker, will block the linebacker directly positioned over him.

As was mentioned previously, any action in the backfield, such as the blocking previously described, can be utilized. Wedge plays are effective. If the offense is receiving a great deal of pressure from the two defensive guards, the draw, middle screen, and some type of shuffle pass should be employed. A type of block for the draw is a trap block by the offensive guards and center with the remaining line using draw blocking techniques.

If the defensive guards are angling and stunting in the middle area, area blocking techniques should be employed. Stepping toward the play and picking up

THE WIDE TACKLE-6 DEFENSE

loops and angles must be accomplished. If the offensive play is going to the outside, scramble blocking with the offensive guards on the defensive guards can be done, especially if the defensive personnel is bigger and stronger. Pulling can easily be accomplished with the onside and offside guards and/or the offensive center and onside-offside tackles.

The offense should attack the number 1 defensive man. If he is aligned to the inside, the offense should attack outside. If the defensive guard is positioned to the outside the offense should go inside. A quick halfback or fullback dive at the defensive guard can be employed with a quick cut to either side by the offensive back depending on the reaction and movement of the defensive guard. The offense should fake inside and go outside or fake outside and run inside the defensive guard. The inside and outside drive series is an example.

Another method to attack over the offensive guard position is to cross block between the offensive guard and tackle. The offensive tackle will angle block down on the defensive number 1 man and the offensive guard will step around at the linebacker. Any quick-hitting, power, or counterplay at that area could be employed.

The offense should attack over the offensive tackle area. The first question that should be asked is, "Is the offensive tackle bigger and stronger than the defensive linebacker?" If so, then the offense should immediately attack this vulnerable area. Straight blocking can easily be utilized. The offensive guard blocks the defensive guard, the tackle blocks the linebacker, and the end blocks the defensive tackle. The quick dive play, with the halfback driving over the offensive tackle, is effective. The halfback will cut either right or left according to the movement of the linebacker. Counterplays can be employed also.

Power and isolation plays are very effective against the Wide-Tackle 6 defense. Straight blocking with a wing or tailback (Diagram 8–25) on the defensive linebacker can be utilized.

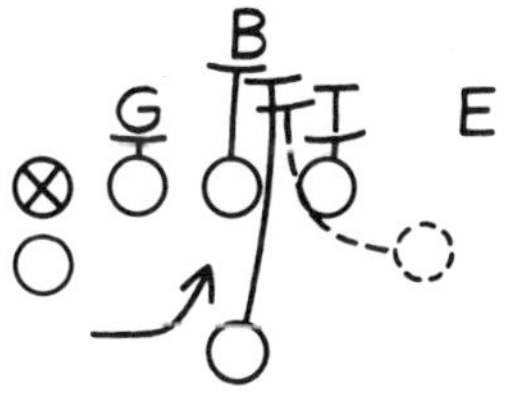

Diagram 8–25

Out blocking, with the offensive tackle on the defensive tackle and the offensive end on the defensive end, can be employed. The wingback or tailback blocks the linebacker. This type of blocking (Diagram 8–26) is excellent whether the defensive tackle aligns to the inside, head up, or outside the offensive end.

Diagram 8–26

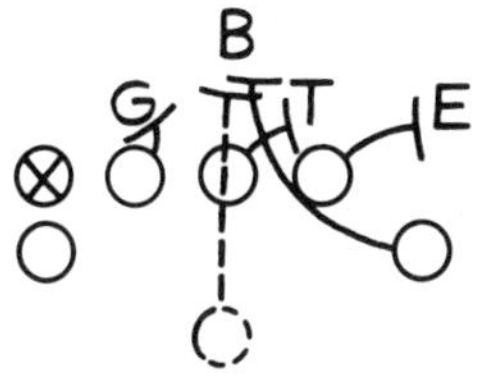

Another method in blocking the off-tackle area is double-teaming the defensive tackle and isolating the linebacker with one or two offensive backs (Diagram 8–27). Still another method is to block out on the defensive tackle with the offensive tackle, and with the offensive end assisting on the linebacker (Diagram 8–28).

In Diagram 8–27 the double-team can be employed whether the defensive tackle is head up outside or inside shoulder of the offensive end. However, in the second case, (Diagram 8–28) it is best to utilize this when the defensive tackle is either inside or outside shoulder of the offensive end, because the offensive end may not be able to get to the linebacker.

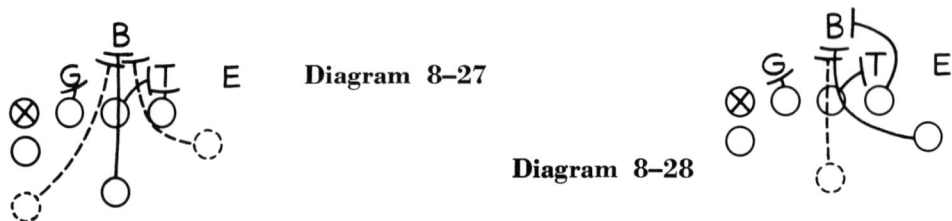

Diagram 8–27

Diagram 8–28

Frank Navarro, head football coach of Columbia University, sent the following play (Diagram 8–29) from the "Pro" set which has been very successful for him. One year it averaged 4.3 yards per carry. Coach Navarro feels the most dangerous man is the defensive tackle and, therefore, double-teams him. John Pont, head football coach at Indiana University, Bloomington, Indiana, sent the

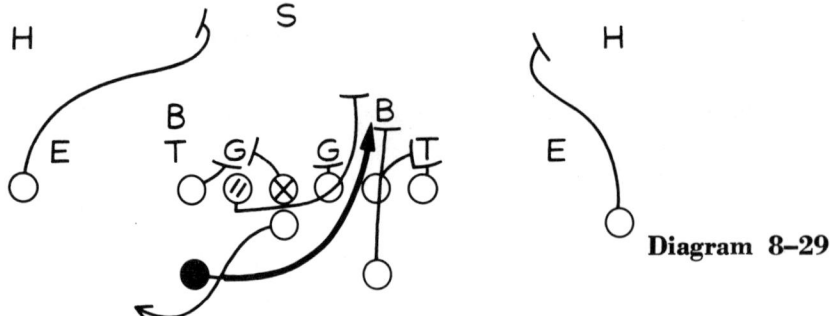

Diagram 8–29

same type of play but from a tight wing alignment, as illustrated in Diagram 8–30.

If the defensive guard is handling the offensive guard, a double-team block on the number 1 man with the offensive guard and tackle may be necessary. The offensive end blocks the defensive tackle and one or two backs double on the linebacker (Diagram 8–31). This, again, can be utilized with any type of backfield action.

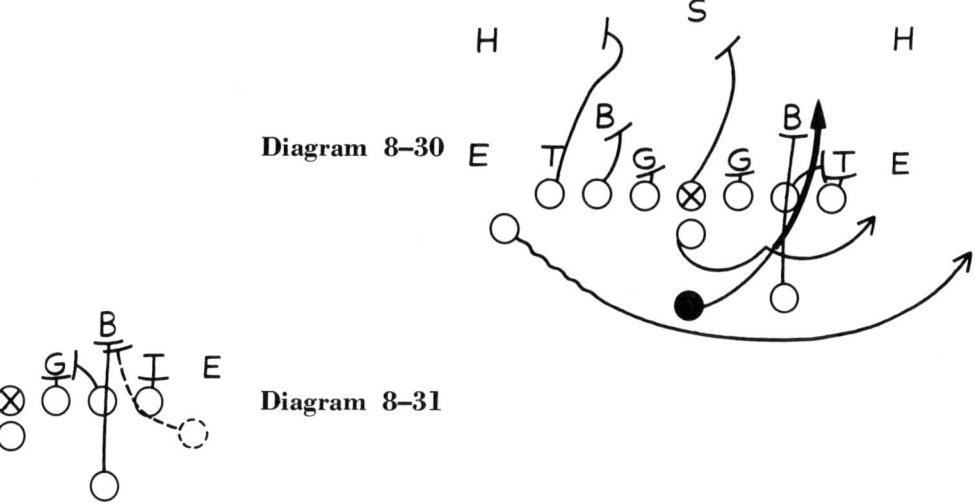

Diagram 8-30

Diagram 8-31

Trapping the defensive tackle can be employed also. The offensive tackle blocks down on the defensive guard and the offensive end steps for the linebacker. The offensive guard pulls out and traps the defensive tackle. The offside guard can pull and trap the tackle, especially on the reverses and counter-action plays.

Another effective method off the tackle area is illustrated in Diagram 8-32. The offensive tackle angles down on the defensive guard and the offensive left guard traps the defensive tackle. The left end blocks out the defensive end and, in this case, the fullback blocks the linebacker. The tailback takes the handoff from the quarterback and looks for daylight.

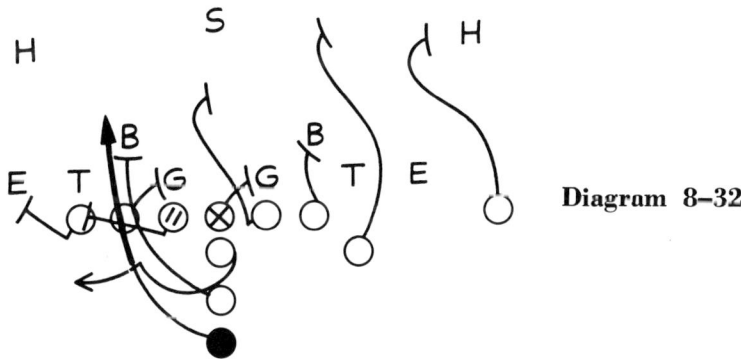

Diagram 8-32

A different type of block at the point of attack is indicated in Diagram 8-33 (next page). The right tackle and end block out on the defensive men as shown. Instead of the wingback coming in on the linebacker, he takes a different course for the linebacker. It is hoped that the fake of the fullback will hold the linebacker for an instant and the wingback will then drive on him.

A cross or fold type of block can be used off-tackle, with the offensive backs employing any action in the backfield. Diagram 8-34 (next page) illustrates a counter-action in the backfield, with the right tackle blocking out on the defensive tackle and the offensive end stepping behind for the linebacker.

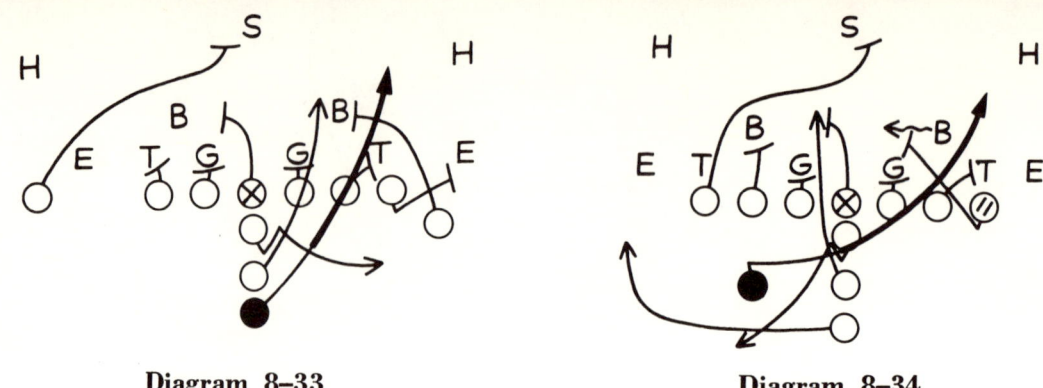

Diagram 8-33   **Diagram 8-34**

Reverses can be run off the tackle area also. The following reverse (Diagram 8-35) was sent by Coach Alex Bell, former head football coach of Villanova University. In this situation, the quarterback rides the fullback at the off-tackle hole to the right. The left halfback will fly one count. The wingback receives an outside handoff and runs for daylight. The offensive guards block the defensive guards, while the center pulls and blocks on the defensive linebacker. The left offensive tackle and end block out on the defensive tackle and end respectively.

It must be remembered that if the number 3 man or defensive tackle aligns and plays to the outside, the offense should attack inside. If the defensive tackle plays to the inside, certain blocking combinations must be used to run in that area. The offense should attack to the outside also. Faking plays inside and outside the number 2 and 3 men should be employed. Making the defensive personnel commit to the fake will assist the offensive play outside.

If the defensive personnel begin to align inside to stop the inside running game of the offense, the offensive linemen should block down and trap the defensive end or number 4 man. Kicking out with the halfback or fullback on the defensive end can be employed, with double-team blocking being executed on the defensive tackle. This situation is illustrated in Diagram 8-36 from both a wide slot and wide flanker situation. In both cases, the wide men come down and seal on the defensive linebacker.

Diagram 8-35

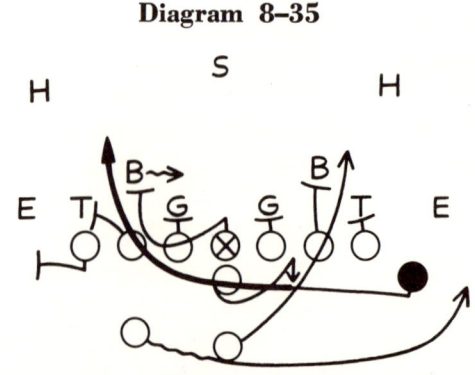

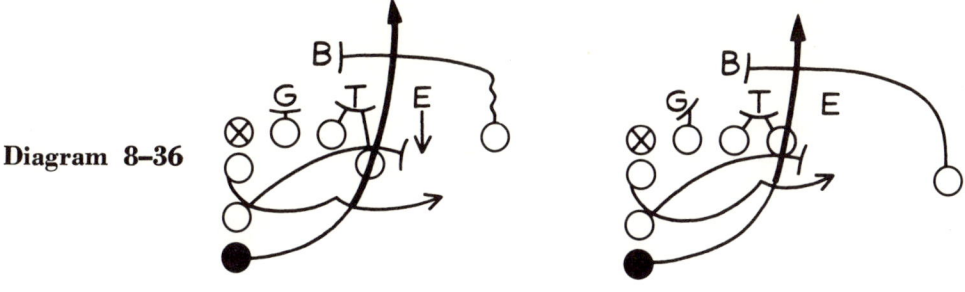

Diagram 8-36

In all the situations presented on attacking the off-tackle area, pulling by the offensive center, offside guard, or offside tackle was not discussed. However, pulling by one or two of these men through the off-tackle hole is very conceivable. Of course, it will depend a great deal on the type of play run and the timing of it. The offensive center can pull easily, because no defensive man is aligned over him. The offside guard can pull with the center angle blocking down on the defensive guard. The offside tackle can pull with the center, again going for the linebacker.

The offense should attack outside the defensive end. Double-teaming can be utilized with pulling executed by one, two, or three offensive linemen. Both offensive guards can pull while the other remaining lineman angle blocks down on the defensive guards. The center and offside tackle can pull also, depending upon the type of play involved. If the defensive personnel align to the inside, angle blocking down with the offensive linemen can be utilized.

Attacking outside with option plays against the defensive end should be employed. Faking to the fullback off-tackle and optioning the defensive end with a trailing halfback is effective. This is especially true if the defensive tackle is closing off to the inside and protecting the off-tackle area. The split "T" running attack should go against this type of defense unless defensive personnel is superior. The fake dive play to "freeze" the defensive linebacker and tackle is another necessity.

Since the defensive end is in a position to halt the outside running attack, the offense should attack the "open" flat areas. Whether the defensive linebacker or the defensive end cover in this area, such a play can cause difficulty for these men. The sprint-out pass is an example of this. The quarterback rolls out creating pressure on the defensive end. A wingback, if stationed outside the offensive end, should get to the flat quickly before the defensive end can recover or the linebacker gets to that area. The quarterback should key the defensive end—if he comes, the quarterback should throw; if the defensive end stays back, the quarterback should run. A halfback pass is effective and the defensive end is in a bind as to whether to rush the passer or stay back for the receiver. All play-action passes should be utilized, especially to hold and freeze the defensive line and linebackers.

The offense should put men in motion to see how the defense adjusts. If no adjustments are made, the offense should capitalize on the motion man. Covering motion by the Wide-Tackle 6 defense may cause difficulties for the defense.

The defensive end or linebacker may have to adjust, which may cause shifting in the defensive line. The offense should find these shifts and attack the weaknesses that may result.

The offense should split ends and put out flankers, and run and pass accordingly. If the defensive personnel cover to the inside, the wide man should angle down and the offense should go outside with options, power, quick pitchouts, bootlegs and reverses. Pass according to the coverage of the defensive backfield: If man-to-man, send out an extra receiver and make a linebacker or defensive end cover him. If the defense covers wide on the spread receivers, the offense should run and throw more to the inside. (Look to Chapter 4 on attacking pass defenses.)

If the defense continually angles, stunts, and blitzes, the offense must area block along the entire line to pick up the different defensive maneuvers. Utilizing the check pass series, going outside, employing wedges, and so forth, are a few methods to be utilized against the stunting game.

Diagram 8-37 illustrates the weakness areas of the Wide-Tackle 6 defense with the strengths, weaknesses, and best plays against the defense, and comments following it. Diagram 8-38 (page 191) indicates the Wide-Tackle 6 card for the "Coaches' Directory of Football Defenses."

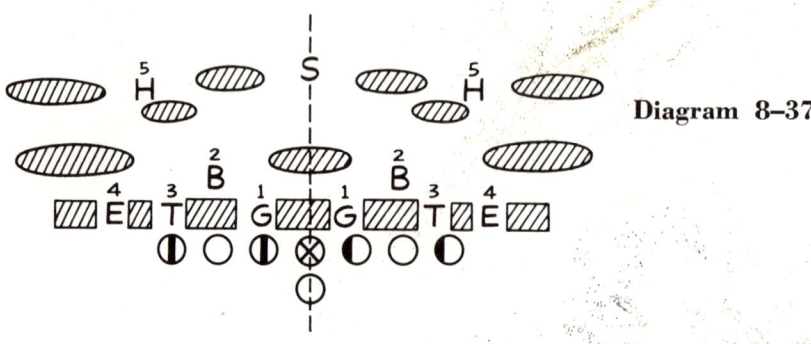

Diagram 8-37

Strength: Certain personnel make the defense strong. The defensive guard and end areas are covered. The defensive tackle can easily hold up the offensive end from releasing the line. The defense is stronger outside than inside. The defense utilizes a three deep secondary. The hook areas are well covered. The defense is a good stunting defense. It can shift to other defenses easily.

Weakness: Certain personnel and improper alignments make the defense weak. The middle area is weak with a three-on-two situation. The offense should attack over the tackle area. The flat areas for the passing game are considered weak. The defense can be vulnerable to traps. The defense is an eight-man front. The split "T" running attack should go against this defense.

Best Plays Against the Wide-Tackle 6 Defense:

1. The offense should utilize straight blocking in the middle area. Double-teaming can be employed with the center and one of the offensive guards also.
2. The pull-around technique can be used up the middle area.
3. Halfback and fullback traps between the two offensive guards should be employed.
4. Any quick-hitting play up the middle area with the blocking described should be utilized.
5. Counters with the blocking mentioned. Sneaks and wedges up the middle are effective.
6. Utilize the draw, middle screen, and shuffle pass if the defensive guards are putting pressure up the middle.
7. The offense should attack the number 1 man or defensive guard. Go inside if aligning outside, and go outside if positioned inside.
8. Is there a bigger offensive tackle on the defensive linebacker? Employ straight blocking with a halfback or fullback dive. Utilize cross blocks between the offensive guards and tackles.
9. Utilize power and isolation at the off-tackle hole by utilizing straight power with double-team blocking on the linebacker, and out blocking with power on the linebacker.
10. Double out on the defensive tackle and block the linebacker with one or two backs, or double in on the defensive guard and isolate the linebacker.
11. Angle down with the offensive end and tackle on the linebacker and defensive guard respectively and trap the defensive tackle with the offensive guard.
12. Angle down with the offensive tackle on the defensive guard and trap out on the defensive tackle. A halfback or fullback can lead on to the linebacker. Utilize cross and fold blocking also.
13. The offense should employ straight, counter, and reverse plays with the blocking mentioned at the off-tackle area.
14. Pulling of offensive linemen, to run off-tackle and go outside, can be used effectively for power, etc.
15. The offense should attack the alignments of the number 2 and 3 men. Go inside the defensive tackle if he is aligned to the outside and vice versa if aligned inside.
16. Go outside with pitchouts, option plays, power sweeps, bootlegs, and reverses. Utilize angle blocks, pulling linemen, and double-team blocking.
17. The offense should employ the option run-pass, play-action passes, etc. at the defense.

SUCCESSFUL RUNNING PLAYS

TO THE LEFT	TO THE RIGHT

SUCCESSFUL PASSING PLAYS

SUCCESSFUL ACTION PLAY PASSES

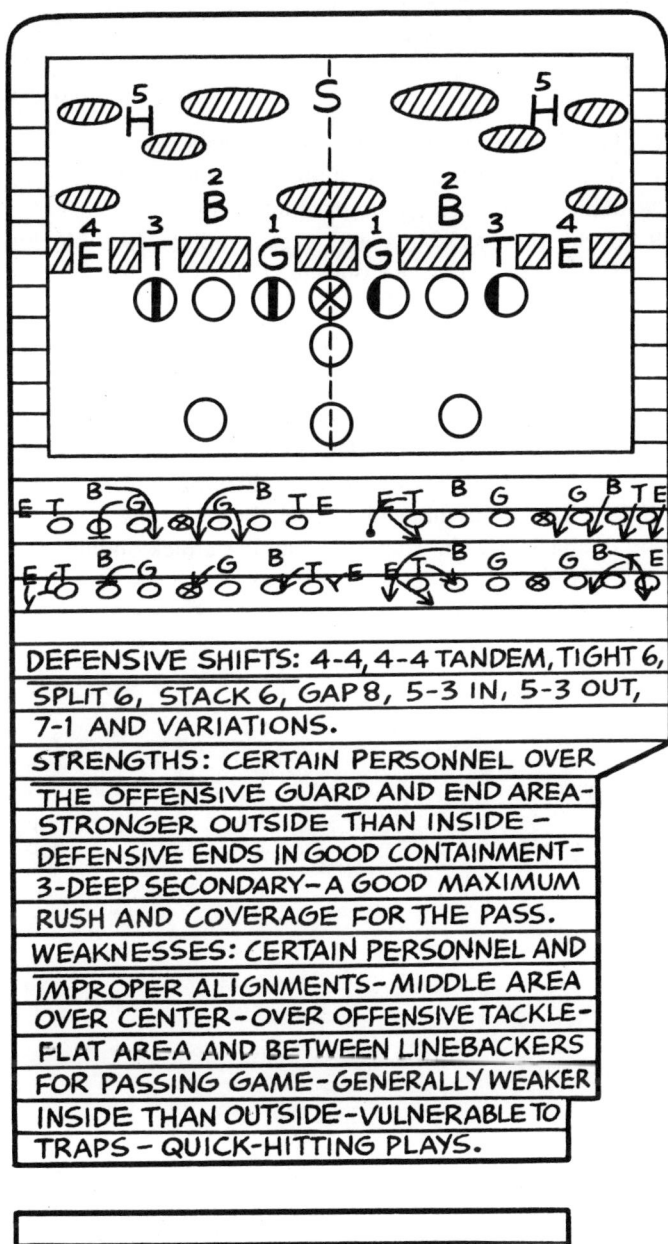

DEFENSIVE SHIFTS: 4-4, 4-4 TANDEM, TIGHT 6, SPLIT 6, STACK 6, GAP 8, 5-3 IN, 5-3 OUT, 7-1 AND VARIATIONS.

STRENGTHS: CERTAIN PERSONNEL OVER THE OFFENSIVE GUARD AND END AREA— STRONGER OUTSIDE THAN INSIDE — DEFENSIVE ENDS IN GOOD CONTAINMENT— 3-DEEP SECONDARY—A GOOD MAXIMUM RUSH AND COVERAGE FOR THE PASS.

WEAKNESSES: CERTAIN PERSONNEL AND IMPROPER ALIGNMENTS—MIDDLE AREA OVER CENTER—OVER OFFENSIVE TACKLE— FLAT AREA AND BETWEEN LINEBACKERS FOR PASSING GAME—GENERALLY WEAKER INSIDE THAN OUTSIDE—VULNERABLE TO TRAPS—QUICK-HITTING PLAYS.

BLOCKING: STRAIGHT, CROSS, FOLD, DOUBLE TEAMS, TRAPS, PULL AROUND, ISOLATION, POWER, ANGLE BLOCKS, PULL LINEMEN, AREA BLOCK VS. ANGLES AND STUNTING, WEDGE BLOCKING.

Diagram 8–38
The wide-tackle 6 even-diamond defense

18. The offense should split ends and flankers and run and pass accordingly. Put men in motion to see the defensive coverage. Capitalize on the defensive movements to motion.
19. If the defense stunts and angles, utilize area blocking, use the check pass series, go outside, employ wedges, put out flankers and split ends, etc.
20. Attack the pass defense according to the defense coverage.

Comments: The defense is strong outside because of the defensive ends' alignment. The defensive guards must protect the inside first. The defensive tackles protect against the off-tackle attack. The Wide-Tackle 6 is a pursuing and containing defense. Throw in the middle area between the two defensive linebackers. The split "T" running attack should go against this defense.

9

THE SPLIT-6 DEFENSE

The Split-6 Even-Diamond defense is an eight-man front with a three deep diamond secondary. The six-man line consists of two defensive guards, two tackles, and two ends. In the variations of the Split-6 defense, the two defensive linebackers are stationed inside the offensive guards. The defensive guards are either aligned on the outside shoulder of the offensive guard or positioned in the gap area between the offensive guard and tackle. The defensive tackle or number 3 man is either aligned in the gap between the offensive tackle and end, or on the inside shoulder, head up, or on the outside shoulder of the offensive end. The defensive end is aligned outside the offensive end and the split of the defensive end is determined by the alignment of the defensive tackle, the formations, the plays of the offensive team, etc. As can be seen, the alignment and play of the defensive tackle and end is approximately the same as the Wide-Tackle 6 defense. The only changes that are made are with the defensive guards and linebackers. Diagrams 9–1a through 9–1d (next page) illustrate a few alignments of the Split-6 defense. In the course of a ballgame the alignments can rapidly change and one side of the line can be slightly different than the opposite side. The offensive coach should attempt to know the exact play and execution of the defensive unit so that the offense can attack the defense with various blocking combinations more easily.

The Split-6 is mainly a pursuing and containing defense. Also, it is a good penetrating defense when necessary. The defense can stunt and blitz for additional pressure. As Vince Dooley, head football coach at the University of Georgia, Athens, Georgia, stated, "We like to put pressure on the offense, so our defensive players play their technique tough and we stunt a great deal." The advantages to this defense are that it puts the defensive linebackers in a position

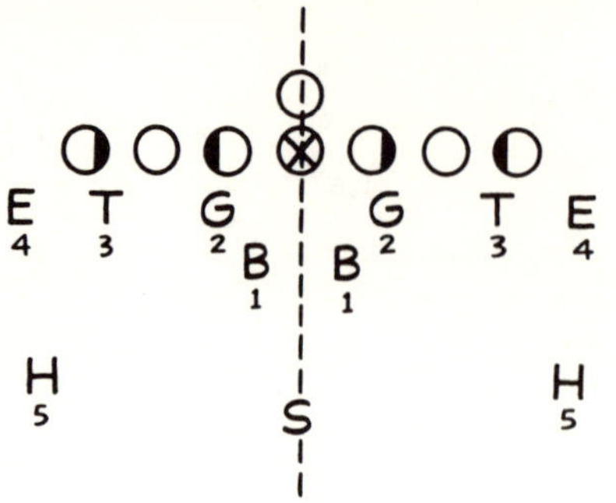

Diagram 9–1a

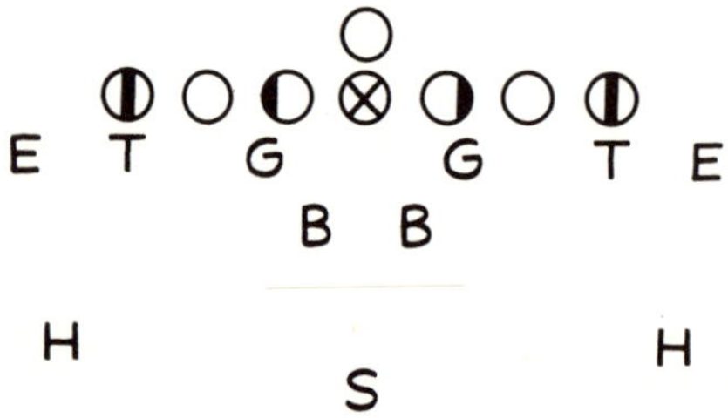

Diagram 9–1b

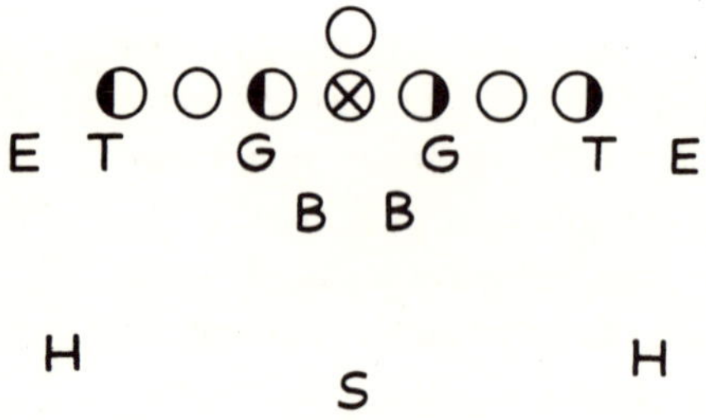

Diagram 9–1c

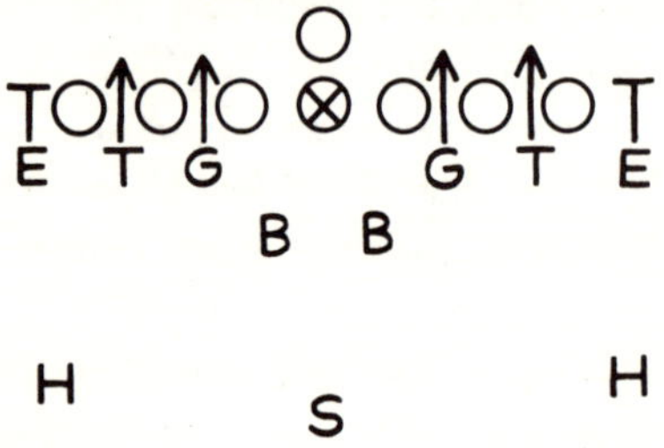

Diagram 9–1d

THE SPLIT-6 DEFENSE

not to be blocked by the middle offensive linemen. However, the linebackers are not in good position to cover certain areas well on pass defense.

THE PLAY OF THE SPLIT-6 DEFENSE

The following is the alignment, stance, initial movement and execution, responsibilities and coaching points of each position of the Split-6 Even-Diamond defense. The different alignments and executions of the eight-man front will be explained and described as was previously mentioned at the start of this chapter.

DEFENSIVE LINEBACKERS (Number 1 Men)

Alignment: Line up either in the center-guard gap or straddling the inside leg of the defensive guard. Be approximately 1 to 3 yards in depth from the line of scrimmage, depending upon the down and distance, etc.

Stance: A low two-point upright stance, with the inside leg forward. Feet can be parallel, but no more than a toe-instep relationship.

Initial Movement and Execution: The basic key is the quarterback, but can include the fullback or another offensive back. Be alert for a play in the middle, such as the sneak, wedge, or trap. If the play is toward, protect the center-guard area. If the play goes outside, step to the outside between the offensive guard and tackle. If the play is away, the linebacker will step up and meet the offensive center and deliver a forearm blow. In many instances the linebacker will react to the movements of the offensive center and not deliver a blow. The linebacker must protect that area. (Look at accompanying diagram.)

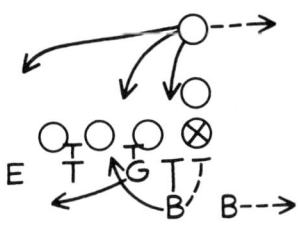

Responsibilities: 1. Play Toward—If an offensive back does not come in the guard-tackle gap, the linebacker will continue to move to the tackle-end area. If the play goes wider, the linebacker will assist with the defensive end on containment and can cover the flat if a pass develops. The defensive end and linebacker can exchange assignments with the defensive end covering the flat and the linebacker helping on containment. (It must be remembered that the more the defensive tackle aligns to the outside, the more the linebacker must protect inside, and vice versa.)

2. Play Away—The linebacker first controls the center area, reacts to his keys, and goes on a proper pursuit angle. If pass develops, go to the onside hook area.

3. Drop Back—Both linebackers will go to the onside hook areas unless involved in a stunt. One or both linebackers can be responsible for the draw.

Coaching Points: Keep shoulders square to the line of scrimmage when delivering a blow to the offensive center. The linebacker should watch for the screen and shuffle pass when going to the hook areas.

DEFENSIVE GUARDS (Number 2 Men)

Alignment: Line up on the outside shoulder of the offensive guard approximately 12 inches off the ball. If penetrating, align in the guard-tackle gap.

Stance: Either a low three- or four-point stance, with the feet parallel or toe-instep relationship.

Initial Movement and Execution: On the snap of the ball, the defensive guard will strike a blow with the inside forearm into the outside shoulder of the offensive guard. The number 2 man will react from there. If penetrating, the defensive guard will charge straight ahead going low and hard. The defensive guard will take approximately two steps, or to a depth of 1 yard.

Responsibilities: 1. Play Toward—Keep the offensive guard off the line-backer. Responsible from the offensive guard

THE SPLIT-6 DEFENSE 197

to the tackle area. If not blocked, watch for the trap by the offside offensive guard. If penetrating, go hard for depth and tackle anything over and around the area. Watch for the trap.

2. Play Away—Go on pursuit. Watch for the draw on sprint-out away. If guard pulls, follow him down the line. If penetrating, go on pursuit.

3. Drop Back—Rush the passer hard and close the middle area off. May be responsible for the draw play.

Coaching Points: Stay square to the line of scrimmage when delivering a blow. Keep the outside arm and leg free. When being trapped, stay low and strike a hard blow to the offensive trapper.

DEFENSIVE TACKLES (Number 3 Men)

Alignment: Can either align in the tackle-end gap, inside shoulder, head up, or outside shoulder of the offensive end. Approximately 12 to 18 inches off the ball.

Stance: Line up in a low three- or four-point stance. This may depend on the defensive technique employed.

Initial Movement and Execution: If aligned inside or in a head-up position, step with the outside foot and forearm and deliver a blow into the offensive end. If positioned on the outside shoulder of the offensive end, strike a blow with the inside shoulder. When stationed in the tackle-end gap, penetrate across the line of scrimmage.

Responsibilities:
1. Play Toward—If aligned inside, protect against the straight dive and the inside area. When outside, protect the territory from the offensive end to the alignment of the defensive end. If aligned inside, do not be driven in by the offensive end. Watch for the trap.

2. Play Away—Chase the play, looking for the bootleg, reverse, etc.

3. Drop Back—Rush the passer hard from the outside in.

4. Play Outside—Move to the outside, fighting blockers. If roll-out pass, attempt to contain the passer. If end drops off, fight for containment.

Coaching Points: When penetrating, go low and hard. Get off the ground and get to the ball immediately. If not blocked, look to the inside and prepare for a trap block. Stay low and keep the shoulder square, meeting trapper with inside forearm, shoulder, and leg. Keep outside arm and leg free.

DEFENSIVE ENDS (Number 4 Men)

Alignment: Line up on the line of scrimmage approximately 1 to 3 yards outside the offensive end, depending upon the alignment of the defensive tackle.

Stance: A low two-point stance, with inside leg forward.

Initial Movement and Execution: On the snap of the ball take a short jab step forward, approximately 6 to 9 inches with the inside leg. Can have keys on the lead offensive back, quarterback, and offensive linemen.

Responsibilities:
1. Play Toward—Come across the line of scrimmage forcing all plays to the inside; nobody must get outside. Do not give ground. The angle of penetration will be determined by the type of play and quickness of it—"Ball comes, I come." If sprint-out toward, can retreat to the flat and have the linebacker be responsible for containment with the defensive tackle.
2. Play Away—Take step forward and wait for the counter, reverse, bootleg, screen pass, etc. Drop off and then go on pursuit—"Ball goes, I go."
3. Drop Back—Can either rush the passer hard or cover in the flat area.

Coaching Points: Keep shoulders parallel to the line of scrimmage when the play comes toward. When dropping off to the flat, go as deep as possible so long as it is possible to come back and cover the offensive ballcarrier to the line of scrimmage. Do not be a floater when forcing the running plays.

DEFENSIVE HALFBACKS (Number 5 Men) Look to Chapter 6 under the 5–3 In Odd-Diamond defense for the defensive halfback play.

THE SPLIT-6 DEFENSE

DEFENSIVE SAFETY Look to Chapter 6 under the 5–3 In Odd-Diamond defense for defensive safety play.

Diagram 9–2 illustrates the defensive coverage of the linebackers, ends, and three deep secondary on a roll-out pass. It must be remembered that the defensive linebacker toward the flow of the ball can exchange assignments with the defensive end. The defensive end could be the contain man while the defensive linebacker covers in the flat area. It must be pointed out that this is very difficult for the linebacker to execute.

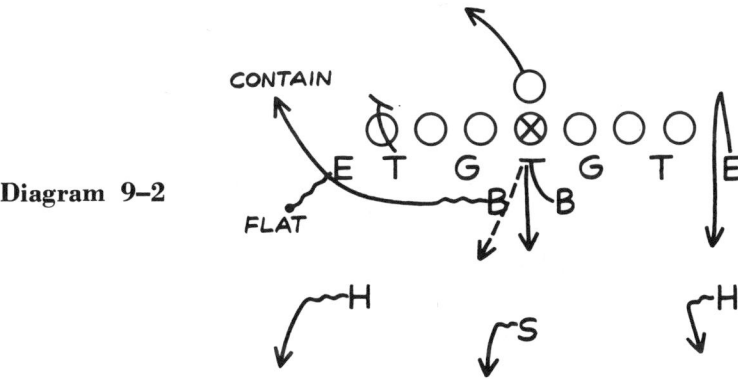

Diagram 9–2

Another method is for both the end and linebacker to rush the passer while the defensive halfback comes up and covers in the flat area. The safety and away halfback would rotate toward the ball. Man-to-man coverage could be employed by the three deep also.

ADJUSTMENTS TO OFFENSIVE FORMATIONS

If the offensive line has abnormally wide splits, the Split-6 must adjust in the gaps. The defensive linebackers align in the center-guard gaps, the defensive guards position in the guard-tackle seams, the defensive tackles station in the tackle-end holes, while the defensive ends adjust slightly inward onto the outside shoulder of the offensive ends.

If the offense splits an end, the defense can adjust in several different ways. The defensive linebacker, guard, and tackle can remain the same, but the defensive end can either play tight, walkaway, or double-up position on the offensive end. The defensive end can stack behind the defensive tackle and maneuver from that position also. Another method is for the defensive guard, linebacker, and end to remain the same while the defensive tackle aligns on the outside shoulder or head-up position on the offensive tackle.

The defensive guard and tackle can align in a head-up position on their offensive counterparts, and the defensive linebacker to the side of the split end can tandem behind the defensive guard. The defensive linebacker to the split end can maneuver out between the defensive guard and tackle or tandem behind the defensive tackle. The linebacker can adjust out, in a tight or walkaway position, while the defensive end can adjust accordingly; i.e., tight, walkaway, or double-up position. The linebacker away from the split end must adjust more over the offensive center if the opposite linebacker is maneuvering out. Another method of adjustment to a split end is the defensive guard aligning in the center-guard gap, the linebacker position in the guard-tackle gap, while the defensive tackle can align outside the offensive tackle, or position on his outside shoulder. Diagram 9–3 illustrates this adjustment.

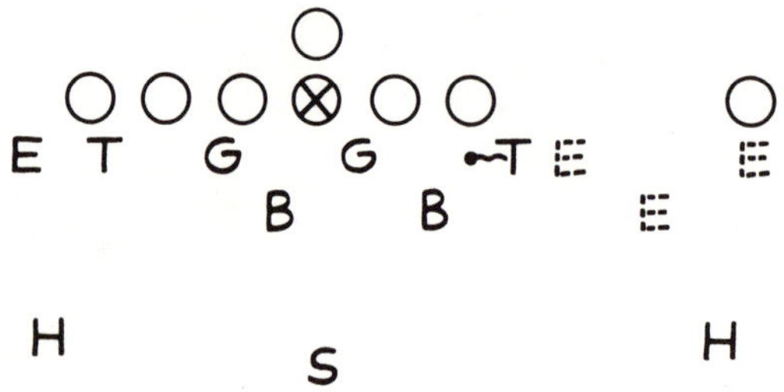

Diagram 9–3

When a wingback appears outside the offensive end, the alignment of the Split-6 can remain the same. However, the defensive tackle can adjust to more of a head-up position on the offensive end, while still protecting to the inside. The defensive end to the side of the wing will position on the outside shoulder of the wingback and have the normal defensive end responsibilities. Another adjustment is for the defensive linebacker toward the wingback to position in a tandem alignment behind the defensive guard.

If the wingback splits out up to 5 yards, the defensive end will play head up. Once the wingback or flanker goes wider, the defensive end will then play either tight, walkaway, or double-up position. The defensive tackle will play either on the inside shoulder, head up, or outside shoulder of the offensive tight end.

When there is a slot formation, the defensive tackle will play the slotback head up to the inside shoulder up to a point of 2 yards outside the offensive tackle. Beyond this point, the defensive tackle will adjust down to his split end adjustments. The defensive end will play the widest receiver head up to a point of 5 yards and then will position on the outside shoulder of the slotback. If the slotback positions wider than 5 yards, the defensive end can maneuver

THE SPLIT-6 DEFENSE

to a tight, walkaway, or double-up position on him. If the slot formation is continually hurting the defense in the slot area, then the defense can station the linebacker toward the slot, to position head up on the slotback. The defensive end would then play tight, walkaway, or double-up position on the defensive end. The linebacker away from the slot will adjust to a head-up position on the offensive center.

Long motion by the offense may create difficulties for the defense. If the offense is using motion to an advantage, then the defense must adjust. The defensive line can remain the same or maneuver slightly. The defensive end may cover the motion man, or the defensive linebacker toward the motion may cover him. If this should occur, the away linebacker will adjust and align over the offensive center.

In all the situations described, it is important for the defensive secondary to adjust to the many offensive formations that can occur. The offense must take advantage of the adjustments made by the defense whether it is at the line of scrimmage or in the defensive secondary.

STUNTS, BLITZES, FIRES, AND ANGLES

The defensive linebackers are in excellent positions to accomplish many defensive maneuvers. As illustrated in Diagram 9–4, a linebacker executes a fire technique, and in Diagram 9–5 a double-fire is indicated. A defensive blitz is shown in Diagram 9–6, with the defensive linebackers, guards, tackles, and ends crashing for penetration. While it is illustrated that the entire eight-man front crashes, a lesser number of players can be employed. Usually this can be executed with six men blitzing while the defensive tackles remain on the line of scrimmage.

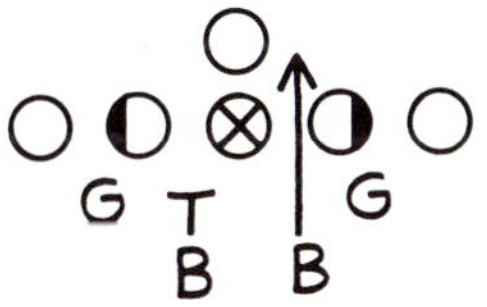

Diagram 9–4

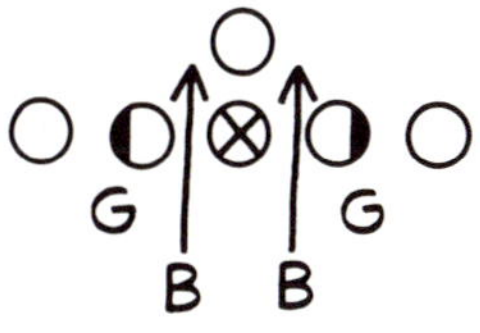

Diagram 9–5

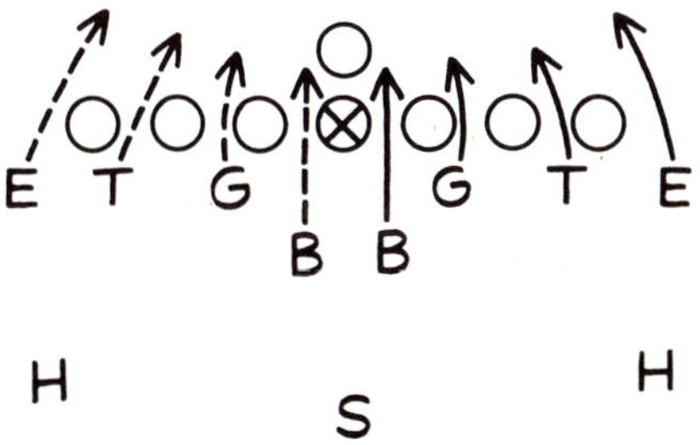

Diagram 9–6

Another double-fire is shown in Diagram 9–7. The defensive linebackers execute similar responsibilities (as was done in Diagram 9–5), however the defensive guards loop out to a head-up position on the offensive tackle. (While not illustrated, the linebackers could jab step forward, protecting the offensive center-guard areas and then pursue to the ballcarrier.) The defensive guards' responsibilities are to square up to the line of scrimmage after the initial hit and be responsible for the inside area between the offensive guard and offensive tackle.

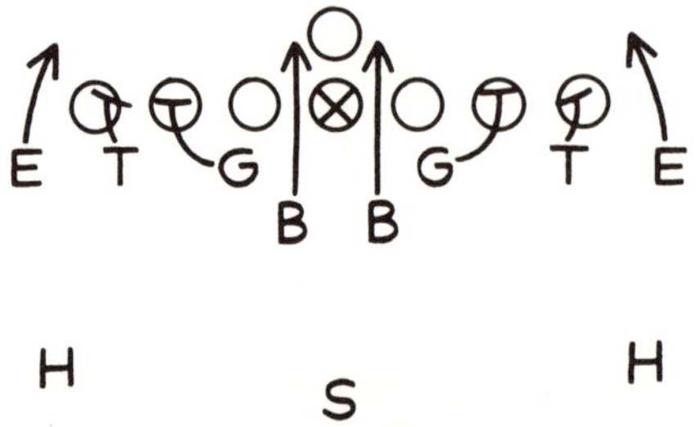

Diagram 9–7

A defensive stunt is illustrated in Diagram 9–8. Either linebacker, but usually the linebacker away from the strength of the offensive formation or field position, will step up hard to a head-up position on the offensive center. He will deliver a hard forearm blow and react to the play. The charging linebacker would not be taken either right or left by the offensive center. The opposite linebacker will shuffle step over the offensive center, behind the charging linebacker, and pursue to the ballcarrier.

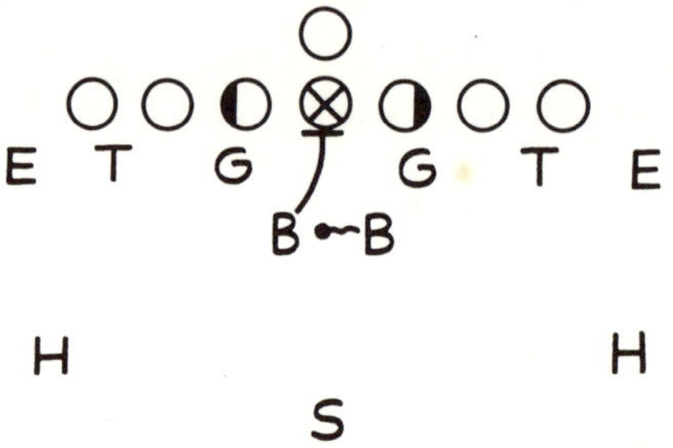

Diagram 9–8

Another defensive charge can be executed between the two linebackers (good against the inside trapping game). As indicated in Diagram 9–9, the two linebackers exchange defensive gaps and fire the seams between the offensive guards and center. Either linebacker can go first. Again, the defensive guards can either play straight or can loop out (Diagram 9–9a) onto the offensive tackles.

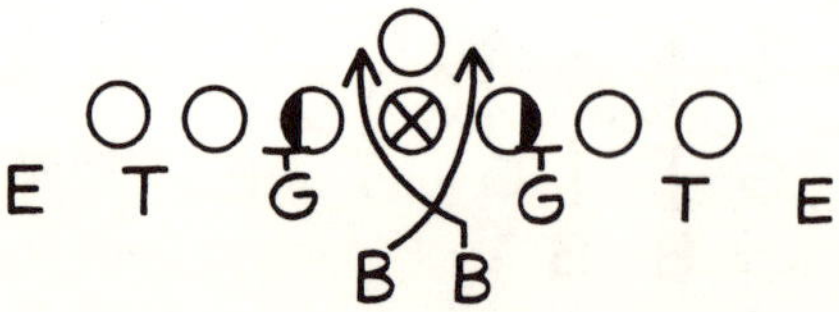

Diagram 9–9

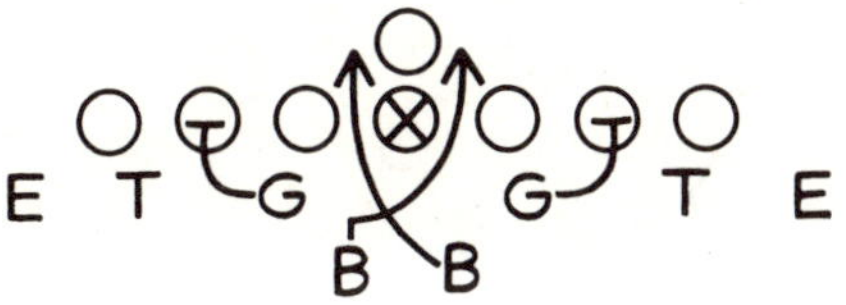

Diagram 9-9a

Still another stunt can be executed by the defensive guards and linebackers (good against the isolation type play). On the snap of the ball (Diagram 9–10), the defensive guards drive on a gap charge into the center-guard area, going for approximately a 1 yard depth. The defensive guards should not be cut off by the center's block and should follow the offensive guard if he pulls.

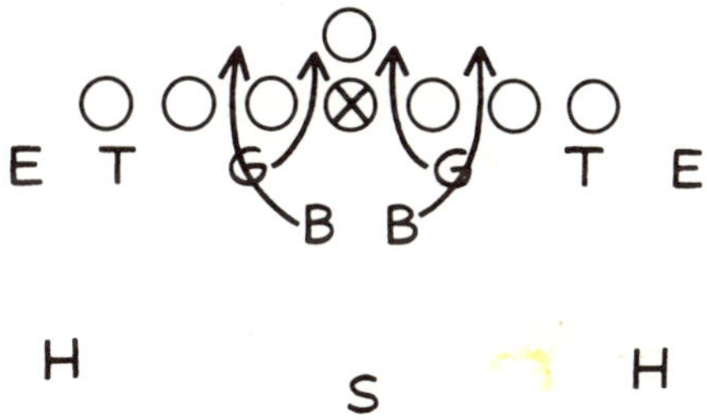

Diagram 9-10

If the offensive guard attempts to reach block the defensive guard, the defensive guard should run around the offensive guard's block if the flow of the ball is away. The linebackers will step and shoot the guard-tackle gap as hard as possible. The linebackers should remain low, ready to take on the offensive blockers.

The same charge can be executed by the defensive guards (Diagram 9–10). However, the linebackers do not have to shoot the guard-tackle gap. In this situation, the linebackers will maneuver over the offensive guard-tackle area. If a dive man or the offensive play comes in that direction, the linebacker should step up to meet the ballcarrier. If no play comes in that direction, the linebacker will slide along the line of scrimmage; he should not be cut off by the offensive tackle. If the flow of the ball is away, the linebackers should check for counter, reverse, and bootleg and then go on pursuit.

Diagram 9–10a (next page) illustrates a slightly different defensive maneuver. In this situation, the defensive guards employ an aggressive charge through the head of the offensive guard, going for the inside shoulder of the offensive guard and finishing up in a position parallel to the line of scrimmage. The defensive guard will pursue the ball from this position. The defensive linebackers will key their responsibility. If the play is toward, the linebacker will scrape off and go through the head of the offensive tackle. He should square up to the line and react to the ballcarrier. If the play is away, the number 1 man will step over the offensive center and play the football from there.

—A stunt by the defensive guard, tackle, end, and linebacker can be accom-

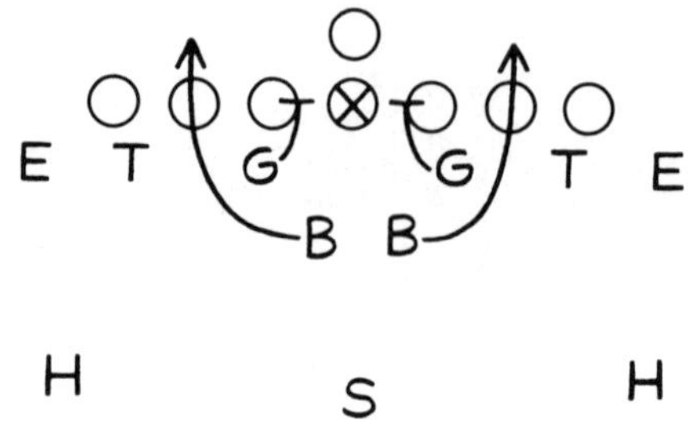

Diagram 9-10a

plished. On the snap of the ball the defensive guard shoots the center-guard gap, the defensive tackle drives for the outside shoulder of the offensive tackle, and the defensive end drives across the line of scrimmage. The defensive linebacker can either fire the guard-tackle gap or shuffle over the guard-tackle area and go on pursuit. This defensive maneuver is illustrated in Diagram 9-11.

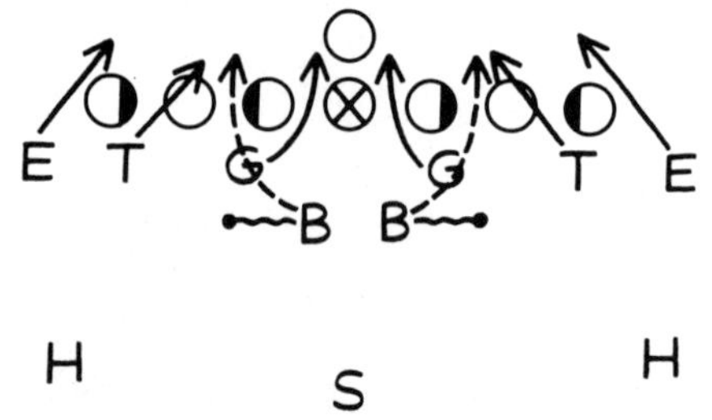

Diagram 9-11

Defensive stunts can be executed by the defensive tackle and end also. Defensive stunts by these two men can be seen in Diagrams 9-11 and 9-12.

Angling from the Split-6 defense can easily be accomplished and executed. An angling line is indicated in Diagram 9-12. The left defensive end slides down onto the outside shoulder of the offensive end, and the left defensive tackle does the same with the offensive tackle. The defensive left guard slants down through the neck of the offensive center, while the right defensive guard slants through the neck of the offensive left tackle. The right defensive tackle loops out onto the outside shoulder of the offensive end and the right defensive end steps out and executes a wide end play. The defensive linebackers slide out over the offensive guards, key into the backfield, and pursue to the ballcarrier.

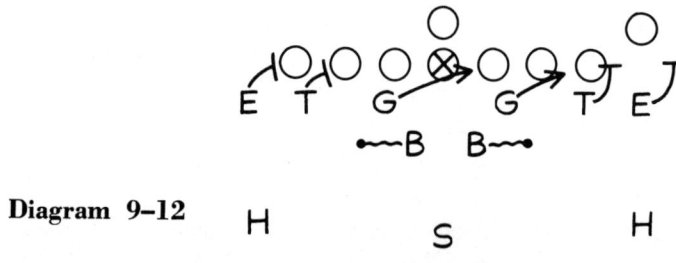

Diagram 9-12

THE SPLIT-6 DEFENSE

DEFENSIVE SHIFTS

The Split-6 defense can easily shift into various defensive alignments. Diagram 9–13 illustrates the defensive tackles aligning on the outside shoulder of the offensive tackles and the defensive ends positioning on the outside shoulder of the offensive ends. The defensive guards and linebackers remain the same. With this type of defensive variation the inside is stronger, while the outside is creating a weakness. The linebackers, however, are more free to pursue outside.

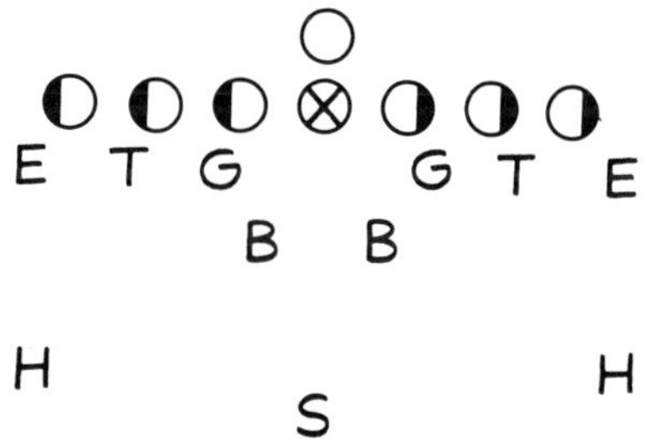

Diagram 9–13

Another defensive shift is shown in Diagram 9–14. The defensive tackles and ends remain the same as in Diagram 9–13; however, the defensive guards align in the center-guard gaps and the linebackers position in the guard-tackle gaps. Diagram 9–15 illustrates this alignment on the left side of the offensive line, while the right side remains in a Split-6 defense. From this same alignment, angling can be accomplished as illustrated in Diagram 9–16 (next page). The linebackers can stunt if necessary. The left side, however, is angling back into a Split-6 while the right side is angling into what was illustrated in Diagram 9–11.

Diagram 9–14

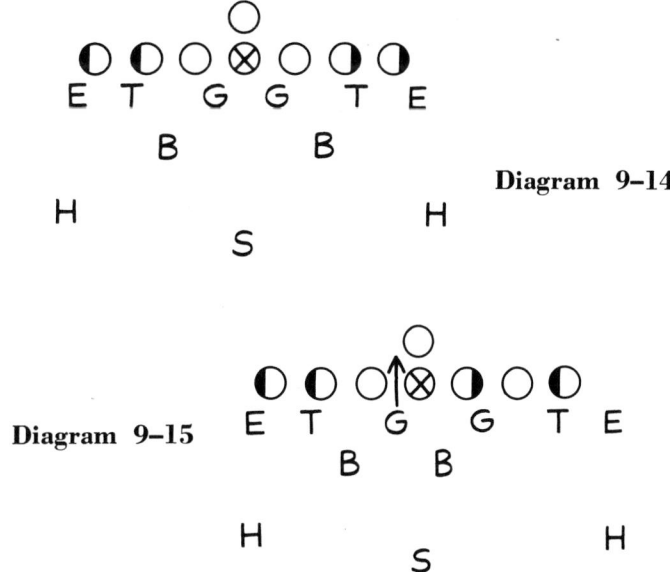

Diagram 9–15

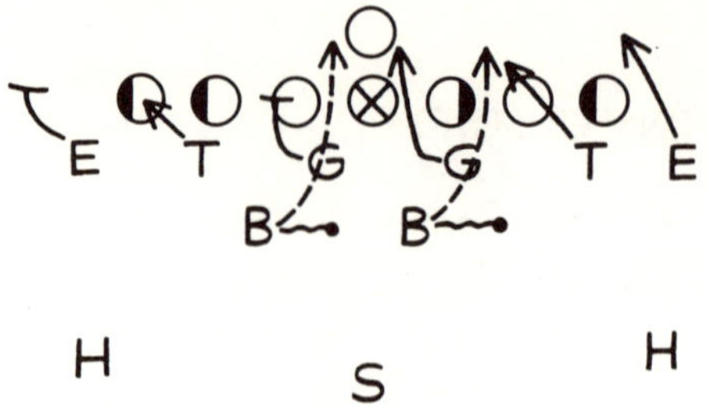

Diagram 9-16

Another defensive shift is indicated in Diagram 9–17. The defensive linebackers remain the same as in the Split-6 defense, the defensive tackles align in a head-up position on the offensive ends, and the defensive ends tandem directly behind the defensive tackles. The defensive tackles and ends can then execute different defensive stunts, with the tackle charging inside or outside, and the linebacker going opposite that of the tackle.

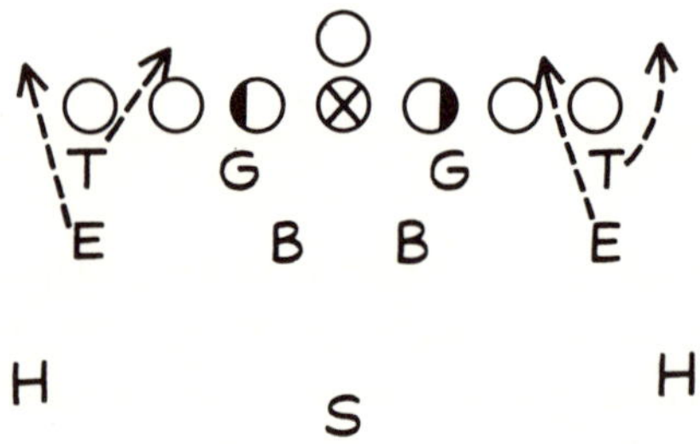

Diagram 9-17

Another tandem alignment can be executed with the two defensive linebackers. One linebacker positions head up in a four- or three-point stance over the offensive center, while the other linebacker tandems directly behind him, creating a seven-man line. The remaining defensive players execute the same assignments and responsibilities (Diagram 9–18).

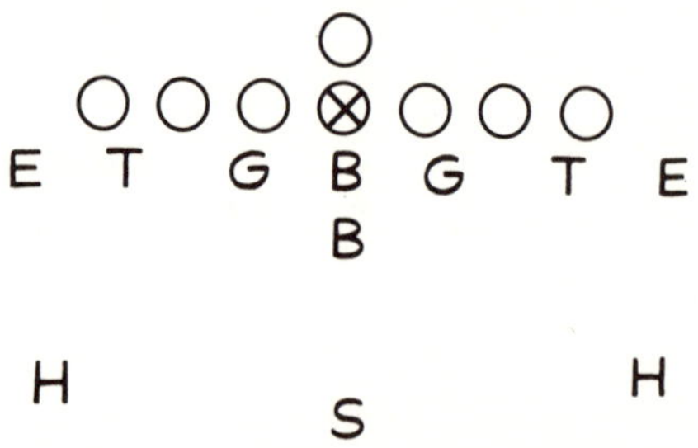

Diagram 9-18

Other defensive shifts can easily be accomplished. Diagrams 9–15, 9–17, and 9–18 illustrate other defensive shifts the Split-6 can easily maneuver into. Other defenses the Split-6 can shift to are the 4–4 Tandem Even-Diamond, the 4–4

THE SPLIT-6 DEFENSE

Even-Diamond and its variations, the 5–3 In and Out Even-Diamond, the Wide-Tackle 6 Even-Diamond, the Tight-6 Even-Diamond, the Stack-6 Even-Diamond, the 7–1 Odd-Diamond, the Gap-8 defense, etc. Overshifts, with a "monster" man stationed to the outside employing a three deep secondary, can be utilized also.

ATTACKING THE SPLIT-6 EVEN-DIAMOND DEFENSE

THE STRENGTHS OF THE SPLIT-6 DEFENSE

The strengths of the Split-6 Even-Diamond defense are as follows:

1. In the middle area over the offensive center where the defense has four men to the offense's three.
2. Over the offensive guard area is strong.
3. Strong off-tackle, if the defensive tackle is aligned inside the offensive end. Stronger outside if the defensive tackle is aligned head up to outside shoulder of the offensive end. Is the defensive tackle bigger and stronger than the offensive end?
4. The defense is generally strong inside if the offensive tackles are aligned inside the offensive end.
5. The defense is a good pursuing and containing defense.
6. The defensive ends are in a good containment position.
7. A great deal of stunting can be accomplished, especially up the middle area.
8. The defense can adjust to offensive sets and shift to other defenses easily.
9. A good defensive rush can be put on the passer.
10. The defense has the ability to defend against the pass with a maximum number of players.
11. The linebackers can cover the middle hook zones adequately.
12. The defense employs a three deep diamond secondary.

THE WEAKNESSES OF THE SPLIT-6 DEFENSE

The weaknesses of the Split-6 defense are illustrated in Diagram 9–19 (next page), and the weaknesses of the defense are as follows:

1. The offense should attack the middle area with an extra offensive man.
2. The area between the offensive guard and tackle is weak.
3. The defense is generally weaker for the running game inside, if the defensive tackles align outside, and weaker outside if the tackles position inside.
4. The offense should attack outside the defensive end.
5. The flat areas for the passing game are weak.

6. The hook areas over the offensive ends are relatively weak.
7. If the defensive tackle must contain on roll-out plays, a weakness results.
8. The quick pass to the tight end should be executed.
9. Putting men in motion may create weaknesses over the middle area or other areas in the defense.
10. Attack the three deep pass defense according to the weaknesses of the defensive coverage.

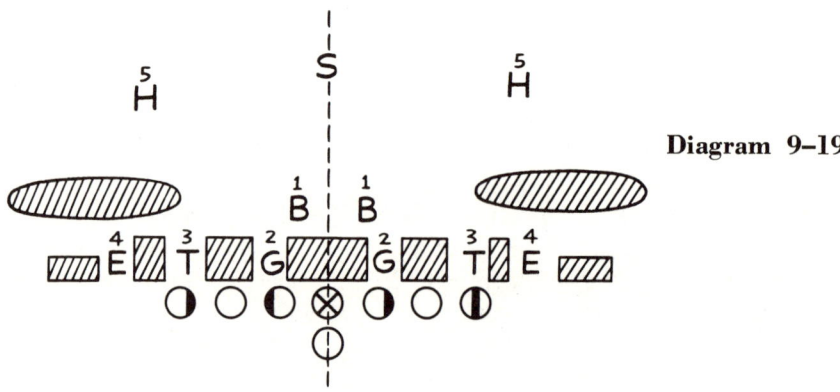

Diagram 9–19

ATTACKING THE AREAS OF THE SPLIT-6 DEFENSE

The offense can attack over the middle area. However, if this is to be accomplished, the offense must add an extra blocker. This can be an offensive lineman or back. The defense has four men (two linebackers and two defensive guards) to three offensive men (an offensive center and two offensive guards). An extra man is essential. Sneak and wedge plays (halfback, fullback wedges) at the two linebackers can be employed. Counterplays, to get the linebackers out of the area, are effective also.

To add an extra man up the middle, a pull-around technique by the offensive tackle can be executed. As illustrated in Diagram 9–20, the left offensive guard blocks on the number 2 man, the center blocks on the away linebacker, the right offensive guard blocks the opposite defensive guard, and the left offensive tackle pulls and leads on the remaining linebacker. Using a pull-around and blocking on the other or opposite linebacker can easily be done. In this case, the offensive guards block the defensive guards while the center blocks the right defensive linebacker. The offensive left tackle pulls and drive blocks on the opposite linebacker. Should the linebacker be firing, the linebacker will be in excellent position to be trapped. Diagram 9–21 illustrates the offensive left tackle pulling

THE SPLIT-6 DEFENSE   209

again and trapping on the left defensive guard. The left offensive guard, center, and right guard block down on their defensive men respectively.

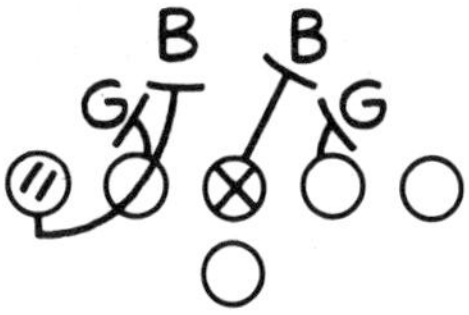

Diagram 9–20

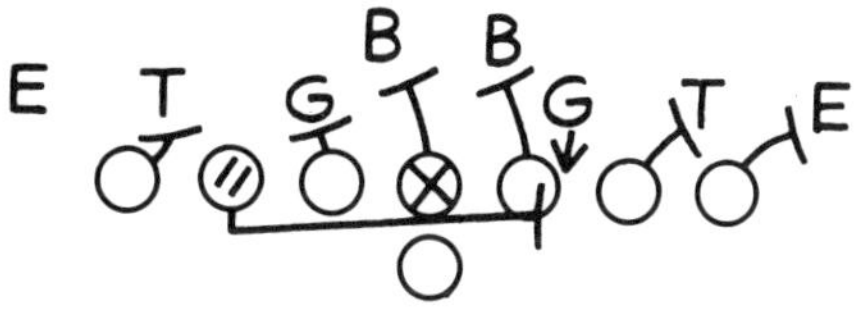

Diagram 9–21

With this type of blocking described, halfback, fullback, and countertraps can easily be installed. An inside reverse, with a wing or slotback coming back, is another excellent play.

Diagram 9–22 illustrates a double pull-around, putting additional offensive men in the middle area. Trapping with the offensive guards can be accomplished also, but the offensive tackle must seal down on the defensive guard who is covering the pulling offensive guard. As shown in Diagram 9–23, the left offensive guard pulls and traps on the defensive left guard. The center blocks the

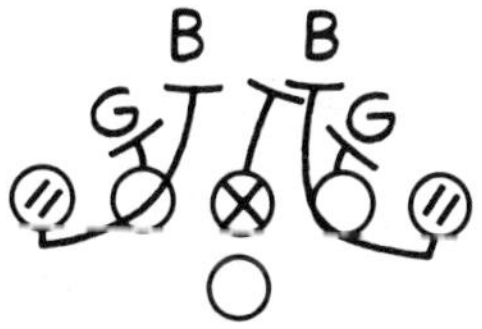

Diagram 9–22

right defensive linebacker one-on-one, while the right guard, tackle, and right end, if necessary, block on the left defensive linebacker. A halfback can be employed to block on the defensive tackle as shown. If the left offensive tackle in

Diagram 9–23

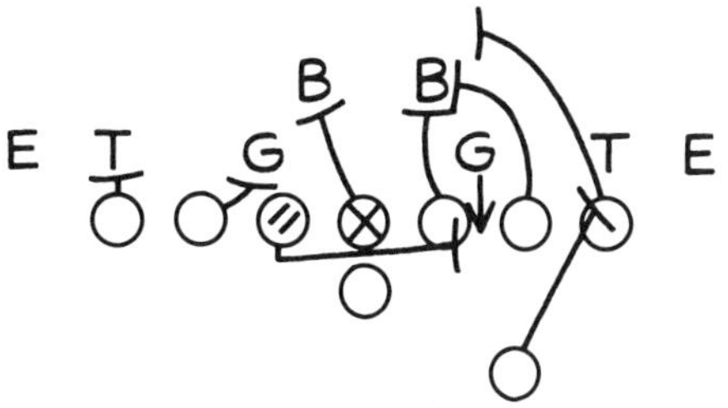

Diagram 9–23 cannot seal the defensive guard, then a trap by the tackle can easily be utilized with the offensive guard blocking the defensive guard.

Isolation can be utilized in the middle area also. A simple isolation play is shown in Diagram 9–24. The offensive guards block the defensive guards, the center blocks on one of the linebackers, while the fullback leads and drives on the opposite linebacker. In this case, the quarterback reverse pivots and hands back to the halfback. As shown, the offensive right tackle assists the fullback on the linebacker.

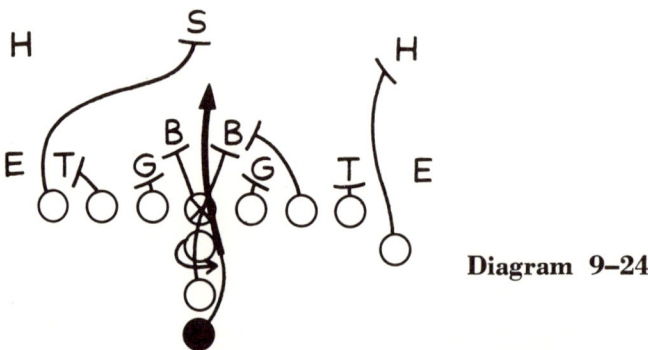

Diagram 9–24

The offense should employ motion to see how the defense adjusts. Many times the linebackers will do the adjusting and if a linebacker goes with the motion man there remains only one linebacker over the center area. Now many of the problems of attacking this area are eliminated. After motion takes the linebacker out, there remains a three-on-three ratio, and many other offensive plays can be run in this area. The offense must, however, *force* the defense out of the two-linebacker alignment. In accomplishing this, a long motion must be utilized for effectiveness. Usually a quick toss out to the motion man, putting a one-on-one situation with the defensive halfback, is good. If the defense does not adjust, the offense should continually utilize the motion man, especially if it cannot move up the middle area. It must be remembered, however, that the defense may maneuver another defensive player, such as a defensive end, to cover the motion man. If this should occur, the offense should attack the weakness that develops in that and other areas of the defensive line.

If the defense is receiving pressure from the middle area due to the defensive guards and linebackers, the defense should utilize some type of draw play or middle screen to slow down or halt the pressure. A shuffle pass to a halfback over the middle can also be utilized.

The offense should attack the alignment of the number 2 man or the defensive guards. If the defensive guards are aligning more to the outside, the offense should go inside and if the guards are maneuvering to the inside, the offense should go outside. Faking plays that hold both the linebackers and guards inside and then go outside should be utilized. Plays that fake outside and then go inside the linebackers and defensive guards should also be used.

THE SPLIT-6 DEFENSE

The offense should look to the area between the offensive guard and tackle. The defensive tackle will determine the amount of attack the offense will utilize in this area. Diagrams 9–25a and 9–25b illustrate the lesser and wider areas present if the defensive tackle aligns inside to outside position on the offensive end. Diagram 9–25a indicates the defensive tackle is aligned inside the offensive end, therefore leaving less area to attack. However, Diagram 9–25b shows the defensive tackle aligned head up to the outside shoulder of the offensive end creating a wider hole over the offensive tackle. The offense, therefore, should attack and block the area according to the alignment of the defensive tackle.

```
     B
  G▓▓T  E       Diagram 9–25a                    B
 ⊗ ○ ○ ○                                      G▓▓T→ E
  ○                                           ⊗ ○ ○ ●
                 Diagram 9–25b                  ○
```

Straight blocking can easily be accomplished over the offensive tackle area. The offensive end blocks the defensive end, the offensive tackle takes the defensive tackle no matter where he is aligned, the offensive guard blocks the number 2 man, the center drives on the onside linebacker, and the offside guard goes for the offside linebacker. The offensive tackle away from the play attempts to seal off the away defensive guard.

In many instances, the linebackers may be very quick and fast. If the offensive center is not as quick, the onside linebacker toward the hole being run could easily step up and plug the hole for the ballcarrier. If this were the case, the center could easily execute a pull-around technique. Diagram 9–26 illustrates the offensive guard, tackle, and end on their respective defensive counterparts, while the offensive center, after snapping the ball, pulls around the offensive guard and drives on the linebacker. If the defensive linebacker were stunting during the course of a ballgame, an area technique could be employed. If the linebacker or defensive guard does not stunt, the offensive center will step, look for the stunt, and then utilize the pull-around maneuver on the linebacker. Once the center realizes that the defensive men are not continually stunting, he can quickly step behind the offensive guard for the linebacker. A counter or false action to hold the linebacker for a second is good with the pull-around technique being employed.

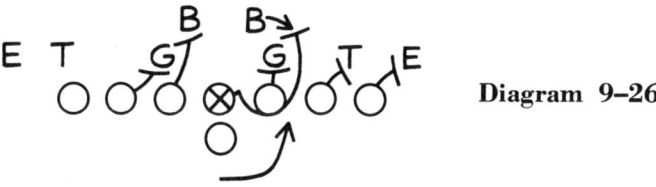

Diagram 9–26

212   THE SPLIT-6 DEFENSE

Another pull-around maneuver is executed by the offensive guard. In this situation (Diagram 9–27) the offensive tackle angles down on the defensive guard and the offensive guard pulls and drives on the linebacker. The center can either assist with a double-team on the linebacker or can block away toward the opposite linebacker. In using this technique, the defensive tackle should be in a position so that the offensive end can block him.

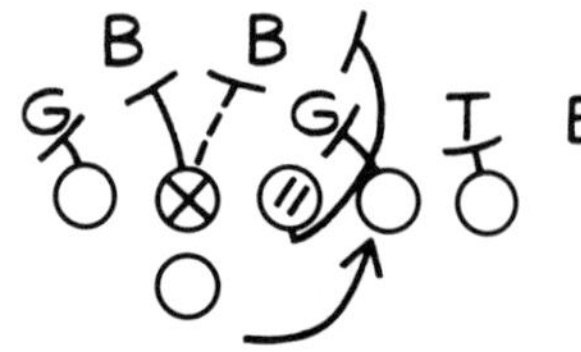

Diagram 9–27

Cross blocking by the offensive guard on the defensive guard and tackle can be utilized also. This is illustrated in Diagram 9–28. A type of cross block is indicated in Diagram 9–29. In this situation, the offensive tackle blocks out on the defensive tackle, while the offensive end steps back and traps on the defensive guard. A slotback can be utilized in place of the offensive end, with the slot blocking on the defensive guard. In another situation, the offensive guard could double-team with the trapping slot or end while the center could drive on the onside linebacker. A fake inside or a counter-action in the backfield is good with the type of blocking described.

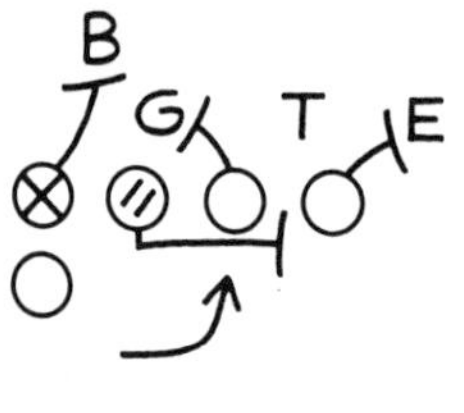

Diagram 9–28

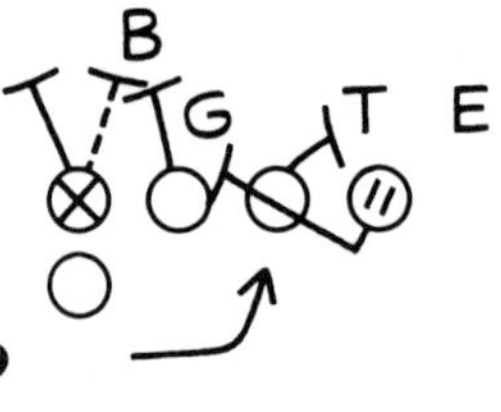

Diagram 9–29

Another method is the employment of double-team blocking on either the defensive guard or tackle. Double-teaming on the defensive guard with the offensive guard and tackle can be used. The center can block the onside defensive linebacker and the offside offensive guard will drive on the opposite linebacker. The defensive tackle must be in a position to be blocked by the offensive end. A pull-around technique by the offensive center on the linebacker can be utilized with the double-team block also.

Double-teaming the defensive tackle, no matter where he is aligned, by the offensive tackle and end can be used. The offensive guard blocks the defensive guard while the center drives on the onside linebacker or utilizes the pull-around maneuver. The offside guard blocks the away linebacker while the offside offen-

THE SPLIT-6 DEFENSE 213

sive tackle seals on the defensive guard. A wingback or halfback can be employed to lead on the defensive linebacker while double-teaming the defensive tackle. This can be utilized when double-teaming the defensive guard also.

Cross-blocking between the offensive guard and tackle, as mentioned previously, can be employed; however the offensive end can assist on the defensive tackle. The center can block the onside linebacker and/or a wing or halfback can drive through the hole and block the linebacker.

Double-teaming the defensive tackle or guard with a set halfback can be used also. As shown in Diagram 9–30 the offensive end and halfback double on the defensive tackle. The offensive tackle angles down on the defensive guard, while the offensive guard drives on the linebacker or pulls around for him. The offensive center can either drive on the onside or offside linebacker. In Diagram 9–31 the halfback and offensive guard double-team the defensive guard. The offensive center blocks the onside linebacker and the offensive tackle blocks the defensive tackle. The offensive end can either out block on the defensive end or double-team the defensive tackle with the offensive tackle. The offensive end could release and drive across the hole on the number 1 man also. If the defensive tackle in Diagram 9–31 were playing head up to the outside shoulder of the offensive end, the offensive end would block the defensive tackle alone, while the offensive tackle would block the defensive linebacker.

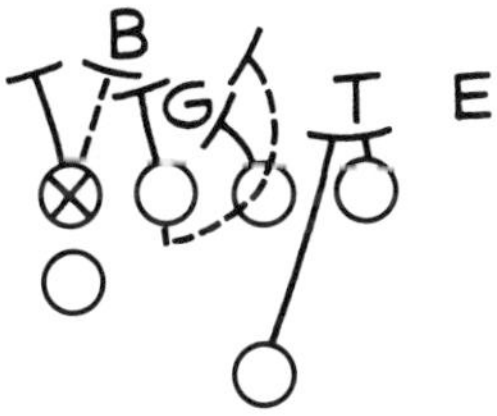

Diagram 9–30

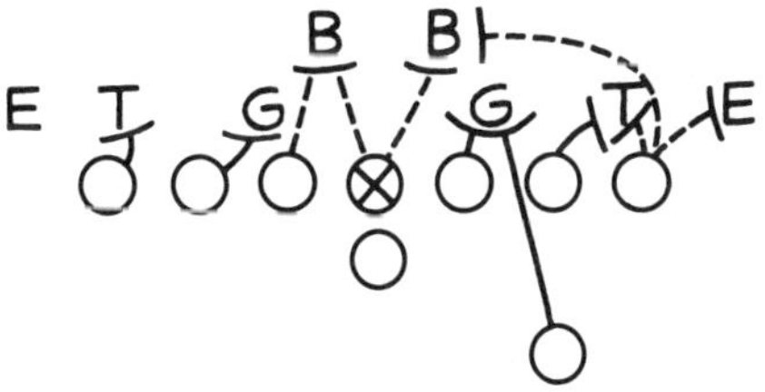

Diagram 9–31

Utilizing a halfback on the onside defensive linebacker, with the offensive center, while the offensive guard, tackle, and end utilize straight, cross, and double-team blocking, can be employed also.

Utilization of a halfback or wingback on the defensive linebacker while leading through the hole is beneficial. Straight, cross, and double-teaming can be used. Another method of exploitation is the employment of the offside guard or tackle trapping the defensive tackle. In this case, the offside offensive tackle would seal block the defensive guard. Another method is for the offensive tackle to trap the defensive tackle with the offensive guard blocking the defensive

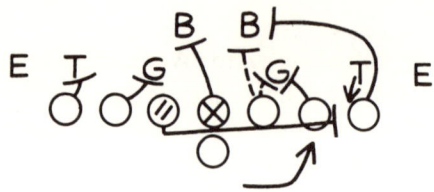

Diagram 9–32

guard. In Diagram 9–32 the offensive end blocks down on the linebacker, the offensive tackle angles down on the defensive guard, while the offensive guard either drive blocks on the linebacker and assists on a double-team with the offensive end, or doubles with the offensive tackle on the defensive guard. An inside reverse or a counter-action utilized in the backfield is effective with this type of blocking.

Many other blocking combinations can be used between the area of the offensive guard and tackle. While many have been shown, numerous others can be employed. In many instances the blocking in this area will be determined by the speed and quickness of the defensive linebackers or how strong the defensive guards and tackles are. It must be remembered that pulling of other offensive linemen over the offensive tackle area can be used with much of the blocking already described. Leading with offensive backs and powering this area can be employed also. Using area blocking principles by the offensive linemen, away from the point of attack, may have to be utilized if a great deal of stunting and blitzing is employed by the defensive guards and linebackers. Pulling the offensive center through the hole, as described, can be used in many of the blocks mentioned.

Alignment of a wingback on the outside shoulder of the offensive end may force the defensive tackle to a head up or outside shoulder position on the offensive end. If this is the case, the point of attack has widened and the offense should attack more over the offensive tackle area. A slight split by the offensive end and tackle may also widen the area over the offensive tackle considerably. Employment of faking plays up the middle area, to hold the defensive linebackers, is effective. Counters and inside reverses should also be employed.

The type of blocking used when attacking outside the defensive tackle or outside the offensive end area will depend on the alignment of the defensive tackle. In many cases the offensive end will block the defensive tackle one-on-one. The question that should be asked is, "Can the offensive end block the bigger defensive tackle?" It should be remembered that if the defensive tackle is aligned inside the offensive end, the offense should attack outside. However, if the defensive tackle is positioned head up to the outside shoulder of the offensive end, the offense should attack inside.

Straight blocking can easily be employed. The offensive end blocks the de-

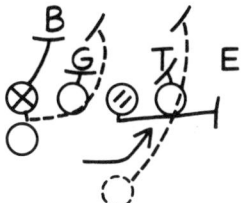

Diagram 9-33

fensive tackle in, the offensive tackle drives on the linebacker, the offensive guard blocks the defensive guard, and the offensive center drives on the offside linebacker. The center can assist on the onside linebacker, utilizing a double-team block with the tackle also. A halfback can then kick the defensive end out. A wingback could station outside the offensive end. If the defensive tackle is aligned head up to the outside shoulder of the offensive end, the wing could utilize a double-team block with the offensive end. If the defensive tackle positions inside the offensive end, the offensive end could take the defensive tackle one-on-one, while the wingback leads through on the quick-flowing linebacker. Leading an extra back and/or lineman through the hole can be employed also. While utilizing these techniques, the offensive guard could use the pull-around technique, with the offensive guard pulling around and driving on the linebacker or any other quick-pursuing defensive man. If the defensive tackle is playing tough, a double-team by the defensive tackle and end can be used if the defensive tackle is positioned inside the offensive end.

Power blocking, with two offensive backs on the defensive end, is effective with the offensive end blocking the defensive tackle. Another blocking combination is illustrated in Diagram 9-33. The offensive end blocks the defensive tackle while the offensive tackle traps the defensive end out. A halfback leading through the hole can also be used. Utilizing the same blocking, but powering a halfback

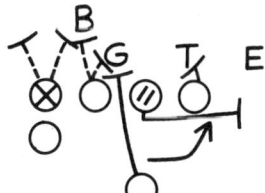

Diagram 9-34

on the defensive guard, can be employed (Diagram 9-34). Trapping the defensive end with the onside guard and using either angle blocking down or double-teaming the defensive tackle with the offensive end and wingback are effective. Trapping the defensive end with the offside guard can be used with some type of counter or reverse being utilized. It must be remembered that any type of pulling or leading through the hole by offensive backs and linemen is effective. Faking inside the tackle and going outside is good, especially if the defensive tackle is committing to the inside. Area blocking up the middle area while attacking outside the defensive tackle can be employed especially if the defensive guards and linebackers are stunting and blitzing.

The offense should attack outside the defensive end. Double-teaming the number 3 man and having a halfback block the defensive end is effective. This is especially good if there is a fake over the offensive end and the defensive end is committing inside. Pulling offensive linemen can be used also. Angling down and pulling is effective. The offense should employ power, reverses, bootlegs, pitchouts, and option plays to attack outside the defensive end. Utilizing the belly or split "T" option is good also.

The offense should immediately attack the flat area for the passing game with flat, flare, and swing passes being employed. The defensive end and linebacker are in awkward positions to cover this area. Sprint-out or roll-out passes are good. Utilize motion in the flat area also. A quick pass to the tight end is effective especially with the alignment of the defensive linebacker. The option run-pass against the defensive halfback should be used also. Play-action passes, to hold and freeze the defensive linemen and linebackers, are very effective. Play-action passes and throwing in the flat area should be utilized. The offense should split ends and put out flankers to see how the defense covers the spread men. The offense should run and pass according to the defensive coverage of the wide men. The coverage will depend on the defensive ends, linebackers, and the three deep secondary.

If the defense continues to stunt, fire, angle, and blitz, the offense must be fully prepared to area block the defensive maneuvers. Utilizing the quick check pass, wedge blocking, going outside, splitting ends, and putting out flankers, etc., are a few of the things that must be done.

Diagram 9–35 illustrates the weakness areas of the Split-6 Even-Diamond defense with the strengths, weaknesses, and best plays against the defense, and comments listed after it. Diagram 9–36 (page 219) indicates the card for the "Coaches' Directory of Football Defenses."

Strength: Certain personnel make the defense strong. The middle area with the defense having a ratio of four men to three offensive men. Strong over the offensive guard area. Strong inside if the defensive tackle is aligned inside. Stronger outside if the

Diagram 9–35

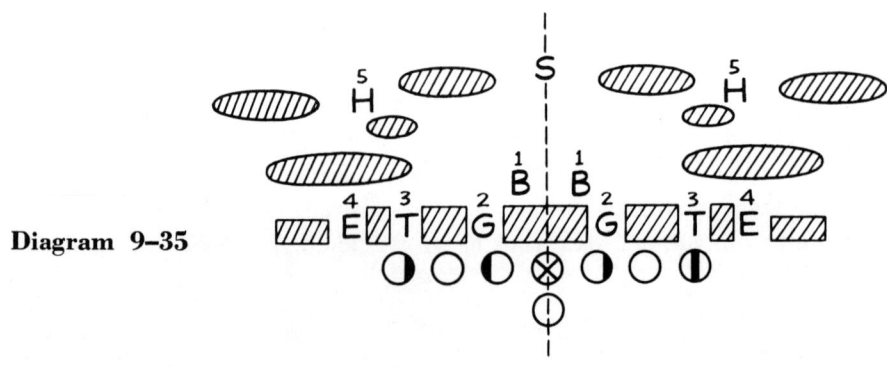

defensive tackle is outside. Generally stronger inside if tackles are inside and vice versa for outside. It is a good containing and pursuing defense. Can penetrate easily. The middle hook areas are well covered. The defense employs a three deep secondary.

Weakness: Certain personnel and improper alignments make the defense weak. Over the offensive tackle should be attacked. Weak inside if defensive tackle is aligned outside or weak outside if defensive tackle is positioned inside. The flat areas are weak. The hook areas over the offensive ends are weak. Over the middle, outside the tackle, and outside the end can be attacked with power blocking combinations. Attack the three deep secondary according to defensive coverage.

Best Plays Versus the Split-6 Defense:

1. Attack the middle area with an extra offensive man. Utilize the pull-around on both linebackers or trap block the opposite defensive guard with either the offensive guard or tackle.
2. Utilize the double pull-around or isolate one of the linebackers up the middle area.
3. Employ sneaks, wedges, counters, halfback or fullback traps.
4. Use the draw, middle screen, or shuffle pass if there is pressure by the defense up the middle area.
5. Utilize motion to see if one of the defensive linebackers leaves the middle area.
6. Attack the alignment of the defensive guard and linebacker. If aligned outside, attack inside and if positioned inside, attack outside.
7. The offense should attack over the offensive tackle area with straight, pull-arounds, and cross blocking.
8. The offense should double-team the defensive guard or defensive tackle and attack over the offensive tackle.
9. Pull linemen and lead halfbacks over the offensive tackle area with the blocking mentioned. Utilizing trap blocks on the defensive tackle is also good.
10. The offense should utilize counters, inside reverses, and faking plays to hold and freeze the linebackers.
11. Attack the alignment of the defensive tackle. Go outside if the defensive tackle aligns inside and go inside if the defensive tackle stations outside.
12. Attack outside the defensive tackle with straight and kick-out blocking. Double-team the defensive tackle with the offensive end and tackle and kick the defensive end out.

SUCCESSFUL RUNNING PLAYS

TO THE LEFT	TO THE RIGHT

SUCCESSFUL PASSING PLAYS

SUCCESSFUL ACTION PLAY PASSES

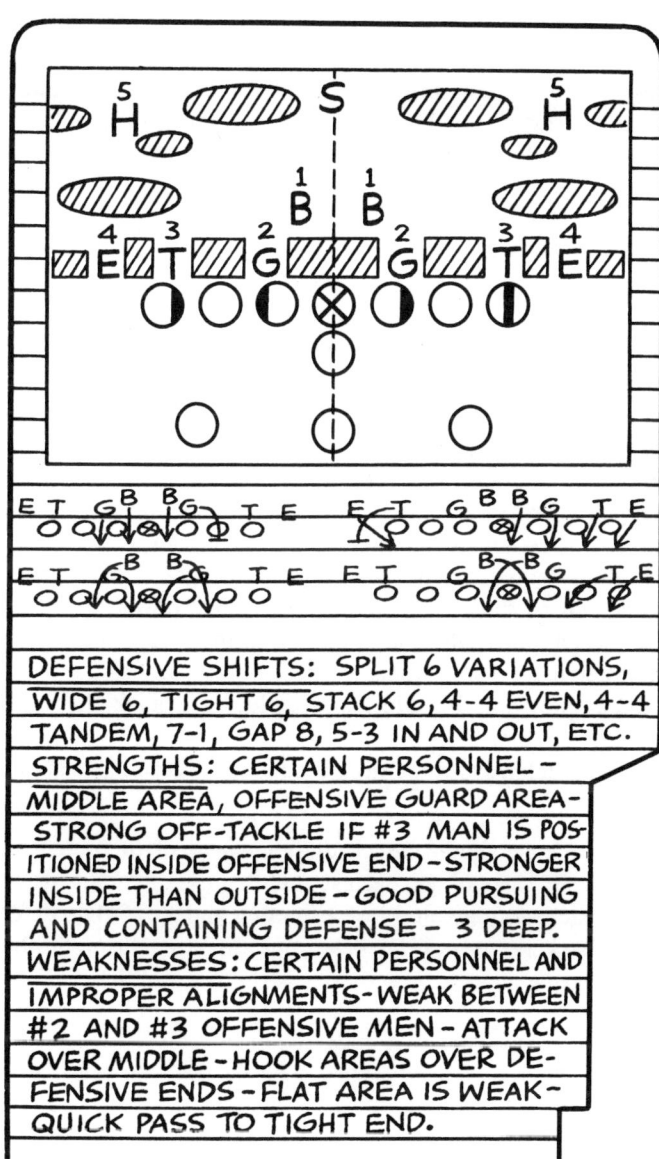

DEFENSIVE SHIFTS: SPLIT 6 VARIATIONS, WIDE 6, TIGHT 6, STACK 6, 4-4 EVEN, 4-4 TANDEM, 7-1, GAP 8, 5-3 IN AND OUT, ETC.
STRENGTHS: CERTAIN PERSONNEL – MIDDLE AREA, OFFENSIVE GUARD AREA – STRONG OFF-TACKLE IF #3 MAN IS POSITIONED INSIDE OFFENSIVE END – STRONGER INSIDE THAN OUTSIDE – GOOD PURSUING AND CONTAINING DEFENSE – 3 DEEP.
WEAKNESSES: CERTAIN PERSONNEL AND IMPROPER ALIGNMENTS – WEAK BETWEEN #2 AND #3 OFFENSIVE MEN – ATTACK OVER MIDDLE – HOOK AREAS OVER DEFENSIVE ENDS – FLAT AREA IS WEAK – QUICK PASS TO TIGHT END.

BLOCKING: STRAIGHT, CROSS, TRAPS, PULL AROUND, DOUBLE PULL AROUND, WEDGES, DOUBLE TEAMS, ISOLATION, POWER (AREA BLOCK IF DEFENSE CONTINUALLY STUNTS, ETC.)

Diagram 9-36
The split-6 even-diamond defense

13. Utilize power, quick traps by the offensive tackle and guard on the defensive end. Lead and pull linemen through the hole.
14. Double-team the defensive tackle with the offensive end and wingback and kick the defensive end out with either an offensive back or lineman.
15. Trap the defensive end with either the offside guard or tackle and employ counters and inside reverses.
16. Attack outside with double-teaming on the number 3 man and "rolling" the defensive end in. Angle block down and pull offensive linemen to go outside.
17. The offense should employ power sweeps, reverses, quick pitchouts, bootlegs, and options to go outside.
18. The offense should attack the flat area with quick passes, utilize the quick pass to the tight end, employ play-action passes and the option run-pass on the defensive end and halfback.
19. The offense should split ends and put out flankers and run and pass according to defensive coverage. Utilize power, bootlegs, reverses, quick pitchouts, and options with the spread men.
20. If the defensive team stunts, angles, blitzes or fires, the offense should employ area blocking, wedge blocking, quick check passes, going outside, etc.
21. Attack the defensive three deep secondary according to its coverage.

Comments: The offense should attack the alignment of the defense. The split "T" should go against this defense. Are the defensive linebackers quick and fast, or strong and slow? The defensive linebackers and tackles determine the strength of the Split-6 defense.

10

THE GAP-8 GOAL LINE DEFENSE

The Gap-8 defense, also known as the 8–3, 8-Goal Line, or 8-Gap, is an even defense with a three deep diamond secondary. While it is considered a three deep, the safety man could be aligned as a middle linebacker. The Gap-8 is usually utilized on the goal line or in any short yardage situation. It is employed by almost every team in the country, including high school, college, and professional football. It should be stated that the personnel aligned in the defensive gaps can change from one team to another. For example, the number 1 men could be defensive guards, while the number 2 men are defensive tackles. Another team, however, may utilize the defensive tackles in the center-guard gaps, while the defensive guards position as the number 2 men. Other coaches will employ four large tackles in the center-guard and guard-tackle gaps, while the defensive guards align in the tackle-end seams. A few other teams may utilize one, two, three, or four linebackers from their basic defense, and will align them in a number of the gap areas also. Linebackers could position in the center-guard gaps, guard-tackle gaps, tackle-end seams, or on the outside shoulder of the offensive ends. Diagram 10–1 and Diagram 10–2 (next page) illustrate numerous Gap-8 alignments, with the different defensive personnel illustrated.

The Gap-8 defense can be utilized anywhere on the field, and in numerous cases, it is employed throughout an entire game against a given offensive team. It could be utilized as an element of surprise, or against a team that does not

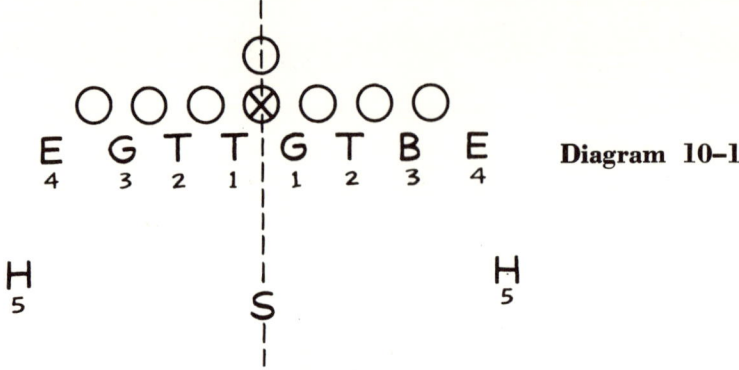

Diagram 10-1

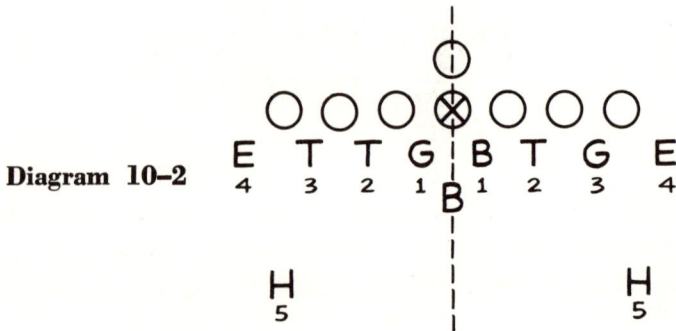

Diagram 10-2

have an offensive passing attack, or on rainy days when an offense has difficulty in passing the football.

Since this defense is mainly utilized on short yardage and goal line situations, it is basically a penetrating defense. The defensive linemen must drive across the neutral zone in order to stop the ballcarrier for no gain or a possible loss. It is a tough, hard-nosed defense that puts pressure on the offensive team. Pursuit by the defensive personnel is executed, however, only after penetration has been made. Usually pursuit is of secondary importance on the goal line when the offensive opponent is ready to score. Therefore, penetration is essential and necessary to stop the ballcarrier. In many instances the defensive linemen will not be able to drive through their respective gaps because of the blocks executed on them. However, the defensive linemen must not let the offensive blockers drive them back. They must hold their ground, keep leverage on their offensive opponent, and get to the football.

In most instances, the defensive coach wants the big, strong football player aligned in the middle to stop the quick-hitting plays of the offense, such as the sneak and fullback wedge plays. The defensive number 1 and 2 men must make penetration and stop any play up the middle and should attempt to force the play outside of them. These men should be rugged and tough and be determined that an offensive play will not make yardage in this area. The defensive linemen in the tackle-end areas should make penetration also, but can hold up the offensive ends from releasing for a pass. The number 3 man's area of responsibility is the off-tackle hole. Usually the defensive ends are positioned outside the offensive ends and are responsible for containment on wide offensive plays. The defensive safety man's alignment will vary. In some cases, he will align directly over the offensive center, behind the number 1 man's heels, or from 1 to 5 yards back from the line of scrimmage. Generally he will be responsible for the quick play over the middle, any offensive back that attempts to hurdle the line of scrimmage, or outside, against an offensive play going in that direction.

The defensive secondary can either employ zone or man-to-man coverage. Usually man-to-man pass defense is employed, because the offense is so near to the goal line. However, many coaches utilize zone defense down in this area with a great deal of success.

PLAYING THE GAP-8 DEFENSE

The following are the alignments, stances, initial movements and executions, responsibilities, and coaching points of the Gap-8 defense. There are many other defensive techniques for the Gap-8 defense and, therefore, many of them will be presented and mentioned under the defensive maneuvers.

DEFENSIVE GUARDS (Number 1 Men)

Alignment: Align in the center-guard gap approximately 6 to 8 inches off the line of scrimmage. Align as close to the line of scrimmage as possible.

Stance: Employ a four-point stance with the inside foot forward. Keep shoulders parallel to the line of scrimmage, with the elbows bent to remain low to the ground.

Initial Movement and Execution: Spring off the front foot, utilizing a low, hard charge, keeping the shoulders parallel to the line of scrimmage and making penetration.

Responsibilities: 1. Play Toward—The center-guard gap. Watch for the sneak and quick wedge plays.
2. Play Away—Pursue to the ballcarrier.
3. Drop Back—Rush the passer from the inside and stop any possible draw play.

Coaching Points: Scramble hard for penetration. Charge low, almost skimming the ground, then coming up looking for the offensive play. Be aware of the trap by keeping the outside arm and leg free.

DEFENSIVE TACKLES (Number 2 Men)

Alignment: Line up in the guard-tackle gaps approximately 6 to 8 inches off the line of scrimmage. Align as near to the line as possible.

Stance: Four-point stance with inside leg forward. Shoulders should be parallel to the line of scrimmage with the elbows bent.

Initial Movement and Execution: Spring off the front foot going for penetration. Stay low to the ground and utilize a hard, low charge when penetrating.

Responsibilities: 1. Play Toward—The guard-tackle gaps. Watch for the halfback wedge play, power, and trap play.
2. Play Away—Go on pursuit. Fight through offensive opponents' block and get to ballcarrier.
3. Drop Back—Rush the passer hard from the inside.

Coaching Points: Keep the outside arm and leg free when meeting the offensive trapper. Come up hard after making penetration.

DEFENSIVE OUTSIDE LINEBACKERS (Number 3 Men)

Alignment: Line up in the tackle-end gaps approximately 6 to 8 inches off the line of scrimmage. Get as near to the line of scrimmage as possible.

Stance: Utilize a four-point stance with the inside foot forward. Keep shoulders parallel to the line of scrimmage.

Initial Movement and Execution: Push off the front foot going for penetration and staying as low to the ground as possible. Go through the gap hard and come up looking for the ballcarrier.

Responsibilities:	1. Play Toward—The off-tackle hole. Be aware of power and trap plays in this area. 2. Play Away—Go on pursuit to the ballcarrier. If blocked, fight through the offensive blocker to the ballcarrier. 3. Drop Back—Rush the passer hard from the inside. If the defensive end drops off to the flat area, the number 3 man contains and must not let the passer get to the outside.
Coaching Points:	Be aware of the trap play. Keep outside arm and leg free. Keep shoulders square when going through the hole. Raise head and look for the football.

DEFENSIVE ENDS (Number 4 Men)

Alignment:	Line up approximately 1 yard outside the offensive end directly on the line of scrimmage.
Stance:	Two-point upright stance with the inside foot forward. Knees should be bent to remain low.
Initial Movement and Execution:	Drive across the line of scrimmage, pushing off the inside foot and going for penetration. Play tough and protect inside. Do not let anyone run inside between the linebacker and yourself. Contain on play recognition. Force play wide and deep.
Responsibilities:	1. Play Toward—Inside to the linebacker. Watch for the trap and kick out blocks by the offensive halfbacks. 2. Play Away—Chase the ballcarrier looking for bootlegs, reverses, cutbacks, etc. 3. Drop Back—Rush the passer hard from the outside-in. Can retreat to the short, flat areas while the defensive number three man contains.
Coaching Points:	Meet the offensive backs with the inside shoulder and forearm. Force the play wide to the defensive halfback. Be aware of the trap block. Remain low to the ground when coming across the line of scrimmage.

The defensive halfbacks align in a two-point ready stance, approximately 3 yards outside the offensive end and 2 yards off the line of scrimmage. Their first responsibility is the run outside and they look through the offensive end to the ball. When the play comes toward, the defensive halfback should not widen the gap between the defensive end and himself. All plays must be met aggressively, because this is a short yardage and goal line defense. If the defense is employed farther up the field, the defensive halfbacks can align approximately 6 to 8 yards in depth and play the football. They can easily defend man-to-man or cover the outside deep 1/3 of the field on zone. Diagram 10–3 illustrates the play of the eight defensive linemen, middle linebacker or safety man, and the two defensive halfbacks.

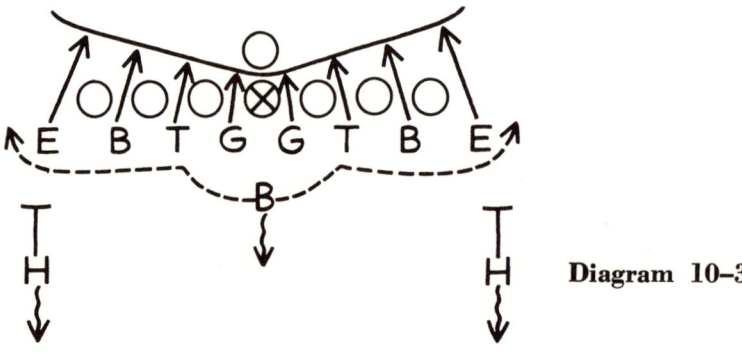

Diagram 10–3

ADJUSTMENTS TO OFFENSIVE FORMATIONS

If the offensive team detaches an end, there can be numerous defensive coverages. The defensive halfback can adjust out and align directly over the split end, while the defensive number 3 and 4 men remain in their similar positions. However, the defensive end could stack behind the number 3 man, double up on the split end, or play a walkaway position. If the number 3 man were a linebacker, as previously mentioned, the defensive end and linebacker could exchange alignments and responsibilities. The defensive end positions outside the offensive tackle, while the linebacker stations out to cover the offensive split end. Another method is for the defensive halfback to remain at his regular alignment, while the defensive linebacker covers the split end man-for-man.

If there is a wingback stationed directly outside the offensive end, the defensive alignment can remain the same or easily adjust. The defensive end can position and charge into the inside shoulder of the wingback looking for any play developing inside. However, the defense can align in a 6–5 alignment to the wingback side also. The defensive number 2 man or tackle, when the wingback has aligned outside the offensive end and there is no halfback in the regular set position, can station head up to the offensive tackle. The number 3 man aligns directly over the offensive end, while the number 4 man or defensive end positions on the wingback or stations behind the defensive linebacker and tackle.

THE GAP-8 GOAL LINE DEFENSE

227

This is illustrated in Diagram 10-4. If the wingback widens to a flankerback position, the defensive end could tandem directly behind the defensive number 3 man or play in a tight, walkaway, or double-up position on the flankerback. It must be remembered, that if the number 3 man were a linebacker, the defensive end and linebacker could exchange defensive positions and assignments easily on the flankerback.

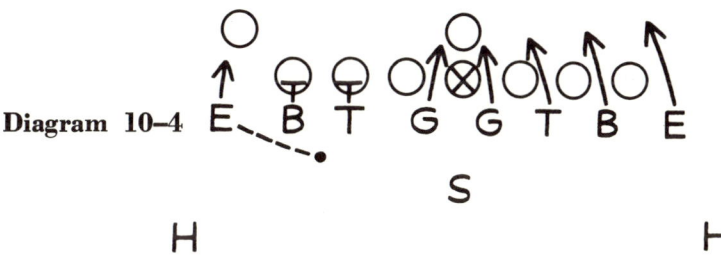

Diagram 10-4

Against an offensive slot formation the defensive alignment can remain the same, with the defensive number 3 and 4 men playing the slotback as if he were an offensive end. However, the defensive alignment can play the slot as if the slot were a flanker formation and align in the 6-5 defense.

Diagram 10-5 illustrates a strong formation to the defense's left. As can be seen, the defensive safety or middle linebacker and the right defensive halfback adjust slightly over to the offensive strength. The defensive eight-man front can adjust into a 6-5 alignment toward the strong formation with the shifting of the safety man and defensive halfback still being executed. Diagram 10-6 (next page) indicates motion by the offensive team. The three deep can adjust as shown or the defensive linemen can maneuver into a 6-5 alignment toward the wingback and motion man also.

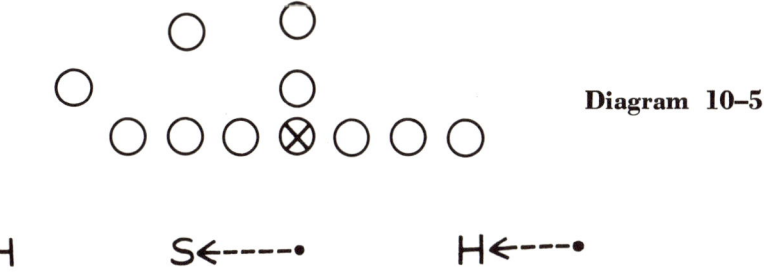

Diagram 10-5

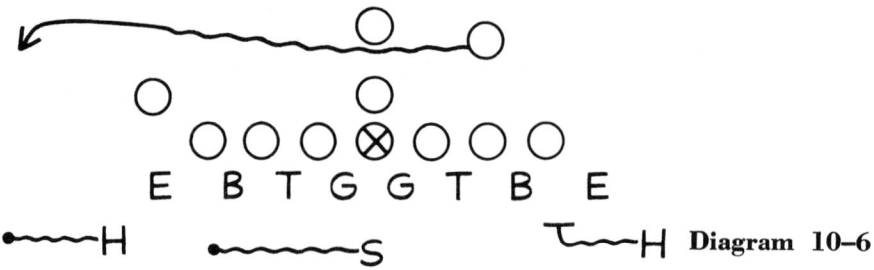

Diagram 10-6

DEFENSIVE MANEUVERS

Stunting by the Gap-8 defense is minimized because of the eight-man front alignment. Also, stunting is not usually desired close to the goal line where the three deep are the only ones to back up the charging linemen. However, certain defensive maneuvers can be accomplished according to field position, down and distance, score of the game, etc.

The Gap-8 "In" charge is illustrated in Diagram 10–7. The "In" charge is usually called on "fourth and one" or any other short yardage situation comparable to it. On the snap of the ball, the defensive number 1, 2, and 3 men step with their outside feet, springing off their inside feet, and aiming their inside shoulders lower than the outside shoulders of their offensive opponents. They attempt to contact their offensive counterparts' outside knees. After penetration has been made, the defensive linemen square their shoulders to the line of scrimmage and go to the ball. In some instances, the defensive men shift slightly from their original position to the outside shoulders of their offensive opponents. The defensive number 4 man or end plays tough and tight, through the offensive end, closing the inside. He should jam the offensive end to the inside and should not let him release for a pass.

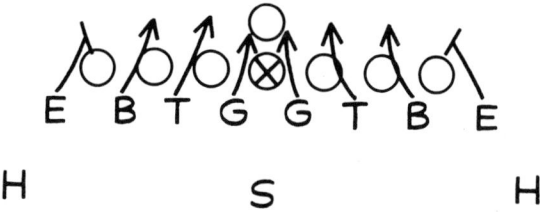

Diagram 10-7

Diagram 10–8 illustrates the Gap-8 "Out" defensive maneuver. This is usually executed when the offensive team needs long yardage for the first down, such as "third and fifteen, fourth and six, etc." The offense does not want to run up the middle, but feels it has a better chance to make yardage outside. With the

THE GAP-8 GOAL LINE DEFENSE

"Out" charge, the defensive number 1, 2, and 3 men spring off their inside feet, lowering their outside shoulders and aiming lower than the inside shoulders of their offensive counterparts. The defensive linemen go for the inside legs of the offensive opponents, drive for penetration, square up to the line of scrimmage, and go to the ball. In many cases, the linemen can cheat for position when executing the "Out" charge to get the job done properly. If a wingback is not aligned outside the offensive end, the defensive end will hit into the offensive end, jam him, and play his regular assignments. If a wingback positions outside the offensive end, the number 4 man will explode with his outside forearm, through the wingback's inside shoulder, and will attempt not to be double-teamed by the wingback and offensive end. The defensive safety or middle linebacker protects over the center-guard gaps and then pursues to the ballcarrier. Diagram 10–9 illustrates the right defensive number 1 man jamming into the offensive center while the middle linebacker prepares to fill aggressively over the offensive left guard.

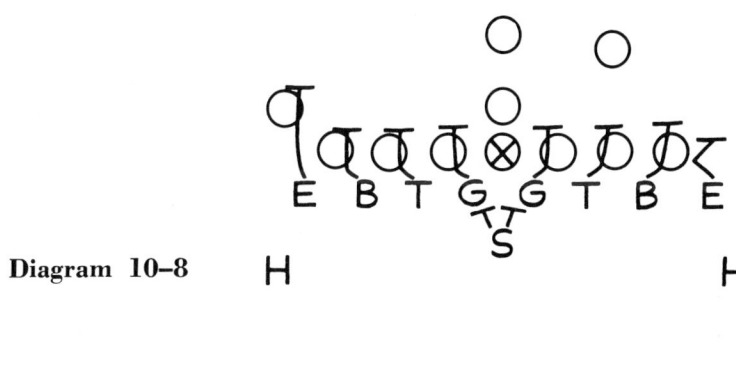

Diagram 10–8

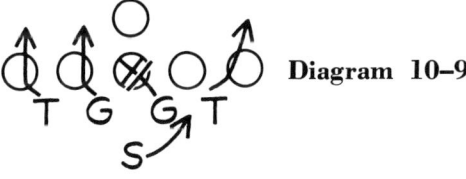

Diagram 10–9

Angling left or right by the defensive linemen can easily be accomplished. Diagram 10–10 (next page) illustrates the line angling to the left. The same procedure could be mirrored to the right. The angling is usually performed to one side of the field, because of a strong formation, wide side of the field, etc. In the indicated diagrams, the left defensive end, linebacker, tackle, and guard angle through the heads of the men to their outside. They strike a blow with their inside forearm and shoulder utilizing a crossover step maneuver. The defensive linemen should not be cut off by the offensive blockers and should square up to the line of scrimmage and pursue to the ballcarrier. The defensive linemen away from the angle perform their regular defensive "In" technique. The middle linebacker is aware of the offensive play directly over the middle and keeps alert to the play away from the angling line.

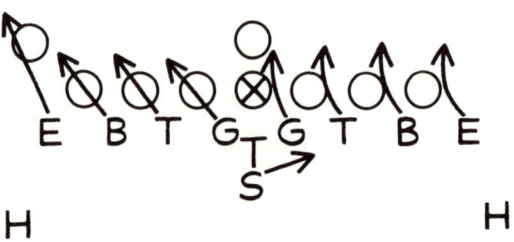

Diagram 10–10

Other defensive maneuvers can easily be accomplished. For example, the defensive guards could pinch hard inside, while the remaining defensive line charges outside. The defensive safety would, therefore, fill over the offensive guard areas. However, the defensive guards and tackles could pinch down hard to the inside, while the outside linebackers and defensive ends loop outside. The middle safety is then prepared to fill aggressively over the offensive tackle area. While not indicated, other examples of angling techniques can be employed with all or a few of the defensive linemen at one time.

DEFENSIVE SHIFTS

The Gap-8 Even-Diamond can easily shift to other eight-man front defenses. They include the Wide-Tackle 6 Even-Diamond, Tight-6 Even-Diamond, Split-6 Even-Diamond, Notre Dame 6 Even-Diamond, Stack-6 Even-Diamond, 5–3 In and Out Odd-Diamond, 4–4 Even-Diamond, 4–4 Tandem Even-Diamond, 7–1 Odd-Diamond, etc. The Gap-8 can shift to nine-man front defenses as well.

ATTACKING THE GAP-8 EVEN-DIAMOND DEFENSE

THE STRENGTHS OF THE GAP-8 DEFENSE

The strengths of the Gap-8 defense are as follows:

1. The inside is generally stronger than the outside. Strong from tackle to tackle.
2. The defensive linemen control the splits of the offensive linemen. The offense must tighten down.

THE GAP-8 GOAL LINE DEFENSE

3. A good pass rush by the eight defensive linemen can easily be executed.
4. The defense is an excellent pressure and penetrating defense.
5. It is an excellent short yardage and goal line defense.
6. The offensive ends can easily be held up and jammed on the line of scrimmage.
7. The defense employs a three deep secondary.

THE WEAKNESSES OF THE GAP-8 DEFENSE

The weakness areas of the Gap-8 defense are illustrated in Diagram 10–11 and the weaknesses of the defense are as follows:

1. The area over the offensive center can be attacked.
2. The off-tackle hole is weak.
3. The defense is generally weaker outside than inside.
4. The defense is weak against the trapping game.
5. The offensive team usually knows what to expect from the defense. Good blocking angles are present with the Gap-8 defense.
6. The hook areas over the offensive ends are weak. The quick pass to the tight end is good.
7. Attack the weakness areas of the three deep secondary. The short hook and flat areas are weak if the three deep are playing back off the line of scrimmage. Throw deep passes if the secondary is close to the line of scrimmage.

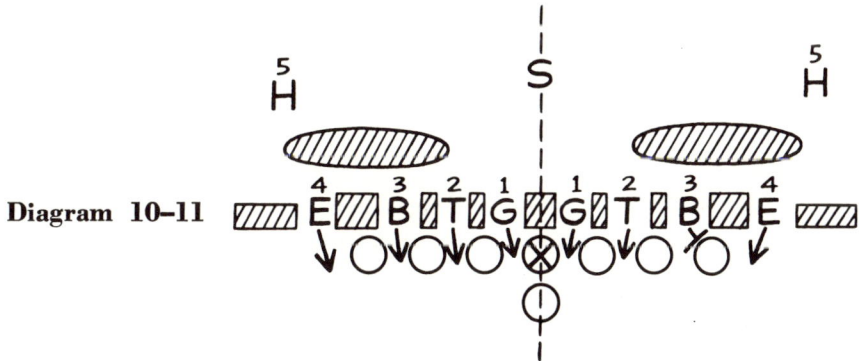

Diagram 10–11

ATTACKING THE AREAS OF THE GAP-8 DEFENSE

When the Gap-8 defense is encountered, the offense should automatically tighten down the splits of its line. This makes it easier for the offensive linemen to block the hard-charging defensive linemen. Another important factor is that the offense must stop the penetration of the defensive linemen. If penetration cannot be made, the effectiveness of the defense is lost in terms of throwing the ballcarrier for a loss.

An extra offensive formation against the Gap-8 can be used effectively. In many cases, the formation adds strength against certain areas of the defense and gives extra blocking, power, etc., at the defense also.

The offense can attack the area over the center. The offense should attempt to know the tactical situation and what the defense will do in certain situations on the goal line. The defense may shoot across the line hard, not pinching inside or penetrating outside with their charges. Other defensive teams will utilize an "In" charge on the goal line when there are inches to run for the touchdown and will employ "Out" charges when a great deal of yardage is necessary. Much of this must be taken into consideration by the offensive team when attacking over the middle area. A quarterback sneak may work if the defensive number 1 men are not pinching hard to the inside. Another important factor is the alignment and play of the defensive safety or middle linebacker. Is he far enough off the line for a sneak or wedge play to go effectively over the middle area? If he is not, the offense should attack elsewhere. In many instances the defensive team will align linebackers directly in the gaps on the line of scrimmage, employing them as linemen on short yardage and goal line situations. If this occurs, the offense should immediately look to these areas for possible exploitation against the "softer" linebackers. On numerous occasions, the linebackers position in the middle area.

The offense should use quarterback sneaks and halfback and fullback wedges over the offensive center area. Possible traps can be executed on the number 1 men also. However, this can only be done depending on the type of play being run, the execution of the defensive charge, etc. Any quick-hitting wedge, power, or trap play should be employed. Counters are good against the middle linebackers. Drop-back passes may be hampered due to the hard rush of the defensive linemen; however, quick shuffle passes and middle screens are effective. Utilizing different offensive formations may shift the defensive linemen and the three deep secondary to different alignments. An example would be a strong formation or a man in motion to get the middle linebacker away from the center area.

The offense should attack the alignment and play of the number 1 defensive men. Are they aligning and playing outside or pinching inside? If outside, the offense should attack inside, and if playing inside, the offense should attack outside. Also, are the defensive number 1 men linebackers or defensive tackles? If the number 1 men are bigger and stronger than the offensive center and guards, attack elsewhere against the defense; but if they are considered weaker, attack this area attempting to drive them back off the line. The offense should attack directly over the offensive guard or between the number 1 and number 2

THE GAP-8 GOAL LINE DEFENSE

defensive men. Wedging over the offensive guard or at the number 2 man is good. A quick dive play by an offensive halfback or fullback and wedging can be effective. Cross and trap blocking can be employed in this area, especially with the defensive linemen penetrating. Trap blocking is illustrated in Diagrams 10–12a and 10–12b, with the offensive guard and tackle executing the trap blocks. In both illustrations, the remaining offensive blockers employ cave blocking away from the hole being run and reach blocking where the offensive trapper has pulled. Some type of faking or counterplay should be utilized with the trap blocking also.

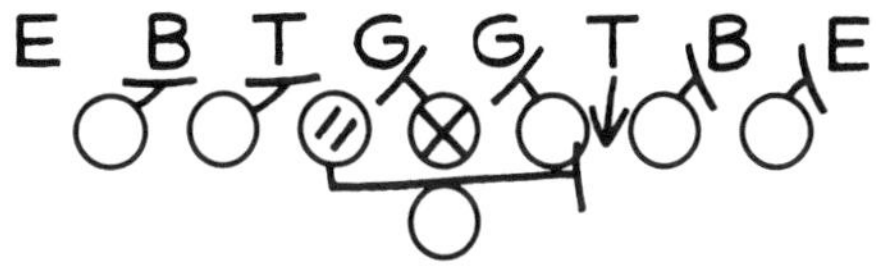

Diagram 10–12a

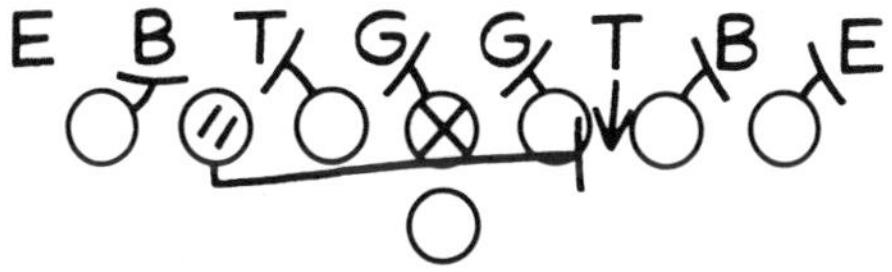

Diagram 10–12b

Powering at the number 2 man should be done. Employment of an offensive back on the defensive linemen can be utilized. Cave blocking with a one-on-one block by the offensive back on the defensive linemen (Diagram 10–13), or reach blocking and executing a double-team block, can easily be accomplished (Diagram 10–14).

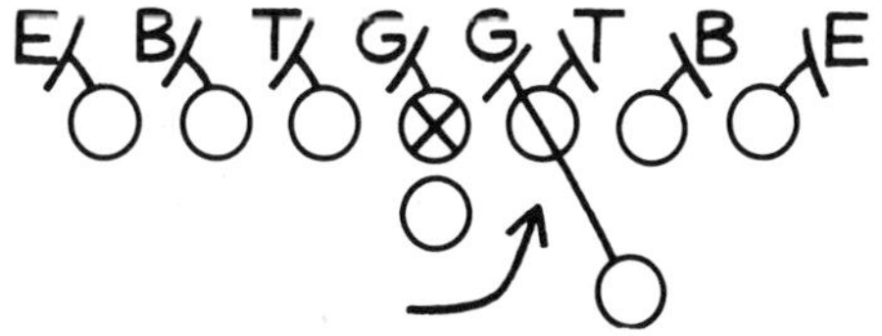

Diagram 10–13

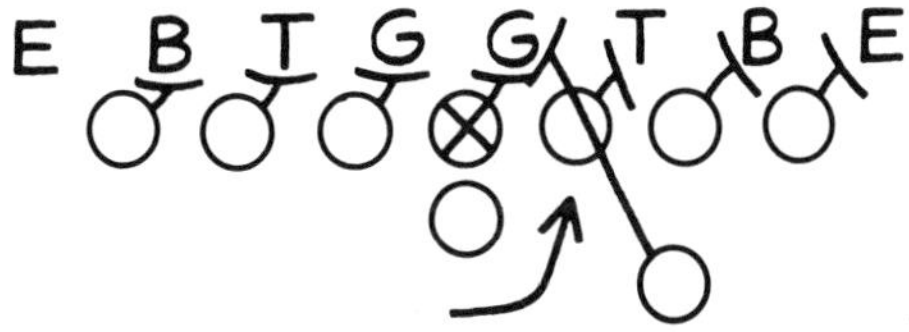

Diagram 10–14

Leading an extra offensive back through the hole can be employed. Quick-hitting power or counter-power plays can be utilized with the blocking indicated.

The offense should attack the alignment and play of the number 2 man. If he is aligning and playing to the outside, the offense should attack inside, and if positioned inside, the offense should attack outside.

The offense can attack the area over the offensive tackle or between the number 2 and 3 defensive men. Wedge blocking, cross blocking (Diagram 10–15), trap blocking with the onside or offside offensive guards can be used. Power blocking with an extra offensive back can be done also. He can either block in on the number 2 defensive man or out on the number 3 man. Diagrams 10–16 and 10–17 illustrate this with either cave or reach blocking being utilized. Any type of offensive play can be used with the blocking mentioned, including power, straight, counters, faking plays, inside reverses, etc.

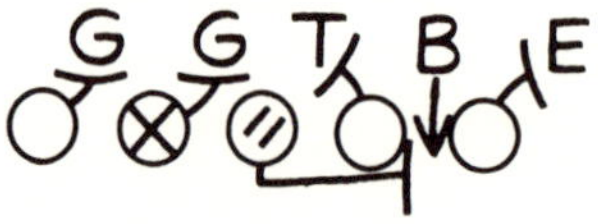

Diagram 10–15

Diagram 10–16

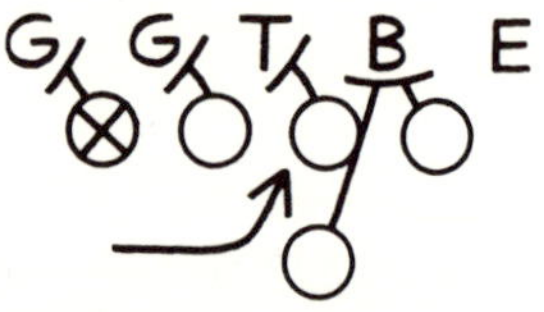

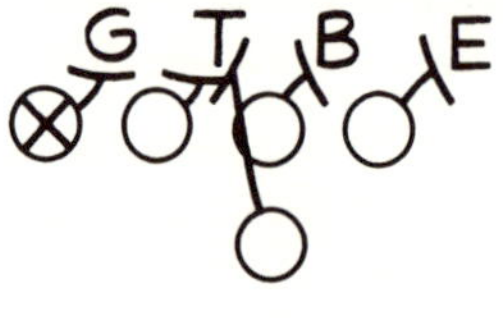

Diagram 10–17

The offense should attack the alignment and play of the number 3 defensive men. If they commit inside, the offense should run outside and if they play outside, the offense should attack inside.

One of the weakest areas of the Gap-8 defense is the off-tackle area directly over the offensive end and between the number 3 and 4 defensive men. While wedge blocking can be utilized at the off-tackle hole, other methods are effective. Angle blocking down with the offensive linemen and kicking the defensive end out with an offensive back, is good. The same can be executed with double-team blocking being employed on the number 3 man and reach blocking principles utilized with the remainder of the offensive line. Diagrams 10–18a and 10–18b illustrate both methods.

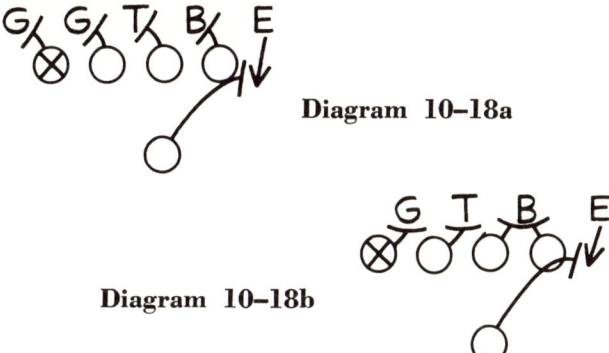

Diagram 10-18a

Diagram 10-18b

Angle blocking down (cave blocking) and trapping the defensive end out, with either the onside or offside guard, can be done. Usually faking plays, counters, and inside reverses can be employed with the trapping. Leading extra backs through the hole should also be done. Diagram 10-19 illustrates a power play at the defensive end, with double-team blocking being executed on the number 3 man and the fullback kicking the defensive end out. The deep tailback influences the defensive end out. Pulling extra linemen can easily be installed.

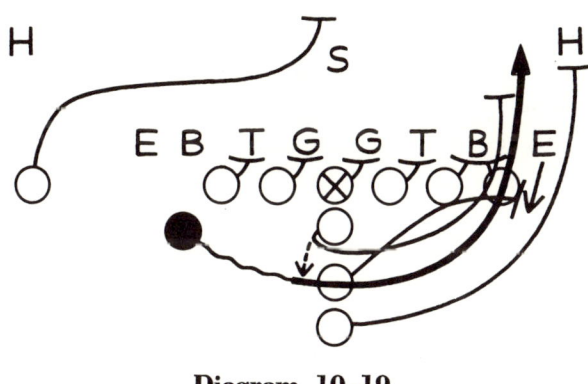

Diagram 10-19

Utilizing an extra offensive formation and leading a back through the off-tackle hole are shown in Diagram 10-20. The entire line cave blocks, while the offensive back aligned behind the tackle "traps" the defensive end out.

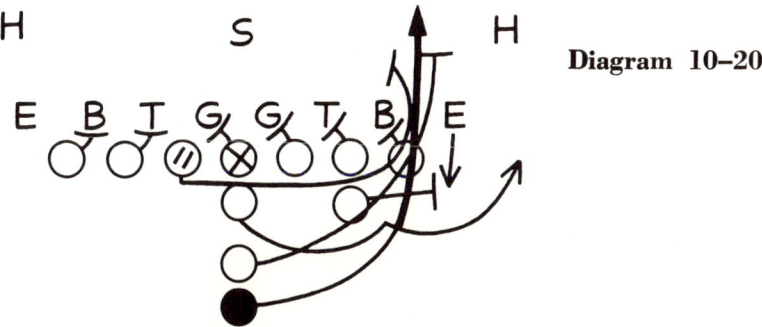

Diagram 10-20

Powering at the number 3 man with an offensive tackle and back can be effective. Diagram 10–21 illustrates this, with the offensive end blocking the defensive end out while the remaining offensive linemen utilize reach blocking.

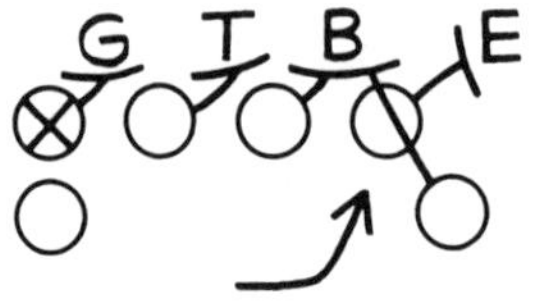

Diagram 10–21

Cross blocking can be utilized off-tackle, with the offensive end blocking down on the defensive number 3 man while the offensive tackle pulls and drives on the defensive end. The remaining blockers employ reach blocking on the defensive linemen.

The offense should attack the alignment and play of the defensive end. If the end is executing inside, the offense should go outside and if he is playing outside, the offense should run inside. Faking plays that make the defensive end commit inside and then go outside should be utilized. The offense should cave block down and run outside the defensive end. Either a wingback blocking down on the end, or a halfback driving the end in is effective. Utilizing power with the offensive backs and pulling linemen is effective. Employment of a wingback and end double-teaming the number 4 man and running outside should be done, with reach blocking used along the line of scrimmage.

The offense should employ option plays against the number 4 man and either run inside or outside the defensive end. Double-teaming the number 3 man or cave blocking is effective. Diagram 10–22 illustrates a quick option play to the deep tailback, with a flanker formation to the side of the option. Notice the defensive halfback is automatically driven deep, creating extra running room outside. Diagram 10–23 illustrates an option play on the defensive end, with a fake up the middle first that tends to hold the middle linebacker and defensive linemen. In this situation, the deep tailback blocks on the defensive halfback, while the left halfback receives the pitch if the quarterback does not keep and run the ball. Notice the possibility, in both option plays, for the back who receives the

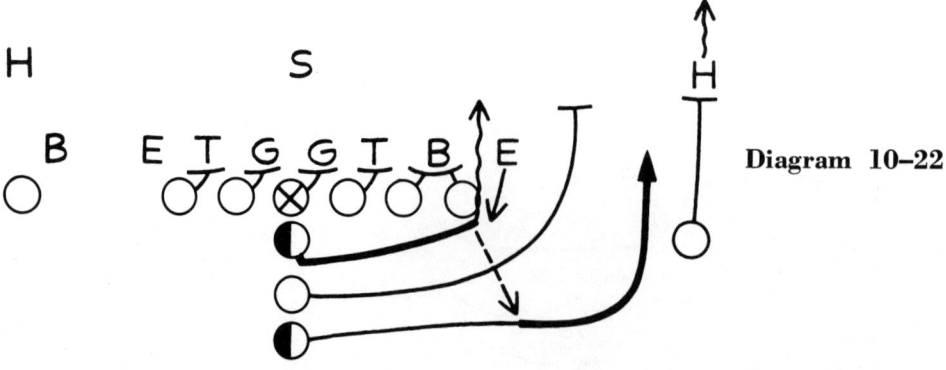

Diagram 10–22

THE GAP-8 GOAL LINE DEFENSE

pitch to throw a short pass to the receiver driving the defensive halfback deep. If the defensive halfback comes up, the ballcarrier throws the ball, and if the halfback drops off the line, the ballcarrier runs the football. The offense should go outside with quick pitchouts against the defensive end and halfback. Utilization of bootlegs and reverses can be employed also.

The offense should pass against the coverage of the three deep. If the defensive number 3 or 4 men are not hitting the offensive tight end a quick pass to him is effective. The offense should utilize sprint-out, roll-out, and option run-passes against the defensive halfback. Play-action and companion passes are good against the three deep and defensive linemen. Throwing in the flat and short hook zones with the play-action pass is effective. Swing, flat, and flare passes in the flat zone are good against the defensive halfback. The offense should know whether the secondary is man-to-man or zone, and should attack accordingly. The hook zones over the offensive end area are weak. If the defensive halfbacks play close to the line of scrimmage, attempt to throw deep and behind them. The offense should employ motion to see the defensive coverage and attack the weakness areas that motion creates.

The offense should utilize different offensive formations to see if the defensive linemen shift. If this occurs, the offense should attack the weaknesses that develop. For example, the defensive team may adjust to a wingback by utilizing a variation of the 6–5 Goal Line defense. Detaching ends and putting out flankers are effective, and the offense should run and pass according to the weaknesses that develop in the secondary and on the line of scrimmage.

Diagram 10–24 (next page) illustrates the weakness areas of the Gap-8 Even-Diamond defense, with the strengths, weaknesses, best plays against the defense, and comments listed after it. Diagram 10–25 (page 241) indicates the card for the "Coaches' Directory of Football Defenses."

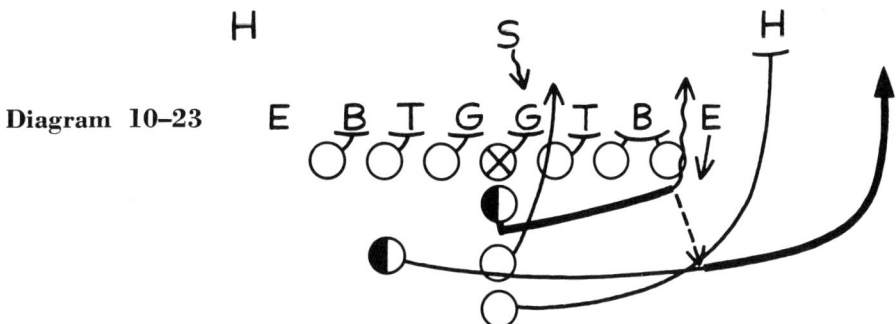

Diagram 10–23

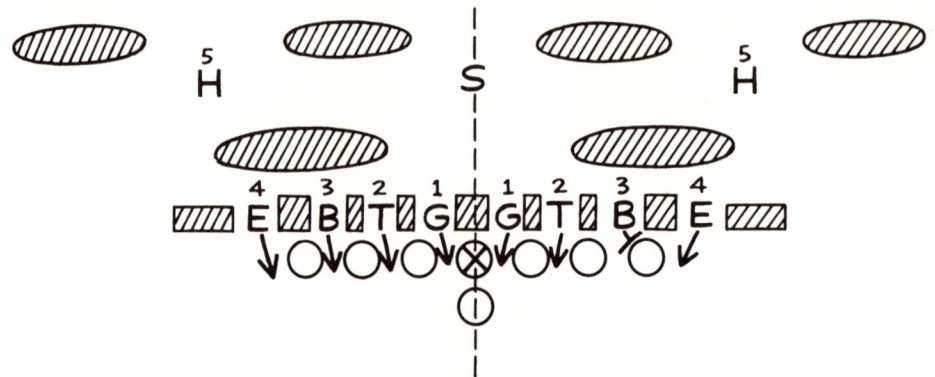

Diagram 10-24

Strength: Certain personnel make the defense strong. Inside, from tackle to tackle, is generally stronger than outside. The defensive linemen control the splits of the offensive linemen. The defense makes the offense tighten down its splits. The defense is an excellent pressure and penetrating defense. It is an excellent short yardage and goal line defense. A good pass rush can be executed by the eight-man defensive line. The defense employs a three deep secondary. The offensive ends can be jammed and held up from releasing for a pass.

Weakness: Certain personnel and improper alignments make the defense weak. The area over the offensive center can be attacked with certain blocking. The off-tackle hole is considered weak. The defense is generally weaker outside than inside. The hook areas over the offensive end area are weak. The quick pass to the tight end is good. Attack the weakness areas of the three deep. Throw deep if the defenders are aligned close to the line of scrimmage and throw short if positioned off the line of scrimmage. The offensive blockers know what to expect from the defensive linemen. Good blocking angles are present. The defense is weak against the trapping game.

Best Plays Against the Gap-8 Defense:

1. The offense should immediately tighten down its splits in order to stop the penetration of the defensive linemen. The offense must stop the penetration if the ballcarrier is not going to take a loss.
2. A different offensive formation may be beneficial for added blocking and power.
3. The offense should see if certain formations make the defense

shift to different alignments creating other weaknesses for the offensive team to attack.
4. The offensive team should attempt to know the different charges of the defensive linemen; i.e., "In," "Out," or angle left or right, so the offense will know where to attack the defense on certain downs and distances, field position, wide side of the field, etc.
5. The offense should attack over the center with quarterback sneaks, wedges, fullback and halfback wedges, etc.
6. Trapping the number 1 man can be executed on certain occasions.
7. Screen and shuffle passes in the middle may be needed against the hard-charging defensive linemen. The drop-back pass may be limited.
8. The offense should utilize quick-hitting plays and counters or faking plays over the middle area. If a middle linebacker is positioned over the offensive center, attempt to move him by the use of counters, faking, motion, strong formations, etc.
9. The offense should attack the alignment of the number 1 man. If playing outside, run inside, and if executing inside, go outside.
10. The offense should attack the number 2 and 3 men with wedges, cross blocks, short and long traps, power plays (utilizing a different formation and adding an extra offensive back), etc.
11. Leading backs through the holes or pulling linemen can be done. Utilize halfback and fullback wedges, quick-hitting plays, counters, inside reverses with the trapping game, etc.
12. The offense should attack the alignments of the number 2 and 3 men. Run inside if playing outside and run outside if charging inside.
13. The offense should definitely attack the off-tackle hole. Utilize either cave blocking or double-team the number 3 man and employ reach blocking. Kick the defensive end out with one or two offensive backs, or trap the defensive end with either the onside or offside offensive guard or tackle.
14. The offense should pull extra linemen and lead offensive backs through the hole.
15. Employing cross blocks and wedges off-tackle can be done. Utilization of straight, counters, and power plays off-tackle is good. Powering the defensive number 3 man with the offensive tackle and another offensive back (wingback or halfback) is effective.
16. Attacking the play of the defensive end should be done. If the end is playing outside, the offense should run inside of him, whereas if he is committing to the inside, the offense should run outside.
17. The offense should attack the number 4 man with option plays. The quarterback can either keep or pitch to the trailing offensive back. Faking inside first and optioning the defensive end is effective.

SUCCESSFUL RUNNING PLAYS

TO THE LEFT   TO THE RIGHT

_____   _____
_____   _____
_____   _____
_____   _____
_____   _____
_____   _____
_____   _____
_____   _____
_____   _____
_____   _____
_____   _____
_____   _____
_____   _____
_____   _____

SUCCESSFUL PASSING PLAYS

_____   _____
_____   _____
_____   _____
_____   _____
_____   _____
_____   _____

SUCCESSFUL ACTION PLAY PASSES

_____   _____
_____   _____
_____   _____
_____   _____

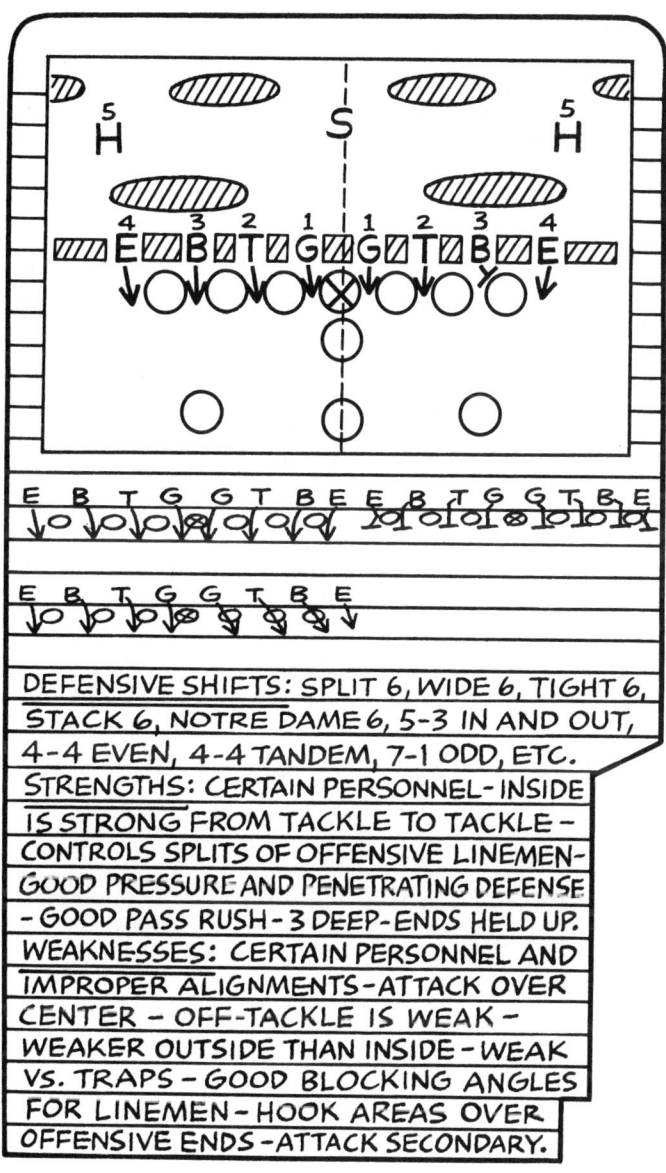

DEFENSIVE SHIFTS: SPLIT 6, WIDE 6, TIGHT 6, STACK 6, NOTRE DAME 6, 5-3 IN AND OUT, 4-4 EVEN, 4-4 TANDEM, 7-1 ODD, ETC.

STRENGTHS: CERTAIN PERSONNEL - INSIDE IS STRONG FROM TACKLE TO TACKLE - CONTROLS SPLITS OF OFFENSIVE LINEMEN - GOOD PRESSURE AND PENETRATING DEFENSE - GOOD PASS RUSH - 3 DEEP - ENDS HELD UP.

WEAKNESSES: CERTAIN PERSONNEL AND IMPROPER ALIGNMENTS - ATTACK OVER CENTER - OFF-TACKLE IS WEAK - WEAKER OUTSIDE THAN INSIDE - WEAK VS. TRAPS - GOOD BLOCKING ANGLES FOR LINEMEN - HOOK AREAS OVER OFFENSIVE ENDS - ATTACK SECONDARY.

BLOCKING: WEDGE, TRAPS, CROSS BLOCKING, DOUBLE TEAMS, CAVE, REACH BLOCKING, POWER.

Diagram 10-25
The gap-8 even-diamond defense

18. The offense should go outside with cave blocking and driving the defensive end in with the wingback or halfback. Double-teaming the number 4 man with reach blocking by the entire line is good also. Pulling extra offensive linemen outside should be utilized.
19. The offense should go outside with power sweeps, reverses, bootlegs, and quick pitchouts.
20. Attack the coverage of the three deep secondary. If aligned close to the line, throw behind and if positioned deep, throw in front.
21. Attack outside with the option-run pass at the defensive halfback. Utilize the sprint-out or roll-out pass. Play-action or companion passes against the defensive linemen and secondary are good. Look to the hook zones over the offensive ends and short flat areas for attacking purposes.
22. The offense should split ends and put out flankers, and run and pass according to the defensive coverage.

Comments: The Gap-8 is a tough, hard-nosed penetrating defense. The offensive linemen must be ready and fully prepared to meet the hard-charging defensive linemen. The blockers must attempt to stop penetration, because this is the objective of the defense. If penetration can be stopped and the pursuit of the defensive linemen somewhat halted, the offensive team should have an excellent chance of making the first down or scoring the touchdown.

11

COACHES' DIRECTORY OF FOOTBALL DEFENSES

The "Coaches' Directory of Football Defenses" was designed as a telephone flip-open directory. When people want to check a phone number to make a call, they simply move the arrow indicator to the first letter of the last name, and the information will flip open and be quickly at hand. The system is easily adapted for football defenses. A coach will have a combination of often used defenses in one compact directory of defenses. Included in the directory will be the strengths and weaknesses of the defense, stunts, fires, slanting and looping lines, defensive shifts, and the best type of blocking against the particular defense. At the bottom of the directory, the offense's best running plays, drop-back passes, sprint-out passes, and/or roll-out passes, which can successfully be executed against the defense, would be included.

ADVANTAGES OF THE DEFENSE DIRECTORY

There are numerous ways in which a coach could benefit from using a "Coaches' Directory of Football Defenses."

1. Every defense can be viewed in a matter of seconds.
2. It provides a reference of defenses that can be used as a guide, to be studied, etc.
3. It can be utilized by a few or many coaches at meetings, discussions, clinics, conventions, etc.

4. The "Coaches' Directory of Football Defenses" can be easily carried. It can be placed on a clipboard, or in a jacket pocket. Bulky books, which normally contain such information, do not have to be used.
5. It can conveniently be taken to team and quarterback meetings and used as a guide and reference for everyone present.
6. It has obvious practical use on the practice field as a quick reference for the coaching staff and quarterbacks.
7. In a game situation, with a new defense confronting the coach, it can be used again as a quick reminder of the strengths and weaknesses of the defense, and the offensive plays and passes that will successfully go against the defense. The "Coaches' Directory of Football Defenses" is a quick quarterback reference during a time-out. Confusion will not occur. The quarterbacks will know exact plays desired.
8. It can be given to the quarterbacks or any other team member to study all defenses in general, and the special defenses which will represent the opposition during the season or on a particular game day. In addition, quarterbacks may retain the "Coaches' Directory of Football Defenses" during the offseason for study purposes.

WHY MAKE A COACHES' DIRECTORY OF DEFENSES?

To prepare a directory requires many long hours, but these hours will be well spent. Although time is involved, there are numerous reasons a coach should undertake and make a "Coaches' Directory of Football Defenses."

1. A coach can benefit considerably because he will be schooling himself about differences and similarities between defenses.
2. He will learn and know why a defense has certain strengths and weaknesses.
3. The coach will better understand fires, loops, and slants that will be employed against the offense.
4. By making the directory, a coach will understand defensive football better and may find an idea or two that can be incorporated into the defense he uses.
5. A coach will become better aware of the offensive running plays and passes that will be executed against each defense and choose these certain plays for employment in the future.
6. The coach will be in a better position to school his football staff, teach quarterbacks and members of the team why defenses are aligned in a certain manner, where the strengths and weaknesses are, the various maneuvers of defenses, and so forth.

HOW TO MAKE THE COACHES' DIRECTORY OF DEFENSES

The coach must first secure a simple flip-open telephone directory. (Photos 11-1 and 11-2 are illustrations of such a directory.) The type of directory the coach desires will be determined by the number of defenses that will be inserted. As shown in Photo 11-1, there are 21 different listings for the indicator; therefore, 21 different defenses can be registered. Other directories will provide more or fewer listings and the coach should choose the one he feels best suits his purpose. The number of defenses selected will depend on the coach. All 21 defenses may be listed, as was done in the case of this directory. If the coach sees this as unnecessary, then he can list only those defenses and their variations which his team will probably meet during the season. For example, the basic 4–4 Tandem

Photo 11-1
Notice there are 21 listings for the arrow indicator; therefore, 21 different defenses can be registered.

Photo 11–2
The telephone directory flipped open.

defense can be recorded on one card, and the 4–4 Tandem with a slanting line can be placed on another.

CONSTRUCTING THE DIRECTORY

The "Coaches' Directory of Football Defenses" can be easily constructed. Use a piece of paper approximately the size of the directory and place it over the front cover where the letters are listed next to the arrow indicator. This is illustrated in the drawing of Diagram 11–1 (page 248). Paste the paper on the directory and put a clear plastic adhering sheet on and over the paper to protect it. With the plastic sheet, smudging, water, ripping, or any other abuse will not damage the cover. As is shown, the defenses should be placed in order, from the first, a four-man line, to the last, an eight-man line. The defenses that were placed on the front cover of the "Coaches' Directory" are the following:

1. 4–4 Even-Diamond
2. 4–4 Tandem-Diamond
3. 4–5 Even-Box-Corner
4. 5–2 Umbrella-Odd-Box-Corner
5. 5–3 In Odd-Diamond
6. 5–3 Out Odd-Diamond
7. 5–4 Inside Odd-Box

8. 5-4 Oklahoma Odd-Box-Corner
9. 5 Eagle Odd-Box-Corner
10. 6 Loose Even-Diamond
11. 6 Tight Even-Diamond
12. 6 Tandem Even-Diamond
13. 6 Split Even-Diamond
14. Notre Dame 6 Even-Diamond
15. 6-1 Umbrella Even-Box-Corner
16. 6-3 Even-Box
17. 6-5 (Goal Line)
18. 7-1 Odd-Diamond
19. 7-2 Odd-Box
20. 7 Box-Odd-Box
21. Gap 8 (Goal Line)

Once the defenses have been inserted on the front cover of the directory, the next step is to place each defense on the appropriate cards. As an illustration, if the 5-4 Oklahoma defense is to be included, place the arrow indicator next to that defense and flip open the directory. For better results, easier handling and writing, take the directory apart, because it will be easier to incorporate the defenses on the cards, and neatness will result.

THE TOP CARD

Classifying the defenses on each card is a simple matter. Needed materials are thin paper (for the defense), red, black, green ink, and paper glue. (The reason for the thin paper is that if thick paper were added, the cover of the directory would not close.) On the paper, the offense should be drawn in black, the defense in red, and the various weaknesses of each defense in green ink. The numbering system of the offense that the coach employs should be placed on the card with the offense. Rotation of the backfield can be shown with a four deep secondary, and at times three deep pass coverage. While this is not indicated throughout the book, it is illustrated in Photo 11-3 (page 251). Diagram 11-2 (page 249) shows, for example, an offense that is used, the 5-4 Oklahoma Odd-Box-Corner defense, and the weakness of the defense as indicated by the areas. The defense should be pasted at the top of the card as shown. Size of the paper for the defense will be determined by the size of the cards. The information for the defenses can be easily secured from this book. Other books, articles, and the coach's own knowledge will, of course, enlarge the directory.

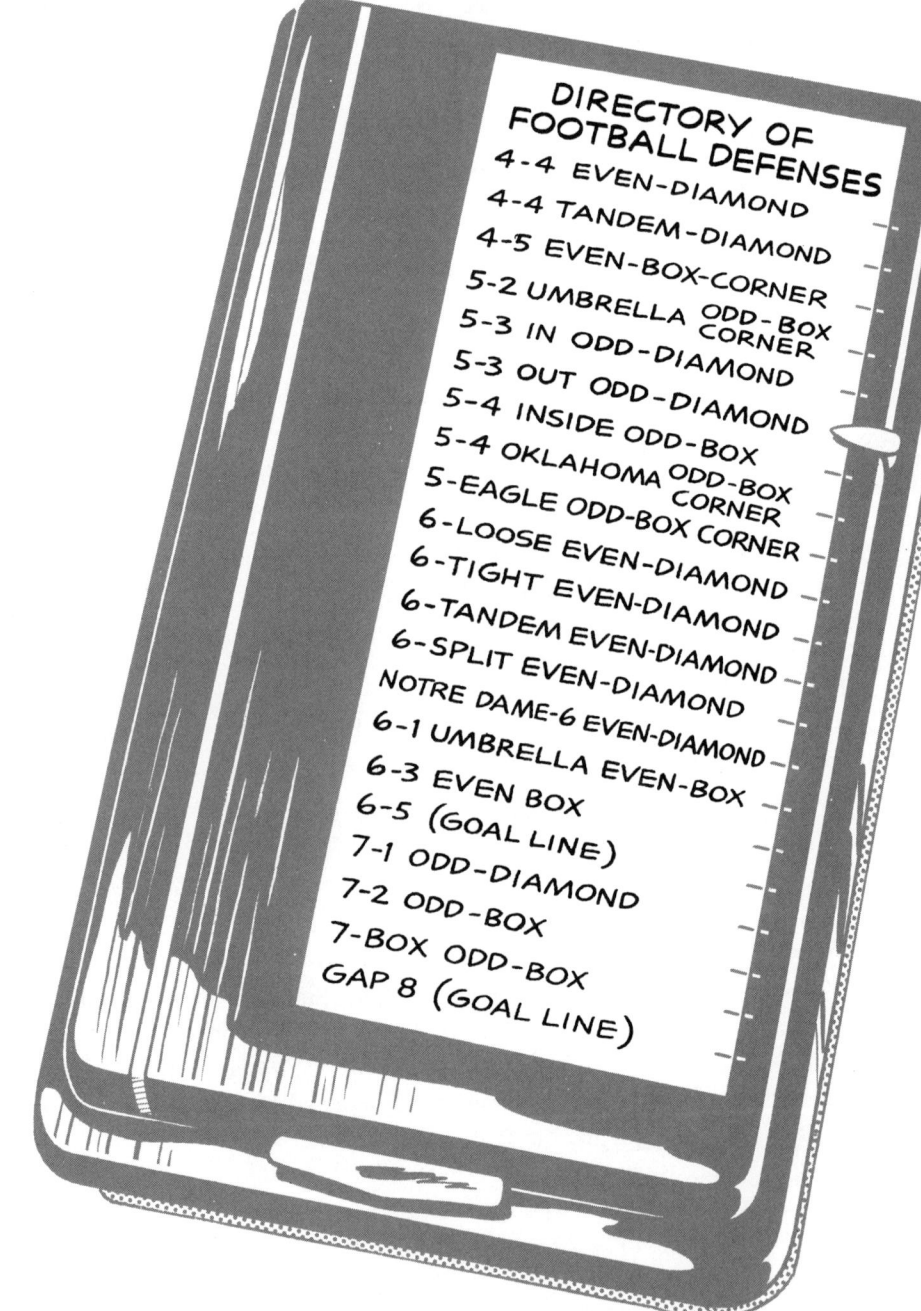

Diagram 11-1
The front cover of the directory. The paper is pasted on to the front cover and a clear plastic adhering sheet is placed over it.

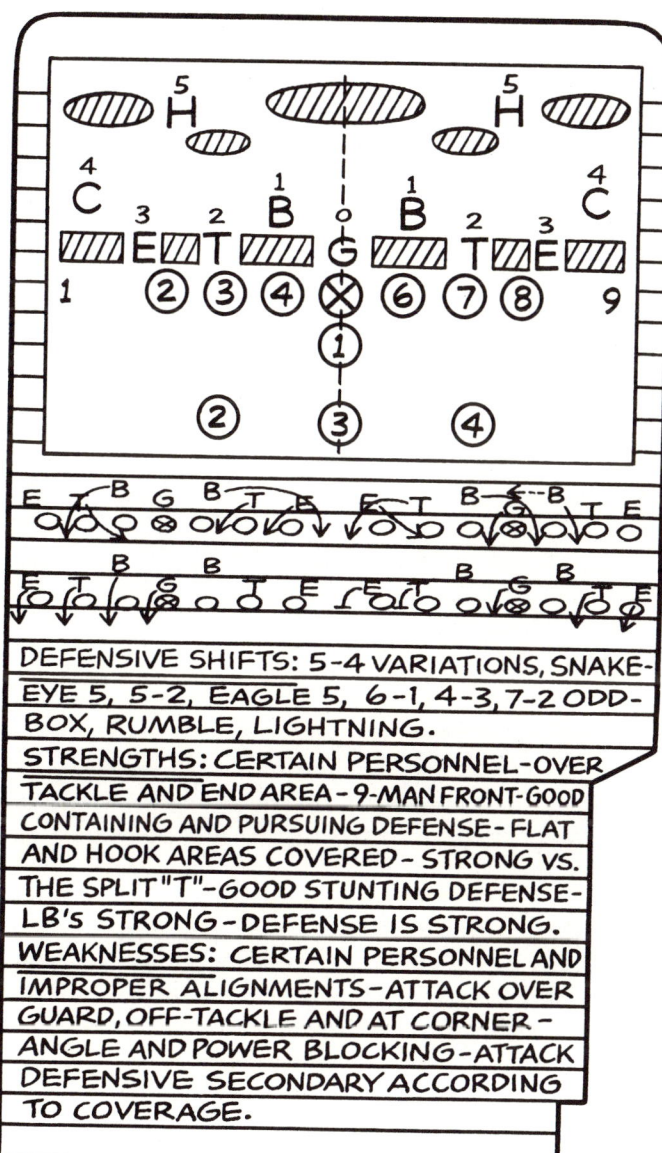

Diagram 11-2

Diagram 11-2 illustrates the top card of the directory. Notice the numbering system of the offense and the weakness areas in the defense. Stunts, fires, and other special maneuvers are shown under the card.

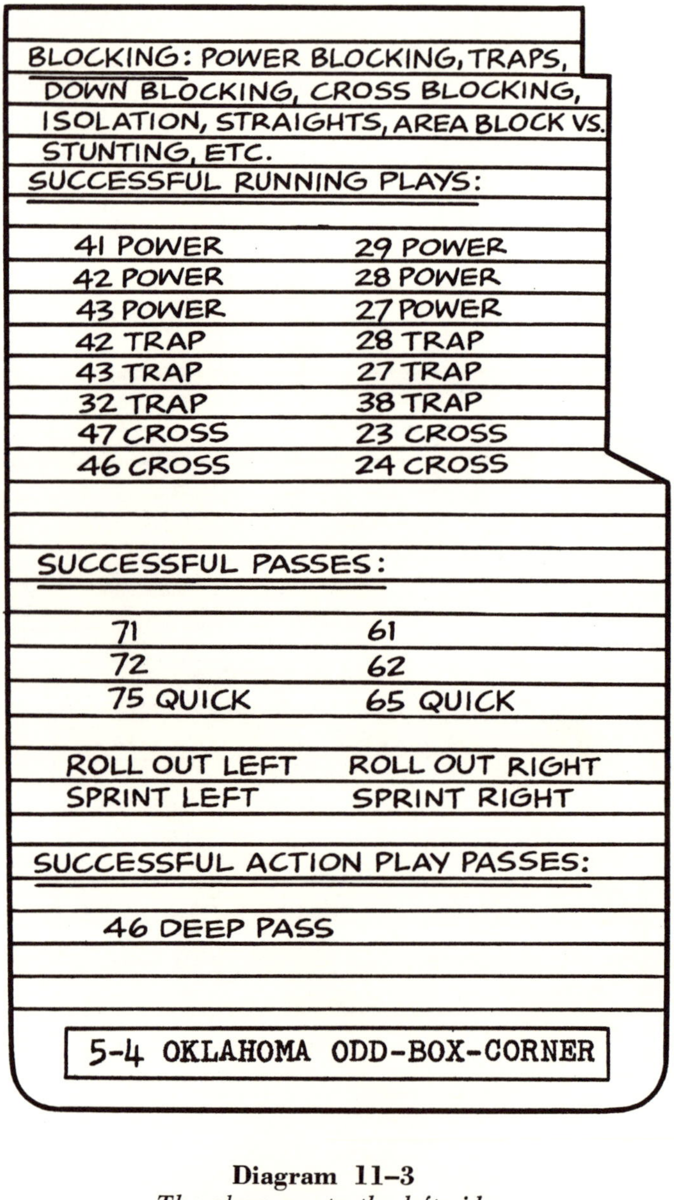

BLOCKING: POWER BLOCKING, TRAPS, DOWN BLOCKING, CROSS BLOCKING, ISOLATION, STRAIGHTS, AREA BLOCK VS. STUNTING, ETC.

SUCCESSFUL RUNNING PLAYS:

41 POWER	29 POWER
42 POWER	28 POWER
43 POWER	27 POWER
42 TRAP	28 TRAP
43 TRAP	27 TRAP
32 TRAP	38 TRAP
47 CROSS	23 CROSS
46 CROSS	24 CROSS

SUCCESSFUL PASSES:

71	61
72	62
75 QUICK	65 QUICK
ROLL OUT LEFT	ROLL OUT RIGHT
SPRINT LEFT	SPRINT RIGHT

SUCCESSFUL ACTION PLAY PASSES:

46 DEEP PASS

5-4 OKLAHOMA ODD-BOX-CORNER

Diagram 11-3
The plays run to the left side of the line are placed on the left side of the card, and the plays run to the right side of the line are placed on the right side of the card.

Underneath the pasted defense there is sufficient space on the card to show special maneuvers (slanting lines, various stunts and fires, etc.). Below this would be written information on what the defense can easily shift to, the strength of the defense, and the weakness of the defense. The material should be placed on the first card, the one which was flipped up. This procedure should be continued with every defense that is listed on the front cover of the "Coaches' Directory."

Photo 11-3
The overall scheme of the top and bottom card as it looks on the telephone directory.

THE BOTTOM CARD

On the bottom card, the best type of blocking that can be used against the defense should be written. Every running play, pass, and play-action pass which can successfully be used against the defense, should then be written on the card in pencil. Writing in pencil will make it possible for the coach to eliminate a play he employed at one time by simply erasing it. Plays that are run to the left side of the line should be placed on the left side of the card, and the plays run to the right side should be placed on the right side of the card.

The name of the defense, in this case the 5–4 Oklahoma Odd-Box Corner, is placed at the extreme bottom of the card. Diagram 11–3 (page 250) indicates this and Photo 11–3 (preceding page) shows the overall scheme of the top and bottom card as it looks on the telephone directory. This should be done with all the defenses that are listed.